TURNING
THE
TABLES

Restaurants and the Rise of the

TURNING
THE
TABLES

American Middle Class, 1880–1920

ANDREW P. HALEY

The University of North Carolina Press   Chapel Hill

Publication of this book was supported in part by a generous gift
from Eric Papenfuse and Catherine Lawrence.

Designed by Courtney Leigh Baker and set in Dante with Sackers
Gothic display by Rebecca Evans. The paper in this book meets the guidelines
for permanence and durability of the Committee on Production Guidelines
for Book Longevity of the Council on Library Resources. The University of North
Carolina Press has been a member of the Green Press Initiative since 2003.

Library of Congress Cataloging-in-Publication Data
Haley, Andrew P.
Turning the tables : restaurants and the rise of the
American middle class, 1880–1920 / Andrew P. Haley.
p. cm.
Includes bibliographical references and index.
ISBN 978-0-8078-3474-9 (cloth : alk. paper)
1. Restaurants—United States—History—20th century. 2. Middle
class—United States—History—20th century. 3. Consumption
(Economics)—United States—History—20th century. I. Title.
TX945.H29 2011   647.9573—dc22
2010043602

15 14 13 12 11   5 4 3 2 1

CONTENTS

ACKNOWLEDGMENTS ix   NOTE ON LANGUAGE xiii

INTRODUCTION
The Tang and Feel of the American Experience
Class, Culture, and Consumption
I

CHAPTER ONE
Terrapin à la Maryland
The Era of the Aristocratic Restaurant
19

CHAPTER TWO
Playing at Make Believe
The Failure of Imitation
43

CHAPTER THREE
Catering to the Great Middle Stripe
Beefsteaks and American Restaurants
68

CHAPTER FOUR
The Restauration
Colonizing the Ethnic Restaurant
92

CHAPTER FIVE
The Simplified Menu
The Case against Gastronomic Ostentation
118

CHAPTER SIX

Satisfying Their Hunger

Middle-Class Women and Respectability

145

CHAPTER SEVEN

The Tipping Evil

The Limits of Middle-Class Influence

171

CHAPTER EIGHT

Ending Linguistic Disguises

The Decline of French Cuisine

192

CONCLUSION

Indifferent Gullets

The Middle Class and the Cosmopolitan Restaurant

222

NOTES 237   BIBLIOGRAPHY 327   INDEX 353

ILLUSTRATIONS

James Wells Champney,
"The Guardian Angel—Eagle Hotel, Asheville"
36

Delmonico's Menu "C"
54

"Two Things Interfere with the Enjoyment of Food,
Too Much Money and Too Little"
66

"Why the Public Restaurants Are So Popular"
73

Walter Brown, "Our Artist's Dream of the Centennial Restaurants"
93

Marty, "Supposedly Foreign Restaurant"
109

"Hotel St. Regis Restaurant"
124

Cover of the inaugural issue of *What to Eat*, August 1896
131

Otto II. Bacher, [Women in Restaurant in High Building], 1903
156

Patent, J. F. Daschner, "Automatic Table Service Apparatus," 1917
188

Bilingual dinner menu (English and French), The Waldorf,
New York, N.Y., April 23, 1896
202

ACKNOWLEDGMENTS

Few endeavors are the work of just one person. I have liberally drawn on the wisdom of those kind enough to give their time, attention, and intellectual prowess to this project and have discovered that many chefs do not spoil the broth.

A considerable number of years ago, I shared with Paula Baker, then at the University of Pittsburgh, an idea I had about the middle class and dining that came to me (I am a little embarrassed to admit) while viewing Martin Scorsese's remake of Edith Wharton's *Age of Innocence*. Half-baked ideas do not always amount to much; however, in this case, Paula not only endorsed the idea but helped me to develop a philosophical and practical approach to studying public culture and class. Paula eventually moved to Ohio State University but continued to support the project, and her rigorous, biting approach to scholarship continues to inspire me.

Meanwhile, Donna Gabaccia, now at the University of Minnesota, joined the faculty at the University of Pittsburgh. Donna's support was invaluable. A marvelous, energetic scholar, she contributed her considerable knowledge about food history. With her advice, a menu was prepared, arguments were expanded, and the project grew from a few disparate chapters to a coherent thesis. Donna shepherded the project to its conclusion while initiating me into the historical profession, and for that I am very thankful.

Three other scholars at the University of Pittsburgh also helped to shape the final work. They read chapters, offered advice, and then patiently reread chapters. Carol Stabile from the Department of Communications tutored me in cultural theory; Dick Oestreicher demanded the highest standard of proof, including (rightly so) a statistical basis for my claims and a consistent model of class; and Bruce Vernarde, like a restaurant steward, made sure that everything came together in the end. Collectively, they challenged me to look more deeply and more thoroughly at how Americans have experienced class.

My education did not end when I left Pittsburgh. Since then, I have had the privilege of teaching at the University of Southern Mississippi and have found myself, once again, surrounded by exceptional scholars and marvelous students. To name everyone would be cumbersome, but I owe special thanks to Phyllis Jestice, my department chair and an accomplished editor, who read the manuscript from cover to cover not once but twice; Amy Milne-Smith, whose work on the "real" aristocracy in Britain has served as an invaluable foil for my research; Jeff Bowersox, whose sharp insights are almost as nourishing as the barbecue in Owensboro, Kentucky; and Kyle Zelner, whose friendship has proven longer than even my longest sentences. Likewise, I wish to acknowledge the advice and encouragement of seasoned colleagues—most notably, Michael Neiberg and Andrew Wiest—who have guided me through my academic career. Finally, it has been a pleasure to work with graduate and undergraduate students at the University of Southern Mississippi, especially those who have taken my cultural history or culinary history classes. You have made me a better scholar and have shaped this work.

My coworkers at the University of Southern Mississippi supplement a national franchise of friends and colleagues who have lent their support over the years. Scott Giltner, now a faculty member at Culver-Stockton College in Missouri, paced me and pushed me. Laura Bier, my closest friend and a remarkable scholar who now teaches at Georgia Tech, debated my quirky ideas on class, culture, and capitalism and constantly reminded me, with characteristic grace, that the facts don't always speak for themselves.

My study was made easier by those who have done the kitchen prep: the scholars and librarians who have made a wealth of material on the Gilded Age and Progressive Era available online and the countless interlibrary loan professionals who have gone to great lengths to track down the most obscure books (especially the staffs at Hillman Library at the University of Pittsburgh and Cook Library at the University of Southern Mississippi). I am particularly indebted to the librarians at Pitt, Southern Miss, Harvard, the New York Public Library (including the volunteers who gave their time to organize the menu collection), the Boston Public Library, the Carnegie Libraries of Pittsburgh, the National Restaurant Association, and the Library of Congress. I am also beholden to those who provided funding for me to write and research, including the committees that awarded me the Andrew Mellon Predoctoral Fellowship, the University of Pittsburgh's Cultural Studies Predoctoral Fellowship, and the Samuel Hay Summer Travel Grant. Additional support came from the Center for Instructional Development and Distance Education at the University of Pittsburgh and the Department of History at the University of Southern Mississippi.

To everyone who contributed the leavening over the years, I owe more than I can repay. I have benefited greatly from the support of the University of North Carolina Press. Sian Hunter and her assistant Beth Lassiter have had to calm my nerves more than once, and I am thankful for their confidence. I particularly appreciate the reviewers Sian and Beth found for this manuscript. Jeffrey Pilcher and Krishnendu Ray, as well as a still anonymous reader, provided some great advice, and I have done my best to incorporate those suggestions. Finally, Paula Wald and Julie Bush and the production staff at UNC Press have taken much of the worry out of finishing and publishing this book.

To my parents and my in-laws, I beg forgiveness for all the missed gatherings and rushed visits. I hope you will find the finished project worthy of the abuse. Likewise, I am grateful for the kindnesses that my brother, John, and my wife's sisters, Chelsea and Hannah, have repeatedly shown. But no one has suffered more for this book than Danielle Sypher-Haley, my spouse and most trusted taster. As an accomplished professional chef, Danielle financially supported my work and nourished it. As a gifted writer, she served as my writing coach and editor. As a brilliant thinker, she helped me to refine the ideas that constitute this study. Money was scarce during graduate school, but Danielle and I would occasionally treat ourselves to an expensive coffee at Prestogeorge, a local coffee roaster. Asked to justify the luxury, Danielle argued that we were not just purchasing coffee but reaffirming class. "Just because we don't have the money doesn't mean we aren't the type of people who drink cappuccino." It is now more than ten years later and I have not formulated a more succinct theoretical explanation of class and consumption than she produced, to use a bit of restaurant slang, "on the fly."

Most of my friends and advisers will have a chance to read this work. One will not. To Chris S. Caforio (1969–2004), whose spirit remains un bounded, this work is dedicated.

NOTE ON LANGUAGE

Cultural history can be more descriptive than explanatory; I hope this work is not. I believe that in the late nineteenth and early twentieth centuries, the middle class displaced the aristocratic elite and emerged as the dominant class when it came to determining the shape of American culture. To make such an argument—to assert that cultural phenomena as diverse as the utopian novel, spaghetti dinners, and smoking women were instruments of the middle class's rise to power—is to understate the infinite variety of cultural experiences and to impose a determinacy on the most indeterminate of life's experiences. To make this process as transparent as possible, I have included extensive notes and have followed a number of conventions. On a practical level, I have tried to reproduce accurately the imprecise and obscure "cook's French" that appeared on menus and in culinary guides. In the United States, "cook's French" referred to a long tradition of using specialized French terms for dishes and to the hackneyed, amateurish efforts of American-born chefs to use these specialized terms. In *Turning the Tables*, I have reproduced the misspellings, misusages, and misplaced accents. To reduce the clutter and simplify reading, these terms are placed in italics instead of quotation marks. Thus, italicized dishes (both English and foreign), unless noted otherwise, should be considered direct quotes from sources and have been cited accordingly. To distinguish these quoted passages from dishes I have described in my own terms, I have not followed the usual convention of placing foreign words in italics.

In addition, I have followed a number of conventions when discussing the major protagonists of the story. I have avoided the more accurate "middle classes" (a term that recognizes that members of the middle class were diverse and that the black middle class, the rural middle class, and a host of other middle classes did not have the same experiences as the largely white, sometimes first-generation immigrant, urban middle class that is the focus of this book) in favor of the simpler, if less precise, "middle class." Similarly, I have chosen to use the historically accurate, if provocative, "aristocrats" to describe America's self-constituted elites. As Matthew M. Trumbull, a former member of the Grant administration, wrote in *The Nineteenth Century* in 1888: "The word aristocracy is used here, not in its technical or dictionary meaning, but according to the sense in which it is generally understood by the people of the United States—not as the old Greeks used it, to express the class composed of the best people; not as the European nations use it, to express the titled classes; but as the Americans use it, to describe a class of pretenders who would be titled people if they could, and a class who assume superior importance on account of money."[1]

TURNING
THE
TABLES

THE TANG AND FEEL OF THE AMERICAN EXPERIENCE
Class, Culture, and Consumption

All I want is a bowl of chop suey,
A bowl of chop suey and you-ey,
A cozy little table for two-ey,
With a bowl of chop suey and you-ey.

For a place that's very Chinesy
Is nice for a hug and squeezy,
Where we can do a billion coo-eys
With a bowl of chop suey for two-ey.

—Ben Bernie, Alyce Goering, and Walter Bullock,
"A Bowl of Chop Suey and You-ey," 1934, as performed by
Sam Robbins and his Hotel McAlpin Orchestra

The Hotel McAlpin was built in New York City in 1912 during a spree of apartment and hotel construction that began with efforts to accommodate foreign travelers on their way to the 1893 Chicago World's Fair and did not slow until World War I. Designed by architect Frank Mills Andrews, the McAlpin was richly appointed. It boasted a rathskeller with colorful Fred Dana Marsh terra cotta murals, a tapestry gallery, a massive marble lobby, a Louis XVI–style dining room, floors that catered exclusively to men or women, and—at the top—Russian and Turkish baths and a vaulted ballroom. Considered the largest hotel in the world when it opened, the McAlpin employed 1,500 staff members to cater to the whims of 2,500 guests, and still the never-ending demand for new features and more rooms led its owners to purchase adjacent land and expand the hotel within five years of its grand opening.[1]

Given the hotel's splendor, it was not surprising that the earliest accounts of the McAlpin failed to mention the hotel's tearoom, but the little shop drew the attention of the press in 1919 when the culinary-industry journal *The Steward* reported that "the McAlpin Hotel teashop is serving a special Chinese luncheon and supper . . . and is proving very successful."

According to *The Steward*, the tearoom's success could be attributed to the decision to "secure a number of dainty little American-born Chinese girls to serve as waitresses" and, when this "proved so pleasing and satisfactory," the hiring of several Chinese cooks.[2] There was no ignoring "the evident pride the Celestials take in preparing and serving the viands which appear to have struck the fancy of the Occidentals," *The Steward* concluded.[3]

The McAlpin's Chinese tearoom was not the first Chinese restaurant in New York, nor was it the most spectacular. Chinese restaurants were popular "slumming" destinations in the late nineteenth century, and by the turn of the century, after a chop suey craze had swept the nation, Chinese restaurants could be found throughout New York's five boroughs.[4] Yet this Chinese tearoom was remarkable in that it was located in one of New York's newest and grandest hotels, and, as a result, it signaled a sea change in dining. For much of the nineteenth century and into the first decades of the twentieth, America's best restaurants and most respected hotels catered to the tastes of elites by serving mostly French food cooked by French chefs.[5] The decision to serve Chinese food recognized the cosmopolitan tastes of the middle class.

The nineteenth-century restaurant culture of French menus and stuffy waiters had been created for and was sustained by America's social and cultural upper class. Although small in number, wealthy families exercised disproportionate influence over cultural fashions and used this influence to shape the better class of restaurants into testaments to their power. While not all restaurants were as French as the nation's most celebrated eating establishment, Delmonico's, the best restaurants and the finest households looked to Paris for inspiration. By consuming the cuisine of Old World elites, society leaders of the late nineteenth century believed they were asserting a claim to membership in a European-style aristocracy. If you are what you eat, then eating like the French nobility made you an aristocrat.[6]

Those in the nascent middle class who were eager to carve out a place for themselves in the urban landscape scoffed at such pretentions. For clerks, managers, and professionals—the occupational byproducts of the ongoing industrial and managerial revolutions—the upper class's claim to cultural authority not only was evidence of foreign frippery and haughty habits but also was unfair. The French restaurant was expensive and alienating; it discriminated against those who could not afford large tips, those who did not read French, and those whose budgets made a nine-course meal a once-a-year extravagance. In newspaper columns and magazines, refer to the vanguard who championed "middle-classness" as the middle class (or the urban middle class), and I occasionally refer to the process as the "middle-classing" of restaurant culture. Yet it is important to be reminded from the start that as influential as this "identity of interests" could be, it did not erase (even if sometimes it challenged) real differences of race, gender, and ethnicity that shaped middle-class lives. The public dining experiences of an African American shopkeeper who faced legal or extralegal discrimination was different from those of a second-generation Irish clerk, even if both men held a similar idea of what it meant to be middle class.[15] Class conscious does not have to mean class unanimity, nor does it mean that everyone who identified himself or herself as middle class experienced class in the same way.

Cosmopolitanism

The struggle over restaurant dining that took place at the turn of the century pitted the cultural influence of the upper class against the aspirations of the middle class. On one side of this cultural and class divide stood members of an urban elite who cast themselves as social leaders and called themselves "Society." In the mid-nineteenth century, these aristocrats styled themselves after Europe's aristocracy and felt entitled by their wealth and breeding to shape the public culture of the United States.

In *Highbrow/Lowbrow*, historian Lawrence W. Levine explored the "sacralization" of high culture. In the nineteenth century, Levine argued, America's somewhat egalitarian urban culture fragmented. Arts that were once accessible to all, such as the works of Shakespeare, were elevated to the status of high culture by influential arbiters who insisted that by dint of their association with Europe, some cultural expressions should be valued more than others. The "sacralization" of high culture placed opera, European painting, and literature into a hallowed category beyond criticism and vulgar appropriation by the masses.[16]

Dining underwent a similar transformation. In the early nineteenth century, French food was admired, but it was not yet sacred. While the fashionable Hotel Astor employed a French chef, he shared responsibility for running the kitchen with an English cook and an Italian cook.[17] By the middle of the century, however, the American elites' patronage and celebration of everything associated with the European aristocracy elevated French food and the aristocratic restaurant, creating markers of status that only those who traveled to Europe or employed a French chef could fully master. In both large cities and small towns, the wealthy who dominated the society columns and set the standard for private and public consumption insisted that French cuisine was the best and then reveled in their monopoly of the cuisine they had ordained.

Opposing this economic and cultural aristocracy was a nascent urban middle class of managers, bureaucrats, small-scale entrepreneurs, and professionals.[18] They were an unlikely group of cultural insurgents. They labored in office buildings, lived in the suburbs, and traveled to work in trolley cars or, later, automobiles. Many were better educated and wealthier than their parents, but they lacked their parents' close ties to a local community. As a consequence, they turned to the public entertainments that the modern city offered to fill their leisure hours. They dined in restaurants, attended the theater, and courted at amusement parks, and in the process of making simple choices about which entertainments they would patronize, they became aware that they were participating in a shared culture with other potential members of the urban middle class. Ethnically diverse, occupationally dissimilar, and residentially sprawled, they were often united by nothing more than their eagerness to enjoy all of the city's pleasures.

Understandably, historians have overlooked the tensions that existed between aristocratic elites and the middle class. As C. Wright Mills wryly observed, the new middle class worked for the wealthy, turning "what someone else has made into profit for still another."[19] Dressed in square-cut, off-the-rack sack suits, turn-of-the-century middle-class businessmen have more often been viewed as conformists than revolutionaries. But in the course of the late nineteenth and early twentieth centuries, the men and women of the emerging middle class became increasingly dissatisfied with their exclusion from upper-class culture and angry at the American aristocracy's unbridled enthusiasm for all things European. Their frustration over class distinctions fueled the Progressive movement's antagonism toward "fat cats," trusts, absentee landlords, and divorce, and found further expression in editorials against the extravagance of aristocratic dining and the impenetrability of the French menu.[20]

Eventually, the middle class countered the "sacralization" of French food by celebrating cosmopolitan dining. For the middle-class patriot, cosmopolitanism was not the philosophical underpinning of a theory of post-nationalist, multicultural globalism, as it has become for modern theorists.[21] In fact, it was often mired in the imperialistic pride of a young nation that was in the process of taking its place on the world stage. Cosmopolitanism was, instead, a celebration of the culinary diversity of America's cities and the incredible variety of ethnic dishes available in the

United States. But cosmopolitanism also posed a challenge to the sacro-sanct monoculture of the aristocrats. Cosmopolitanism maintained that ethnic food could be every bit as good as French cuisine, and in doing so, it undermined the hegemony of aristocratic tradition with the "hetero-geneity of cosmopolitan tastes."[22] Once middle-class diners could enjoy German cuisine on its own terms at the fashionable HofBräu Haus, then French cuisine was no longer the measure of quality, and other aristocratic pretentions—stodgy manners, multicourse dinners, gender-segregated dining, tipping, and French-language menus—were also subject to scru-tiny.[23] Cosmopolitanism introduced relativism and allowed for greater re-spect for individual tastes. It laid the groundwork for a more democratic restaurant experience, and as a result, it has been as influential in the twen-tieth century as the aristocratic tradition was in the nineteenth.[24]

Agency and Culture

Tocqueville observed that "the passion for physical comforts is essentially a passion of the middle classes," and historians have successfully looked to consumption as a means of understanding the essence of the middle class in the late nineteenth and early twentieth centuries.[25] With a larger mem-bership than the upper class and more money than the working class, the middle class emerged as the nation's foremost consumers, and historians of culture and consumption have recorded their stories. Middle-class shop-pers are central to William Leach's account of the rise of the department store, they discover themselves in Richard M. Ohmann's examination of mass circulation magazines, and they purchase comfort and gentility in Richard L. Bushman's history of mid-nineteenth-century America.[26] For historians, the spending habits of members of the middle class—whether they are purchasing vacations, greeting cards, or home furnishings—have provided a window into the collective soul of the nation.[27] These studies and others supplement the broad spectrum of scholarship that has ex-amined the development of advertising and the role of mass marketing in constructing the modern economy, a literature that implicitly and ex-plicitly addresses middle-class consumerism. Nor are such musings about the central role of the middle-class consumer in American life limited to the hindsight of historians. America's corporations at the end of the nineteenth century looked to the middle class as the turbine of future economic growth, and extant evidence suggests that the middle class em-braced that role.[28] If budget studies of early-twentieth-century family ex-penses are to be trusted, it seems that middle-class Americans dedicated increasing portions of their household income to consumer goods, amusements, and vacations, and in the consumer economy, disposable income was the basis for cultural power.[29] Thus, it was not especially surprising that an article in the *Denton Journal* in 1927 declared that the middle class had become "the dominant social body" in America.[30]

Yet some of these studies, past and present, have treated the role of the middle-class consumer as inevitable and uncomplicated.[31] Desperate to demonstrate their distance from the teeming masses, those of the urban middle class are alleged to have surrendered their collective fate to advertisers and image makers. Whereas studies of the early-nineteenth-century middle class granted extensive agency to middling folks, studies of the turn-of-the-century middle class emphasize the inherent economic power of corporations rather than the autonomy of middle-class consumers.[32] Scholarship on the topic of advertising has been especially willing to depict middle-class moderns as pliant shoppers whose sad existences are filled with fruitless consumption. In these works, middle-class Americans are at best pawns, at worst hollow men and women wallowing in the false promise of consumer luxury.[33]

The persistence of studies that describe members of the middle class as dupes in a corporate world is surprising, given the widespread recognition of agency in less privileged and less empowered groups. Working-class and subaltern histories view class as constructed by a full range of life experiences, shaped but not determined by the dominant ideology. In recent years, studies of the American working class, from Roy Rosenzweig's *Eight Hours for What We Will* to Nan Enstad's *Ladies of Labor, Girls of Adventure*, have stressed the self-determination and dignity of laboring men and women.[34] Yet this sensitivity to a class's ability to shape its own experience has not always been in evidence when the subject is the middle class.[35] There are exceptions, but even these have tended to focus on marginal activities without fully relating these transitory acts of autonomy to the larger development of a modern middle class. Those of the middle class may have occasionally reimagined their place in the world, these works concede, but trapped in a seductive paradise of tin baubles and ceramic gewgaws, they lacked the power to challenge the underlying cultural and class hierarchy.[36]

Studying restaurants has allowed me to reexamine the middle class without the white noise of mass consumption, and what has emerged is a story that differs from previous examinations of the middle class in the late nineteenth and early twentieth centuries. First, as only a few works have done previously, *Turning the Tables* does not take the existence of the middle class for granted. It maintains that the middle class and the modern consumer economy were forged in tandem through the interplay of small consumer preferences. Second, without downplaying the eagerness of members of the middle class to separate themselves from the working class, *Turning the Tables* contends that a willful and self-conscious middle class was produced when middle-class urbanites began to distinguish themselves from elites. Finally, I argue that the ascendance of the modern middle-class consumer reshaped the cultural life of the United States in the twentieth century.

My approach, I concede, stems from my sympathy with the middle class. I was raised in a middle-class household in New Hampshire. My father was an electrical engineer at a local printing press manufacturer, and my mother stayed at home to manage the house and raise two children. When I arrived at the University of Pittsburgh to do my graduate work, I was shocked to find that the middle class was so often characterized by academics as a group of culturally bankrupt yes-men or insidiously repressive reformers. These reputations, contradictory as they seem, may not have been entirely undeserved, but they contrasted sharply with my family's story, a history in which first-, second-, and third-generation immigrants strove for economic security but were neither submissive consumers of culture nor status-anxious antagonists of progress. The middle class in which I was raised renegotiated its relationship to consumption daily. My parents cut coupons, supplemented family recipes for Lebanese dishes with newfound recipes for Chinese stir fry, and saved money that they might have spent on vacations so that their children could go to college. We had our favorite brands of butter and soup and avoided restaurants with indifferent food or bad service. Although as a historian I have tried to look at the late nineteenth century's middle class with a critical and objective eye, it was my own experiences that led me to reconsider the middle class and to take seriously the legitimate and sometimes noble efforts that members of the middle class made to define their place in the modern consumer economy.

Restaurants and Consumption

The restaurant provides a remarkably untarnished reflection of class, culture, and consumption at the turn of the century. Although the first American restaurants were founded in the 1820s and 1830s (prior to that, city dwellers and travelers dined at taverns, coffeehouses, and boardinghouses), until the Civil War, restaurant-going was a fairly uncommon event.[37] Restaurants—eating establishments that served food on demand—were located in urban business districts, transportation centers, or hotels and were patronized by both social elites and harried businessmen. Only the elites, however, dined out for pleasure, and they increasingly distinguished themselves from the middle class by ordering French dishes that were too expensive and too unfamiliar for most Americans. By the middle of the nineteenth century, the upper class effectively exercised a monopoly on fine dining.

It was not until the end of the nineteenth century that the upper class's influence over dining for pleasure was challenged. Beginning in the late 1870s, newspapers took notice of the growing number of middle-class urbanites who were patronizing restaurants. As the number of these middle-class (as well as working-class) diners increased, restaurant culture underwent material changes, adopting new menus and new forms of service, and these changes are the basis of this study. Through the examination of menu cards, cartoons, editorials, essay contests, photographs, diaries, poems, advertisements, and a host of other sources, including culinary journals and restaurant industry journals (many of which have been previously overlooked), I have tracked the most important material changes that restaurants underwent between 1880 and 1920. These sources, from restaurateurs, patrons, and publishers around the country, offer concrete evidence that the rise in middle-class patronage transformed public dining.

The turn-of-the-century restaurant is a uniquely valuable historical location in which to study the possible influence of the middle class on consumption. Unlike department stores or mass-market magazine ventures, restaurants were relatively modest entrepreneurial enterprises subject to the whims of the marketplace. Although a few local chains emerged in the late 1880s, the vast majority of America's restaurants in the late nineteenth and early twentieth centuries were locally owned.[38] Even many of the largest hotel restaurants, until just before World War I, were independent operations. As such, these restaurants were necessarily sensitive to the needs of their patrons. The records of R. G. Dun & Company, a nineteenth-century credit rating service, regularly attributed a restaurant's success to the owner's "connections" and the loyalty of his or her customers, and, as late as World War I, economists noted the industry's remarkable sensitivity to changes in demand.[39]

The small scale of restaurant enterprises meant that large numbers of restaurants were built and competition was stiff. National employment statistics, adjusted for increases in population, demonstrate that restaurant, café, and lunchroom employment grew over 400 percent between

1880 and 1930, dwarfing the expansion of other service industries such as saloons and hotels.[40] To succeed in this competitive market, restaurants were necessarily sensitive to customers' expectations and desires. Restaurant industry publications in the late nineteenth and early twentieth centuries consistently preached adaptation and innovation, recommending everything from decorative menus to automated kitchens. Likewise, restaurant managers and employees formed associations and published trade journals to disseminate new ideas about how to attract and retain customers. Since the costs of making changes in service or cuisine were relatively low, restaurateurs experimented. Unlike a department store that might require months and a substantial investment to develop a new clothing line, a restaurant could introduce a new menu, hire an orchestra, or change its waiters' uniforms with little planning or expense.

This is not to say that restaurateurs were given to capricious changes. In the following pages, I will argue the opposite. Restaurant owners were remarkably slow to adapt to the emergence of middle-class patronage, but their reluctance was not born of institutional sluggishness or fears about the costs of renovations. If restaurateurs did not immediately shift focus from the upper class to the middle class, it was because they were, no less than their customers, under the sway of the aristocratic class's cultural hegemony. Despite considerable economic incentives to embrace the reforms the middle class sought, restaurateurs at elite establishments identified with the interests of their wealthy customers and, for a time, saw themselves as protectors of aristocratic culture. When change came, it was because the managers of more modest dining rooms were quicker than their privileged counterparts to see the opportunity that middle-class dissatisfaction with upper-class dining offered. Their adaptations created competition that eventually forced even elite restaurants to take notice.

Restaurants are also ideal sites of historical study because they did little to create demand, unlike many of the large-scale consumer enterprises that emerged in the early twentieth century. Restaurateurs were slow to advertise, as they believed that modernization, urbanization, and the popularity of kitchenless apartments guaranteed the future of the restaurant trade. Most turn-of-the-century restaurants—indistinctly named after their owners (Mike's Restaurant, for example)—depended entirely upon word of mouth to survive. It was not until the founding of the National Restaurant Association in 1919 that restaurants began to advertise regularly.[41] As a result, changes in restaurant dining at the turn of the century are attributable to customers' desires more than marketers' skill at creating demand.

The rapid growth and entrepreneurial nature of restaurants provided the middle-class consumer with an opportunity to influence the course of dining in America. They also make it possible for the historical investigator to demonstrate that middle-class patronage had real and tangible effects on the consumer economy, both locally and nationally. For while restaurants were often small and independent, they were not insular. Restaurant managers, chefs, stewards, and waiters were rarely attached to a single establishment for their entire careers and instead changed jobs often, frequently traveling from state to state seeking better positions.[42] Cookbooks, trade journals, and shared menus (at a time when menus were printed daily and saved as souvenirs) also contributed to the construction of a national restaurant culture in which new dishes and new forms of service quickly spread from one coast to the other.[43]

At the center of this national culinary network were a few major cities (San Francisco, Chicago, New Orleans, Boston, and Washington), and at the top of the restaurant hierarchy was New York, the culinary capital of the United States. Although every major city made an occasional claim to culinary novelty, New York dominated America's dining culture. Culinary journals from across the country regularly reported on the fashions of Gotham—often to the exclusion of local restaurant news. The short-lived Boston-area culinary journal *The Dining Room Magazine*, for example, survived long enough to include a feature article on New York's restaurants, but it never ran a single story on Boston's restaurants. And *The Dining Room Magazine*'s devotion to all things New York was not exceptional. Both *What to Eat*, published in Minneapolis and later Chicago, and *The Southern Hotel Journal*, printed in Atlanta, had regular columns written by New York correspondents.[44] Even the folksy Indiana-based journal *Cooking Club*, which rarely addressed public dining, nonetheless conceded that the "world's greatest kitchen[s]" were to be found in New York. For restaurateurs and restaurant-goers throughout the country, New York was a crucible where the culinary controversies of the day were debated and dining fashions were established. Typical of the sway that New York held over American dining, southern hoteliers did not replace the locally grown oranges they served at breakfast with fresh squeezed orange juice until they were assured that "Sherry, Delmonico, Hotel Astor, The Knickerbocker, The Plaza, The Waldorf-Astoria, The Belmont, and all the other strictly first-class establishments [in New York] serve oranges exclusively this way."[45] Reflecting this historical centrality, New York remains at the center of this study, although extensive efforts have been made to recognize regional variations when and where they existed.[46]

Sensitive to change and national in scope, restaurants offer the historian an ideal vantage point from which to view the emergence of the consumer economy, but if restaurants were unique among turn-of-the-century businesses, they were not so unique as to make them isolated cases of change without historical significance. Restaurateurs faced the same challenges that most small businesses faced. They worried about the cost of raw materials, experienced hardships during economic downturns, and were pragmatic about government regulations (endorsing, for example, pure food laws and opposing Prohibition). Nor were restaurants isolated from larger shifts in urban culture. Changes in restaurant dining were closely tied to all aspects of public life, and the restaurant was often the public proving ground at the center of controversy. Debates about the role of women, public smoking, tipping, nationalism, internationalism, and nutrition accompanied the growth of restaurants in the twentieth century. As *Printer's Ink* observed in an article reprinted in *The Caterer* in 1900, restaurants were "colleges of living": "[When one] pauses to think of the vast number of people who regularly or occasionally lunch or dine in hotels, clubs or restaurants, and of the many thousands, hundreds of thousands, who for some weeks or months of every year, traveling on business and pleasure, make these establishments their temporary homes and refreshment places, one readily sees how widely disseminated is the influence of these colleges of living, the American 'Standard of Taste.'"[47]

Food has always been a central part of national cultures. In the United States, material changes in how Americans dined in public offer evidence of new, class-based ideas about consumption. Nonetheless, one should not overestimate what restaurants can tell us about the middle class or public culture at the turn of the century. Material changes in restaurant culture reflect attitudes, but they cannot directly reveal the feelings and dispositions of the middle class, and restaurant-goers have left only limited personal accounts of their feelings about dining. Restaurant dining was so quickly accepted as a normal part of urban life that it was generally taken for granted and received scant attention in memoirs and surprisingly commonplace coverage in newspapers. While we can see the changes, we can only speculate—carefully, and with as much corroborating evidence as possible—on the meaning of those changes to middle-class patrons.

Finally, restaurants were largely an urban phenomenon, and the historical record is richest with regard to those dining establishments located in America's largest cities. Although a national restaurant culture emerged in the late nineteenth century, it would be foolhardy to assume that small, local establishments in the hinterlands experienced the rise of their local middle class in the same way that urban institutions did. Urban restaurants were worldlier, more concerned with European opinion, and, with moneyed socialites in abundance and a steady stream of well-heeled tourists, less concerned with middle-class patronage than were restaurants in smaller cities. In fact, contemporary restaurant industry journals warned rural establishments not to borrow ideas wholesale from the city.[48]

While *Turning the Tables* is not the first account of the development of public dining in the United States to acknowledge the special role restaurants played in the emergence of American consumer culture, it does differ from previous studies in locating the nexus of change in the late nineteenth century and in arguing that clashes between classes played a central role in the emergence of twentieth-century consumer culture.[49] In particular, while I owe a great debt to Harvey A. Levenstein's foundational works on American dining, I have come to believe that Levenstein did not pay enough attention to the deliberate class struggle over dining. Before World War I, this struggle was the central factor in the transformation of dining that Levenstein ascribed to modernization, the emergence of new scientific ways of thinking, and Progressive activism.[50] Ultimately, modern restaurant culture was not the product of a new consensus around the role of science or ideas of cleanliness but rather a clash between the upper and the middle classes, and new diets were not the inevitable result of progressive change but the end result of a hard-fought battle in the marketplace.

The Menu

Turning the Tables is organized around an overlapping chronology that highlights three periods of transformation. In the first two chapters, I examine how French restaurants in the mid-nineteenth century served the interests of elite Americans seeking to buttress their social standing by invoking the culture of Europe and also look at the efforts middle-class Americans made to imitate their social betters. In the two chapters that follow, I explore how the failure of imitation led to the development of middle-class restaurants and cosmopolitan tastes. Unable to master the cultural capital of elites or to find affordable food in upper-class restaurants, the middle class colonized lower-class restaurants, businessmen's dives, and even ethnic restaurants and, by the late nineteenth century, aggressively championed the superiority of middle-class dining. Finally, in the last four chapters, I consider the growing economic and cultural influence of the middle class in the early twentieth century and contend that aristocratic restaurants changed to accommodate middle-class tastes.

Smaller, English-language menus and accommodations for women diners represent, I argue, the triumph of the middle-class ideal of cosmopolitanism over aristocratic ideas of dining. Over time, eating out became more democratic even as members of the middle class replaced elites as the arbiters of culture. However, the middle class's influence was not without limits, and those limits, especially with regard to the elimination of tipping, are also explored. Finally, throughout the development of modern restaurant culture, I maintain that the middle class came to know itself as a social and consumer class.

Corralling cultural changes, organizing them into a chronology—even an overlapping one—and using that chronology to demonstrate how cultural power was exercised invariably does some violence to the historical record. Cultural change is messy, often unorganized, slow, and sometimes contradictory, and changes in restaurant dining rarely fit into neat typologies. The newspaper columns, songs, menus, images, novels, and advertisements used in this study offer only partial glimpses and inexact accounts that have to be interpreted, refined, and organized to tell a story. With few first-person accounts to confirm my findings (restaurant-goers occasionally recorded where they ate in diaries but rarely discussed what the meal meant to them), I had to use my judgment and avoid dwelling on the exceptions, including the occasional rant of a cranky middle-class diner who loved French food. However, American cultural histories have too often described events without fully explaining them, and while I respect the challenge that imposing order on a chaotic past entails, I believe strongly that the most vital job of the historian is to interpret.

Handmaiden of the Middle Class

The middle-classing of American restaurant culture created a new cosmopolitan restaurant experience that caused much dismay among self-proclaimed gourmets and Francophile chefs. Few, however, were as discerning as Edward R. J. Fischel, the managing steward of the Piedmont Hotel in Atlanta. In a forum on the future of the culinary crafts that appeared in *The Caterer* in 1911, Fischel complained that "the art of cookery is slowly [being] stifled by commercialism[;] the great chefs are still with us but these chefs [have] had to bend to commercialism."[51]

Commercialism was the handmaiden of the middle class. In the nineteenth century, upper-class restaurants embraced an elite, aristocratic tradition that emphasized luxury, exclusivity, and complex rules of social behavior. These restaurants were elegant and their decorations were grand,

and they made their profits by charging extravagant prices to a small sliver of the population. Although not formally off-limits to the middle class, these establishments were exclusive. By 1911, however, the restaurant business had changed. As the middle class began to exert its economic and cultural influence, restaurateurs discovered—in much the same way that Henry Ford embraced mass production—that profits were to be had by lowering standards, increasing efficiency, and catering to the largest number of customers. The shift from exclusive to mass dining offered the middle class, whose numbers and collective wealth made them attractive to restaurateurs, an opportunity to promote cosmopolitan ideals and to exercise unprecedented influence over how Americans dined. The new restaurants were never exclusively for members of the middle class, but in the end, these restaurants served their interests by selling middle-class values to rich and poor alike and, in doing so, helped to establish the hegemonic status of the middle class in modern society.[52]

TERRAPIN À LA MARYLAND
The Era of the Aristocratic Restaurant

In 1842, Charles Dickens visited the United States and left unimpressed. He was received warmly; as Dickens admitted, "There never was a King or Emperor upon the Earth, so cheered, and followed by crowds, and entertained in Public at splendid balls and dinners." The admiration, however, was not mutual.[1] While Dickens's feelings toward America ultimately soured over copyright law, in his autobiographical account of the trip, *American Notes*, and his subsequent novel, *Martin Chuzzlewit*, the great democracy's eating habits were singled out for ridicule:

> The poultry, which may perhaps be considered to have formed the staple of the entertainment—for there was a turkey at the top, a pair of ducks at the bottom, and two fowls in the middle—disappeared as rapidly as if every bird had had the use of its wings, and had flown in desperation down a human throat. . . . Great heaps of indigestible matter melted away as ice before the sun. It was a solemn and awful thing to see. Dyspeptic individuals bolted their food in wedges; feeding, not themselves, but broods of night-mares, who were continually standing at livery with them. Spare men, with lank and rigid cheeks, came out unsatisfied from the destruction of the heavy dishes, and glared with watchful eyes upon the pastry.[2]

Dickens, whose aspirations to respectability included a love of French cuisine, found the culinary life of America barbarous.

The American public was not amused by lurid descriptions of its dining habits, and a heated, transcontinental exchange of barbs ensued. Encapsulating the views of the harshest of Dickens's American critics, editor and poet Park Benjamin Sr. wrote in *The New World*, "Mr. Dickens, whatever may be his merits as a writer, is, as will readily be admitted by those who have been most in his society, a low-bred vulgar man."[3] But the public outcry only made Dickens more recalcitrant. "I have nothing to defend, or to explain away," the aggrieved author added in a new preface to *American Notes* published in 1850. "The truth is the truth; and neither childish absurdities, nor unscrupulous contradictions, can make it otherwise."[4]

Twenty-five years later, Dickens returned to the United States. The trip, intended to secure Dickens's financial future, was carefully managed to protect the aging author's frail health. Dickens attended only one public dinner, spent most of his time in Boston and New York, and reserved ample time to rest privately in his hotels. His hosts made every effort, grudgingly or not, to demonstrate that the United States of 1867–68 was a very different place from the young country that Dickens had encountered in 1842. Gone were the pesky reminders of democratic unruliness, from the gargantuan, disordered meals to the slinging of tobacco juice, and in their place was a new, distinctly European refinement. In New York, Dickens was housed at the Parisian Westminster Hotel, where he had exclusive use of the back stairs and a French waiter, the former to protect his privacy and the latter to flatter his appetites. And when Dickens eventually consented to a public dinner, it was not surprising that it took place at Delmonico's, the nation's most European restaurant, where French cuisine—and only French cuisine—was served.[5] Perhaps the gambit worked. At the dinner at Delmonico's, Dickens offered a surprising (and, admittedly, financially opportune) retraction of his previous libels. "I have been received with unsurpassable politeness, delicacy, sweet temper, hospitality, consideration, and with unsurpassable respect for the privacy daily enforced upon me by the nature of my avocation here and the state of my health," Dickens proclaimed to an enthusiastic crowd of reporters and dignitaries. Given these "gigantic changes," Dickens resolved that "so long as I live, and so long as my descendants have any legal right in my books," those books would include an appendix testifying to his revised opinion of America.[6]

It would be folly to ascribe Dickens's change of heart to any one cause. He hoped to repair a costly rift with the book-buying American public, and undoubtedly his revised sentiments were a byproduct of his restricted itinerary. Still, Charles Dickens, like most people of means in Europe, equated a country's civilization with its culinary fare, and perhaps nothing better symbolized the new America that Dickens admired than the ready availability of French cuisine. His American hosts understood this. Instead of the massive hotel dinners featuring as many as seventy dishes with which he was feted during his first visit, immigrant chefs renowned for their mastery of French cuisine prepared his farewell dinner at Delmonico's. And, as a correspondent for the *Boston Transcript* noted, it was when Dickens spoke of "gigantic changes" in the "graces and amenities" of American life that "every man rose to his feet and acknowledged by loud hurrahs the compliment so beautifully expressed."[7]

In the decades that followed Dickens's second trip to the United States, members of America's elite became more refined in their tastes and more imitative in their aspirations. Unprecedented economic opportunities following the Civil War created a wealthy class of capitalists who, seeking to distinguish themselves in a democratic nation that had traditionally spurned class distinction, turned to Europe to find markers of their social standing. Along with imported marble, Old Master paintings, and haute couture, they imported French culinary culture (and the chefs and waiters required to prepare and serve it). By the end of the century, French cuisine dominated the menus of the best restaurants and, supported by the economic and cultural elite, gained hegemonic status. French cuisine was the best, and Americans, if they had any taste at all, wanted to eat French food.[8]

The American Aristocracy

By the second half of the nineteenth century, an American aristocracy of wealth dominated the cultural contours of consumption. The growth of large cities, the mass arrival of cheap immigrant labor, and the concentration of large-scale business enterprises in the hands of a few made unprecedented luxury possible; the dour egalitarian ideals that had suppressed extravagant displays of wealth in the days of the early Republic were a distant memory. The Gilded Age was a period of conspicuous consumption, the heyday of aristocratic culture.

Only 1 or 2 percent of the population, buoyed by America's four thousand millionaires, was rich, but these capitalists, merchants, manufacturers, and landowners controlled 27 percent of the nation's wealth by 1870.[9] Although the distribution of wealth is difficult to measure between 1880 (when census takers stopped asking about real estate and personal property) and the introduction of the income tax in 1913, it was widely believed at the time that the economic equality that characterized Toqueville's America was quickly fading as the eastern capitalist establishment consolidated its control of the nation's riches. Recent economic studies lend credence to these beliefs.[10]

Money made the capitalist, but wealth alone did not make the American aristocrat. Historian Michael E. McGerr argues that the wealthy were a homogenous group with a shared history and shared values. They were primarily of English descent, Protestant, from middle- and upper-income families, and generally college graduates. "Above all," McGerr observed, "the upper ten shared a fundamental understanding about the nature of the individual. Glorifying the power of the individual will, the wealthy held to an uncompromising belief in the necessity of individual freedom."[11] Yet these were intangible characteristics and hardly exclusive to the wealthiest Americans. To distinguish themselves publicly, members of the upper class engaged in unprecedented conspicuous consumption. In the years that followed the Civil War, American elites invested their surplus wealth in mansions, fancy balls, extravagant dinners, elaborate carriages, charities, and collections of paintings.[12] Not every newly minted businessman sought the social sanction that prodigal spending might bring, but a significant number—calling themselves "Society"—did, and once "Society" had taken root, it inspired competition and even more extravagant acts of splendor. Consumption, particularly the conspicuous consumption that economist Thorstein Veblen described in 1899, was an honorific investment in social reputation, an effort to secure membership in elite society through the purchase of the right address, the right clothes, and the right table at a restaurant.[13]

Lavish consumption had a practical purpose. Elaborate spending, and the standards of taste and imposed exclusivity that accompanied it, created bonds among the men and women of old wealth and pedigree (in their vernacular, the "nobs") and the industrial magnates whose fortunes were less than a generation old (the "swells").[14] In their private dining rooms, these wealthy Americans enacted the intricate parlor games that settled their internecine claims to status and secured their place in local blue books. Arbitrary but acknowledged distinctions, the stuff of Edith Wharton novels, determined who belonged and who did not. But it was in public venues—opera houses, restaurants, theaters—that subtle distinctions in food, clothing, and manners were transformed into public declarations of class membership. Extravagant spending, conspicuous leisure, and sanctioned manners established the legitimacy (and the hegemonic sway) of wealthy Americans' claim to aristocracy.[15]

An early historian of society life noted that New York elites (and, for that matter, Pittsburgh, Chicago, and San Francisco elites) were "frantically eager to adopt any earmarks of social distinction."[16] But the rapid growth of the ranks of America's millionaires in the late nineteenth century posed a challenge for any aristocrat seeking to demonstrate success through conspicuous consumption. A relatively young nation without a history of aristocracy, America had failed to develop homegrown accoutrements of wealth, the socially certified markers of aristocracy.[17] American fashions, paintings, architecture, and cuisine, the traditional indicators of honorific value and economic success, were, at best, in their infancy. For those Americans who chose to be conspicuous in their spending, it was necessary to look to Europe, where an authentic, hereditary nobility set the standard for what constituted enviable wealth. By the late nineteenth century, wealthy Americans were purchasing dresses in France, paintings in England and Italy, and titles in Spain, and were also eagerly embracing European manners and cuisine.[18] As French novelist Paul Bourget wrote after visiting the United States in 1893, "[American millionaires] do not admit they are different from the Old World, or if they admit it, it is to insist that if they chose they could equal the Old World, or, at least, enjoy it."[19]

Aristocratic Dining

By the mid-nineteenth century, adventurous visitors to America's cities could find rough taverns serving beefsteaks, pie, and beer as well as exotic Italian restaurants featuring spaghetti, olive oil, and—shockingly!—garlic. Yet this diversity belied America's culinary orthodoxy. Like their counterparts throughout Europe, wealthy Americans demanded French cuisine prepared by French chefs and served by professional waiters who knew how to flatter their patrons.

FRENCH RESTAURANTS

French cuisine had not always been the hallmark of excellence in the United States, although it had always signaled pretension. Historian Dixon Wecter noted that in the 1780s, Philadelphia society was "startled" by Mrs. William Bingham's Francophile "innovations" at dinner parties, and contemporary chroniclers noted "a prejudice against dishes with French names."[20] As late as the 1820s and 1830s, Americans looked to England more than France for guidance regarding correct culinary fashions (ignoring, apparently, the growing importance of French cuisine in London), and French restaurants were familiar only to the most fastidious residents of a few American cities, including New York and Philadelphia.[21] But in the years just prior to and immediately following the American Civil War, as the Industrial Revolution churned out steel, jute, and millionaires, French cuisine transformed the upper-class menu.[22] In 1857, August Belmont, the wealthiest of New York's parvenus, caused a sensation when he hired a

French chef for his private home, and a few years later, Pierre Blot—a transplanted Frenchman and author of *What to Eat and How to Cook It*—opened a cooking academy in New York dedicated to spreading the gospel of French cuisine among the city's fashionable families.[23] Trips to Europe on the "Grand Tour" further stimulated the elites' interest in French fashions and cuisine, and soon New York's millionaires were offering exorbitant salaries to lure French chefs (many of whom were actually Swiss or Austrian) to the United States. As New York's late-nineteenth-century cultural arbiter Ward McAllister wrote in *Society as I Have Known It*, "The French *chef* then literally, for the first time, made his appearance, and artistic dinners replaced the old-fashioned, solid repasts of the earlier period."[24]

Delmonico's restaurant in New York set the national standard.[25] Founded by Swiss immigrants in the 1820s, Delmonico's brought French restaurant cuisine to the United States. Sam Ward, banker and bon vivant, recalled the first Delmonico's restaurant, located on William Street in the business district, as a "primitive little café" with excellent food and "prompt and deferential attendance, unlike the democratic nonchalance of [its rivals]."[26] Yet if the atmosphere was "primitive," the menu was not. An 1838 menu—printed in both French and English—was ten pages long (excluding the wine menu) and featured such dishes as *Pâté de volaille aux truffes* (described as Chicken Pie with Truffles) and *Salmi de becasse* (Woodcock Salmi).[27]

"Del's," as the restaurant was affectionately called, grew in pretension as New York emerged as the nation's capital of capitalists. By midcentury, Delmonico's cuisine was celebrated throughout the United States and in Europe. In an 1848 *New York Daily Tribune* article extolling the virtues of Delmonico's (at a time when French food was still a novelty), reporter George Foster remarked that Delmonico's was the "only complete specimen" of the "expansive and aristocratic *restaurant*" in the United States, an "equal in every respect, in its appointments and attendance as well as the quality and execution of its dishes, to any similar establishment in Paris itself."[28] Many Europeans agreed. British illustrator and travel writer George Augustus Henry Sala claimed that Delmonico's was the best French restaurant in the world.[29]

As fashionable New York moved uptown, Delmonico's moved with them, and its reputation and commitment to French refinement grew.[30] In 1862, the restaurant moved to Fifth Avenue, abandoned the two-language menu for a French-only menu, and acquired the services of Charles Ranhofer, a French-born and Paris-trained chef who would soon become America's most celebrated cook.[31] The Fifth Avenue restaurant, Delmonico family biographer Lately Thomas wrote, "marked the dividing line between Delmonico's as purely a restaurant—foremost of its class, which was the foremost—and Delmonico's as a social institution, influencing the manners, tastes, and customs not only of the city but of the nation for decades to come."[32]

Following the Civil War, wealthy New Yorkers increasingly entertained outside their homes, and "Del's" was the site of many of the formal and informal gatherings of New York's rich and famous. It hosted the select Patriarch Balls, gatherings of clubs and business associations, and the private dinners of the Astors and the Vanderbilts—and every event was decidedly French. As one patron recalled, Delmonico's "afforded a Parisian aspect" to New York.[33] Even when French food seemed incongruous, a French dinner at Delmonico's bestowed prestige. Celebrating St. Patrick's Day in 1884, the Society of the Friendly Sons of St. Patrick ate *poularde braisée, Montpensier,* and *croquettes de Ris de Veau, Parisienne.* The menu was decorated with green ribbons, but the cuisine was unmistakably French.[34] Likewise, Delmonico's dubbed a number of dishes "à la Centennial" to celebrate America's hundredth birthday in 1876, but despite their "American" names, the dishes were French to a fault.[35]

In time, Delmonico's influence on American dining extended beyond New York. The restaurant's kitchens served as a training ground for some of America's more elite chefs and stewards, and its menus were passed along by patrons and reprinted in magazines and newspapers.[36] Dishes created at Delmonico's (such as Lobster Newburg) were imitated throughout the nation, and as America's first culinary brand name, dozens of restaurants throughout the country borrowed the "Delmonico" sobriquet.[37] The first dining car on an American railroad was named "Delmonico"; restaurants in New Orleans, Chicago, San Francisco, and Albia, Iowa, were called Delmonico's (although they were not owned by the Delmonico family); and almost any restaurant known for excellence might informally earn the title.[38] In New York in the early twentieth century, the best Chinese and Jewish restaurants in the city were known as the "Chinese Delmonico's" and the "Yiddish Delmonico's."[39] Acknowledging its influence in 1895, historian James Ford Rhodes wrote in his *History of the United States from the Compromise of 1850*: "Any person who considers the difference between the cooking and service of a dinner at a hotel or restaurant before the Civil War and now, will appreciate what a practical apostle of health and decent living has been Delmonico, who deserves canonization in the American calendar."[40]

Delmonico's success inspired imitation, although in the mid-nineteenth century it was usually pale imitation. With the exception of a few vanguard French restaurants like Antoine's in New Orleans or the Poodle Dog in San Francisco, few American restaurants in the early 1870s had the chefs or the expertise to prepare a complete French menu.[41] Yet in large American cities, French terms and French dishes occasionally appeared on the bill of fare of respectable establishments. A November 1873 menu at the Fifth Avenue Hotel in New York, a favorite meeting place for New York's Republican Party, prominently featured corned beef and cabbage, beef tongue, roast beef, mutton, Mallard duck, and chicken pie *American Style*. Nonetheless, a growing number of items on the menu were sauced in the French style: the pig's feet were served with Madeira sauce, the turkey livers with Champagne sauce, and the rice croquettes *à la crème*.[42] Similarly, in 1873 the Gardner House in Chicago used the term "entrée" on its menu, and, along with baked pork and beans, turkey with cranberry sauce, and smoked beef tongue, offered dishes with French names, including *fried pickerel, a la Tartare*, and *croquettes au chocolate*.[43] But outside of the largest cities, the traditional Anglo-American menu printed predominantly in English remained the midcentury norm. The Falmouth Hotel in Portland, Maine, used no French in its September 1870 menu. The courses were listed in English (entrées were referred to as "side dishes"), and even the most exotic item on the menu, rice croquettes, was simply described as *Rice Balls with Jelly*.[44] Likewise, The Oceanic, a resort hotel on Star Island in New Hampshire's Isles of Shoals that attracted wealthy vacationers, featured an 1874 menu that seemed insulated from the growing trend toward French cuisine with entrees that included *Stewed Lamb, Country Style; Lobster Salad*; and *Fricassee of Chicken*.[45]

By the end of the 1870s, however, all major cities, and a good many small towns, were home to a French restaurant. While no American restaurant rivaled Delmonico's reputation in the nineteenth century, and few cities could challenge New York's claim to the culinary vanguard, restaurants across the country gallicized their bill of fare, serving French food—or at least dishes with French-sounding names—to a public that was beginning to consider French cuisine a mark of high culture. New York, Philadelphia, Jacksonville, St. Louis, Denver, and San Francisco all hosted well-known restaurants that served French food, as did resort locations like Saratoga, St. Augustine, and Portsmouth.[46] One wit claimed that a California mining boomtown was not complete until it had a saloon, a billiards hall, and a French restaurant.[47]

Although the Anglo-American menu did not disappear entirely, these upper-crust restaurants featured French dishes described with French terms. The fashionable Brevoort House in New York offered entrées such as *ris de veau piqué aux épinards; côtelettes of salmon à la Victoria;* and *salmi of partridge au chasseur* (alongside Irish stew and fried halibut with salt pork) on its 1886 "Carte du Jour."[48] Sunday dinner at the West Hotel in Minneapolis in 1886 included *tenderloin of beef, larded, a la Lucullus; sweet breads en caisses a la Reine; cutlets of lobster a la Genoise;* and *pate de foie gras* washed down with *punch a la Cardinal* and followed by *carlotte russe a la vanilla* and *petit four Melis.*[49] And even the fashionable but isolated New Hampshire tourist destination The Oceanic, which ten years before had featured stewed lamb and lobster salad, served *Beef a la Mode with Noodles; Chicken Livers Sauté, Fine Herbs;* and *Tripe Stew a la Lyonnaise* in 1884.[50] In fact, it was nearly impossible to find a respectable restaurant in any mid-sized American city after 1880 that did not supply at least a few French entrées with French sauces. French cuisine—particularly the expensive and exacting cuisine of Paris—had become de rigueur for any exclusive party or banquet. In the Gilded Age, one could attend a gathering of physicians over *Ris de Veau Braise, aux petits pois nouveaux* at the New Willard Hotel in the nation's capital; banquet with brewers serving *Pompano au beurre de Montpellier* at the St. Nicholas Hotel in St. Louis; enjoy the company of southern planters over *Filet de Bœuf, Pique aux Champignons* at the St. Charles Hotel in New Orleans, or join a meeting of tailors in Buffalo for *Timbale de volaille à la reine* at the Hotel Iroquois.[51]

Despite this enthusiasm for French food, the shared ideal of an elite cuisine did not ensure that every respectable restaurant in the country could find the staff, ingredients, and patrons to support a genuine Parisian-style French restaurant. The rigorous training that French chefs received kept their number in the United States low for much of the nineteenth century. Only at the very end of the century, as travel costs decreased and the general prosperity of America drew the attention of newly minted European chefs, did the number of chefs begin to meet demand.[52] In the meantime, restaurateurs made compromises. Many restaurants gallicized their menus even when French names did not always indicate genuine French cuisine. As a result, the menus of the nineteenth century are sometimes a hodgepodge of culinary traditions: part southern plantation, part English tavern, and part French restaurant. Yet the effort to appear French was nearly universal among the better class of restaurants, and the pains restaurants exerted to appear French, no matter what was being served, suggests the cachet that French cuisine had achieved in the United States. In 1885, vacationers at The Antlers in Colorado Springs were offered a curiously "American" dinner featuring *consommé a la Cleveland; sweet breads braise a la Tilden; turkey wings stuffed a la Harrison;* and, for dessert, *inaugu-ration pudding with reform sauce, a la Cleveland and Hendricks*.[53] Even mani-festly American dishes were given French names. The United States Hotel in Saratoga was so determined to enhance its status by the repeated use of French terms that the celebrated American specialty, turtle soup, was transformed into the French-styled *terrapin stew à la Maryland*.[54]

THE MENU'S MYSTIQUE

Restaurants that sought an elite patronage attracted wealthy customers with elaborate rules governing dress and manners, attentive service, and elegant decor, but more than anything else it was the menu that estab-lished a restaurant's reputation. French menus augured European distinc-tion. They promised that the restaurant was exclusive and that the restau-rant's patrons were sophisticated. In 1893, when New York's social gadfly Ward McAllister recommended in an open letter that "Chicago society import a number of fine French chefs" in advance of the World's Fair, Chicago newspapers lashed out at his presumption that New York had a right to dictate fashion to the Midwest. Few denied, however, the underly-ing assumption that the formal test of American civilization would be its command of French cuisine.[55]

The appeal of the French menu rested on its mythic origins: in particu-lar, the widely held belief that the first French restaurants were established in Paris by private French chefs reduced to commercial pursuits when the French Revolution deprived them of their aristocratic patrons.[56] A 1900 textbook used by primary school teachers to teach domestic science re-peated the well-worn tale. "The era of fine cookery in France began dur-ing the reign of Louis XIV.[*sic*], in [the] seventeenth century," the textbook claimed, "when the nobles vied with each other in compounding delicate dishes. . . . After the Revolution, the cooks of the nobles, being obliged to provide for themselves, established restaurants where the most delicate and elaborate products of their skill were at the service of the one who could pay the price. The world has adopted the restaurant system, and French cookery is the standard of excellence."[57] But there was no truth to the legend. Rebecca L. Spang has demonstrated that the restaurant, ironically, owed its origin to France's pretentious pre-revolutionary bour-geoisie, who sought to demonstrate their sensitivity by taking restorative soups in public (the word "restaurant" is derived from the French word *restaurer*, "to restore"), and not to roving bands of unemployed chefs set adrift by the Revolution.[58] Nor was the restaurant uniquely French. The Chinese, as early as the thirteenth century, had restaurants that served customers individual dishes made to order.[59] Nonetheless, this august, albeit mythic, tradition stamped French cuisine with the imprimatur of European aristocracy. Tropes of kings, courtiers, and cooking, when repeated in the United States, bestowed aristocratic distinction on those who could now command the services of French chefs.[60]

Thorstein Veblen argued that conspicuous consumption was not about beauty or utility but rather the honorific value a purchase embodied.[61] This was true of French cuisine. Nineteenth-century accounts of elaborate and expensive meals made only passing reference to taste. Etiquette guides emphasized table decorations, flower displays, and china; menus were elaborately decorated with ribbons, art, and calligraphy; dishes were named in honor of famous Europeans. The gallicizing of the American menu mattered not because it guaranteed flavor, since there was no well-circulated standard by which one judged whether a particular French meal was more satisfying than another; rather, the French menu embodied a culinary aesthetic that promised status, a guarantee that by ordering the dish, the restaurant patron would acquire social standing. In 1902, when rumors of a decline in Parisian standards of cooking reached the United States, American food historian George H. Ellwanger confidently concluded that the French menu would never disappear because "French cookery has been tacitly accepted as unparalleled on the same principle that a titled personage is supposed to possess superior accomplishments."[62] The American aristocracy banked its reputation on that principle, but for an emerging middle class, it was this intangible and timeless value, disempowering to the patron who might not like aspic or terrapin, that made the aristocratic restaurant so intimidating.

THE FRENCH CHEF

The honorific value of French cuisine was enhanced by its founding myths, but it also derived from the belief that French chefs were more accomplished. Although generally the French chef's skill was accredited to rigorous training, many nineteenth-century observers also believed that the French were inherently better chefs.[63] In 1885, *The Caterer* observed that "chefs are made, not born; but to attempt to make one out of any other stuff than a Frenchman, would, we fancy, present as many insurmountable difficulties as are presumed to surround the task of making a silk purse out of a—well some other material than silk."[64] Regardless of the reason, French chefs were widely admired. As one culinary historian observed at the turn of the century, the "championship of gastronomy has for centuries been held by French chefs."[65]

In America, native-born chefs—even the best—learned their trade haphazardly, without formal training or an organized system of apprenticeship. In contrast, a chef trained in France in the nineteenth century underwent a well-choreographed and intensive apprenticeship that might last twenty years. This training, the professionalization of the culinary trade, made the French chef "a personage of consequence."[66] At a time when wealthy Americans were establishing their reputations by purchasing European art and marrying their daughters to cash-strapped sons of European nobility, the ability to command the labor of a trained French chef was a recognized means of enhancing one's reputation.[67] Some wealthy Americans were reported to have paid exorbitant salaries, as much as $10,000 a year (nearly ten times a modest middle-class salary), to their chefs, and restaurants seeking to attract a well-heeled clientele were compelled to compete.[68] The *New York Times* reported in 1895 that there were "at least five hotels and restaurants in this city where chief cooks draw a salary of $6,000 a year, with perquisites that will easily net $10,000 a year more." "Civilized man," the newspaper concluded, "cannot live without civilized cooks; and a cook who knows his business can command a higher salary in New-York to-day than a man who is equipped to take the Chair of Languages and Literature in a college."[69]

The large salaries paid to French chefs were in recognition of the French chef's mastery of culinary skills, but, as with the menu, myth enhanced the reality. Although the French culinary arts were undergoing change as celebrities such as Marie-Antoine Carême in the early nineteenth century and Auguste Escoffier in the late nineteenth century standardized and simplified haute cuisine, in the view of many Americans the French culinary tradition represented a timeless, regulated tradition of excellence. As described in the *New York Sun*, the iron-fisted Académie de Cuisine ruled the French culinary world:

> Since the day of Napoleon I[,] the Académie de Cuisine has regulated the art of the French kitchen just as the forty Immortals look after the language of the French nation. The cookery academy conducts classes, has its big corps of apprentices, sits in solemn conclave, for instance, on whether wax flowers can be legitimately used in the decoration of banquet pieces, decorates its members and bestows medals and diplomas that mean everything to the ambitious and artistic French cook. . . . That is one of the reasons why French cookery is kept up to its present lofty standard, and why it is taken

so seriously by its pupils and master workmen. It is on the whole a very big thing to be a first-class cook in Paris.[70]

While in practice the various culinary associations that sprang up in France in the 1880s, including the Académie Culinaire de France (originally, Union Universelle pour le Progrès de l'Art Culinaire) and the Société des Cuisiniers Français, did not exert the influence that the *Sun* attributed to them, the newspaper's exaggerations reflected the widespread belief that French chefs practiced a form of culinary alchemy, the ability to transform a basic human activity—eating—into something luxurious and exclusive.

The French chef's skills seemed to transcend the laws of science. Although some foods might cost more than others, in the end, a baked potato was still a baked potato, and it tasted the same to the king as it did to the pauper. The French chef defied this apparent truism. The "veritable chef," "French to his finger tips," could transform the common article of food into an aristocratic dish. As M. E. Carter told readers of *What to Eat* in 1901, "The plebeian potatoes likewise, through chef's transforming wand, will seem to belong to the elite vegetable."[71] Similarly, Ward McAllister compared the French chef to a novelist, "an educated, cultivated artist," "almost as much inspired as writers."[72] The metaphor McAllister used suggests that the chef created a literary masterpiece, a narrative of tastes that—if told well—promised social recognition and advancement.

On occasion, McAllister's metaphor seemed to take tangible form. Developed by French chef Antoine Carême in the early nineteenth century, grande cuisine was renowned for the construction of ornate, inedible food sculptures. These elaborate decorations, created from sugar at great expense, served no other purpose than to decorate the table and to celebrate the wealth of the men who commissioned them. At New York's annual French Chefs Ball in 1891, W. K. Vanderbilt's "kitchen" produced "a reproduction of his yacht, while Mr. Cornelius Vanderbilt's chef contributed galantines *décorées sur socle* [molded white meats in jelly on a decorated pedestal]." Size, realism, and pomp were the prized attributes. "The collection occupied one whole table and numbered eighteen distinct pieces," a reporter observed. "The first of these to catch the eye was an American villa, a massive structure built on a rocky elevation decorated with trailing vines and blossoming flowers. On the balconies of the villa and from its windows appeared ladies and gentlemen in elegant dresses, and altogether the effect was exceedingly realistic."[73] These "pieces de fantaisie," as an 1896 *Times* society reporter aptly labeled them, were a public celebration of the estates and the restaurants that produced them.[74] They were grand, showy spectacles designed to flatter the creator's patron, not feed the guests. Like Vanderbilt's actual, seaworthy yacht, his chef's confectionery yacht was a conspicuous display of aristocratic wealth.

THE FRENCH LANGUAGE

With French cuisine and the French chef came the French-language menu. By the 1890s, it was unusual to find an elite menu that did not use French to describe its cuisine, whether the food was genuinely French or not. The persistence of the French language ensured that even as the middle class entered the restaurant, the restaurant remained an aristocratic institution. The French-language menu was more than a subtle allusion to the aristocratic origins of the restaurant; it was a passkey to culture that excluded those who were not wealthy, traveled, and educated.

In the nineteenth and early twentieth centuries, French was not a language of education and business but of breeding, diplomacy, and culture. Educators required that secondary and college students learn the classical languages (Latin and Greek), arguing that the rigor of mastering these languages contributed more to the intellectual development of pupils than mastery of French or German. In 1900, only 14 percent of American public high school students in grades nine through eleven studied French, and fewer and fewer students would learn to speak French in the early twentieth century.[75]

The paucity of French-language education in the United States increased the symbolic value of French to the elite. For the American aristocrat, speaking French was a sign of cultural superiority and a worldly education. Trips to Europe and a language tutor were, after all, among the privileges enjoyed by the scions of the wealthy.[76] As a professor at the New England College of Languages wrote in 1895, if one observes French "speakers" in America exhibiting "self-satisfaction . . . you may conclude they have acquired their knowledge of the tongue in a fashionable boarding-school."[77]

A thorough knowledge of French made it easier to read a restaurant menu and to place an order, but speaking French was not enough; the French-language menu posed other challenges to the uninitiated diner lacking the appropriate cultural capital. French menus employed truncated French, derogatorily referred to as "cook's French," a complex language with its own linguistic conventions. Phrases were mysteriously abbreviated ("à la mode," for example, was written as "à la"), and meanings changed with the context. "À la mode anglaise" was written as "à l'anglaise" and connoted different preparations when modifying a potato, fish, or custard dish.[78] And to make matters worse, descriptive phrases were often honorific, defying direct translation. A 1902 anecdote illustrates this well. As the story was told, one Colonel Sam Reed was breakfasting at Delmonico's when he decided to have some fun with his waiter. After looking over the French menu for a few minutes, he called to his astonished server: "You may bring me some eggs blushing like Aurora, and some breeches in the royal fashion with velvet sauce; and for dessert be sure you bring a stew of good Christians and a mouthful of ladies."[79] Each and every item he asked for was a direct translation of a dish on the menu; for the uninitiated diner, however, these terms were meaningless.

Complicating matters further, American chefs, many with only a passing knowledge of French, routinely created faux French names for the dishes they served. Macaroni and cheese, a staple entrée in the 1870s, was described by the Fifth Avenue Hotel as *Macaroni, au Parmesan cheese*. But that description was hardly universal. In other menus dating from the same period, the dish is described as *Macaroni au gratin au Parmesan*; *Macaroni lié, aux fromage, à la Milanaise*; *Macaroni a la Neopolitaine*; *Macaroni à l'Italienne*; *Macaroni lie au fromage, à la crême*; and *Macaroni de Naples au gratin*. This endless, slapdash variation made it impossible for those who did not know French to memorize a few easy terms before going to a restaurant, although those who dined regularly at elite restaurants (or employed a French chef at home) might learn both the conventions and idiosyncrasies of "cook's French."[80] Confusing as the system of naming dishes could be, an aristocratic American diner steeped in the rituals of dining and experienced with spoken French could order dinner without risking the waiter's scorn.[81] Middle-class upstarts, without the linguistic skills to decode the elaborate names given to French dishes, were outsiders, even if they occasionally had the money to purchase a full-course dinner at an elite restaurant. As the *Chicago Post* noted in 1914: "To order plain sweetbreads and peas, instead of ris de veau [and] petits pois, identified a person as an aborigine who would tuck his napkin into his collar and eat his sweetbreads and peas with his knife. . . . We do not pretend to understand this; we only know from experience that it is so."[82]

ARISTOCRATIC SERVICE

The commitment of the elegant restaurant of the nineteenth century to flattering its wealthy clientele extended beyond the menu and the food to every aspect of service. Maîtres d'hôtel and waiters were servants, and the best restaurants were imitations of the baronial dining rooms of America's millionaires.

The aristocratic dining experience began at the door. Here the head-waiter met the patron and passed judgment. Patrons who looked like they might not be able to pay were refused service; the rest were seated according to their social standing. Jessup Whitehead's 1889 stewards' manual explained the process of social sanctioning entrusted to the headwaiter: "He has obscure tables, lower end tables, middle-class tables, upper-class tables and exclusive tables, and he sorts strangers as they come and allots them to their tables according to their appearance or their deserts generally, without their being at all aware of the sorting process they are subjected to. That is what he is at the door for."[83]

Patrons were not as unaware as Whitehead's promise of discretion implied. A table near a well-established family was considered an opportunity for social advancement, a table near a window was a chance to be seen, and a table near the kitchen was universally recognized as a snub. This process of selection and exclusion assured the elite diner that his or her standing in society was acknowledged by the restaurant and advertised to the other guests, and when, on rare occasions, mistakes were made, the restaurant's reputation might suffer.[84]

Once the headwaiter had seated the guests and withdrawn, a waiter arrived with the bill of fare. The waiter's appearance was an integral part of the restaurant's atmosphere. "Waiters must be promptly in line at roll-call," one guide to waiting tables stated, "clad in the proper uniform, with shoes neatly polished."[85] Although dress varied from establishment to establishment, the most common uniform consisted of black pants, polished shoes, vest, bow tie, and a white or black jacket depending on the time of day.[86] Uniforms were a guarantee that the staff was there to wait on the restaurant's patrons, and the uniformity of dress suggested the interchangeable unobtrusiveness of elite service. Guides for wait staff repeatedly advised waiters to be "neat and clean in their general appearance" and provided detailed instructions on proper hygiene. One guide even warned waiters "to avoid having your face com[e] in too close contact with your guests, as your breath may be offensive."[87]

Appearance was more than a clean collar and a well-scrubbed face, however; race and ethnicity reinforced the honorific value of service. No group was viewed as more fit for restaurant service in the nineteenth century than African Americans. Evoking images of slavery, the black waiter became a part of a restaurant's aesthetic, a physical reminder of servitude. As E. A. Maccannon, an African American waiter, explained, "[P]atrons in the majority of classes prefer colored waiters. . . . [An] intelligent polished piece of ebony is just the thing needed to give force of contrast to the marble guests and at the same time properly distinguish the servitor from those he serves, and gives the exquisite and artistic variety of color-blending to the splendor of the surroundings in the dining room."[88]

Yet by the time that Maccannon was writing in 1904, racial attitudes were shifting. Racism spurred by the great migration of African Americans to the North, the availability of low-wage immigrant labor, and the increasing identification of wealthy Americans with European aristocracy contributed to the marginalization of black waiters in northern and western cities.[89] While black waiters continued to find employment in the South and Midwest, new ideals of servitude emerged on the two coasts.[90] On the West Coast, restaurateurs prized Asian waiters for their alleged docility, and on the East Coast, western Europeans, especially those with a continental accent, were preferred. "White" waiters, who had apprenticed in France or Switzerland, were especially sought after, for they signified America's mastery of European expertise.

Appearance was not the only determinant of good service in the nineteenth century. A waiter was expected to be ever attentive to the needs of a guest but never intrusive. To ensure good service, early-nineteenth-century waiters were dressed and drilled like an elite military corps.[91] Waiters would march into the dining room in lockstep and serve dinner in synchronized fashion. This required extensive drilling and a military-style chain of command. In 1848, Tunis G. Campbell, an African American headwaiter with experience in Boston and New York (and a leading abolitionist), suggested "[w]aiting-men should be drilled every day, except Saturday and Sunday."[92] As restaurant hours became more flexible and dining rooms larger in the second half of the century, choreographing the wait staff became less common, but military discipline was still required. W. F. Cozart explained in 1898, "[O]f all the army of people employed for one of these occasions [a club dinner], perhaps the head waiter's duty is the most strenuous and exacting. . . . Under his command are an hundred men, trained with military precision, each to know his exact place and duty and attend to that alone."[93]

At most elite establishments, each table had its own waiter who stood quietly by the table waiting (as the title implies) to serve as needed. "Politeness, obedience, and submission" were considered the essential qualities in a good waiter, and waiters were regularly warned never to "assume or show too much authority over a guest [or] . . . become officious in any respect."[94] But while the waiter had to veil his authority, he exercised

James Wells Champney, "The Guardian Angel—Eagle Hotel, Asheville."
From *Scribner's Magazine*, March 1874. Courtesy of the Picture Collection,
The New York Public Library, Astor, Lenox and Tilden Foundations.

tremendous power over the success of the meal. Until the late nineteenth
century, most American hotels and many independent restaurants served
table d'hôte dinners.[95] For a fixed price, a restaurant patron was offered a
broad menu featuring up to seven or eight courses with as many as ten
items for each course. No one was expected to sample everything on the
menu, but there were also no formal restrictions. The nineteenth-century
diner viewed this broad bill of fare as an opportunity to demonstrate his
artistry by carefully constructing a choice dinner. The expert waiter quietly assisted; he would subtly guide the diner, informing him or her of
what was fresh and assisting with the selection of appropriate wines. Expert waiters were taught to "anticipate the wants of the guests," and a
kindly waiter might even bring two or three entrées to the table, allowing

the diner to select what he or she liked best.[96] As a poem from 1901 noted, the talented waiter was a student of human psychology:

> Pick out some first-class waiter,
> I'll tell you what you'll find,
> A man of keen perception,
> One with an active mind,
> Who reads a guest like magic,
> And tells quick as a flash
> If he will call for sweetbreads
> Or make his order "hash."[97]

Such tributes were rare, for if the waiter was very skilled, his assistance was barely noticed and the aristocratic diner would claim credit for the imagination and skill needed to select the meal.

Disciplined, unobtrusive, and obedient, a well-trained wait staff secured a restaurant's reputation for exclusivity and flattered the egos of aristocratic patrons. Like the French menu, the waiter evoked an aristocratic past (whether it was Bourbon France or the plantation South) where wealth commanded loyalty.

ELITE PATRONAGE

The European chef and the well-trained waiter embodied the aristocratic ideal, but it was the continued patronage of wealthy clients that made a restaurant "aristocratic." Wealthy Americans who had established aristocratic credentials through private acts of conspicuous consumption lent their reputations to the public sphere of dining by being seen in restaurants and hotel dining rooms. Newspaper society columns lauded and publicized the restaurants of the wealthy, and in time, elite guests, no less than the chef and waiters, became a part of a restaurant's reputation. As Ward McAllister reminded New York Society, "the success of the dinner depends as much on the company as the cook."[98]

Elite restaurateurs understood the important role that popularity among the society set played in their continued success. Wealth begat wealth, and restaurants carefully cultivated reputations to attract aristocratic patrons. In New York, society men were sometimes paid secret commissions in order to influence the choice of venue for aristocratic balls and other upper-class gatherings.[99] George Boldt, the proprietor of the Waldorf-Astoria, purportedly said: "I'd rather see Mrs. Stuyvesant Fish enjoying a cup of tea in an all but empty Palm Room than a dozen lesser-known guests there feasting."[100]

Perhaps the best evidence of the symbiotic relationship between elite restaurants and their patrons appears in the obituaries of restaurants that closed their doors. No restaurant or hotel in one of America's major cities moved, closed, or remodeled without a paean to the patrons who made it famous. Delmonico's move to Madison Square in 1876, for example, warranted a *New York Times* article recounting the famous banquets held in its dining rooms as well as a list of more recent diners. "For about ten years . . . society has given its dinners at Delmonico's," the paper recalled, "and among the names which have marked its annual lists of guests are Henry Wilson, Schuyler Colfax, Gen. Sherman, Rev. Dr. Hitchcock, J. Lothrop Motley, Major Gen. McDowell, Edwin P. Whipple, Judge Hoar, William Cullen Bryant, Mr. Evarts, Senator Conkling, Secretary Robeson, and Charles Sumner."[101] Nor was this eulogy atypical. The shuttering of the Fifth Avenue Hotel in 1907 (the *Times* gently called it the "passing of the Fifth Avenue") led to a similar tribute. In the dining room of the Fifth Avenue, readers were reminded, one "met men who made and unmade Presidents and Governors and who decided political questions of highest importance."[102] The half-page story recalled dozens of dinners attended by the historically significant, the wealthy, and the merely influential.

Such tributes were so commonplace that any association with the upper class was worthy of mention. The closing of the Stevens House produced a typical tribute to its aristocratic past in the pages of *The Steward* in 1918. Popular with shipbuilding magnates, regular guests included "George Steers, builder of the famous yacht *America*; John Ericsson, inventor of the *Monitor*; John Englis, and Joseph Francis, inventor of the lifeboat bearing his name, while Commodore Vanderbilt was an occasional patron." But a return visit was not required for the magazine to make note of a famous patron. The article recorded that "like every popular hostelry the Stevens House had its tragedies," including the 1858 suicide of "Henry William Herbert, better known as Frank Forester to three generations of lovers of healthful, open-air sports."[103]

Cultural Capital and Social Darwinism

Thorstein Veblen explained in his 1899 study of the leisured class's conspicuous consumption that "superior gratification" stemmed not from utility but from costliness "masquerading under the name of beauty."[104] The French restaurant with its European service and foreign trappings was among the symbolic goods that allowed the upper class to distinguish itself from the lower classes in the late nineteenth century.[105] It embodied luxury, tangibly represented aristocratic taste, and, when necessary, monitored the boundaries of polite society. Dominated by the aristocracy, the fashionable restaurant of the nineteenth century may have appeared to be open to anyone who could afford a meal, but it was never a democratic space.

French sociologist Pierre Bourdieu argued in *Distinction* that it is the command of cultural capital as much as economic capital that serves to differentiate one class from another. Cultural capital is knowledge, an inherited expertise in cultural matters that can be "cashed in," in much the same way that money can be spent, to achieve prestige. "Knowing that 'manner' is a symbolic manifestation whose meaning and value depend as much on the perceivers as on the producer," Bourdieu wrote, "one can see how it is that the manner of using symbolic goods, especially those regarded as the attributes of excellence, constitutes one of the key markers of 'class' and also the ideal weapon in strategies of distinction, that is, as Proust put it, 'the infinitely varied art of marking distances.'"[106] Buying a mansion on Fifth Avenue distinguished the wealthy from the middle-class New Yorker because it represented an enviable expenditure of money, but dining at Delmonico's, unselfconsciously selecting a meal, ordering in perfect French, and speaking to the waiter with the correct tone of polite condescension, was no less effective in setting aristocratic Americans apart from their social inferiors. Wealthy society men and women's familiarity with the symbolic language of wealth was flagrantly on display when they dined out, and elite restaurants—eager to retain the patronage of these families—created environments that reinforced class distinctions.[107]

Mastery of French restaurant cuisine—its etiquette, language, and multiple courses—also made growing class disparities seem natural. By implying that there were no hard and fast barriers to participation in upper-class culture, restaurants made it appear that opportunities existed for the enterprising young man with a French dictionary and a pocketful of savings to participate fully in aristocratic culture. As a result, those who could not afford a meal or who were intimidated by the waiter were not victims of an increasingly stratified society but of their own failings, and those who could afford a meal and were not intimidated by the waiters were merely enjoying the legitimate fruit of their labors. Reiterating the gospel of wealth—the prevailing belief that affluence was evidence of superiority—the aristocratic restaurant allowed America's elite the opportunity to demonstrate the justness of their claim to cultural and economic influence by ordering blue point oysters and charlotte russe.

The stability of this cultural hierarchy stemmed from peculiar notions of social evolution popular in Gilded Age America. The tenets of social

Darwinism held that the survival of the fittest applied not only to the natural world but also to man's social interactions. It promulgated the belief that a racial hierarchy existed in which all societies paled in comparison to the accomplishments of western Europeans. Influenced by theories of civilization advocated by the social Darwinists—Herbert Spencer, William Graham Sumner, Andrew Carnegie, and a cadre of other elite thinkers—food chroniclers in the late nineteenth and early twentieth centuries held that "good taste" was a product of good breeding. As Britain's most famous nineteenth-century culinary historian, Abraham Hayward, wrote, there was a "hereditary quality [to] taste."[108]

Historians have justly questioned whether social Darwinism created the laissez-faire economy of the late nineteenth century, but in doing so they have often overlooked the cultural significance of distinctions grounded in economic and biological determinism.[109] Social Darwinism may not have been the underlying source of business decision-making in the late nineteenth century, but these ideas were nonetheless embedded in popular discussions about race relations, immigration, women's roles, and eating. In an article titled "The Cultured Palate" that originally appeared in *Self Culture* in 1900, A. H. Gouraud distinguished himself as one of the most ardent proponents of a link between high birth and gastronomic discrimination. Gouraud argued that "superior taste" was "absent in most animals, and its deficiency in savages is evident from their manner of eating, their rapid swallowing, their silence and gravity, their intensity of action, and finally from the fury and fierce desire that gleams from the eye as it rests upon the food." While the savage's experience of food had not yet been "wholly eliminated from civilization," Gouraud argued that only when the basest instincts cooperated with man's "intellectual facilities" could the pleasures of the table be fully appreciated. The finest food, therefore, offered the "highest gratification to the most cultured intelligence."[110]

For Gouraud, as for many American social Darwinists in the nineteenth century, civilized tastes were not a strictly biological inheritance but rather the effects of cultural evolution. However, ascribing discriminating palates to elite cultures sanctioned those who, influenced by the emerging science of nutrition, sought to establish dietary laws based on racial hierarchies. M. O. Warren, writing about the science of dietetics, made the claim forcibly in *The Steward* in October 1903:

> It is obvious . . . that the practices of the more successful races and
> the more affluent classes of a nation are more likely to yield good
> [dietary] dictate models than the practices of backward races and

poorer classes. The former have had greater freedom of choice, and their success in the struggle for existence is evidence of the suitability of their food habits. Now the British race and the other races of western Europe, together with their descendants in different parts of the globe, are, on the grounds stated, best able to supply us with a body of dietetic customs that may serve as a model.[111]

Tapping into century-old beliefs that a civilization could be judged on the sophistication of its cuisine, both Gouraud and Warren believed that western Europe represented the highest advancement of culinary culture.[112]

Not every scientist agreed with Gouraud and Warren, but popular understandings of diet and biology echoed social Darwinist sentiments and applied the idea of a racial culinary hierarchy to differences in class and occupation.[113] In a letter on French cooking that Carl Benson wrote to the editors of the *New York Times* in 1873, he argued that "[t]he man with an iron constitution, who has passed the greater part of the day in manual labor, or hunting or shooting, may eat the same dinner month and month, but those not able to up the like amount of Spartan sauce [that is, work, exercise, hunger, and thirst] require variety, and here the French art comes in."[114] Likewise, Ward McAllister's suggestion to the planners of the 1893 Chicago World's Fair that they import French chefs stemmed not only from eastern snobbery but from the deep-seated belief that the wealthy, if not biologically ordained to eat fancy food, were at least culturally disposed toward foie gras. "In these modern days, society cannot get along without French chefs. The man who has been accustomed to delicate fillets of beef, terrapin, pâté de foie gras, truffled turkey and things of that sort would not care to sit down to a boiled leg of mutton dinner with turnips."[115] And the reverse was true as well. Popular conceptions of nutrition at the turn of the century, shared by some in the medical profession, held that the refined foods of the elite were not substantial enough for the laboring classes. Dr. Stephen Smith Burt, the house physician at the upper-crust Hotel Astor in New York, displayed his belief in the social Darwinism of dining in comments he made in 1905. Misappropriating studies that demonstrated the relationship between exercise and calories, Burt asserted that the quality of a man's steak should reflect the work he performed:

> [A] working man, one who is employed out of doors at hard manual labor, needs rugged food—something upon which his digestive organs can work for a protracted period. Give such a man a delicate tenderloin steak for luncheon and he would become faint before the

day ended, simply because it is too easily digested—for him. But, as it is an ill wind that blows nobody good, poverty is often a blessing in disguise, since people in very moderate circumstances are not heirs to the ailments which haunt and afflict the highly prosperous. On the same line of reasoning, high prices are frequently a means of deterring people from overeating.[116]

Burt's understanding of the relationship between diet and the social hierarchy underscored thinking about nutrition in the years before most people fully understood the science of calories and nutrients. Refined foods, everything from tenderloin to white bread, were the birthright of the rich and sedentary; hearty foods, course cuts of meat and whole-grain breads, were (conveniently) more appropriate for the poor.[117]

Social Darwinist theories helped to justify the pretensions of the wealthy and explain the exclusion of both workers and many in the middle class from the elite dining rooms of the Hotel Astor.[118] If only the aristocrat was born and bred with the sensitivity and taste necessary to appreciate pâté de foie gras or terrapin soup, then the exclusion of other classes was, as Dr. Burt suggested, in their own best interest. However, social Darwinist ideas about food were only an undercurrent in the rise to prominence of the aristocratic French restaurant. The raison d'être for the aristocratic restaurant was its symbolic role in publicly certifying the wealthy as the social and cultural elite.

Conspicuous consumption helped to undermine early-nineteenth-century ideals of equality and ushered in a new age where cultural and economic capital established one's station in life. The aristocratic elite thrived on distinction and exclusion and made the aristocratic restaurant, with its elaborate cuisine and complex etiquette, a guardian of privilege. In the Gilded Age, an elite corps of diners set the standard for what constituted a proper and respectable dinner, and they guarded that privilege jealously.[119]

PLAYING AT MAKE BELIEVE
The Failure of Imitation

In the 1890s, it was the custom on New Year's Day for elite New York hotels to serve buffets in the men's dining rooms.[1] Respectable restaurants
offered these free-of-charge buffets, prepared by the city's most notable
chefs, each jockeying for accolades, hoping to win the patronage of bachelor gentlemen during the coming year. The menus at these "free lunches"
were elaborate. In 1893, the Savoy's offerings included *consommé en tasse*;
aspic d'hiútre, Bresilienne; *saumon à la Parisienne, sce. verte*; *galantine de dinde
d'Adirondack, Renaissance*; *pièce de bœuf, à l'Anglaise*; *chaud-froid de Cailles,
Perigord*; *jambon d'York, à la gelée*; *pain de foie gras en Bellevue*; *langue de bœuf,
à l'Ecarlate en lyre*; *faisans Anglaise en Vollière*; *pâté de grouse en croustade,
truffé*; *salade de homard à la Russe*; *mayonnaise de Volaille à l'Americaine*; *petits
fours*; and *pièce montes*.[2]
Although there is no evidence that middle-class diners were turned
away from these New Year's Day banquets, reporters who attended the
events described a homogeneous crowd drawn from the fashionable set:

> Several of the leading hotels yesterday set out in their cafés sumptu-
> ous and inviting free lunches, although the chefs who set out the dis-
> plays of delicacies did not call them by the vulgar name by which they
> are commonly known. They were patronized largely by the unfortu-
> nate and fashionably-attired men about town, who are comparative
> strangers to the comforts of domestic life.
> Chef Fari's display in the Plaza Hotel café attracted a throng of
> well-dressed men, *who would doubtless feel ashamed to stand up at a table
> and eat the ordinary free lunch*. They were not there because they really
> desired anything to eat, but mainly to gratify curiosity, kill time, and
> pay compliments to the artistic skill of the chef.[3]

What kept the less-fashionably attired middle class away? The dining rooms were open to the public, the food was free, and (as the reporter implies) middle-class men were accustomed to free lunches (served by bars with the purchase of a beer). The sugar sculptures of the Columbus Arch and life-sized Graces that adorned a number of the banquets were imposing but surmountable barriers.[4] Looking back, we can only assume that a less tangible obstacle barred the middle-class bachelor from availing himself of the best that New York's restaurants could offer.

The comments of a newspaper reporter, presumably a fledgling member of the middle class, provide clues that help explain the reticence that middle-class men felt about patronizing an elite restaurant or hotel. Intimidated by the use of French terms on the bills of fare of the uptown restaurants' buffets, the anonymous reporter favorably contrasted the modest Murray Hill Hotel to the elite man-about-town's favorite establishment, the Hoffman House. On New Year's Day, the reporter observed, the Murray Hill Hotel served an English-language menu "in thoughtful consideration of the few patrons of the house who do not understand French," while at the Hoffman House "the chef did not deem it necessary to use English in naming his produetious [productions?]" in "recogn[ition] of the fact that the Hoffman House patrons all understand French."[5] For the correspondent, command of the French menu separated the aristocrat from the middle class. Two years later, another *Times* reporter drew similar conclusions from his New Year's Day forays. At the end of an article on the free buffet, he reflected, "No one who knows the ropes need start in hungry for the New Year."[6]

The middle class did not "know the ropes." With its foreign menu, dress codes, and intimidating service, the elite restaurant was an alien and unforgiving space. Etiquette guides might talk about manners and French cuisine, but books could not substitute for the extensive experience of those who regularly dined at the Waldorf, Hoffman House, or Savoy. Rather than feel like an outsider, many middle-class New Yorkers spent their New Year's Day at home, where the cuisine was familiar and the dishes were described in a language everyone understood. Those middle-class bachelors who had no other choice but to eat out on New Year's Day seem to have ventured downtown to the familiar business district, where hotels like the Murray Hill served friendlier fare—"roast beef, bologna, crackers, cheese, *potatoes à la Irlandaise* and pigs' feet"—with fewer linguistic disguises.[7]

The French restaurant operated for the convenience of its aristocratic clientele. Its food and service, while theoretically available to all who could pay, were unfamiliar and intimidating to middle-class Americans who lacked the right breeding and training. At first, with few options available, middle-class arrivistes sought to master the language of the French restaurant and imitate the culinary experiences of the restaurant-going wealthy, but when imitation failed and the costs of dining out seemed too great, nascent members of the middle class rejected the codes of etiquette that the aristocrats had championed and began to create a public culture that catered to their own tastes.

The era of imitation stretched from the end of the Civil War well into the first decade of the twentieth century, but as early as the 1870s some middle-class critics bemoaned the extravagance of elites, complained that the middle-class diner was a second-class consumer, and celebrated the man who measured his wealth by a healthy appetite and not the cost of his dinner. In the end, the high cultural and economic costs of elite dining set in motion a middle-class revolution in public dining that transformed the class structure and cultural hierarchies of the United States.

The New Middle Class

During the years in which America's social elites were establishing a claim to aristocratic authority based on what they ate, how they dressed, and who they entertained, the middling folks were undergoing their own economic and cultural upheaval. Early in the nineteenth century, artisans, merchants, lawyers, and ministers constituted America's first substantial, urban middle class. As a whole, this producer and professional class owned their own enterprises and did not do manual labor.[8] The industrial expansion that happened midcentury, however, undermined the economic and structural base of the producer and professional middle classes. While some merchants grew wealthy by turning small factories and mercantile establishments into large competitive firms, others found that the growth of big business threatened their livelihoods. As historian Stuart Blumin observed, these producers were undermined at the moment, ironically, when "the term 'middle class' was achieving a quite stable form and a widely understood meaning within the American language."[9]

Yet even as economic growth threatened members of the producer middle class, new opportunities emerged for their children. In the late nineteenth century, a managerial revolution created a need for clerks, salespeople, professionals, lawyers, managers, and administrators to organize the burgeoning economy.[10] While few of these employees could expect, as perhaps their parents had, that they would one day own their own commercial enterprises, their jobs were secure and their prospects of owning a home, hiring a maid, and sending their children to college were good. Joined by the most fortunate sons of Irish and German immigrants, they went to work in white collars, they were comfortable enough to purchase luxury items and take vacations, and their wives and children did not work. Many lived in cities where corporate headquarters would soon reach to the sky.[11] These beneficiaries of the Industrial Revolution—urban, white-collar men and women with middling salaries—would form the nucleus of a new middle class in the late nineteenth century.

Little quantitative historical research on the occupations and incomes of the middle class in the late nineteenth and early twentieth centuries exists, in part because few historians accept that these imprecise measurements offer an accurate picture of what it meant to be a member of the middle class.[12] Income, for example, is at best an awkward measure of membership. In 1900, a unionized factory worker could earn over nine hundred dollars a year, more than the average annual salaries of employees in health services, state and local government, public schools, and the retail trade, and nearly as much as federal civilian employees or clerical workers in the manufacturing and transportation sectors.[13] The higher income, however, did not necessarily mean that the unionized laborer identified more with the midlevel clerk in a department store than he identified with his lower-paid coworkers in the trades. Further, individual income rarely reflected a family's resources or lifestyle. Income might be supplemented, hidden, or squandered; real income must account for familial contributions, the vicissitudes of contract work, and successful and unsuccessful investments.[14] Luck and lifestyle—inheritance, investments, credit, lottery winnings, number of children, drinking habits, and a host of other variables too numerous to count—also determined the real income of a family.

Nor is occupation a stable predictor of class. When viewed over time, occupational categories changed meaning.[15] A clerk in the nineteenth century, Richard Ohmann argued, was often second in command of a business and might someday own a shop of his own, while a clerk in the twentieth century was more often counter help or a secretary holding a low-paying job with little opportunity for advancement and little job security.[16] In Booth Tarkington's *Alice Adams*, the protagonist's ridiculous scheming is precipitated by the desperation felt by the family of a middle-class department store clerk as the breadwinner's job gradually lost its prestige.[17] Likewise, in an age in which professional standards were still evolving, even a doctor's social status was dependent upon more than his job title. A country doctor might consider himself local gentry, an urban doctor hired by a large hospital might see himself as a member of the middle class, and a self-described doctor in an immigrant community with little or no formal medical training might consider himself as working class (as is the case with Frank Norris's character McTeague, a dentist).[18] Surveys conducted in the twentieth century have suggested that class identity is rarely a simple reflection of earned income or the job one holds.[19]

Although income and occupation cannot tell us with certainty who belonged to which class, viewed in aggregate they demonstrate the growing material base of professionals and managers at the turn of the century.[20] Limited data from manufacturing firms suggest that real daily wages of all employees (adjusted for inflation) nearly doubled between 1860 and 1914, increasing by more than 25 percent in the 1890s alone.[21] In part, these increases were a product of the emergence of a large number of salaried workers. The number of professional occupations, as P. K. Whelpton argued in 1926, doubled (when adjusted for increases in the population) between 1820 and 1920.[22] Managerial positions alone grew from 161,000 to approximately 1 million between 1880 and 1920 (more than doubling the percentage of the population that worked in management), and the number of male clerks, just one occupational group within the new white-collar workforce, rose 300 percent from 1880 to 1900, substantially outpacing overall increases in the labor force.[23] Other, less direct measures of middle-class growth—from increases in home ownership and the size of the government workforce to decreases in the length of the workday and increases in leisure time—all suggest that more and more Americans had the time and money necessary to enjoy a moderately prosperous life.[24] Taken collectively, these statistics suggest that potentially 10 to 20 percent of Americans might make a claim to membership in the middle class at the turn of the century.[25]

Historians' failure to find an accurate scale with which to measure the middle class reflects the lack of middle-class cohesion in the 1870s and 1880s. Neither owners of capital nor exploited workers, the new managers and professionals initially found little basis for class solidarity. The home, the mid-nineteenth-century cultural foundation of the middle class, was increasingly under assault from commercialization, urbanization, and the sporadic booms and busts of the economy. New roles for women, suburbanization, and the ethnic diversity of the emerging middle class further undid traditional markers of middle-class identity, and while scattershot efforts at professional organization (from the American Medical Association to Harvard alumni organizations) brought some members of the urban middle class together, these efforts were limited.

Yet despite the lack of a clear, cohesive middle-class identity, the lines between success and failure were well drawn in the middle third of the nineteenth century. As historian Scott A. Sandage has demonstrated, the modestly prosperous family with money in the bank and a home could distinguish itself from the "born losers."[26] Financial security, even if it was often fleeting in the topsy-turvy overheated economy of the second industrial expansion of the nineteenth century, was concrete evidence of success. This success created material differences in the lives of the middle class, including a better diet, which made manifest the distance between the middle and working classes.[27]

Yet a coherent middle class would not emerge until middling folks could also distinguish themselves from the rich, and in the middle of the nineteenth century it often seemed as if those of the nascent middle class were more interested in joining the wealthy at their lavish hotel tables than in highlighting class differences. The clever social climber honeymooned at Niagara Falls, dined at the Clifton House on the Canadian side of the Falls, and, in imitation of the truly wealthy (whose honeymoons often involved the Grand Tour of Europe), let it be known that he had spent the summer abroad. He might conduct a business meeting in the lobby of the Astor House, eat dinner in the hotel's restaurant, and feel that he was—at least superficially—part of the upper class.[28] The wealthy, however, were raising the bar for membership in the elite; public dining, in particular, was becoming the exclusive province of the upper class. Many a social novice would try and fail to imitate the lifestyle of the well-to-do, only to learn that a modicum of economic success did not necessarily entitle one to the respect and social recognition that set the American aristocrat apart from the rest of society.

This failure to imitate the wealthy forced middle-class urbanites to reconsider their status. Shaped by their role as consumers rather than producers, the fledgling middle class constructed an identity in the public spaces of urban centers, the virtual spaces of mass-marketed books and magazines, and—ultimately—in the dining spaces of American restaurants. While restaurants were just one space among many that middle-class urbanites contested, their struggle to find a respectable restaurant in which to eat a decent meal proved important in their effort to distinguish themselves from the overweening avarice of elites. In the end, this effort would not only birth the modern middle class but also transform dining in America.

In 1870, however, there were hardly any signs of the impending transformation in dining. Fashionable restaurants, mostly in hotels, catered specifically to the tastes of elites, and only a few options existed for those who sought respectability but could not afford a French meal. While lunch places offered quick meals to hungry businessmen and travelers, the urban landscape was largely dominated by a dizzying array of saloons, oyster venders, and other establishments too squalid for many white-collar men and unquestionably off-limits for their genteel wives and children. Faced with few choices and aspiring to raise their social standing, many in the nascent middle class initially gravitated to the respectability that elite French restaurants and hotels promised, despite the high cost and unfamiliar menu. Only when these efforts at imitating the wealthy failed did middle-class urbanites begin to create the markers of their own class identity.

The Cult and Culture of Imitation

The aristocratic restaurant was theoretically open to all, but its exclusivity was never in doubt. An informal system of discrimination embedded in the requirements of cash and culture made aristocratic restaurants uncomfortable for those who were neither rich nor intimately familiar with the intricacies of dining in a French restaurant. If members of the middle class were rarely barred from dining in aristocratic restaurants, they were nonetheless marked as second-class consumers, imitators of a culture they did not fully understand.

Upper-class culture had not always been so exclusive. In the intimacy of the early-nineteenth-century city, the upper and middle classes were residential neighbors who shared markets and dining establishments.[29] Early-nineteenth-century eating establishments served table d'hôte dinners at long, common tables where members of the upper class and middle class mingled.[30] Distinctions existed, but a strong republican culture suppressed ostentatious displays of wealth while promising that the separation between the hard-working, middle-class merchant and the hard-working, upper-class merchant was traversable. By the second half of the nineteenth century, however, great fortunes, products of the industrial expansion that followed the Civil War, were increasingly accompanied by great acts of conspicuous consumption that widened the divide between the millionaire and the merchant. The rise of the French restaurant was one indication of this growing disparity.

Yet even as the wealthy purchased larger homes and entertained on a grander and grander scale, the restaurant—unlike the urban gentlemen's club—remained an ostensibly public space in which elites and the middle class might mingle. The restaurant was fashionably exclusive, yet formally unrestricted, because it served the interests of the aristocratic class to keep the restaurant public. Spaces where the classes met were necessary for social reproduction. In the restaurant, the nouveaux riches auditioned for inclusion in the city's social register, and boundaries between society, the unfashionably rich, and the middle class were drawn. As one of the first chroniclers of America's upper crust observed, the "assimilation of plutocracy to aristocracy has been the vital problem of society in America since its beginnings, but particularly since the rise of great industrial fortunes."[31]

Seduced by the prospect of advancement for a time, the most social-climbing element in the middle class embraced the French restaurant and its cuisine, expecting that imitation of upper-class culture would lead to acceptance. An 1888 article first published in the *New York Telegram* recounted the story of a young man who invested his money in clothes, "dine[d] conspicuously at first-class restaurants at least once a month," and spent his free time in the lobbies of expensive hotels. Although he lived in a menial boardinghouse, he kept this information from his acquaintances and employers, hoping that if they saw him in first-class establishments they would assume he came from money. "My income is only $1,200 a year, yet people think my income five times that amount; consequently I am sought after. . . . By and by I am invited to dinner, and I get acquainted with the ladies of the family. My promotion to an important position follows."[32] Similarly, Ward McAllister, long before he had established his reputation as the majordomo of dining in New York, gave a dinner for Commodore Vanderbilt at the New York Hotel. The carefully chosen meal was an attempt to ingratiate himself with the Vanderbilts, and McAllister was gratified by the judgment of the hotel's manager: "My young friend, if you go on giving such dinners as these you need have no fear of planting yourself in this city."[33] Other social aspirants set up fully funded accounts in advance of dining at fashionable restaurants so that they could make it appear that they were regular guests who had been extended credit, a luxury restaurants typically reserved for well-heeled patrons.[34]

For those aspiring to eat like the wealthy, knowledgeable guides offered assistance. Arthur M. Schlesinger estimated that before the Civil War, when distinctions between the middle and upper class were still muted, an average of three new etiquette guides were published each year; following the war, as both the fledgling middle class and the publishing industry boomed, between five and six new publications were released annually.

Another scholar has identified over two hundred etiquette guides published in the United States before 1900, and etiquette books were only one source of advice on manners and dining in the Gilded Age.[35] Articles on how to map out the social landscape were the bread and butter of dozens of late-nineteenth-century magazines and newspapers.[36]

Etiquette guides promised to help the ambitious middle-class family acquire, through careful study, the subtle codes of dress, manner, and behavior that set the elite apart from the parvenus. "Behind endless manuals of etiquette and blue books of behavior, scrapbooks of culture and outlines of knowledge, and all the nostalgia for European titles as well as Old Masters," historian Dixon Wecter wrote, "lies the aspiration of a rising middle class attempting to seize, even by casual symbols, upon some guiding wisdom, upon the art of being rich gracefully, which Americans are accused of lacking."[37] Manners maven Abby Buchanan Longstreet, while conceding the advantages of birth, assured readers of her 1883 guide to etiquette that "elegant manners should not be considered beneath the attention of any man or any woman. They will carry a stranger further up the heights of social ambition than money, mental culture, or personal beauty. Combine elegance of manner with thoughtfulness and any other of the three powers, and the world is vanquished."[38] Although advice manuals never promised it would be easy, they nonetheless held out the promise that entry into polite society was possible.

Etiquette manuals addressed a broad array of subjects. "One could learn to act, build, calculate, carve, cook, dance, draw, dye, and so forth through an alphabet of attainments," and how to dine was a significant concern of most.[39] From the myriad of etiquette books and articles, middle-class women could learn how to set a table for dinner, arrange flowers, manage servants, purchase china, and select entrées. Middle-class men might learn how to dress, which fork to use, how to read a menu, and what to order when purchasing on a budget. Most exacting were the guides written specifically for the ambitious urban social climber. *The Bazar Book of Decorum* published in 1870 advised dinner-givers not to invite "more than the Muses [nine], or less than the Graces [three]" to dinner and, in an effort to condemn ostentation, recommended that a hostess serve an "ordinary French dinner" at dinner parties. The suggested menu, simplified for the "sovereign people of a republic," consisted of "soup, salmon and peas, a pair of boiled chickens, and a roast joint, with the various vegetables, followed by a good pudding or tarts, and the usual knicknackeries of confectionery." If a brace of partridges or a pair of canvasback ducks could be found to supplement the chickens, and a salad course was inserted after the roast, the "banquet will be one which ought to satisfy the most exacting of guests in this democratic country."[40]

Perhaps because public dining was relatively new and etiquette guides were hopelessly committed to time-honored rules, restaurants received only passing attention in many of the book-length guides. However, in the more urbane guides where specific advice on restaurants, chaperones, and public manners appeared, the rules governing public dining were often more rigorous than those provided for private dinners.[41] As Robert Tomes, author of the *Bazar Book*, explained, attention to the rules of etiquette was more important if a restaurateur catered the event since the host, freed of material concerns, had more time to focus on manners and civility.[42] In *The Social Etiquette of New York*, Abby Longstreet warned her presumably middle-class reader that the formal opera and theater party at a restaurant might "belong peculiarly to the province of the wealthy"; nonetheless, she offered guidelines for public dinners.[43] The rules she set out were Byzantine. A woman invited to a party at a restaurant had to be accompanied by both a chaperone and a waiting woman. The chaperone was obliged to stay for the gathering; the waiting woman returned home and then reappeared when the party was over. Within a few days of the dinner, the female guest was required to pay a visit to her chaperone to express her gratitude, and the host, if he was a bachelor, was obliged to visit his guests' homes in order to thank "mother and daughter . . . for the honor and pleasure he has received."[44] All this, of course, was in addition to the table manners expected at any formal dinner.

If the "blue books of behavior" were slow to address the growing trend of entertaining in restaurants, middle-class magazines were quick to fill the gap, offering specific advice on navigating menus and behaving courteously. Culinary magazines such as *What to Eat* and *Table Talk*, although often unsympathetic to aristocratic restaurant culture, published menus and recipes authored by renowned chefs, dictionaries of French culinary terms, and rules for public dining. *What to Eat*'s Paris correspondent, Frank Tryon Charles, offered typical advice in an 1897 series entitled "Don'ts for the Table":

Don't pronounce MENU "may-nu," but "men-ue."
Don't pronounce the A long in "A LA."
Don't cross the knives and forks.
Don't use butter at dinner, except with cheese.
Don't use the same knife for more than one course.

Don't use the same fork for more than one course.
Don't use a spoon for ices or ice-cream.
Don't serve peas, beans, cauliflower, etc., with meat.
Don't eat sugar with salad.[45]

Such lists offered a blueprint for social interaction and hinted at the possibility that class boundaries were surmountable. Memorize a few rules, demonstrate some common sense, and the wall between the middle class and the aristocracy would fall.

Newspapers offered advice that was even more practical.[46] Two articles published at the turn of the century in the *New York Times*, for example, offered suggestions on choosing a restaurant, selecting from a large and varied French menu, and managing the costs of eating out. Both articles addressed aspiring young men seeking to entertain female companions, both assumed the reader was unfamiliar with the workings of an elite restaurant, and both made it clear that it was preferable to eat a "dainty" feast at an established aristocratic restaurant than a more substantial meal at a lower-class establishment.

Published in 1897, "Cheap and Dainty Feast" promised to show a young man how he might invite "two young women" and "their escorts, a chaperon and himself" to dinner without the bill surpassing twenty dollars. This strange date, six people in all, was possible if the young man planned carefully, "abjure[d] wine altogether," and consulted the menu in advance so that he would be able to "cultivate the study of arithmetic as well as the tastes of the prospective guests."[47] To assist the neophyte gastronome, the *Times* provided a selection of suggested menus: three from Delmonico's and three from the Waldorf. The shortest of the menus recommended six courses, the longest proposed nine, and while the actual menus in these restaurants were in French, the *Times*' recommendations were translated and self-consciously printed "almost entirely in English."[48]

Less than a decade later, with the etiquette of dating and dining in flux, the *Times* once again offered to open the doors of the aristocratic restaurant to the middle-class romantic. "'Covers for Two': A Gastronomic Study" addressed the young man seeking to impress a date with a fancy dinner. Again, the *Times* offered a step-by-step guide to when, how, and what to order at a "smart" New York restaurant, including select menus from three of the city's most fashionable restaurants: Delmonico's, the Café Martin, and the Hotel Astor. Fortunately for the young man on a budget, it was now acceptable to leave the chaperones and escorts at home.

Delmonico's Menu "C"

Blue Points [Oysters], six orders at 25 cents . . . $1.50

SOUP
Chicken Gumbo, three orders at 60 cents . . . 1.80

FISH
Sea bass, shrimp sauce, three orders at 65 cents . . . 1.95

SIDE DISHES
Olives, pickles, celery . . . 1.50

ROAST
Sirloin beef with fritadelles, three orders at 75 cents . . . 2.25

VEGETABLES
Spinach, three orders at 40 cents . . . 1.20
Potatoes duchesse, three orders at 30 cents . . . 90

GAME
Quail, larded, three orders at 75 cents . . . 2.25

SALADS
Watercress, three orders at 40 cents . . . 1.20

DESSERT
Biscuit glace, six orders at 25 cents . . . 1.50
Nuts and raisins, three orders at 25 cents . . . 75
Assorted cakes, two orders at 25 cents . . . 50
Cheese, gorgonzola, two orders at 30 cents . . . 60
Coffee, French, six orders at 15 cents . . . 90

Waiter . . . $1.20

Total: $20.00

Delmonico's Menu "C." From "Cheap and Dainty
Feast," *New York Times*, October 17, 1897.

Further, "fashions in eating [had] changed very much within five years," and women, now "afraid of becoming corpulent," could be counted on to "abstain from many things which they like." As a result, a "very good little dinner" could be purchased for between ten and twenty dollars—although, curiously, all three of the newspaper's recommended menus cost over twenty dollars.[49]

"'Covers for Two'" offered a variety of practical tips for uninitiated diners. The newspaper told middle-class readers that it is "bad form at a dinner in a private house to have these refreshers [cocktails] served, and more than bad form to partake of them at restaurants." They were instructed to order a "clear soup rather than a puree or a thick one" and were told that a glass of sherry, preferably Xeres, would complement the soup. The newspaper also suggested that "if you desire to appear to have a correct judgment of wines you should order a bottle of red Burgundy" with the roast rather than the common choice, champagne. Finally, culinary terms such as "timbale" were defined, and the *Times* provided information on the mechanics of dining out. Readers were reminded to dress formally for dinner, were prepared for the dinnerware they might expect to see at some of the better restaurants ("The Astor and Rector's have peculiar shapes designed for them"), and were instructed that seven in the evening was the ideal time for a meal (unless you were going to the theater afterward).[50]

"Cheap and Dainty Feast" and "'Covers for Two'" were not written for the sons of aristocratic families who had been initiated in restaurant culture at the Patriarch or French Chef's Ball or had learned the basics of gourmet eating from the family's private chef. The newspaper's audience was the rising class of new urban professionals with the money and leisure to go out for an occasional dinner. The authors noted the names and locations of the city's best restaurants and led readers painstakingly through course after course, offering tips on proper manners and culinary fashion. Like etiquette books, these newspaper columns sought to provide enough information that middle-class urbanites might feel comfortable joining aristocratic diners in the city's best restaurants. Follow our advice, the newspaper columnists suggested, and you will "demonstrate that you are not only generous, but likewise you are an epicure and that you know the ropes."[51]

Ordering a single meal to impress a date, however, was not the same as social acceptance. For a few, these etiquette guides and newspaper advice columns may have provided the blueprint for social advancement, but the majority of middle-class Americans would never achieve either the financial success or the social grace demanded by the elite restaurant. Mastering the rules of aristocratic dining required a lifetime of learning and the financial resources to dine out regularly, and it quickly became clear that full and equal access to elite culture was nearly impossible. Lacking the necessary funds and the required cultural capital, the middle class faced the likelihood of remaining second-class consumers in a world in which what and where one ate mattered.

"Ordinary Mortals": The Failure of Imitation

Despite the advice manuals, many in the urban middle class failed to breach the ramparts of high society. While the middle class's economic power, spurred by industrial growth and corporate consolidation, continued to grow, the same economic forces further widened the gap between elites and the middle class. In 1860, the richest 1 percent of society controlled 29 percent of the nation's wealth. By 1912, the first date for which economic data allows comparison, the richest 1 percent had increased its share of the nation's wealth to 56 percent.[52] Equally important, as Michael G. Kammen contends, the 1870s marked a turning point in which the upper class began to exclude the masses from "high culture."[53] In New York, the establishment of the Patriarch's Ball (1872), the publication of the Social Register (1887), and Ward McAllister's list of the four hundred society families (1888) represented an effort to establish discrete lines between old money, new money, and the hopeless parvenu.[54] These attempts at establishing class hierarchies (even if only intended to manage distinctions within the aristocratic class) restricted opportunities for informal contact between elites and members of the middle class and made the restaurant, if only because it was open to all, the cynosure of middle-class frustration with the limits of their social advancement.[55]

Occasional newspaper accounts of lavish conspicuous consumption drew the wrath of some in the fledgling middle class, but their limited ability to emulate and imitate was most apparent when members of the middle class screwed up their courage and penetrated the hallowed halls of the French restaurant. Imitation generally failed. First, middle-class families found it difficult to afford the costly dinners at elite restaurants. Second, no degree of study could overcome the deficient cultural capital of the middle class. Imitation assumed a fluidity of class that was unrealistic in the late nineteenth century; the social registers did not swell to accommodate every middle-class aspirant who remembered to use a fork to eat ice cream.

The aristocratic restaurant was public, but it was anything but cheap. While collectively the large and growing middle class was a significant economic force credited by contemporary economists with the purchasing power necessary to keep the American economy growing, individual members of the emergent middle class lacked the financial resources to share fully in elite urban pleasures. While a middle-class couple might dine at Delmonico's once every few months, they would never be regular patrons.

"Cheap and Dainty Feast" and "'Covers for Two'" promised to reduce the cost of eating at a restaurant, but the economies such articles recommended did not make Delmonico's, Sherry's, and the Waldorf affordable. A twenty-dollar dinner—possible only if the diners shared single orders, under-tipped, and avoided alcohol—was still beyond the means of most urbanites.[56] The average weekly salary (nationally) of clerical workers in the manufacturing and railroad sectors in 1900 was $19.44. The average weekly salary of civilian employees of the federal government was $18.08. For those employed in finance, insurance, or real estate, the weekly salary was around $20.00—and these were among the highest paid members of the middle class. Wholesale and retail trade workers earned only $9.77 a week, while public school teachers brought home $6.31.[57] The scion of a wealthy manufacturing family might have managed to take a date to one of New York's elite restaurants at the turn of the century and have felt frugal spending only twenty dollars, but the middle-class clerk would go home knowing he had spent at least a week's salary. Few in the middle class could afford such expenses on a regular basis.

A letter to the New York Times made explicit the expense of dining out. Writing in 1908, H. Schuyler compared the cost of a meal for five at a restaurant to the cost of a similar meal at home. Schuyler did not specify what type of restaurant he chose except to say that he was "not dealing with the 'highest price restaurant,'" but he offered an item-by-item cost comparison of a menu consisting of cocktails, oysters, soup, chicken, peas, potato gratin, celery, cranberry sauce, lettuce, French ice cream, coffee, cheese, wine, liquor, and cigars. The restaurant meal (including the cost of tipping the waiter) came to a total of $24.30; the home meal (including the cost of fuel and other sundries) cost $10.45.[58] Eating out, even without calculating the costs of incidental expenses such as transportation, clothing, and jewelry, cost twice as much as eating at home, and even when prepared at home, this elaborate meal was beyond the means of many in the middle class.

The high cost of dining out not only discouraged middle-class urbanites from eating at aristocratic restaurants but also diminished their enjoyment on the occasions they did eat out. Frugal diners found that the prices of some items on the menu prohibited indulgence. As the *New York Times* reported in 1904, "many thousands of men, not rich, not poor, earning a fair competency" found that the prices at better restaurants made it impossible to order a complete meal. "When the average all-the-year-round patron of hotels or restaurants goes into a place of the better class he finds nowadays that unless he wishes to be extravagant he must deny himself strawberries; more than one vegetable for dinner is out of the question, too. . . . Of course, if a man can't have strawberries for breakfast he isn't going to cry about it; but that is merely one item by way of illustration. There are many others."[59] Although clever diners might try to shave costs by ordering a single portion and sharing it, restaurants discouraged more than two from sharing, and only a seasoned restaurant-goer was likely to be bold enough to defy such dictates.[60]

Penny-pinching patrons also faced the likelihood of poor service and inferior food—especially if they left the 6 percent tip recommended in "Cheap and Dainty Feast." Quality of service depended upon establishing a relationship with a waiter and nurturing that relationship over the course of many visits to the restaurant; waiters sized up and often gave poor service to occasional visitors.[61] Charles Fellows, a popular author of books on restaurant management, explained the importance of the gratuity in his 1910 "dissertation" on tipping. "The bill of fare is handed you by the waiter," Fellows explained. "You order from it, and give the waiter instructions as to the way you wish it cooked and served." What happened next depended upon the tip. "If the waiter sizes you up as a good TIP, you may get your desires. If he thinks otherwise, you may even, before he takes the order to the kitchen, be told, We are out of this or that to day [*sic*]; and you inwardly register a kick about the bill of fare and its maker."[62] Experienced waiters readily distinguished between middle-class and aristocratic patrons, and they reserved the best food and service for those who promised a big tip.

Given the obstacles that the cost of dinner posed and the few rewards that the adventurous middle-class diner could expect, it is not surprising that culinary journals warned the middle class to avoid entertaining in restaurants. Writing in 1877, Mary F. Henderson told readers of *The Dining Room Magazine* that no matter how unskilled they were at entertaining and no matter how many difficulties they may face in getting domestic help, they should avoid looking to restaurants to provide the "social board" that "hospitality demands." "In some of the larger cities satisfactory dinners and trained waiters may be provided at an enormous cost at the famous restaurants where the meal may appear homelike and elegant. But unfortunate is the woman, generally, who wants to do 'the correct thing,' and, wishing to entertain at dinner, relies upon the sense, good taste, and management of the proprietor of a restaurant," lamented Henderson. "She may confidently rely upon one thing—an enormous bill; and, generally, as well upon a vulgar display, which poorly imitates the manner of refined private establishments."[63]

Middle-class couples took such advice to heart and retreated from the aristocratic restaurant. Contemporary observers noted how rare it was in the late nineteenth century for anyone other than the wealthiest city dwellers to eat at fancy restaurants. Elizabeth Tompkins observed in 1889, "Swell places like Delmonico's and the Brunswick are mainly for the pretentious and exclusive fashionables, who go there more for the sake of being seen there by their friends than for the sake of their stomachs. In these places can always be seen a sprinkling of strangers, who are taking in the town and who don't mind paying the extortionate prices just once, in order to tell what the famous places look like when they get home." "These fancy-priced places," Tompkins concluded, "are only favored by occasional visits from ordinary mortals."[64] "Ordinary mortals," try as they might, could not easily deny the limits that income placed on imitation.

CULTURAL CAPITAL ON DISPLAY

Dixon Wecter succinctly described the poise of the American aristocrat in his 1937 book, *The Saga of American Society*: "The self-assured aristocrat—who can most readily be distinguished from the arrivist[e] by the nonchalance with which he invites the world in general to go to hell—has passed beyond the servility of regarding wealth as the measure of success," the historian wrote. "Rich enough to take it for granted, or else poor enough to ignore it, he under no circumstances crooks the knee."[65] The self-assurance that Wecter attributed to aristocratic Americans was not shared by the middle class. What the aristocrat took for granted, the middle class had to learn. What the rich ignored, the middle class fretted over. The middle class arriviste lacked the knowledge and experience to be nonchalant.

For the fledgling middle-class diner, ordering a dinner in French, selecting which fork to use, or choosing the correct wine to drink with a beef entrée required study and practice. While etiquette book writer Abby Longstreet maintained that manners could be learned, she acknowledged that the social graces that came naturally to the rich could only be "imitated" by those not to the manner born:

> Fortunate are those who were born in an atmosphere of intelligent refinement, because mistakes to them are almost impossible. They know no other way than the right one in the management of their social affairs.
>
> As to the unfortunates who have been reared at remote distances from the centres of civilization, there is nothing left for them to do but to make a careful study of unquestionable authority in those matters of etiquette which prevail among the most refined people. High breeding may be imitated, and a gentle courtesy of manner may be acquired through the same process by which other accomplishment is perfected.[66]

Other etiquette guides were more circumspect but offered a similar message. When Clara L. Cousine told readers that "if the father and mother be so unfortunate as not to have had proper training themselves, they should study to correct any bad habits they may have, for the sake of their children," she inadvertently conceded that the process of inculcating aristocratic manners was a generational undertaking and not a quick cure for a middle-class social aspirant.[67] Elizabeth Ellet was more explicit and warned against any effort to mimic the wealthy. She instructed readers that "every one [sic] ought to live according to his circumstances, and the meal of the tradesman ought not to emulate the entertainments of the higher classes."[68]

Subtle suggestions that the social order was impermeable did not prevent the fledgling middle-class urbanite from trying to imitate the manners of the wealthy, but by the late Gilded Age, such efforts were often portrayed as foolhardy. Dozens of novels in the late nineteenth and early twentieth centuries warned about social climbing. In William Dean Howells's 1885 *The Rise of Silas Lapham*, the Lapham family's efforts to ingratiate themselves with Boston's wealthy aristocrats, despite their considerable wealth, earn them little more than pity. In Edith Wharton's 1905 *House of Mirth*, a young woman's search for a place within society leads to her death. In David Graham Phillips's 1917 *Susan Lenox: Her Fall and Rise*, financial success comes only at the expense of middle-class moral rectitude. In Booth Tarkington's 1921 *Alice Adams*, the Adams household sacrifices its dignity and economic security in a disastrous pursuit of respectability. In Theodore Dreiser's 1925 *American Tragedy*, the protagonist's desperate pursuit of a distant relative's wealth leads to murder and imprisonment.[69]

If not every tale focused explicitly on the middle class, nonetheless the message was clear: aspiring to live beyond one's station leads to failure and tragedy.

Nor were accounts of the perils of social climbing limited to works of the literati; they also appeared routinely in stories and travel accounts published in popular magazines. T. S. Winslow's "When We Get In with Nice People," published in the *American Mercury*, was typical of stories in the popular press. Winslow was a journeyman magazine author with hundreds of stories published in *Smart Set*, *Cosmopolitan*, and the *New Yorker*. "When We Get In with Nice People" tells the tale of a young couple, Laurence and Irene Turner, who turn their backs on Camden, Illinois, since there was "no one here to go with who is our sort," and move to New York.[70] Laurence is a financial success in the metropolis, and with each economic advancement the couple move to a more prosperous neighborhood and frequent more elite restaurants—from delicatessens to "the smartest and one of the most expensive places in town."[71] Despite their best efforts, however, they remain outsiders, too focused on social climbing to form genuine relationships with their peers. They go largely unnoticed by the elites they seek to befriend. Winslow's tale, a sort of reverse Horatio Alger story, is a cautionary tale for the urban middle class. Modest financial success did not promise social acceptance.

More explicit admonitions about the foolishness of emulating the wealthy appeared in nonfiction travel accounts. Travel offered members of the middle class opportunities to escape their local castes and experience the anonymity of consumer culture. Public dining was a potential moment of transgression, an opportunity to test one's social standing. Accounts of travel, however, regularly included cautions for those who might seek to escape their class. In a 1910 article for the culinary journal *Table Talk*, Hilda Richmond wrote about those who "'put it on' to use an expressive bit of Western slang." "The instant they enter a [railroad] car they make themselves felt, and it is impossible not to see and hear them," she observed. "Often to know the talkers is to get the impression that they are playing the old game of 'Make Believe' indulged in by little children." To illustrate her point, she recounted stories of inexperienced diners who tried to fake a high-class upbringing. In one, a "sensible couple, who always got much amusement out of every journey, listened to the accounts of a young man just ahead of them as he told of the hotels at which he had stopped." At first glance, the young man appeared to be a gentleman, a seasoned traveler with a taste for the finest. "He rolled off the delicacies served at the various famous hostelries together with the prices in a way to convince the most skeptical, and lamented that the service in dining cars was beastly. In fact [the young man complained], it was impossible to get decent food outside a few exclusive hotels of the state, and going away from them was a hardship refined travelers could hardly endure." Yet a week later, the young man's web of lies unraveled. Dining in a "modest restaurant in a large city, where expensive hotels abounded to care for the wants of wealthy tourists," the "sensible couple" from the train was only mildly surprised to see the young man, "who had almost starved on board the train because he could find nothing to which he had been accustomed," seated at a nearby table. "He ordered a dinner for about thirty-five cents from the bill of fare, and ate as if he enjoyed it, much to the amusement of the couple who had listened to his complaints a week before."[72]

While the young man in Richmond's story was unmasked by accident, most social climbers were easily identified. Helen Bruce Wallace observed in 1911 that dinner was a particularly dangerous moment for the upstart. "Some women are chronic abusers of the food. They will sit at a hotel table and growl in loud tones at the cooking, make unnecessary demands on the waiter's time and ostentatiously send dishes from the table. Naturally they are disliked and get poor service while they are terribly mortifying to the rest of their party," she wrote in *Table Talk*. "The disgusted onlooker never fails to wonder if that woman is not 'very plain' and used to miserable cooking at home. She who is accustomed to a good table rarely is loud in complaint of her food in traveling."[73] For Richmond and Wallace, such grotesque acts of social climbing not only betrayed the parvenu's lack of cultural capital but also offered a warning to those who might pretend to be something they were not. Wallace's advice to middle-class readers was to accept their class status: "Those others who go places and do things they actually dislike because they think it 'the thing' . . . come home worn out, have had a miserable time and no one thinks any more of them than if they had been unfashionable and gratified their own tastes."[74]

These stories, both fictional and real, resonated because they reflected the everyday struggles of middle-class families who failed, despite the etiquette guides, to acquire the cultural knowledge necessary to order a French meal at an aristocratic restaurant. The reader of "Cheap and Dainty Feast" or "'Covers for Two'" would have to have been extremely clever, self-assured, and suave to put the articles' advice into action, even with the newspaper providing the menu. The promised savings would have been achieved by ordering fewer dishes, dividing them among the diners, avoiding alcohol, and giving the waiter a puny tip. All of this would have to have been accomplished without appearing stingy and, in contrast to the menus reprinted in the newspaper, while ordering in French.[75] Acknowledging these potential difficulties, the author of "Cheap and Dainty Feast" made mention of acceptable table d'hôte dinners (where the menu and price were fixed) that might be found at some of the less expensive hotels in New York, but the newspaper gave only passing attention to these alternatives and advised against the "progressive" dinner where guests might go to Delmonico's or the Waldorf for appetizers and then to a less expensive restaurant for dinner. The paper conceded that "the young man . . . would undoubtedly feel embarrassed if he were obliged to take his guests from the Waldorf or Delmonico's," but would he be any less embarrassed to ask guests to share entrées or to order from a French waiter in English?[76]

The author of an 1896 article in the *New York Daily Tribune* on "how to make the best" of a restaurant dinner was less sanguine about the chances of a novice ever enjoying the fruits of restaurant life. "It is pitiable," the author conceded, "to see a person quite unused to restaurants trying to order a meal. . . . Everyone who frequents such scenes knows the poor wretch whose sole idea of luxurious novelty is fried oysters, and also the one who always orders rare roast beef, of which he is tired to death, for fear he might get something that he would not like so well." While the reporter gamely suggested a hodgepodge of practical advice aimed at improving the inexperienced diner's chance of enjoying a restaurant meal— from ordering what one might have at home, to "order[ing] things by guess," to following the advice of waiters—ultimately he suggested it was best not to dine out at all. "Life in restaurants is bad enough for those who know how to live it; for those who do not it is inexpressibly pathetic," the advice writer conceded. "Do not suppose that the humble effort here made to mitigate an evil can turn it into a good. It can't."[77]

Despite the promise that anyone—at least anyone who read the *New York Times* or the *New York Daily Tribune*—might succeed in ordering a dinner in a fine restaurant, the assurances of etiquette guides were never to be taken too seriously. Their purpose was not to expand the numbers of the upper class but to win the middle class's acquiescence to the hegemony of upper-class culture. Often written by members of the upper-middle or aristocratic class (or by those trying to feign membership in the elite), these books celebrated the trappings of European society that wealthy Americans had adopted as their emblems, and in doing so they sought to preserve those trappings as evidence of civility and success.[78] In the end, the guides did more to demonstrate the growing divide between the cultural capital of the established wealthy and the aspiring middle class than they did to bridge it.

The Middle Class Speaks

For many, imitation was a phase, a short-lived and unsuccessful experiment that rarely succeeded. Although each year new social climbers made the same mistakes and suffered the same disappointments, more middle-class Americans, as they became aware of the growing concentration of wealth and cultural authority, increasingly viewed promises of social mobility and republican equality with jaundiced disbelief. As James Huston argued in *Securing the Fruits of Labor*, Americans generally believed in the first part of the nineteenth century that a free and open market was the best guarantor of egalitarianism, but by the Progressive Era, the illusion of emergent equality had become difficult to sustain. "Unlike earlier years, when discussion of American wealth distribution was usually a signal for self-congratulations, the articles and speeches appearing in the 1880s and 1890s were lamentations."[79] This disillusionment was expressed in mass protests over the extravagant Bradley-Martin ball and in Thomas Nast drawings of the railroad trusts, but it was not the sole province of the working class or muckraking journalists. For middle-class urbanites, the conspicuous consumption of the upper class—and the growing distance between elites' economic successes and those of the middle class—made it increasingly difficult to believe that the mere imitation of social codes of etiquette and behavior would provide entry into the circles of social power in America's cities. No reader of the daily newspaper could fail to contrast the wealthy elites' lavish parties and extravagant banquets to the businessman's staid repasts.

In the last quarter of the nineteenth century, some members of the middle class rejected imitation and began to distance themselves from elite restaurant culture. The rebellion was generally economic and cultural, but occasionally vocal critics of how the wealthy dined made themselves heard. While the discontent rarely reached a fever pitch, its persistence exposed a simmering resentment toward those who stood in the way of middle class advancement. Dio Lewis, a food reformer, an early and influential advocate of physical exercise, and a founder of the temperance movement, was, like many spokespersons for the early Progressive movement, deeply suspicious of worldly pursuits. In *Talks about People's Stomachs* published in 1870, Lewis argued that it was as difficult for a rich man to live a healthy life as it was for the biblical camel to make it through the eye of a needle. To illustrate, Lewis told the story of two "ordinary pale, round-shouldered Americans." Both men are "engaged in the struggle for success. One gives up body and soul to making money, the other, a generous part of his life, to laying up this inestimable wealth of health." Now, some years later, Lewis reviewed the progress the two men had made. "The greedy merchant counts his gold by the million; but he is twenty years older than when we saw him first. He is thinner and paler; he is dyspeptic, nervous, anxious, old, thoroughly unhappy. That man has made a wretched failure in life. Every large heart sincerely pities him." Meanwhile, the man who has invested in his health has fared much better. He is "erect, broad-chested, muscular, vigorous, healthy, happy, buoyant, [and] victorious. We will not trouble ourselves to ask how much money he has collected. We cannot look upon him without feeling that he has achieved a grand triumph."[80]

Lewis's account drew a link between dyspepsia and wealth that would become a standard refrain of the critics of the aristocratic table. Echoing Lewis's story a few years later, the *New York Times* expressed pity for the "man whose name is worth millions, and to whom Delmonico or Suther- land would be only too happy to extend unlimited credit," but who has dined out so often at luxurious restaurants that he has ruined his appetite and is now "obliged to content himself with a hard biscuit and a glass of sherry."[81]

Dio Lewis's parable trumpets an up-and-coming hero, the less acquisi- tive, "broad-chested," and "happy" man whose wealth is measured in a healthy appetite rather than in material goods. This metaphorical middle- class diner, a paladin of the palette, emerged in the 1870s and was still meaningful forty years later. In a cartoon from the *New York Times Sunday Magazine* in 1913, a stocky, spectacled man in a dinner jacket and white tie stands alongside an unshaven hobo in a battered hat. Both are looking longingly through the window of a restaurant. The caption read: "Two Things Interfere with the Enjoyment of Food, Too Much Money and Too Little."[82]

While no more than a small minority of Americans voiced such explicit condemnations of the rich gastronome, these early complaints demon- strate that it was class conflict and not the emergence of consumer markets that led to the development of a distinct middle class. Although members of the middle class were active consumers in the mid-nineteenth century (as scholars such as Richard Bushman, Mary P. Ryan, and Susan Williams have demonstrated), the modern mass-consumption marketplace was still taking shape in the 1870s and 1880s.[83] Fabled institutions of commercial-

"Two Things Interfere with the Enjoyment of Food, Too Much Money and Too Little." From the *New York Times Sunday Magazine*, November 23, 1913.

ism, most notably the department stores, did not exist yet and would not exert their influence until the 1890s.[84] There were no chain restaurants, little restaurant advertising, and few alternatives to the aristocratic restaurant. Etiquette and dining guides—such as those printed in the *New York Times*—would continue to advise middle-class diners to embrace the high culture of the elite restaurant into the twentieth century.[85] Although embryonic changes in the landscape of shopping and dining may have contributed to the middle-class revolt against the aristocratic restaurant, members of the emergent middle class were not a mere byproduct of consumer culture but were active participants in shaping it. Alienated from elites, they sought out alternatives to the aristocratic restaurant.

Those of the middle class rejected the elite restaurant not only because the upper-class aristocratic restaurant was expensive and inaccessible but also because they found that the values they were coming to see as their own—commitment to family, love of plain food, simple civility—were manifestly not the values enshrined in the elite restaurant. Frustrated and disillusioned by the failure of the emerging commercial sphere to live up to its democratic promise, conscientious middle-class diners began to avoid aristocratic restaurants; lacking a ready alternative, they colonized and cannibalized a hodgepodge of disparate urban restaurants until their patronage created an alternative public sphere—the cosmopolitan restaurant—where neither price nor European standards of elite dining prevented the middle class from exercising cultural authority.

In retrospect, it is easy to view the protests of middle-class diners with cynicism. Middle-class white men had nearly unequaled access to the public sphere and, as historians have documented, often played an important role in restricting the participation of women, non-whites, and the poor in these arenas. Their complaints about inequality and exclusion often sound hollow and naive. Nonetheless, imagining an alternative public sphere in which the modest, well-mannered diner was as respected as the captain of industry was the first step in creating both the modern middle class and modern restaurant culture, and it was an integral part of a larger critique about equality emerging in American society in the late nineteenth century.[86] Progressive reformers' concerns about monopoly businesses and corporate greed, if not synonymous with middle-class complaints about dining, stemmed from the same frustration: a nagging concern that the gulf between classes was broadening and that elites were less interested in preserving democracy than in establishing a European-style aristocracy.

CATERING TO THE
GREAT MIDDLE STRIPE
Beefsteaks and American Restaurants

In 1869, illustrious former war correspondent Junius Henri Browne published *The Great Metropolis*, a vivid portrayal of life in New York City. Browne estimated that New York had "five or six thousand restaurants" segregated into one of two tiers: the "elegance and costliness of Delmonico's and Taylor's" and "the subterranean sties where men are fed like swine, and dirt is served gratis in unhomœopathic doses." In between the fashionable restaurants and the dirty dives, there were few choices for the middle-class dining public. "One advantage of New-York is that a man can live here very much as he chooses," Browne cynically conceded. "He can live fashionably and luxuriously for from one to five hundred dollars, or meanly and poorly for six to eight dollars a week. The latter method very few Americans adopt unless compelled by absolute necessity; and not then [for] very long, for laudanum is not dear, and the rivers are very deep."[1]

By the turn of the century, Browne's New York had been transformed, and a new class of restaurants was emerging to cater to the needs of an ever-expanding middle class. Twenty-three years after Browne wrote *The Great Metropolis*, *Appleton's Dictionary of Greater New York and Its Neighborhood* described a city where "the habit of eating away from home is a very general one," and a "wide range" of restaurants "of every grade" catered to every class. "From the 'coffee and cake' saloons, indigenous to basements in certain parts of New York, to the palatial and perfectly appointed mansion of Delmonico, in 5th av., is a wide range," the guidebook announced. "Within this come oyster-saloons, chop-houses . . . , lunch-counters, 15-cent-restaurants, commonly called 'hash houses,' foreign restaurants, the restaurants attached to first-class hotels kept upon the so-called European plan, dairies, and restaurants proper."[2] This remarkable transformation of dining in New York—and in most of the great American metropolises—was a triumph of the economic and cultural power of the middle class. Unable, by dint of cash and culture, to become full participants in the fashionable world of the elite nineteenth-century restaurant, middle-class men and women sought out the "subterranean sties where men are fed like swine" and through their patronage transformed these sties into respectable restaurants. The appearance of a new class of restaurants that embodied the values and expectations of the middle class offers evidence of the growing influence of the middle class over the emerging culture of consumption.

Historians often conflate the cultures of the upper and middle classes and minimize the tensions that existed between the two, although the consumer culture of the twentieth century has been shaped as much by the struggle between the rich and the middling folks as by any other factor. Shunned by the elite restaurant, the middle class developed values and nurtured class cohesion that—simultaneously and reflexively—shaped consumer institutions. The collective purchasing power of the emerging middle class encouraged restaurant entrepreneurs to cater to their tastes, and, over the course of forty years, small preferences about how to dine begot cultural changes that eventually birthed both middle-class restaurants and the modern middle class itself.

The "middle-classing" of public dining began in urban America and only slowly penetrated the hinterland, but by the 1920s and 1930s, restaurants that catered to the middle class were commonplace. In the decades to follow, they became ubiquitous. By then, the rough contours (constantly renegotiated and recast) of the middle-class restaurant were apparent. It promised good service, a clean dining room, a well-mannered staff, and quick service, but it was ecumenical and adaptive. It counted among its numbers the ubiquitous faux Dutch restaurants of the 1920s, the family restaurants of the 1930s, the roadside inns of the 1940s, and the continental restaurants of the 1950s. It represented the democratization of dining, although the food was not free and often a shirt and tie were required. It served women and oftentimes had women servers. It promised good food, sometimes labeled "homemade," although it also embraced the modernization of dining and, as menus in the 1920s proudly advertised, did not shy away from brand-name canned goods, bottled sauces, and frozen meats. The middle-class restaurant was, and is, more of an idea than a specific place. That idea had its origins in the late nineteenth century as members of the middle class, excluded by the elaborate codes of conduct that governed elite dining, transformed the disparate and dirty working-men and ethnic restaurants of major American cities into establishments in which they would feel comfortable.

Precursors

In the mid-nineteenth century, few restaurants catered to the emerging middle class.[3] Although a great variety of quick lunch establishments provided meals to middle-income urbanites unable to get home for the traditional midday dinner—the most substantial meal of the day—these establishments put a premium on speed, not quality or service, and offered little to attract families. George G. Foster's 1849 city exposé *New York in Slices*, like Browne's later account, divided respectable dining into two classes: elite aristocratic restaurants and chophouses. Restaurants in the second category served "stringy meat and tepid vegetables" to the "great middle stripe of [the] population." Business boomed from noon to three as city workers sought quick "lunches." Dining at these establishments was a pragmatic, hurried experience. "A regular down-towner surveys the kitchen with his nose as he comes up-stairs—selects his dish by intuition, and swallows it by steam and the electro-galvanic battery," Foster wrote. "As to digesting it, that is none of his business."[4] Looking back after thirty years, Edgar Fawcett, a popular turn-of-the-century novelist, recalled that "in the main, 'eating houses' predominated whose atmosphere would now be defined as vulgarity itself." In the "very crude hostelries" of 1864, Fawcett recollected, "the waiters were 'colored,' and not always of the tidiest type," the china was "cumbrous," the linen appeared "hieroglyphed by coffee stains," and the food lacked "French skill."[5] These were restaurants of convenience that served only men and were rarely open at night.

The short business day of a downtown chophouse—midday meals only—meant that a middle-class couple, married or dating, had few choices if they stayed in the city to shop or take in a performance at the theater. Couples were compelled to patronize either one of the elite restaurants that catered to the fashionable set or to wolf down a dinner at one of the working-class restaurants that Browne had described as "sties." For those with sufficient funds and experience, the choice was easy. In the national imagination, the French restaurant was the pinnacle of public dining. Located in hotels or, in the largest East Coast cities, as stand-alone restaurants, the "*aristocratic* restaurant[s]"—to use George Foster's term—served a French dinner "which is not merely a quantity of food deposited in the stomach, but is in every sense and to all the senses a great work of art."[6] In these establishments, there was "no confusion, no bustle, no jostling, no door-slamming," Browne observed, and "ladies elegantly and elaborately dressed go . . . in handsome equipages, amid flower and toilette odors, and with all the suggestive poetry that night lends to a fine woman."[7] But for those without the economic or cultural capital to enjoy fully the pleasures that the elite restaurant offered and for those who were unwilling to accept the cold food and few amenities of the working-class restaurants, the best choice was often to return home with a few cents in one's pocket.

Demand Rises

Public dining, however, was on the verge of a significant and lasting transformation. After 1870, the new urban lifestyles that commercial growth imposed on middle-class Americans, as well as the siren song of public entertainments and department stores, encouraged the fledgling middle class to engage actively in the public life of their cities—and to reconsider and reassess the restaurant. Newly married couples living in small apartments or residential hotels without kitchens were soon eating at restaurants.[8] Bachelors tired of the unchanging fare at boardinghouses also sought out restaurants.[9] Young women earning an independent living patronized lunchroom saloons (even if they returned home for their supper).[10] Shoppers, unwilling to travel long distances to uptown or suburban apartments for a simple meal, frequented department store restaurants. And, as more urbanites took advantage of the entertainments that the modern city offered, eating at a restaurant made it possible to entertain friends and sweethearts before or after the theater.[11]

The "servant problem" also made restaurants an attractive alternative to domestic help for many middle-class families. Etiquette guides routinely advised women to secure servants to help with the management of a respectable middle-class household, but obtaining help became more difficult as the economy expanded and working women sought the higher wages and greater freedom of industrial jobs.[12] Immigrant women eager for work stemmed the decline, but in most cities the number of domestic servants dwindled in the Gilded Age and Progressive Era. In New York, for example, there were 188 servants for every 1,000 households in 1880, 141 in 1900, and only 66 in 1920.[13] As it became increasingly rare for middle-class families to have a full-time, live-in servant, restaurants offered an alternative to eating and entertaining at home. An English visitor to the United States observed in 1913, well after the servant problem had been enshrined in popular folklore, that "this entertaining at public restaurants probably arises a good deal from the complexity of the servant question. Servants may be a difficult problem in England, but they are nothing as compared with the States."[14] A cartoon accompanying the article in the *New York Times* depicted a bayonet-toting servant forcing a middle-class couple into a public restaurant.

More generally, the growth of the city, including the development of apartment living (or conversely, the long commutes from suburban homes), brought about significant changes in dining. Midday dinners shrank in size and importance (reflected in the linguistic migration from "dinner" to "luncheon" and eventually to "lunch"), and the evening meal, the formal dinner, rose in significance.[15] The late hour of the main meal allowed husbands to return home for dinner, but it also made it possible for couples who lived in or regularly visited the city to take their meals together in urban restaurants. As a result, middle-class families began to seek out affordable restaurants that had formerly catered to the working class or that specialized in providing quick meals to businessmen. Existing restaurants soon expanded and adapted to meet the needs of their new middle-class clientele, and new restaurants were built.

U.S. Census figures on restaurant occupations offer a glimpse of the rapid growth of the dinner trade in the late nineteenth and early twentieth centuries.[16] Over the course of fifty years, from 1880 to 1930, the number of restaurant, café, and lunchroom keepers counted by the census increased from 13,000 to approximately 165,000. Decade by decade, the number of restaurant managers grew more rapidly than the population. Per capita growth in the number of restaurant keepers in the United States exceeded 18 percent in the 1880s, 45 percent in the 1890s, 49 percent in the first decade of the 1900s, 26 percent in the second decade, and 62 percent in the 1920s. Cumulatively, the number of restaurant, café, and lunchroom keepers per capita increased nationally by over 400 percent from 1880 to 1930.[17]

These national trends were replicated at both the local and state levels. In a sample of restaurant proprietor census counts from ten major American cities and ten states, the number of proprietors increased at a rate that usually outstripped population growth. At the city level, only Boston and San Francisco experienced any per capita decrease in the number of restaurant keepers between 1880 and 1930, and then for only one decade, from 1910 to 1920.[18] Likewise, states had sustained rates of restaurant growth. The average decade-to-decade growth rate in restaurant occupations from 1890 to 1930 in New York State, for example, was

"Why the Public Restaurants Are So Popular."
From the *New York Times*, March 23, 1913.

about 39 percent, for Massachusetts 29 percent, and for California 28 percent, and restaurant growth was not limited to the cultural centers on
the coast. Inland and southern states—Colorado, Missouri, Louisiana,
Kansas, and Illinois—all experienced per capita growth rates exceeding
20 percent.

These levels of employment growth were notable even during a half
century marked by considerable commercial expansion. Although the
number of boardinghouse keepers, hotelkeepers, and saloonkeepers also
grew at the turn of the century, these industries seldom kept pace with
the population. In Louisiana, one of the fastest-growing states in terms of
hotel employment, hotel occupations grew at a per capita rate that was
one-third that of restaurant occupations. While specific industry-wide circumstances help to explain some of these differences (saloons, for example, suffered with the rise of the temperance movement), the expansion of
the restaurant industry was remarkable for its ability to weather economic
downturns, food quality scares, labor strife, and war.[19]

In part, the restaurant industry continued to expand because the middle
class continued to expand. Contemporary observers acknowledged the relationship between the increasing number of professionals, managers, and
clerks living in the city and the growth of the restaurant trade. An 1866
article in *Harper's* made note of the "sundry restaurants near Wall Street
where Mr. Omnium can find good, wholesome cuts from well-cooked
joints, and old-fashioned mealy potatoes, boiled in their jackets, and com-
forting beverages in abundance." Likewise, an 1877 *New York Daily Tribune*
article cataloging the variety of middle-income urbanites who were now
dining out concluded that businessmen, women shoppers, lodgers, and
fun-seekers—all members of the rising middle class—"have given encouragement to almost innumerable eating-houses which are to be found scattered all over the city."[20]

Similar observations were being made on the West Coast. In 1868,
Noah Brooks remarked on the large number of restaurants in San Francisco that catered specifically to middle-class urbanites. "The Californian
love of good living is as prominent in these middle-class restaurants as
anywhere. Respectable citizens and well-to-do businessmen dine luxuri-
antly for fifty or seventy-five cents, though, of course, they do not have
a bottle of table claret with their roast, nor cognac with their coffee."[21]
A little more than twenty years later, a reporter in Los Angeles, a small
city of barely fifty thousand residents in 1892, came to similar conclusions.
In addition to its "first-class metropolitan restaurant[s] . . . where luxury
runs riot from solid gold and silver service and broadcloth swallowtails of

the attendants, to the ponderous aristocracy of the patrons," Los Angeles hosted numerous establishments that catered to "that class of people called the middle classes, who are neither financially independent nor squalidly poor."[22]

Scant evidence of these restaurants has survived. In the 1870s and 1880s, city directories used a kaleidoscope of terms—eating houses, oyster houses, eating saloons, oyster saloons—to designate places where food might be acquired, but the taxonomy was notoriously imprecise and offers few clues as to who and what was being served. Consisting of long lists of restaurant names—often no more than the proprietor's surname—directories demonstrate that restaurants were becoming increasingly important, but little more.[23] And since restaurants rarely advertised prior to the second decade of the twentieth century, and restaurant-goers (then and now) seldom recorded their dining experiences, there is little to illuminate the cryptic lists of restaurants that appear in the directories.[24]

It was Foster's protégés, reporters in New York, Washington, Chicago, Los Angeles, and San Francisco, who assembled the most detailed accounts of the middle-class restaurants that were soon crowding the avenues of America's cities. These reporters, themselves members of the emerging middle class, described a rich variety of restaurants, many once frequented only by businessmen and working-class bachelors, that in the second half of the nineteenth century began to cater to the men and women of the "middle stripe."

Restaurants for the Middle Class

While middle-class men continued to patronize saloons (at least those located in respectable neighborhoods) for the infamous free lunches that accompanied nickel beers, during the Gilded Age more and more men and women began to dine at establishments that demonstrated the same commitment to food as they did to drink. As early afternoon dinners—a luxury not readily available to an increasingly regulated workforce—gave way to lighter, earlier lunches and more substantial evening dinners, middle-class Americans sought eating-places that stayed open late and offered moderately priced, well-cooked meals.[25] Hurried clerks might tolerate "stringy meat and tepid vegetables" when a brief noontime break required it, but the more leisurely pace of the evening dinner raised expectations, created a demand for restaurants that served women as well as men, and spurred calls for more dining choices and better food. Restaurants responded by staying open later, improving their service, and offering more elaborate dinners during the early evening hours. Soon, kitchenless families and theater-going couples joined the bachelor ranks at public restaurants. By 1893, L. J. Vance could reassure readers of *Frank Leslie's Popular Monthly* that "for the great army of men and women who must live on moderate incomes, who have long abandoned the dull cares of housekeeping, there is an abundant supply of good dinners, ranging in price from fifty cents for a table d'hôte with wine at Charlemagne's in Houston Street to the expensive à la carte restaurant at the Brunswick."[26]

In reality, dinner at the expensive Brunswick in New York was beyond the means of many in the middle class, but for urbanites who felt excluded from elite restaurants, the city of the 1870s and 1880s offered a variety of restaurants serving everything from simple, inexpensive meals to higher-priced table d'hôte dinners. A full taxonomy of restaurants that accounts for regional preferences is impossible, but newspaper accounts suggest that the rough hierarchy of urban restaurants that the emerging middle class frequented ranged from clean, inexpensive, and reasonably good lunchrooms to late-night coffeehouses. While a vocal minority argued that public dining was, at best, a necessary evil to be avoided, there is little doubt that those of the middle class were increasingly comfortable venturing out of their homes for evening meals.

Among the most respectable of the late-nineteenth-century restaurants (for both midday and evening meals) were the lunchrooms. William Dean Howells, the editor of *Harper's*, described a typical lunchroom restaurant of the 1870s in his novel *A Modern Instance*. In Howells's story, a young couple elope and move to a kitchenless apartment in Boston. When Marcia, raised in the country, experiences a public lunchroom for the first time, she is initially "bewildered":

> There was a great show of roast and steak and fish, and game and squash and cranberry pie in the window, and at the door a tack was driven through a mass of bills-of-fare, two of which Bartley plucked off as they entered, with a knowing air and then threw on the floor when he found the same thing on the table. The table had a marble top, and a silver-plated castor in the centre. . . . The marble was of an unctuous translucence, in places, and showed the course of the cleansing napkin on its smeared surface. The place was hot, and full of confused smells of cooking; all the tables were crowded, so that they found places with difficulty, and pale, plain girls, of the Provincial and Irish-American type, in fashionable bangs and pull-backs, went about taking the orders which they wailed out towards a semi-circular

hole opening upon a counter at the further end of the room; there they received the dishes ordered, and hurried with them to the customers, before whom they laid them with a noisy clacking of the heavy crockery.[27]

The fast pace and constant din that characterized the lunchrooms were both fascinating and intimidating for many first-time diners, but these small restaurants proliferated in the late nineteenth century.

Famous for their large, à la carte menus, lunchrooms occasionally experimented with their menu selections, but most offered some variation on the Anglo-American bill of fare. At Howells's Boston lunchroom, "a great many of the people seemed to be taking hulled-corn and milk; baked beans formed another favorite dish, and squash-pie was in large request."[28] At a typical New York lunchroom, diners feasted on oysters, fish, cold meats, and a selection of "specials" that might include "beef a la mode, lamb pot-pie, knuckle of ham with spinach, hashed turkey with poached eggs, chicken and oyster patties, roast pork and apple sauce, roast turkey and cranberry sauce, roast venison, wild duck, roast Spring chicken, and a dozen other things to make your mouth water."[29] Regional cuisines—Boston baked beans, Virginia hams, and southern chicken—also appeared regularly on the menu. In San Francisco, where the dining public tended to be more worldly, middle-class lunchrooms might also serve bastardized French cuisine.

Many lunchrooms featured both table and counter service. In New York, for some "unaccountable reason the lunch counter was nearly breast high, (as it always is), and when a man sat on one of the stools his feet were far above the floor and rested upon an iron bar."[30] Although custom rather than law governed these establishments, the lunch counter was most often reserved for men while the dining room, sometimes with its own entrance, was for couples and families. In less formal establishments without separate dining facilities for women, a small section of the restaurant might be screened off for families during the evening dinner hours. The decorations were invariably simple.

By the late 1870s, lunchrooms were considered respectable and increasingly middle-class. The food was moderately priced, at least in comparison to aristocratic restaurants, and generally well liked. But price and service varied from city to city. In 1892 in Los Angeles, the popular businessmen's "restaurants and lunch-rooms" served meals that cost anywhere from $0.25 to $1.25 with the cost dependent on the restaurant's "style" as well as what was ordered.[31] In nearby San Francisco, à la carte dishes—"and a 'dish' is a lavish portion, all that a hearty man could eat"—cost ten cents each, but frugal diners could go to "three-for-two" places where three dishes were served for two bits (twenty-five cents).[32] And San Francisco establishments were somewhat unusual in their willingness to deliver food to the apartments of families who wished to avoid the annoyance of dining at a restaurant.[33]

The lunchroom's stiffest competition came from table d'hôte restaurants. Table d'hôte restaurants served a multicourse meal, occasionally including wine, for a fixed price. Although the offerings were seldom as select as those at aristocratic restaurants, the large number of inexpensive and popular tables d'hôte gave middle-class diners a broad range of culinary experiences from which to choose. Many table d'hôte restaurants were ethnic—Italian, German, or French—while others served a generic American meal. The *Washington Post* described the diversity of table d'hôte restaurants in an 1898 article:

> The table d'hôte dinner, served in every style and at variegated prices to that ever-increasing army of Bohemians here who know not, and care less, where to lay their heads, is a deservedly popular institution. I have sampled them in every language, in a corresponding variety of localities, and my ennuied and satiated personality has absorbed everything from a New England boiled dinner to a meal at which spaghetti by the furlong was supposed to supply every want, all under the same tempting title. Some of these dinners have nothing unusual in their composition, and begin at the blue points and proceed decorously through entrée, roast, and salad, to the black coffee in the usual stereotyped style; and again, at others, you are supposed to enjoy cloves of garlic and pods of red peppers, eaten in all their virgin purity and strength.[34]

Although the ethnicity of the restaurants' offerings varied, the middle-class table d'hôte was universally known for its large portions at comparatively low prices.

While all agreed that the tables d'hôte offered plenty of food, the quality of the offerings was both widely praised and widely ridiculed. A newspaper exchange over the merit of table d'hôte dining in New York offers a glimpse at the cantankerousness of the debate. In 1899, the pseudonymous "American" wrote to the *New York Times* to denounce the French table d'hôte at which he had recently dined as little more than "Alsatian humbuggery." The menu, "American" complained, consisted of "soup made of Croton water and colored with beef extract," a small portion of fish and half a potato, chicken that tasted like the "rim of an old straw hat," "roast beef," "a few sprigs of spaghetti," cheap wine, coffee, and dessert. Aware of the class implications of dining at a popular table d'hôte restaurant, "American" concluded that "it is fair to assume . . . that some of the dishes served at these tables d'hôte may have been [previously] chewed on by the guests of the Fifth Avenue Hotel or Waldorf-Astoria. It is time New Yorkers had learned some common sense, and either buy their own food and cook it or patronize honest restaurants."[35]

But not everyone agreed with the dour assessment of "American." For many, the table d'hôte restaurants' shortcomings were easily forgiven. Readers of the *Times* quickly responded to the litany of complaints leveled by "American." "H. S. H." wrote to report that respectable men and "their wives and daughters" regularly visited tables d'hôte for the healthy food, while "Housekeeper" reminded readers that the table d'hôte might not promise excellence, but it delivered ample portions cheaply.[36] "No intelligent being could expect, no hotel keeper could give, both the quantity and the quality 'American' wanted for the price paid," "Housekeeper" observed. "But there is a class of people not over-particular, who, not being accustomed to anything better, neither require, desire, nor expect other than what they obtain at cheap restaurants. . . . It is absurd to demand the first and best quality for third-rate prices."[37] Faced with a choice between the daunting cost of the aristocratic restaurant and the need to be frugal at the à la carte lunchroom, the table d'hôte restaurant's large servings, dozens of extras, and fixed price were an affordable alternative, especially for middle-class families. "At a great many of the first-class [table d'hôte] places somebody has let the cook go out for the evening, and an entire family, including a small boy, are dining there," one observer noted.[38]

Lunchrooms and tables d'hôte topped the hierarchy of possible alternatives to the aristocratic restaurants and hotel dining rooms, but they were not the only choice for middle-class diners. In 1881, the *New York Times* described a number of other downtown restaurants that had once been avoided by middling families but were increasingly popular with the fledgling middle class: the inexpensive beefsteak restaurant, the American restaurant, and the "coffee and cake saloons."

The beefsteak or chophouse, "modeled on the plans of British cities," was a favorite eating place for a broad variety of American men.[39] As a reporter for the *Times* observed after visiting a New York chophouse in 1881, "The tables were full, and the customers were of all sorts and kinds—well-dressed people, evidently with plenty of money in their pockets, marketmen, countrymen, clerks, store boys—a regular gathering of clans scattered at Babel." Despite the "cheapness of the articles on the bill of fare" and the "rush and tumble of waiters," the food was usually considered above average. The *Times* reporter, although probably not speaking from personal experience, concluded that "it is doubtful whether Delmonico serves better steaks or roasts."[40]

The beefsteak restaurant was equally popular on the West Coast. In Los Angeles as in New York, the "chop-houses and beefsteak shops" (where "several stalwart chefs arrayed in immaculate white caps, aprons and jackets, [attend] to the wants of half a hundred hungry maws flanking the high counter") provided inexpensive, quick meals. "The bill of fare at these places is very simple, comprising chips and beefsteak and a two-story cup of coffee, the tariff for which is 'two bits,'" a reporter for the *Los Angeles Times* wrote, "but anyone who has indulged in this simple fare will be sure to try it again, as some of the cooks who have made a study of this branch of cookery have attained a very high proficiency in the art of grilling meats, and what is left out in accessories is added in bulk of meat, so that altogether one has to confess that he has received a most satisfying meal and gotten the worth of his money."[41] Businessmen, bachelors, and gamblers were the primary customers of the West Coast beefsteaks; it was only in the early twentieth century that these restaurants began to cater to women.[42]

If the beefsteak was considered "superlative in both quality and quantity" by most commentators, the same could not be said of the "average 'American' restaurant." Nonetheless, the relative expense of eating at a chophouse compared to an American restaurant, as well as the rough male atmosphere, forced even moderately well-off families to patronize the "average American caterer" on occasion—even at the risk of being "stuffed and crammed with dyspepsia."[43] Featuring an à la carte menu with an impossibly large bill of fare, the typical American restaurant, especially in New York, was known for the poor quality of its food, the belligerence of its waiters, and the bottles of condiments on the tables.

> The dishes were evidently those used by Noah in the ark, nearly all of them having been nicked and otherwise damaged when the tigers began to chase the lambs around the ship. The waiters were of that bleached type of darkies that express their contempt for the whole human race, in face and manner. . . . But it was a cheap place, very. Roast meats, 15 cents; all sorts of vegetables, 5 cents; pies, tea, coffee, bread and almost every other edible and inedible thing, 5 cents.

The bill of fare was long, but the waiters had an unpleasant habit of returning, after a piece of pie, for instance, had been ordered, with the telegraphic message: "Ain't no pie!"[44]

Not everyone was as critical of the "American restaurant proper," and not all cities were as disparaging of their American restaurants as New York.[45] Culinary conservatives in Boston took pride in the city's plain American restaurants, and those in Chicago felt it was a mark of sophistication that New England seafood was available in the city's restaurants after 1873.[46] But these were exceptions. The American restaurant, with its large but unremarkable bill of fare, generally offered little or no pleasure to discriminating diners until technological innovations in the late nineteenth century resurrected it. Buffets and Automats, introduced in New York and Philadelphia in the 1880s and 1890s, may not have improved the quality of the food, but they eliminated the contemptuous service and replaced the chipped dishes with a dedicated effort to provide clean, antiseptic dining rooms.[47] Department store restaurants, introduced at Wanamaker's in Philadelphia and Macy's in New York in the 1870s, also helped to repair the reputation of American restaurants by capitalizing on the profits generated from the high volume of women shoppers to establish reputations for better food and pleasant surroundings.[48] Finally, some American restaurants secured a steady clientele by specializing in regional cooking, especially southern dishes (in restaurants sometimes operated by African Americans) and New England cuisine.[49]

At the bottom of the hierarchy of culinary experiences, if only because of their limited menus, were the "coffee and cake saloons." Open early for breakfast and late for evening revelers, the coffee shop served sliced cold meats, corned beef, beans, and desserts. The food was often better than that served at the typical American restaurant, but the coffee and cake saloon's popularity rested entirely on its late hours and its inexpensive fare: twenty-five cents bought a satisfying meal.[50] "Now look on the picture of A CHEAP DINNER, such as the guests of the Morton house or the Marble Saloon sit down to," the *Washington Post* remarked. "That looks pretty fair, and it *is* fair for twenty-five cents, one-sixth the price of the big dinner, and the probability is that in no place on the Continent can more be had for a quarter than in this very city."[51]

Coffee and cake saloons were given different names and specialized in different foods depending on the city visited, but all shared a reputation for respectability that attracted both men and women. In Boston and New York, small restaurants and beaneries, including vegetarian restaurants for women, predominated.[52] In Chicago, cafés—"tolerably respectable imitations of the German *conditorei*, and cheaper places which are a sort of parody on the French *cremeries*"—served inexpensive meals.[53] In Los Angeles, the "Waffle Foundry"—where "a large waffle, swimming in melted butter" and covered with "enough maple sprup [*sic*] to float the Chilean navy" could be had for ten cents—established a "large patronage."[54] In Washington, D.C., the coffee and cake saloon enjoyed success in the form of the twenty-four-hour dairy lunch.[55] And in San Francisco in 1892, Charles S. Greene estimated that there were "a hundred . . . establishments that pass under the less pretentious name of 'Coffee Saloons.'"[56] No matter what title they had, however, these restaurants—and more ornate ice cream parlors specializing in small lunches, sweets, and, of course, ice cream—were often the only restaurants outside department stores where a woman unaccompanied by a male escort could dine without raising eyebrows.

By the close of the nineteenth century, middle-class restaurants were established urban institutions that fed thousands daily.[57] If some cities—Atlanta and Pittsburgh, for example—seemed to lag behind New York, Chicago, and San Francisco, most major cities had nonetheless developed restaurants that catered to managers, clerks, women shoppers, and their families. For the most part, these restaurants were small enterprises, subject to the vicissitudes of the economy and the subtle influence of middle-class preferences. It was these factors that made restaurants a reliable measure of the emergence of a cohesive middle class that was able to shape dining culture to cater to its preferences.

An Economic Revolution

Because of the rapid growth of the restaurant industry in the nineteenth century, individual restaurants struggled constantly. While relatively low entry costs encouraged former waiters and beer retailers to venture into the restaurant trade, fickle patronage and the growing variety of restaurants led to intense competition and a substantial rate of failure. Historical geographer Richard Pillsbury estimates that only 2 percent of the restaurants, oyster houses, and coffeehouses operating in 1850 stayed open more than ten years, and surviving business records suggest that the restaurant industry was no more stable in the later decades of the nineteenth century.[58] The account books of R. G. Dun & Company, the first commercial credit agency in the United States, offer a glimpse of the difficulties that restaurateurs faced in the 1870s and 1880s. Correspondents for the company regularly reported that an apparently successful enterprise had changed locations, been sold, or declared bankruptcy. Typical are the stories of the partners Thomas Hanlon and James McCafferty and the misfortunes of Carl Schalk. Hanlon and McCafferty opened an oyster saloon on 14th Street in New York City around 1874. McCafferty had experience in the liquor business and the place was "nicely fitted up," but the partners were saddled with debt and Dun's assessors concluded: "Are not doing a great deal of business. It is an experiment for them both and it is hard to tell whether it will be a success." Four years later, the business, now called a "Bar & Restaurant," was successful enough that the partners had invested in other restaurant concerns, and it looked as though they would experience continued prosperity. However, by 1883 the restaurant had closed.[59] Carl Schalk's experience, although ending in greater tragedy, was similar. Schalk opened a "bier garden of sort" at 120 Nassau Street in New York in 1869, but it had closed by 1876. Schalk did not give up; he opened a second business shortly after the first closed. Although Dun's correspondents thought Schalk a generous man who was popular with his customers, on August 12, 1878, he committed suicide. Dun's account books attribute his suicide to "bus[iness] embarrassments."[60] Hanlon, McCafferty, and Schalk's experiences were not unusual. More casual industry observers acknowledged the precariousness of owning a restaurant: intense competition and the expectation of low prices led many restaurateurs "to give up the business for the reason that it does not pay."[61]

PUBLIC DEMAND

For the restaurateur, the instability of the restaurant industry required that he take risks that often culminated in bankruptcy; for the urban middle-class customer, instability translated into economic and cultural power. While the individual clerk or manager acting alone exercised limited influence on what was served or how it was served, the nascent middle class acting in concert created "public demand" that no successful restaurant owner could ignore. As more and more middle-class families entreated restaurants to cater to their expectations of cleanliness, accessibility, and attentive service, restaurateurs responded.

The precariousness of the restaurant business empowered the middle-class patron. In an age when restaurateurs named their restaurants after themselves and rarely advertised, catering to the public meant, as Dun's assessors regularly noted, forming a personal bond with the clientele and adapting to their wishes. "The great desideratum for caterers is to first acquire and then retain patrons," J. Fanning O'Reilly proclaimed in a 1910 article for *The Steward*. "Eating in restaurants is more or less a luxury and our friends should remember that nothing is easier in this life to break away from than luxury."[62]

A brief story reprinted in the *New York Times* in 1885 illustrates the willingness of restaurateurs to accommodate middle-class patrons. A visitor to a table d'hôte restaurant in Manhattan offered the proprietor of the restaurant a ten dollar bill to pay a one dollar check. The proprietor did not have the money to make change and refused the guest's offer to pay the bill with pocket change. Instead, the proprietor suggested the young man pay him the next time he was in the restaurant. When another customer asked the restaurateur why he would take such a risk, the man explained: "He's a gentleman, and he would no more think of cheating me out of that dollar than he would of selling his soul. . . . Besides he'll have to come in again to pay that, and of course he'll stay for dinner. I've done the same thing again and again and I never lost a cent by it. . . . It's convenient sometimes to men who receive weekly or monthly salaries."[63] The restaurant proprietor's attitude was remarkable enough to warrant a mention in the newspaper, but his willingness to pander to men on salaries speaks to a more widespread readiness on the part of restaurant owners to cater to the growing influence of the middle-class consumer. In the "long run," as the *New York Daily Tribune* summed up the business philosophy of the late-nineteenth-century restaurateur, "it is altogether for the restaurant keeper's interest to do the best that he can for his customers. The questions are, who his customers are to be and what they will like best."[64]

Attention to the public's taste was a new concern for the restaurant industry of the late nineteenth century. In the elite aristocratic restaurant, the chef was selected for his expertise and skill; although no one felt that the chef was immune to criticism, generally he was the expert and his customers trusted him to provide the best that was possible. In the middle-class restaurant, the tables were turned—the customer was the ultimate authority.[65] Customers who did not like what was being served simply went elsewhere. An 1885 article in *The Cook* acknowledged the growing influence of the new restaurant patrons. Quoting the *Commercial Advertiser* at length, *The Cook* noted that in the past, restaurant-goers had to choose between the "ridiculously high" prices of the various aristocratic restaurants in New York and "places that are squalid and otherwise unattractive." Now, however, there were "new cheap restaurants that furnished meals at very low prices." "A sign of the times," *The Cook* observed, these restaurants were not "selfishly unjust to the public that has paid them so much money" as were their elite counterparts; rather, the new ten or twenty-five cent restaurants courted their customers and responded to "public demand."[66]

MICROMOTIVES

When shared by enough people, simple preferences can produce dramatic changes in a marketplace. Studies of micromotives help to explain why restaurants reacted to the preferences of their middle-class clientele. In the late 1960s and early 1970s, Harvard economist Thomas C. Schelling undertook a study of racial segregation. Public opinion polls at the time of Schelling's study suggested that attitudes about race were changing, but, despite the more progressive outlook, most Americans continued to live in all-white and all-black neighborhoods. Schelling's simple mathematical model (illustrated by the manipulation of pennies on a checkerboard) led to a theory of micromotives. In the case of racial segregation, the subtle, often unstated desire to live near at least one or two neighbors of one's own race explained the nearly absolute segregation of American cities. As Schelling stated, "The interplay of individual choices, where unorganized segregation is concerned, is a complex system with collective results that bear no close relationship to the individual intent."[67]

In the late nineteenth century, micromotives brought about the gradual expansion of restaurant dining and created, as contemporaries acknowledged, "the fascinating and exasperating peculiarities of the various refectories scattered over New-York, and, in a less degree, over other cities."[68] Micromotives undermined the hegemonic domination of the aristocratic restaurant by creating a more diverse world of dining organized by unstated middle-class preferences.[69] Although there was no coherent, mass movement by a delineated middle class, the subtle interplay of individual choices that amounted to a preference for restaurants where the middle-class diner felt comfortable brought managers, clerks, and professionals together. Coupled with the economic pressure their collective wealth exerted, their patronage transformed the restaurant. Restaurants that had once served only the lunch-hour businessman now stayed open late to attract the patronage of middle-class couples and families. Eating establishments notorious for their lack of service soon hired more waiters and covered their tables with checkered linens. Chophouses that once served only steak now offered a variety of simple, inexpensive dinners. Saloons installed family dining rooms, cellar restaurants moved to storefronts, downtown restaurants migrated uptown, and ethnic restaurants began to serve American dishes. New restaurants opened specifically for the urban middle class, and other restaurants opened new dining rooms to accommodate the growing patronage.[70] As early as 1873, *The Table* observed that "a vast improvement has taken place in the style and service of the cheaper kind of restaurant," and by 1885, the *New York Times* considered the transformation nearly complete.[71] "A decade or two ago it would have been practically impossible for many thousand people to live as they are living now. Flats were unknown and restaurants—of the right kind—a rarity. . . . The restaurant system is now so complete that if they live in anything like proximity to the central part of the city they need not fret about a cook—at least in so far as the principal meal of the day is concerned."[72] Restaurants "of the right kind" were now found in every corner of most American cities.

Within a few decades, these restaurants would be as closely associated with the middle class as the French restaurant was with elites. In 1892, a reporter for the *Los Angeles Times* observed that restaurants that catered to the middle class were distinguishing themselves from elite restaurants. "These places are conducted and patronized by people whom any respectable person can meet on equal terms, but are as exclusive in their way as some others with the most aristocratic pretensions, inasmuch as there are no other places where the rules of good breeding are more strictly demanded and observed," the reporter noted.[73] This new exclusivity, a distinctly middle-class exclusivity, rested on the specific demands that middle-class restaurant-goers made. While rejecting the cost, pretension, and wholly French cuisine of elite restaurants, middle-class diners imposed their own standards of economic value and polite service and forced changes in the common restaurant.[74]

The middle-class restaurant had evolved over the course of less than forty years into a new urban institution. It was cleaner than its lunchroom forerunner. Its menu was larger, its service more expeditious, its location closer to the centers of shopping and entertainment. Comfort and value were at a premium. In 1899, at Haan's in New York, a West Side restaurant popular with the middle class, a cushioned divan (precursor of the booth seating found at modern restaurants) ran along the walls, an eight-piece band played softly, and "the gourmet finds he can order any dish he can get elsewhere, cooked in any style he ever heard of." At the Endicott, a favorite of architects and contractors, a table d'hôte breakfast could be had for sixty cents, luncheon for another sixty cents, and dinner for a dollar (without the wine).[75] Again and again, the turn-of-the-century restaurateur innovated on behalf of his new clientele. By 1901, some middle-class restaurants in Chicago featured phones that could be plugged in at the table so that the "Chicago rusher" could "transact business by telephone while he eats his luncheon," while hundreds of restaurants across the country introduced open-air dining rooms for middle-class families that "can't afford to go into the country" during the summer months.[76]

Critics of the new restaurants complained that gourmets were becoming "rare creatures" and that the new middle-class restaurants were bastions of mediocrity.[77] An 1896 article in the *New York Daily Tribune* expressed the contempt many felt at the "dullness" of the middle-class restaurant. "Now and then the most skilful diner will stray into such a place. Its walls are bare. . . . The linen is not much soiled and neither is it perfectly clean. The waiter is not actually dilatory, but he shows no interest whatever in serving or pleasing the guest. Nobody can say that any of the dishes are bad, but nobody ever says 'How good this is!' . . . There is a general oppression of dullness and dissatisfaction, but nothing that can be made the ground of complaint."[78] Yet, saddened as he was, the reporter for the *Daily Tribune* acknowledged the popularity of dull restaurants with "sham luxury." "The saddest thing about it is the keepers of the places have estimated the tastes of their customers as accurately as any of the others have," the reporter observed. "The customers come here because, however much they may complain, on the whole, they like this sort of thing."[79] Reporters further noted that restaurateurs who sought a middle-class patronage but were unwilling to surrender their staid aristocratic traditions or their working-class informality often struggled to stay open.

Perhaps nothing was more galling to the old guard than the insistence of members of the middle class on combining eating and entertainment.[80] Although the cabaret and the dinner show were still in the future, music was heard in some middle-class restaurants as early as the 1870s, and by the end of the century, many restaurants featured orchestras.[81] A "Contributor's Club" submission to the *Atlantic Monthly* in 1907 ranted: "I am personally convinced that music at meals is a crime against nature no less than against art; and the glass of hot milk I now have to force down my throat before retiring, and the pills I forget to remember to take during the day, and the stern injunction against fried foods and sweet desserts, are a direct result of that barbaric adjunct to our modern life, the café orchestra." Of even greater concern than digestion, however, was the way in which music changed the fundamental nature of dining. Critic after critic complained not only that music and digestion were not complementary but also that the fine art of table conversation was being undermined by noisome entertainments. "No sooner," continued the editor at the *Atlantic Monthly*, "have you got the conversation turned into pleasant lanes and jogging nicely along, than—biff, scrape, clash, twang, and you are inundated by the Congo on its way to the sea or whelmed in the beautiful blue Danube. Some fool at the table invariably hums the words of the tune, which are invariably inane, and all further talk on the topic at hand is at an end."[82] A writer for the *New York Times Sunday Magazine* found both his conversation and his appetite for brook trout "put to rout" by the "awful din" of a nearby orchestra playing the "William Tell Overture."[83] Editors at *The Chef* predicted that "pretty soon we will hear of some progressive manager advertising a Punch and Judy show, ballet dancing on the counters or a slack-wire performance while you wait."[84]

At its heart, the strong reaction against dining-room music was not surprising since the introduction of musical entertainments was the most immediate indication that aristocratic standards were being defied. The aristocratic restaurant was a place to be seen, and the "entertainment" was provided by the guests themselves who flitted from table to table, priding themselves on their social graces and table talk. Peacock Alley, the famous entrance to the dining room at the Waldorf-Astoria where diners could survey arriving guests, was the epitome of aristocratic sociability.[85] In contrast, middle-class restaurants, more numerous and less personal, provided professional entertainers to an atomized public that visited restaurants not as clans but as couples. Married diners were not looking for an opportunity to chat, something that could be accomplished at home, but for an entertaining experience that would while away the hours.[86]

Stubbornly resistant to change, the conservative critic was too harsh. Middle-class consumers were not opposed to good food, but they were attracted to places where families could get the best value for their money. Establishments that prized value as well as quality and offered entertainment as well as comfort won the patronage of the middle class. No single archetype of the middle-class restaurant emerged (as happened with the aristocratic restaurant), but the business formula for attracting middle-class patronage, as D. F. Pride wrote in 1912, was simple. "The average patron wants something appetizing to eat, pleasant surroundings and good service."[87]

"Real Progress in the Art of Feeding the People"

Within the last ten years the luncheon and dinner hours have stretched longer and longer, not only in the better class of eating places, but even in
cheaper ones. The building of dozens of skyscraping office buildings and
the congestion of the downtown district not only have made troubles for
the transportation lines but have made crushes for the restaurants.
—*Chicago Daily Tribune*, 1903

Of course, the rich and luxurious are here as in larger cities . . . offering a variety and elegance of cuisine which can be approached by but
a few cities in the world. . . . But it is not in respect to the more expensive places that San Francisco is peculiar, for these naturally approximate
in style and manner to the pattern set by restaurants for the well-to-do
everywhere. The cheap restaurant . . . is at once the pride of the city
and the wonder of tourists. And there are literally scores of them.
—R. Whittle, "Humbler Restaurants of San Francisco,"
Overland, 1903

By the early twentieth century, it was no longer necessary, as a conde-
scending 1911 article in *The Steward* noted, for the middle-class diner who
"merely wants food and cares nothing for the manner in which it is served
to him . . . [to] 'chuck a bluff'—to also use the vernacular—by going to
fashionable dining places where naturally he would feel out of place, and
where he could not possibly have any appreciation of the refinement and
elegance of his surroundings."[88] In New York in 1911, as in Chicago and San
Francisco, the middle-class diner could find "restaurants of all degrees and
adapted to every man's wants and purse."[89]

The "middle-classing" of the restaurant was a process so subtle that
for some it may have appeared that little changed. But in the middle of
the nineteenth century, public dining culture was the province of the rich.
Those with money determined restaurant, clothing, and reading fashions,
and those without substantial resources followed their lead. By the early
twentieth century, while elite business owners still controlled the nation's
manufacturing enterprises, they no longer wielded exclusive power over
how Americans consumed. Small changes in preference had enormous
consequences.

By the end of the 1920s, *The American Restaurant Magazine* estimated
that one out of four urbanites dined out at least once a day. For the most
part, they did not eat in elite hotels and aristocratic restaurants. They ate
in simple, affordable establishments and were a part of what the most enthusiastic American boosters viewed as the golden age of dining. As *The
American Restaurant Magazine* concluded, "[I]t is common knowledge that

restaurants existed in foreign lands long before their appearance in this country," but "we can look to the United States for real progress in the art of feeding the people."[90] This "real progress" was not the development of a new cuisine but the proliferation of quick, clean, and reputable restaurants where families could secure an affordable meal in the evening. As John R. Thompson recalled in 1922:

> Fifty years ago there was practically nothing but railroad eating houses, with occasional all night lunch counters, in which one could eat a sandwich or drink a cup of coffee from heavy earthen ware cups and saucers, made for durability, not for looks or comfort. Ten years later the march of progress began, but it was not until the beginning of the present century that the possibilities of the business of feeding the world attracted the attention of the men who subsequently became the great organizers and money makers of the industry. One might almost say that it was not until the last score of years that the masterminds began to see their dreams come true. . . . The public today is more quickly served and better fed than at any time in the history of the world.[91]

Thompson's not-so-humble account of the rise of the American restaurant belies a genuine expertise on the growth of the industry. By the 1920s, as Thompson recognized, a revolution in dining was well under way.

For some historians and other scholars of class, the hierarchical social structure imposed by cultural capital is unassailable. French sociologist Pierre Bourdieu believed that over the course of a generation or two, a middle-class family might master the codes of civility imposed by the upper class and raise their children's status, but the cultural pecking order remained constant. One might eventually learn to appreciate *jambon d'York, à la gelée* rather than pig's feet, but in doing so one accepted that *jambon d'York* was the superior dish. Cultural preeminence is, in other words, the purview of elites. It is conservative and resistant to change over time. The futility of challenging the cultural hierarchy of class, the inability of a class to overcome the limits of the social structure of cultural capital, led Bourdieu to argue in *Distinction* that the class system is entrenched.[92] These "deep-seated disposition[s]" were for Bourdieu not necessarily "incompatible with revolutionary intention," but they did create a "modality which is not that of intellectual or artistic revolts."[93]

The emergence of the middle-class restaurant at the turn of the century and its influence on dining in the twentieth century suggest that Bourdieu's model is too rigid.[94] In the mid-nineteenth century, a nascent urban middle class composed of professionals, managers, and clerks had few public commercial institutions of their own. Yet thrust into the rapidly expanding metropolis and alienated by an elite culture that they could neither understand nor afford, middle-class urbanites began to patronize restaurants favored by other middle-class urbanites, restaurants where the middle class felt comfortable. These inadvertent individual acts of consumption turned the tables on the upper class. Over time, the middle class made manifest its emergent class identity in codes of conduct that privileged its own cultural capital and established a beachhead that not only celebrated middle-class cultural preference but also undermined the hegemony of the aristocratic restaurant.

THE RESTAURATION
Colonizing the Ethnic Restaurant

In 1876, the United States celebrated the hundredth anniversary of American independence. The culmination of the fanfare was the Centennial Exhibition (formally known as the "International Exhibition of Arts, Manufactures and Products of the Soil and Mine") that opened in Philadelphia in May. Thirty-seven nations participated in the event, and nearly nine million visitors toured the Centennial site on the banks of the Schuylkill River during the exposition's six-month tenure.

A few months after the fair opened, *Harper's Weekly* published a special supplement dedicated to the Centennial. Slipped in among the etchings of Centennial architecture was a sketch by Walter Brown, a Rhode Island–born artist and illustrator best remembered for his drawings in Mark Twain's *A Tramp Abroad*. Brown's "Our Artist's Dream of the Centennial Restaurants" depicts a clutter of restaurants and stalls grouped on a hill with various signs advertising their offerings. In the left forefront is a small Russian restaurant, dwarfed by two burly men with fur-trimmed hats and signs that advertise "Castor Oils on Tap," "Charlotte Russe," and "Turkey Wanted." Towering above, on unsteady posts, is an African restaurant bedecked with hand-lettered menus offering "Natives on the Half Shell" and "Elephant á la Stanley." Dead center are a Turkish and a French restaurant. Behind a turbaned, hookah-smoking Turk, the sign reads "OTTO Roses by the Glass," while at the nearby French restaurant, a waiter, nose in the air, offers "Bull Frogs," "Vin," and "Snails." Meanwhile, just visible to the right, a crowded German "Bier Garten" stacked on top of a Chinese restaurant is almost obscured by various Chinese signs for "Cat Sup," "Rat Pie," and "Hashed Cat." Sundry other booths offered missionary sandwiches (Sandwich Islands), mud pies ("Digger Indians"), Camel's

Walter Brown, "Our Artist's Dream of the Centennial Restaurants."
From *Harper's Weekly*, July 1, 1876. Courtesy of the Print and
Picture Collection, Free Library of Philadelphia.

Milk Punch (Arabia), Roman Punch (the Papal State), and whale on toast
(Greenland Eskimos?).[1]

The racial stereotypes of Brown's "Dream"—the narrow-minded, if
clever, xenophobia—may have accurately depicted Americans' fears about
foreign cuisine, but the illustration was a poor representation of the fair.
Brown envisioned a curiously multiethnic dining experience, a quixotic
panoply of American and ethnic cuisines. In practice, however, the fair offered little to challenge the adventurous eater. Exposition organizers provided for seven major restaurants: two French restaurants, three loosely
defined as "American" (including a southern restaurant featuring, as William Dean Howells noted, fried chicken "served by lustrous citizens of
color"), the Vienna Bakery Café, and Lauber's German Restaurant. The
most fashionable of the restaurants was the Trois Frères Provençaux, an
aristocratic French restaurant that rivaled the best restaurants of New
York or Philadelphia in cost and elegance, but all of the restaurants were
relatively expensive and exclusive.[2] As a result, many visitors to the fair ate
at their hotel, and those who dined on the fairgrounds visited the Great
American Restaurant or the comfort station lunchrooms that featured

typical "American" fare: cold meats, raw oysters, ice cream, and, in a nod to internationalism, "foreign bottled malt beverages."[3]

Cat, rat, whale, elephant, camel, and dog were not served. Spaghetti, tamales, and Hungarian goulash were also not available. Notably absent, as Donald Mitchell wrote in *Scribner's Monthly*, were restaurants that meaningfully expressed the diversity of the thirty-seven nations that had sent representatives to the Centennial.

> We are at the fair to measure so far as we may all the outcome of the civilization of our sister nations, the world over; and when we have grown wearied with study of their art, their guns, their cloths, their jewels, what better can we do in the noontide of rest, than test the dinners they cook? It is a pity, indeed, that the opportunity is not larger in this direction. We can try a cup of Tunisian coffee, and the excellent bread and chocolate of Vienna; but there is no Hollander to regale us with Deventer gingerbread, or his cheese, or herring; no Spanish service of an *olla-podrida*; no Provençal flavor of garlic, even at the *Trois Frères*. There is no Indian specialty of curry, or of mulligatawny; no sight of chopsticks, unless one follows the Chinamen to their private haunts.[4]

There is no telling how Americans would have received more diverse culinary offerings had they been provided. Journalists remarked on how receptive Americans were to the multicultural exhibits at the fair, but culinary adventurism was not a trait typically ascribed to Americans in the nineteenth century. In the United States in 1876, French food was recognized as the world's only great cuisine, and neither American nor ethnic dishes had many defenders. While Walter Brown and the fair's organizers envisioned the Centennial Exhibition differently, both acknowledged the provincialism of American appetites and agreed that America was not ready to experience the diversity of the world's cuisines.

In the closing quarter of the nineteenth century, however, restaurant dining in the United States was transforming. New immigrants flooded into American cities, bringing diverse foods and entrepreneurial traditions of restaurant ownership.[5] Initially, these restaurants offered culinary reminders of home for immigrants in an alien land, but ethnic restaurants did not stay long on the margins of urban life. Members of the emerging middle class, eager to find alternatives to inaccessible aristocratic establishments, colonized and transformed foreign eateries into restaurants that catered to middle-class tastes.

By the turn of the century, many middle-class urbanites had become champions of ethnic dining. Claiming that the United States' culinary diversity made it the envy of the world, the middle class trumpeted America's cosmopolitan culinary culture with patriotic passion. In doing so, they not only celebrated the multicultural menu but also advanced their own class interests. Twenty-five years after the Centennial celebrations slighted foreign cuisine, cosmopolitan dining created a wedge between upper- and middle-class culture that ultimately brought about the end of the aristocratic restaurant.

Foreign Food

In the early 1870s, only a few visionaries thought that Americans would embrace foreign cuisines. An 1872 editorial in the *New York Times* argued that the United States could become a great culinary nation if Americans learned to celebrate the diversity of dining experiences found in its cities, but the *Times'* editorial staff admitted that the moment had not yet arrived. "New-York, we all say, is getting to be very cosmopolitan . . . [and] it might be supposed that eclectic modes of cookery would spring up, wherein all the best customs of the various nations might be combined into one harmonious whole, and a system thus produced which in its entirety should be superior to any of its parts." But while New Yorkers had embraced architecture, theater, and fashion from around the world, New York remained a culinarily segregated city where foreign cuisines could be found only in inaccessible immigrant restaurants. Ethnic cooking might be the "Cuisine of the Future," the *Times* editors concluded, "but our trouble is, it is not the Cuisine of the Present."[6]

The *Times* viewed the ruling class's stranglehold on restaurant culture as a major obstacle to Americans' adoption of ethnic food. The United States, the *Times* stated, had "restaurants and hotels perhaps equal to any in the world," but these establishments were only for the "opulent classes." For the "middle orders as regards the purse," there were few choices. "We may be ever so cosmopolitan, progressive, and modern in other things," the editors wrote, "but in this we are still far behind hand, and our cookery, as adapted to the persons named, is little better than that of the Middle Ages. . . . Unless you can pay for the best of everything, you will, for the most part, have to put up with the worst."[7]

The *Times* did not address the issue, but the rise of the middle-class ethnic restaurant faced a second obstacle. Before the ethnic restaurant could become a staple of urban life, deep-seated stereotypes attached to foreign cuisines had to be confronted. In 1866, C. W. Gesner writing in

Harper's New Monthly Magazine surveyed New York's culinary fare. While Gesner—like the editors at the *Times*—condemned the "up town" restaurants as "unsatisfactory" and "expensive," he did not believe that the German restaurants that were proliferating in ethnic neighborhoods could serve as an acceptable alternative for the middle class. "Greasiness in various degrees distinguishes the German dishes," he inveighed. "Dirt in all degrees is present at the German restaurants. Plates and cups with pieces chipped out . . . and knives which know no cleaning, are always found. When the grease, which is so freely used, takes fire in the kitchen below, or in the rear of the dining-room, there is a suffocating odor which attends the decomposition of animal fat dispersed through the room."[8] Gesner's account of New York's ethnic restaurants was not unusual for the middle of the nineteenth century. Most Americans, excepting recent immigrants, avoided ethnic cuisines, which they found too greasy, too garlicky, or too spicy, and looked askance at restaurants where the smells and tastes were unfamiliar.

In San Francisco, although ethnic restaurants had provided inexpensive Chinese, German, and Italian meals to the founding generation of bachelor prospectors in the 1850s, few positive accounts of the city's foreign fare were published before the 1870s. Typical was an 1868 article in *Overland Monthly* written by newspaper editor Noah Brooks. Brooks, a former confidant of Abraham Lincoln's, was a regular denizen of San Francisco's small French restaurants. "French cookery," Brooks claimed, had "in the cosmopolitan city of the republic . . . predominance over that of all other peoples," and thus it was not surprising that his account of the city's ethnic restaurants was not flattering.[9] While he was aware of one Italian restaurant frequented by "traveled people, gourmands and blasé diners-out" looking for "a new sensation," for the most part Brooks felt foreign restaurants were solely for ethnic immigrants. "Germany has several restaurants—not especially distinctive, but essentially Germanesque in their customers," wrote Brooks, and "in the lower part of the city are numerous Italian restaurants, few of which are really first-class, if prices indicate such grades. . . . The Italian restaurants, however, are more exclusively patronized by the people of their own nationality than is true of any other class."[10] Even in the city's famous Chinatown, already a tourist attraction, Brooks argued that the restaurants were "liberal and bountiful to [their] guest," but "few western palates can endure even the most delicate of their dishes."[11]

Like Gesner and Brooks, *The Cook*, one of the first culinary newspapers in the United States, regularly disparaged ethnic food. Polish dishes were a mixed bag: a beetroot soup called *barszoz* was acceptable, but the magazine warned travelers that *kapusniak*, a sauerkraut beef soup, was "nasty."[12] Likewise, a traveler's account of the "unwearying round of pork fat, black beans and rice or mealio" popular in the Brazilian countryside sported the title "Barbaric Feeding."[13] And while the editors bowed to pressure from middle-class readers to print German recipes (conceding that "the cooks of the Vaterland prepare many delicate, delicious, nutritious compounds"), they showed no such magnanimity toward the Swedes. A venomous 1885 article reprinted from *Lippincott's Magazine* labeled Sweden's sideboard appetizers (smorgasbord) "a nightmare of gastronomic horrors" and concluded that "long before the unhappy tourist has finished his tour he is a hopeless dyspeptic or a raging Swedophobe."[14]

Hostility toward foreign food was not surprising. The modern idea of taste—a liking for foods learned in childhood and modified through experience and education—did not exist in the nineteenth century. To the extent that taste was discussed, it was generally assumed that an appreciation for a particular cuisine was hereditary and that each civilization had its own palate. This was one of the reasons why the elite's embrace of French food conveyed such a powerful message about their membership in the aristocratic class, and it was one of the risks associated with eating what were viewed as inferior foods. While nothing prevented an American from trying German or Chinese cuisine, it was widely believed that foreign dishes (as one observer noted of Turkish cooking) "are all seasoned so highly and are so rich in oils and fats that our plain American digestive apparatus loudly rebels against them."[15] It was also assumed that only inferior races could enjoy inferior foods. Given these attitudes, venturing into an ethnic restaurant was a challenge to established understandings of cultural difference.

Nonetheless, by the end of the nineteenth century, middle-class urbanites were embracing a new culinary adventurism that trumped the culinary xenophobia of the mid-nineteenth century. Lacking the economic and cultural capital necessary to enjoy fully the elite French restaurant, middle-class consumers sought alternatives. They ate in lunchrooms and chophouses and small American restaurants. And they also increasingly ate in ethnic restaurants. Although jokes about odorous German concoctions and garlicky Italian food remained a staple of many journals and newspapers, the middle class ventured into ethnic neighborhoods and experimented with new foods. Familiarity bred tolerance, patronage brought accommodation, and, by the turn of the century, middle-class Americans had become champions of a new culinary adventurism. While some of the earliest guides to ethnic dining offered specific advice on how to avoid food unsuitable for American palates, in time the cosmopolitan ideal, the belief that worldliness was good, became more important than supposed hereditary predispositions.

The Inexpensive Dinner

Middle-class urbanites, many who lived in rooming houses with repetitive boardinghouse fare or apartments without cooking facilities, discovered the ethnic restaurant in the 1870s and 1880s. Despite scurrilous reviews and negative stereotypes, ethnic restaurants—in New York and San Francisco and a number of other cities—won patronage by offering good, abundant, inexpensive food without the annoyance and expense of elite restaurants. An 1885 *New York Times* article subtitled "How Foreign Fashions Are Acclimatized in New-York" described the qualities that attracted the typical middle-class diner:

> Eating at a first-rate restaurant à la carte means a very large expenditure, in addition to the trouble of ordering—a trouble the average American shrinks from as naturally as the average Frenchman or Italian welcomes it. Eating at a second-rate restaurant of the same description implies dyspepsia if not worse. But frequenting a passable [ethnic] restaurant . . . the [diner's] outlay is determined at once and the danger of the repast being followed by indigestion reduced to a minimum. The restaurant may be French, Italian, Hungarian or even German, and the price may be 30 cents or $1.25 a head; the consequences, at any rate, will in all cases cause no annoyance.[16]

Middle-class diners, another reporter observed, "choose restaurants from preference," and the foreign table d'hôte restaurant offered the "cheapness and abundance" they sought. The process of "acclimatizing" to ethnic cuisines and immigrant restaurants, however, was not accomplished quickly.[17] Between the 1870s and the turn of the century, middle-class diners engaged in a process of discovery that led them from German food to a full embrace of the nation's growing culinary diversity.[18]

In eastern cities, German restaurants were the first to establish a reputation among the urban middle class.[19] Germans had been migrating to the United States since colonial times, and by the mid-nineteenth century, over a million German-born immigrants were living in the country. In large cities, these immigrants clustered in ethnic enclaves and supported dozens of restaurants. The prominence of German immigrant communities—and the fact that by the 1870s, many Germans were fully assimilated members of the American middle class—undermined culinary inhibitions and made it easier for middle-class Americans to find and experiment with German food.

German restaurants were initially located in working-class neighborhoods where, in order to secure cheap rents, they "generally occup[ied] the basements of stores and dwelling-houses, and from the exterior [did] not, therefore, present as inviting an appearance as they would were they located on ground floors."[20] Reflecting the stereotype that German food smelled foul, reporters who visited these restaurants invariably commented on the "smells from the kitchen," but they generally pronounced the establishments clean and inexpensive. Recounting a visit to a German restaurant in the 1870s, a reporter for the *New York Times* noted that the "table furnishings are simple but clean, and the floor generally sprinkled with fresh white sand." For thirty-five cents, he observed, you could get a five-course meal: "Though the meat is not always of the best quality, it is sure to be good, and well-cooked, though in a distinctly national manner."[21]

Extolling generous portions and low prices, newspaper accounts of German restaurants cautiously encouraged middle-class diners to try the new cuisine. "So entirely German are the dinners in this latter particular, that Americans can, by partaking of them, become acquainted with dishes of whose existence they had never before dreamed, though in this respect much that is served may be distasteful to the native palate."[22] *Lentil and bologna soup*, *beef à la mode* with macaroni ("a very peculiar but highly satisfactory way of eating it"), *Wiener schnitzel* ("a tremendous name, which, however, when bought, is only veal cutlet with the bone removed"), and *Hamburger steak* ("simply a beefsteak redeemed from its original toughness by being mashed into mince-meat and then formed into a conglomerated mass") were deemed particularly suited to American tastes by a *New York Times* reporter in 1873. The reporter also assured readers that many German restaurants offered—"for the Americans only"—"roast beef, as well as the odd things that foreigners love, and . . . pumpkin pies and dumplings baked."[23]

German food remained among the most popular of the ethnic cuisines throughout the late nineteenth century, especially in cities like Buffalo, Detroit, and Milwaukee where the native-born middle class joined a growing German middle class in patronizing the best-known restaurants. But as the 1870s waned, German table d'hôte restaurants faced competition for middle-class patronage from French and Italian establishments. In New York, French and Italian tables d'hôte were located a little farther uptown than their German counterparts and, while still found primarily in basements, often charged an additional five or ten cents and featured more elaborate menus.[24]

French table d'hôte restaurants, although serving simpler fixed-price dinners than the grand hotels and elite restaurants, were familiar to middle-class patrons who had experimented with French cuisine—and in some cities, the immigrant restaurants' reputations suffered as a result of the comparison. But if the food was occasionally disparaged, French table d'hôte restaurants were applauded for the low prices and informal service unheard of in their aristocratic counterparts. "[T]he wonder is how they can do so much," Charles S. Greene, an editor of the *Overland Monthly* and later the city librarian of Oakland, California, wrote about San Francisco's French restaurants in 1892. "They serve soup, a salad, a choice of several kinds of fish, and any one of half a dozen entrees, either of two kinds of roast, fruit, cheese, and black coffee with kirsch or cognac (only don't try to light the spirit), and of course, the half bottle of ordinaire to each guest. The cooking is fairly good, too,—French cooking that conceals the nature of the materials, and desires you only to accept the results and be thankful."[25] Yet French cuisine remained tainted by its association with elites and never was as popular with the emerging middle class as other ethnic foods. It was Italian food that eventually won the hearts and stomachs of members of the fledgling middle class.

Italian cuisine had experienced a brief period of popularity with male clerks in New York during the 1860s and 1870s but remained less familiar among middle-class diners than German or French cuisine (although some macaroni dishes were served in formal French restaurants) until the end of the nineteenth century. As a result, contemporary accounts of the first Italian restaurants favored by the urban middle class included reassurances that Italian dishes were palatable to middle-class tastes. Encouraging experimentation, a reporter for the *New York Times* favorably compared Italian cuisine to its German counterpart in 1871. "The manner in which the different dishes are cooked, or compounded, is better suited to the American taste than the [German], though at the same time it is distinctively national. It is only by visiting these restaurants that New Yorkers who have never been in Italy can really know how macaroni should be properly prepared."[26]

Such reassurances were effective, and Italian cuisine's popularity mushroomed. By the mid-1880s, the *New York Times* could claim that Italian restaurants were the most accepted foreign restaurants in the city, and by 1901, the *New York Sun* observed that "the larger part [of their patronage] is American."[27] Taste increasingly mattered, but as with other foreign eateries, the Italian restaurant's popularity rested primarily on low costs and ample portions that compared favorably with those served at aristocratic restaurants. "For a good soup, a dish of macaroni—and plenty of it—fish, excellent lamb chops and kidneys, two or three kinds of birds in season, lettuce, salad, two or three kinds of cheese, as many kinds of fruit, coffee, and half a flask—in quantity at least a quart—of light Italian wine," a reporter for the *New York Tribune* enthused in 1884, "[Moretti] charges $1.25; with vin ordinaire, $1. . . . Charles Delmonico would have charged at least $5 or $6 for the same dinner."[28]

German, French, and Italian remained the staple foreign cuisines in most American cities, but by the end of the nineteenth century, New York's rapid growth as an immigrant destination brought new ethnic communities and new culinary experiences for the adventurous diner. Hungarian, Spanish, Chinese, Japanese, South American, and Syrian restaurants developed middle-class clienteles, and a variety of ethnic restaurants provided for the middle class in other American cities. Although the most popular cuisines varied from city to city—a reflection of different patterns of immigration and regional prejudice—by the 1890s, middle-class restaurantgoers across the country had embraced new restaurants and new cuisines.

In San Francisco, Charles Greene bragged that "[s]o far as the education of the stomach goes, one may obtain all the benefits of the grand tour without leaving San Francisco."[29] Greene's "grand tour" included a German-Jewish restaurant featuring herring salad, "a full variety of sausage," and matzos; a Mexican restaurant "where the visitor can burn out his alimentary canal in the most approved Spanish style"; and a genuine Italian restaurant where, unlike the uptown restaurants that "only differ from the French in having a course of Italian pasta in the shape of macaroni, tagliarini, spaghetti, or ravioli," the "food was surprisingly good."[30] As for a true "Celestial repast," he suggested a prearranged dinner in Chinatown: "they will give you a wonderful assortment of viands, even to shark's fins and birdsnest soup, if you are willing to pay for such great delicacies."[31] And Greene's grand tour was not yet complete. In eager anticipation of future delights, he confessed that he had not yet dined in San Francisco's Russian, Scandinavian, and Japanese restaurants.

Journalists in other cities also took note of the growing number of foreign restaurants patronized by middle-class urbanites. In 1892, the *Los Angeles Times* claimed that "a person must have come a long distance from a very obscure corner of the earth if he cannot find something to suit him among all the variety there is to choose from, and Los Angeles restaurants are justly popular and well patronized."[32] Los Angeles's restaurants included many that "cater to particular nationalities, where the German can satisfy his taste for sauer-kraut, limburger and pigs-feet, the Frenchman enjoy[s] his patent mixtures with absinthe in his coffee; the Italian his favorite macaroni and the Spaniard his fiery chilli-con-carve [sic], and the writer once heard a 'Tarheel' order 'some fa-at pork an' some dandelion greens with a few morlasses onto hit,' which was instantly forthcoming."[33]

Likewise, Washington, D.C., celebrated its "cosmopolitan" dining opportunities at the turn of the century. In 1901, the Washington Post noted the opening of the city's first Tex-Mex restaurant featuring Hot Tamales and Chile Con Carne, foods so "biting hot because of the peppers" that "those who eat, partake freely of iced water on the side." But chili was not all the city had to offer. "Der Vaterland is by far the best represented here of any nation in the matter of national eating places," the Post reported. "Washington has rathskellers and beer tunnels galore, where pumpernickel, boar's head, Brauchweiser, leberwurst, schnitzels, Bismarck herring and limburger may be had ad libitum." And the city also boasted three French restaurants, one near the Capitol building; a dozen or more Chinese restaurants; and an Italian restaurant where "[t]he intruder is not looked upon with great favor, but the proprietor willingly serves the visitor with one of the coarse bowls of slippery spaghetti."[34]

For a growing number of middle-class urbanites in New York, San Francisco, Los Angeles, Washington, and a host of other Progressive Era cities, ethnic cooking had become a seminal part of public dining by the 1890s. In 1897, Rosa Belle Holt shared with the readers of What to Eat her experience of living in New York on a fixed budget. Initially she split expenses with a friend and engaged the services of a maid to assist with meals. But when Holt's friend left, she dismissed the maid and began to explore the city's restaurants. Quickly she discovered, and exploited, the variety of restaurants in New York. "Within a radius of one mile from our home we [she often dined with her brother] know the cooking in all the good French, Italian and German restaurants. Finally we settled on three special places, each one presided over by a chef of a different nationality, and each one all that could be desired. The French and Italian served a table d'hote dinner, fifty cents, consisting of from five to eight courses, and smile as you may, they were good. It was, indeed, hard to choose between them."[35]

Holt's experience was not unusual. By the turn of the century, middle-class diners had embraced the foreign restaurants where, even if the food was sometimes unfamiliar, they commanded the cultural authority they lacked in elite restaurants.

Culinary Adventurism

By the start of the twentieth century, it was clear that middle-class restaurant-goers were embracing a new culinary adventurism and that this adventurism increasingly trumped the culinary xenophobia of the mid-nineteenth century. While some of the earliest guides to ethnic dining offered specific advice on how to avoid food that would be unsuitable for American palates, in time novelty became more important than cultural and hereditary predispositions.[36]

In a 1903 widely reprinted article, the *New York Sun* encouraged diners to eat in the "small and cheaper priced Italian eating places [that] abound on the upper side streets off Broadway and are gaily decorated within and extremely clean." While the article conceded that these restaurants had faults—the soup and the spaghetti "are always good" while the oil and the wine "are apt to be bad"—Italian food was viewed as a welcome alternative to aristocratic French cuisine.[37] "It is a generally admitted fact," the *Sun* observed, "that French cookery palls very quickly upon the palate of some people, and the fact was often commented upon that one of the leading restaurant keepers of New York was wont to steal away to less fashionable dining rooms than his own quite frequently for dinner."[38]

The *Sun* was not alone in challenging Americans to seek novelty. Employing a conversion trope that was common in articles on ethnic dining, Lucien Adkins recounted in an 1898 essay how, as a "friend and guide," he had introduced many of his fellow New Yorkers to chop suey:

Take a friend to Chinatown for the first time and watch his face when the savory chop-suey arrives. He looks suspiciously at the mixture. He is certain it has rats in it, for the popular superstition that the Chinese eat rats is in-bred. He remembers his schoolboy history, with the picture of the Chinaman carrying around a cage of rats for sale.

He quickly puts aside the chop sticks, which are evidently possessed of the devil, and goes at the stuff with a fork. It is a heroic effort, but it is not sustained. The novice gets a mouthful or two, turns pale, all the time declaring that it is "great."

It is a long time before he can be persuaded to go again, but he is sure to surrender eventually to the enchanting decoction, and soon there are times when the knowing hunger for chop-suey, and for nothing else, draws him to dingy Chinatown, alone and solitary, if he can find no one to accompany him. For awhile he half believes there must be "dope" in the stuff. He is now certain that there are no rats in it. He is a confirmed chop-suey eater.[39]

While the fear of eating rats, cats, or dogs was a powerful deterrent to cosmopolitan dining, daring to eat in an ethnic restaurant also served as a badge of courage. Facing and overcoming stereotypical fears about unaccustomed cuisines promised culinary rewards. A 1901 report from a German restaurant in Milwaukee suggested that the negative traits of some ethnic foods were obstacles that could and should be overcome in pursuit of a unique culinary experience:

"You don't like it, no?" [the waitress said] with a quaint German drawl. "If you will taste it once you will not be disturbed by the smell."

So with an inward prayer to the special little god that watches over your health and well-being you sample, timidly and hopelessly, the dainty she holds out to you on the tip of a fork. The fear vanishes and something akin to joy fills your soul, for you have experienced a distinctly new gustatory sensation. It may or may not be pleasing. The joy in the sensation lies in its novelty.[40]

These conversion stories celebrated a new culinary philosophy that challenged the underlying social Darwinism of aristocratic dining and called into question biological taxonomies of taste, race, and class. If every cuisine held the promise of gustatory pleasure, then French cuisine's preeminence rested on empty honorifics, not biology, and the cosmopolitan connoisseur whose knowledge of cuisines extended beyond the culinary achievements of France might claim the greater command of cultural capital.[41]

Similar articles celebrating ethnic food appeared regularly in city newspapers and culinary magazines at the turn of the century. Guides to German, Spanish, Scandinavian, or Italian restaurants encouraged middle-class readers to seek out new and challenging culinary experiences.[42] *What to Eat*, for example, kept popular naturalist Felix L. Oswald, MD (author of *Physical Education* and *The Remedies of Nature*), occupied for much of 1901 and 1902 with an extensive series titled "International Food Studies," and *Table Talk* repeatedly published ethnic recipes requested by readers.[43] New foods—Japanese *raufish* and Venezuelan *hallacas*—were discovered and applauded.[44] Not all the tendered advice was accurate—a writer for the *Washington Post* was confused when an Italian restaurant placed grated Parmesan on the table at the start of the meal, mistaking the pasta topping for the postprandial French cheese course—but all challenged Americans to seek variety.[45] And in an era of national expansion, some middle-class diners embraced the new cosmopolitanism with almost patriotic zeal. Rosa Belle Holt, after attending an Armenian dinner, explained her new appreciation for Middle Eastern cooking. "The various dishes, so unique from the American stand-point, were relished with true American adaptability."[46]

The transformation of the marginal foreign restaurant into the mainstream ethnic restaurant challenged nineteenth-century elite ideas that French cuisine was the only cuisine of merit and made it possible for middle-class diners to distinguish themselves from American elites who imitated European aristocracy's manners and mores. The tables were turning, and the aristocratic palate increasingly seemed narrow and outmoded.

A Middle-Class Institution

In the 1870s, the *New York Times* speculated that as foreign tables d'hôte became popular with the middle class, "it is highly probable that in the next few years their influence will work great changes in the present very expensive style of living."[47] By the end of the nineteenth century, these "great changes" were readily apparent. The ethnic table d'hôte had become a practical alternative for the middle-class diner who lacked the resources to eat regularly at the more expensive French-influenced hotels and restaurants. But middle-class patrons did more than eat in ethnic restaurants; they colonized them.[48] Like contemporary imperialists, they occupied, appropriated, and transformed the restaurants they patronized.

As middle-class patrons chose to eat in ethnic restaurants and restaurant owners began to cater to this relatively well-off clientele, the character of immigrant eateries changed. Ethnic families, "the small band of Italian and polyglot intimates who gave [the ethnic restaurateur] his first 'lift,'" were crowded out by the rush of wealthier patrons.[49] In 1885, a reporter for the *New York Times* observed that it was the "quieter people," middle-class couples and families, who formed the majority of the patrons at the more respectable ethnic restaurants of cities like New York. "Young couples who dwell in furnished rooms and have no cook and no servant visit these restaurants constantly; people who have country cousins 'dine them' there as a 'treat,' and when materfamilias has been given ten minutes notice by Bridget she often proposes to paterfamilias that the whole brood shall, for a day or two, tone up their stomachs by means of the masterpieces of Signor Bottesini's chef."[50]

The urban middle class now regularly patronized restaurants that had "taken root in basements . . . or in parlor floors in side streets," and some restaurateurs, eager to capitalize on their success, moved to new locations where they would be more accessible to the professional and managerial class. By 1885, ethnic eateries in New York could be found "amid brownstone abodes in fashionable byways within sight of the main arteries of the metropolis."[51] This migration from ethnic enclaves to middle-class neighborhoods advanced year after year. Looking back in 1920, a writer for the *New York Times* recalled that in the first decade of the twentieth century, the twenties and thirties blocks of Manhattan had been home to the city's French and Italian restaurants. More recently ("within the last half dozen years"), the reporter had witnessed the migration of ethnic restaurants to the lower forties. By 1920, inexpensive middle-class restaurants occupied the "high stooped brownstones" between Forty-Third and Forty-Seventh Streets near Times Square, neighborhoods that had only recently been "doing service as private homes or boarding houses." The writer concluded that "the increasing presence of Italian and French restaurants is an unfailing mark of the decadence of the former homelike atmosphere and the preparation for a hustling and commercial life."[52] More accurately, these restaurants chased their clientele, following them uptown and even to the suburbs. Historians Michael and Ariane Ruskin Batterberry observed that by the 1920s, fashionable uptown Manhattan played host to Italian, German, Chinese, Russian, and Romanian restaurants, while studies of New York and Chicago during the same period have shown that Chinese restaurants followed middle-class patrons to the suburbs as well.[53]

Not every ethnic restaurant chased after middle-class patronage. Many remained in ethnic enclaves and continued to cater to working-class families; others attracted uptown "slummers" and remained in vogue with adventurous middle-class bohemians. The demand for ethnic cuisine grew quickly enough, however, to keep pace with the rapid growth in the number of ethnic restaurants. Lee Wing, a merchant who lived in New York's Chinatown, told the *New York Daily Tribune* in 1901 that new Chinese restaurants "along Third and Sixth aves. and in the other parts of the city" had not hurt the business of older establishments in Chinatown. "On the contrary," Lee told the reporter, "they tell me that the proprietors are doing a larger business than ever."[54]

The move uptown, however, coincided with changes in the menu at both the enclave restaurants and the newer establishments. Ethnic restaurants developed "hybrid" menus that featured an assortment of both ethnic dishes and American favorites. As we have already seen, the earliest German restaurants made concessions to their new clientele by grafting American dishes onto their menus.[55] Italian restaurants soon made similar compromises. "Then the intelligent Boniface has bettered his service, added a course to his bill of fare, poured less water into his ordinaire, and levied an additional tax of 10 to 25 cents," observed a New York reporter. "It is a curious fact that, as the quality of the guests and food improves, the national dishes disappear, and the Italian cook shows a stronger inclination to a hybrid cuisine than to the unadulterated and savory dishes of his mother land."[56] Likewise, Chinese entrepreneurs learned to accommodate a variety of tastes. In a 1903 interview, police captain Burfriend recounted a discussion he had with a Chinese restaurateur:

> I once asked a chop suey man why he did not confine himself strictly to Chinese dishes and not have a bill of fare mixed with such commonplace things as ham and eggs and mutton chops with French fried potatoes. He told me that it was necessary for him to do this in order to satisfy his customers. A man might wish to treat his wife or a friend to a dish of chop suey after a [sic] theatre, but could not eat the stuff himself. He must either go hungry or be satisfied with tea and rice. Consequently, he lets his wife have her chop suey, while he orders from the American side of the bill.[57]

In making these accommodations, ethnic entrepreneurs demonstrated their business acumen. They also tacitly recognized the growing power of the middle-class diner—and his wife—to influence cultural changes in dining.

This trend continued into the twentieth century. A 1915 fixed-price, multicourse menu at one of New York's most celebrated German restaurants, the HofBräu Haus, featured polyglot choices, including a first course that featured two French dishes (*Broiled Spanish Mackerel, Maitre d'hotel* and *Fried Filet of Sole, Ravigote*) and an English dish (*Boiled Beef [with] Horseradish Sauce*); a second course of *Spaghetti a l'Italienne*; and a third course that offered a choice of turkey or *Gefuellte Kalbsbrust*.[58] The

Gefuellte Kalbsbrust, a stuffed veal breast, was the only decidedly German dish among the entrées listed. Similarly, the "special Sunday course dinner" at Chin Lee Company's First Class Chop Sooy and American Restaurant in Providence, Rhode Island, in December 1914 included only one Chinese dish, *Veal Chop Sooy with Green Peppers*, among an assortment of western soups, entrées, roasts, vegetables, and desserts.[59] And Ye Olde Dutch Tavern in New York, an ostensibly Dutch/German restaurant, served such a multicultural mix of German and American dishes in 1914 that it might not be fair to class it as an ethnic restaurant at all. Of the twenty-nine entrées listed in its December 1914 menu, only four were clearly German.[60] Recounting a similar experience visiting a Danish coffee shop, food writer Charles J. Rosebault observed that "if there was any fault to find it was in the bewildering variety of offerings. It was as though it aimed to be the whole world at once: French, Austrian, German, Italian, English and American cuisines were all represented, as well as the Danish."[61]

Menus, however, do not reveal more subtle changes, and it is likely that ethnic restaurants adapted dishes and service to accommodate middle-class tastes. Garlic and other spices unfamiliar to Americans were eliminated, and dishes considered too ethnic for American tastes disappeared from menus. In Chinese restaurants, restaurateurs began to offer knives and forks for those unaccustomed to chopsticks; salt, rare on Chinese tables, became a staple in the 1890s; and some restaurants experimented with providing bread.[62] For those early middle-class adventurers who had developed a passion for "authentic" food, these changes were cause for complaint. A cartoon from 1913 spoofed the "supposedly foreign restaurant." Set in the dining room of a restaurant with a sign proclaiming it to be a "Real Italian Restaurant," the cartoon featured a German restaurant proprietor warning the chef, "Der's an Eyetalian guy dat actually wants some Eyetalian grub," while his Irish co-owner takes the order.[63] In the article that accompanied the cartoon, the writer bragged that he had found two authentic immigrant restaurants—one Arab, the other Italian—but refused to name them because he feared that they would quickly be overrun and co-opted.[64]

Changes in patronage and cuisine were not the only changes that foreign restaurants underwent at the turn of the century. As middle-class diners colonized immigrant restaurants, they demanded more service and more elaborate decor, demands that drove up prices—and profits—and ultimately gentrified the ethnic restaurant. Restaurants patronized by the

Marty, "Supposedly Foreign Restaurant."
From the *New York Times*, November 23, 1913.

"middle classes" became, the *Los Angeles Times* noted in 1892, "exclusive in their own way."[65] In turn, these restaurants, polished and polite establishments, became gateways to cosmopolitan eating that encouraged more and more middle-class urbanites to experiment with ethnic food.

Middle-class diners, like empire-building imperialists, embraced the ethnic cultures they "discovered," but only to the extent that those cultures furthered their own interests. While middle-class diners tried new dishes, they also expected restaurants to provide familiar American foods alongside exotic new cuisines. They ventured into ethnic neighborhoods when necessary, but they also encouraged ethnic entrepreneurs to move uptown, to establish restaurants that met middle-class expectations of cleanliness and service, and to cater to the middle class at the expense of working-class clients. The new cosmopolitanism was as much a celebration of middle-class consumer power as it was an embrace of ethnic diversity, and middle-class urbanites championed and supported those ethnic restaurants that best catered to their preferences.

The Restauration

All the chefs of all the nations juggle all the cookbooks into one culinary
anthology, until there is surely no city on earth where such elaborateness and
variety distinguish the menus. Verily, we are in the period of the Restauration.
—Robert Hughes, *The Real New York*, 1904

The "restauration" coincided with the emergence of the United States
as an economic, diplomatic, and cultural world power and subsequent
efforts to win recognition of America's ascendance from Old World nations. In 1895, Americans invoked the Monroe Doctrine and insisted that
the United States should arbitrate a border dispute between Great Britain
and Venezuela; in 1898, the United States went to war with the dying Spanish Empire and won; a year later, American secretary of state John Hay
unilaterally (although unrealistically) announced European support for an
open-door policy toward China; and in 1905, Theodore Roosevelt negotiated an end to the Russo-Japanese War. Meanwhile, American cultural
entrepreneurs were enthusiastically promoting American culture abroad.
In 1887, Buffalo Bill made the first of a number of trips to Europe with his
Wild West Show, and in 1888, Albert Spalding set out on a world tour to
publicize baseball. Five years later, the World's Columbian Exposition in
Chicago formally introduced the world to American technology and culture, and over the course of the next couple of decades, global interest in
American music, film, and chromolithographs increased dramatically.[66] It
was in this context that culinary adventurism was soon transformed into a
mark of national pride. Eager to demonstrate that Americans' culinary accomplishments matched their economic and military successes, boosters
seized upon "cosmopolitan" dining as America's distinctive contribution
to the historical development of cooking.

The new cosmopolitan creed of dining was simple, although packed
with irony. Other nations might have older culinary cultures, but no nation could match the culinary diversity of the United States. American
cities, teeming with immigrants, sheltered a great variety of gastronomic
expertise that when combined with the fruits of American farming produced a multicultural cuisine superior to anything that the most intrepid
globetrotter might find abroad. This conception of what it meant to be
cosmopolitan argued that worldliness was proof of national superiority
and, without apology, viewed immigrant entrepreneurship as evidence of
American accomplishment.

Scholars now recognize that cosmopolitanism manifests itself in diverse
ways.[67] Cosmopolitans generally believe that we are citizens of the world

with a sense of our shared humanity, but while many cosmopolitans argue that worldliness can mitigate local and national attachments, not everyone believes that respect for diversity has historically undermined nationalism. This complexity was evident in the early-twentieth-century invocation of cosmopolitanism. Members of the emergent middle class celebrated culinary diversity in terms that were global but also patriotic and filled with local pride. Ultimately, however, the contradictions mattered less than the results. Cosmopolitanism provided Americans with their first distinctive culinary tradition, and, since the middle class promoted the idea, it served as a vehicle for middle-class interests. The cosmopolitan creed made ethnic cooking and diverse menus into a powerful counterweight to the aristocracy's Francophilia.

NEW YORK'S COSMOPOLITANISM CHIC

New York had been the center of American culinary culture since Delmonico's first opened in the 1830s, and no city in the United States—and possibly no city in the world—was better poised to claim the mantle of cosmopolitanism than New York in the late nineteenth century. As the nation's commercial capital and the arrival point for hundreds of thousands of immigrants, it hosted dozens of ethnic communities, each with its own culinary traditions and restaurants.

In the 1890s, New York began a decades-long celebration of its culinary cosmopolitanism. L. J. Vance, writing in *Frank Leslie's Popular Monthly* in 1893, was one of the earliest authorities not only to trumpet the city's immigrant offerings but also to suggest that the city's diverse ethnic eateries placed it among the great culinary centers of the world. "The New Yorker may [travel] without leaving the city," Vance observed. "He can breakfast in London, lunch in Berlin, dine in Paris and sup in Vienna. On a wager he could dine differently four times a day for a week, and have each repast composed of foreign dishes, served by foreign waiters, and eat with foreign-born men and women as his convives. No better than that could be done in Paris, the city of rare and artistic *plats.*"[68] Three years later, a brief notice in *What to Eat* expanded on Vance's claim that New York was a world-class culinary city. The anonymous article, echoing early-nineteenth-century bon vivant Sam Ward's claim that he had traveled the world and feasted "in all languages," declared that one could dine in "eleven languages and innumerable dialects" in New York. "If a man only knows 'What to Eat,' and has the wherewith to obtain it, he will have little trouble in satisfying himself in the metropolis."[69]

An avalanche of boasts followed. *The Steward* declared in 1910, for example, that "there is hardly a nationality on the face of the earth that has not a representative restaurant within the limits of . . . [this] most cosmopolite city." In that, the magazine asserted, New York was "distinctive."[70] Advertising expert D. F. Pride declared in 1912 that the "restaurants of New York are probably unequaled in any other city in the world, either in number or variety. The cuisine and national dishes of every nation, as well as dishes peculiar to certain sections of the United States, can all be found within the limits of the Metropolis, and, as a rule, creditably and faithfully represented."[71] Early-twentieth-century dining guides—published for tourists as well as for city dwellers—also began to celebrate New York's foreign cuisines. One of the first guides to the city's restaurants, *Where and How to Dine in New York*, included only a few upscale ethnic establishments, but later dining guides were more catholic.[72] George S. Chappell's *The Restaurants of New York*, for example, promised New Yorkers they could "tour the world gastronomically, with a purse for a passport and a menu for a ticket."[73]

The celebration of New York's cosmopolitanism was more than civic pride; it was an explicit rejection of Europe's claims to culinary superiority. Charles Multerer, a waiter at a leading New York restaurant, credited cosmopolitanism with establishing America's culinary reputation. The United States must, Multerer wrote in 1911, "concede that the older world has given us the initiative in gastronomic science, but we have been apt pupils. . . . Where in all the world can you find its equal in the gastronomic world? . . . [We] serve the national dishes of every civilized country at least as well, if not better, than they are cooked at home."[74] Similarly, "La Billie," the European correspondent for *The Steward*, argued that European cooking had become stale while American cooking had advanced. "The sauce that was said to please Francis I, or Henry VIII, or Louis XIV, is expected to please the denizens of Europe—and to change it would be heresy," the journalist wrote. "Europe lives on tradition, America lives on variety. . . . The New York hotel manager hears of the Southern fashion of the preparing [of] one dish, of the New England manner of cooking another, of the French and Italian specialties, and he never rests until he provides them all for his guests."[75] It was this remarkable diversity of cuisine that led Robert Hughes to wax poetic, "Verily, we are in the period of the Restauration."[76]

COSMOPOLITAN COMPETITION

New York was not alone in celebrating cosmopolitanism; other cities competed for the same crown of sophistication.[77] Since the mid-1800s, San Francisco had boasted a diverse, restaurant-going population and a wide variety of restaurants. Noah Brooks, although not a fan of ethnic restaurants, described the city in the 1860s as lacking a "distinctive local dish" but having compensated with a fare that was "cosmopolitan."[78] Charles Greene described restaurant life in San Francisco in 1892 as a "grand tour."[79]

In the early twentieth century, accounts of San Francisco's cosmopolitan culinary offerings grew more fervent and frequent. Roland Whittle informed readers of the West Coast journal the *Overland Monthly* that San Francisco "is known to the globe trotter as the very metropolis par excellence." In a 1903 article titled "Humbler Restaurants of San Francisco," he made it clear that the city's reputation rested not on the fame of its elite restaurants but on the diversity of its middle-class establishments. "The semi-tropical life, the cosmopolitan population, and the absence of the home life in the beginning of its history, all combined to make the inhabitants of the city by the Golden Gate enthusiastic diners out; and it is to be questioned if any city in the world can show such diversity and individuality in public places of refreshment as can San Francisco," bragged Whittle.[80] He went on to describe the breadth of San Francisco's restaurants—from the genuine Mexican restaurant "where the meals are cooked by Mexican women before your eyes in the approved Mexican fashion" to the popular Italian restaurant "with all its noise and all its crowded revelry."[81]

Clarence Edwords, a self-styled middle-class bohemian, was the most enthusiastic champion of San Francisco's cosmopolitan culture.[82] Writing in 1914, the former editor of the *Kansas City Journal* reported that even those who had been to Paris believed that San Francisco was the place "where you get the best there is to eat, served in a manner that enhances its flavor and establishes it forever in your memory." What accounted for this reputation? Edwords asked. "Do not other cities have equally as good chefs, and do not the people of other cities have equally as fine gastronomic taste?" The answer for Edwords was the indisputably cosmopolitan nature of the city, the "queer little restaurants, where rare dishes are served, and where one feels that he is in a foreign land, even though he be in the center of a highly representative American city."[83]

San Francisco's cosmopolitanism is peculiar to itself. Here are represented the nations of earth in such distinctive colonies that one might well imagine himself possessed of the magic carpet told of in Arabian Nights Tales, as he is transported in the twinkling of an eye from country to country. It is but a step across a street from America into

Japan, then another step into China. Cross another street and you are in Mexico, close neighbor to France. Around the corner lies Italy, and from Italy you pass to Lombardy, and on to Greece. So it goes until one feels that he has been around the world in an afternoon. . . .

This aggregation of cuisinaire, gathered where is to be found a most wonderful variety of food products in highest state of excellence, has made San Francisco the Mecca for lovers of gustatory delights, and this is why the name of San Francisco is known wherever men and women sit at table.[84]

Impartial observers seemingly bore out Edwords's observations. A study conducted in the 1920s by the Department of Commerce concluded that the "highly cosmopolitan nature of the city's population is an important factor in diversifying the character of its restaurant industry." In San Francisco, the study's author noted, "it is possible to eat in any language."[85]

San Francisco, with its long tradition of ethnic dining, posed the most serious challenge to New York's claim to be the nation's most cosmopolitan metropolis, but it was not alone. Even some smaller, less diverse cities made claims to culinary cosmopolitanism in the early decades of the twentieth century. Journalists in Los Angeles, still a small city at the turn of the century, declared that it "may modestly boast of consuming more cooked food than any other city . . . and [having a population] who may enjoy a greater variety of meals in a greater variety of eating places than in any other city." In the "melting pot of epicures," the *Los Angeles Times* boasted, "the appetite may enjoy a tour of the world, touching almost every nation of the universe without passing beyond the city limits."[86]

Washington, D.C., with its embassies and foreign diplomats, also had a vibrant ethnic restaurant culture by the first decade of the twentieth century and was eager to make its own claims to cosmopolitanism. In 1901, the *Washington Post* argued that "[o]ne does not have to leave Washington and seek the Pan-American midway for novelty in the line of foreign restaurants, for there are any number of quaint dining-rooms in the Capital City to accommodate the cosmopolitan population."[87] A year later, the paper implied that the city's Chinese restaurants were as much a part of the Washington experience as the White House and the Washington Monument. "The person who sets out to see the sights of the Capital and fails to visit the Chinese restaurants misses one of the features of the city."[88]

Only Boston, proud of its baked beans and cod (and seat of the conservative Boston School of Cooking), seemed content to leave ethnic food to the ethnic masses. A 1908 article entitled "Boston Women Well Fed" passionately made the case that a restaurant-goer in Boston, unlike New York and Chicago, "may eat better for less money than in any other capital in the country, and she doesn't have to go to a foreign restaurant to do it, either."[89] But Boston's regionalism was increasingly unfashionable. While not every claim to cosmopolitanism was as grand or as well-founded as New York's and San Francisco's, the rush of cities seeking the title suggests that a revolution in dining had taken place.[90] Over the course of little more than thirty years, ethnic cuisine had established a place in middle-class Americans' diets and had gone far to supplant elite French cuisine as the nation's ideal of culinary excellence.

One Hundred Teachers

In 1910, one hundred teachers joined the Nebraskan state superintendent of public instruction on an excursion to the National Education Association's convention in Boston. When the party passed through New York, they visited the Statue of Liberty, Grant's Tomb, the Bowery, the Ghetto, and the bread lines outside Fleishman's. And they ate. First they visited Chinatown, where they "were served a dish of dry cooked rice, chop suey, golden lime preserves, and tea, with chop sticks thrown in."[91] Later the group visited the "Little Hungarian Restaurant" where, according to Bessie Casebeer of York, Nebraska, "[a]fter being served soft drinks (as requested by our leader) we went below to the famous wine cellar, with barrels and barrels of the most expensive wine stored around the sides, where too, all good Hungarians must be married and have their wedding feast."[92]

By the early twentieth century, an ethnic dinner at a restaurant was a commonplace experience for many urban middle-class Americans and a daring—but not too daring—adventure for midwestern tourists. To the dismay of the bohemian who witnessed his exotic adventure turned into a tourist attraction in 1913, groups of "dissipating school teachers" exploring Chinese and Hungarian restaurants had become a regular occurrence. "From every little town in the Middle West they come, making New York their place for holiday. In parties of three or four they timidly enter little restaurants with foreign names; timidly, but with a certain delicate bravado. A sip of Chianti is an adventure, the fork that lifts spaghetti trembles with excitement."[93] The transformation was remarkable. In the period from 1876, when the Centennial provided a few French restaurants for its wealthiest guests and assumed (correctly, if surviving accounts are accurate) that most of the fair's middle-class visitors would be content to eat cold meats, oysters, and ice cream, to 1910, when tourists from Nebraska sought out ethnic restaurants with the fervor usually reserved for the Old North Church or Grant's Tomb, the middle class had remade dining in America.

It is tempting to view this change as merely another indication that the United States was becoming a melting pot and to claim that this is a story of immigrants triumphing over ethnic prejudice. Such an explanation is accurate but too simple. Although immigrant restaurateurs, in their willingness to adapt their cuisine to the public, contributed to the acceptance of the ethnic restaurant, the ethnic restaurant could not have become a part of the American experience without the patronage of the middle class.

Conversely, it is not possible to argue that the growing patronage of ethnic restaurants in the first two decades of the twentieth century was evidence that Americans were becoming more tolerant of ethnic or racial differences. In recent years, scholars have vigorously debated the social and political meaning of cosmopolitanism. Some see it as the first step toward rejecting patriotism, while others argue that cosmopolitanism can involve both pride of place and openness to the diversity of cultural experiences the world offers. Beautifully articulating this second position, Kwame Anthony Appiah argues that "the cosmopolitan patriot can entertain the possibility of a world where everyone is a rooted cosmopolitan, attached to a home of his or her own, but taking pleasure from the pleasure of other, different, places that are home to other, different, people."[94] Remarkable for their time, turn-of-the-century middle-class cosmopolitans embodied and even expanded this definition. They wedded their celebration of American cities to a celebration of world cuisine, implicitly recognizing that national pride might be grounded in local cultural diversity. But this re-envisioning of public dining was not necessarily accompanied by the social tolerance that scholars of cosmopolitanism generally assume. Middle-class diners embraced only the food (and often a tamed version at that). Dining at a Chinese restaurant did not undermine support for the Chinese Exclusion Act; eating spaghetti did not bring an end to nativism. Although some anti-immigrant activists worried that a culinary "grand tour" might undermine support for restrictive immigration legislation, there is no evidence that it did.[95]

Cosmopolitan dining had a limited influence on attitudes toward immigrants because it was so self-centered. The plight of the ethnic restaurateur, whose entrepreneurialism served as a bridge to cross-cultural understanding, was not an essential concern of the middle-class diner. "Cosmopolitan" described the diner, not the restaurateur, and embracing the label did not eliminate intolerance. In an article on the merits of chili con carne and tamales that appeared in *What to Eat* in 1898, M. Lane Griffin stated bluntly what others invariably felt: "I see no reason why Mexican viands, prepared by clean American hands and served in a comfortable dining room, should in any wise depreciate in value, or taste at least, simply because of the absence of Mexican picturesqueness and dirt," Griffin wrote. "And between our American selves, the viands, instead of losing by clean, intelligent preparation and cooking, actually gain in both savory flavor and appearance."[96] Tamales made without the help of Mexican immigrants were no less cosmopolitan.

The middle-class celebration of cosmopolitanism, as a result, was not as politically powerful as it was culturally meaningful; nonetheless, it signaled a sea change in American restaurant culture. As middle-class urbanites dined on spaghetti and borscht, they articulated a culinary credo that challenged the aristocratic sanction of French cuisine. Cosmopolitanism was an alternative means of valuing culinary experiences (similar to what sociologists have termed "omnivorism") that equated excellence with a diverse knowledge of cultural experiences rather than mastery of a single highbrow tradition.[97] Fifth Avenue society mavens might order their meals in perfect French, but middle-class cosmopolitans had tasted shark's fin and shish kabob. For the middle class, this breadth of experience trumped the narrow Europhilia of the wealthy.[98]

If cosmopolitanism rejected scholasticism and snobbery, it was not "indifferent to distinctions."[99] To the contrary, cosmopolitanism celebrated the power of the middle-class diner and marked the emergent class's first claim to cultural and consumer authority. Motivated by their own self interests, disparate groups of diners—hungry bachelors, adventurous bohemians, servantless families, parched shoppers—emerged from ethnic restaurants as a consumer cohort with distinct preferences that even elite restaurateurs would come to recognize, making cosmopolitanism the cultural wedge that transformed dining in America.

THE SIMPLIFIED MENU
The Case against Gastronomic Ostentation

Cultural critic Julian Street recalled a dinner party he attended around 1910 at the home of a wealthy family in Buffalo, New York. The gala was held to celebrate the formation of a new club for society women, the Simplicity League, "the members of which bound themselves to give each other moral support in their efforts to return to a more primitive mode of life." Following an elaborate meal featuring caviar, multiple roasts, salad, ices, and Turkish coffee as well as cocktails, sherry, burgundy, port, sauterne, and cigars, Street asked one of the women about the league's plan to adopt the simple life:

> "We don't intend to go to any foolish extremes," said one who looked like the apotheosis of the Rue de la Paix. "We are only going to scale things down and eliminate waste. There is a lot of useless show in this country which only makes it hard for people who can't afford things. And even for those who can, it is wrong. . . . A dinner can be delicious without being elaborate. Take this little dinner we had to-night—"
> "What?" [Street] cried.
> "Yes," she nodded. "In [the] future we are all going to give plain little dinners like this."
> "Plain?" [Street] gasped.
> "Yes," [the hostess] put in. "You see, the league is going to practise [sic] what it preaches."
> "But," [Street explained,] "I did n't [sic] think it had begun yet! I thought this was a kind of farewell feast."

The hostess looked aggrieved; Street had failed to notice that she had not served champagne.[1]

Buffalo's society women were not the first of America's elites to adopt the "more primitive mode of life." Wealthy aristocrats in New York and other major cities engaged in similar efforts. Mrs. John Jacob Astor made headlines in 1905 when she embraced "a diet of remarkable simplicity" in an effort "to protect her beauty from the spoilating [sic] attacks of the relentless hand of Time," and some years earlier, a reporter for *The Cook* had interviewed famous Wall Street robber barons on their eating habits, and most had claimed that they preferred, as Jay Gould explained, "the simplest food [they] can get." But Gould's idea of simplicity, like that of the women of Buffalo, was relative to the luxury to which he was accustomed. Gould's plain breakfast consisted of "a piece of steak, a mealy baked potato, some graham bread and a glass of milk."[2]

Although bolstered by the new science of nutrition during the Progressive Era, health-food evangelists and domestic doyens had been advocating simple dining since the early nineteenth century, and many in the emerging middle class had already adopted these culinary reforms by the turn of the century.[3] If simple dining among the elite was often no more than a passing fad, for many in the middle class it was a way of life, a demonstration of moral and economic frugality. The sudden embrace of simple eating by upper-class society leaders, half-hearted as it was, demonstrated the rising influence of the middle class with regard to food and diet.

The newfound clout of vocal, middle-class urbanites was made possible by cultural and economic changes at the turn of the century. The celebration of cosmopolitan dining did more than unleash a craze for chop suey; it also challenged the sanctimonious claims of the upper class to cultural authority. By offering an alternative way of valuing the choices that consumers made about what to eat, cosmopolitanism undermined the hidebound traditions of the aristocracy, legitimated the competition that elite restaurants faced from foreign tables d'hôte, and ultimately made it possible for upper-class restaurants to embrace middle-class ideas of dining. Yet this transformation would not have been as quick or as complete had it not been for economic changes in dining at the turn of the century. As more and more hotels and restaurants opened in America's cities, even the finest restaurants needed the patronage of the middle class to fill their cavernous dining rooms. The subsequent adoption of bills of fare that appealed to middle-class diners, including smaller menus and plate dinners with the entrée and side dishes on a single plate, marked a watershed moment in the middle class's efforts to champion a new approach to dining.

The Cosmopolitan Vanguard

By some estimates, professional and managerial workers and their families made up about 12 percent of the national population by 1910.[4] They were a diverse lot. There were rural middle-class Americans and urban middle-class Americans. There were shopkeepers, clerks, and schoolteachers as well as doctors, lawyers, and engineers. There were the Progressive activists, and then there were the silent masses whose only political acts were to vote every four years. There were middle-class women, middle-class Irishmen, and middle-class African Americans. There were self-proclaimed bohemians whose middle-class credentials were every bit as credible as those of their more staid and stodgy suburban counterparts.

Not everyone in all of these "middle classes" tried Chinese food, nor did everyone long to eat at Delmonico's, and not everyone would participate in the coming battles over restaurant culture. For some, dining in the best restaurants was not as important as family or travel or religion or politics. For others, restaurants were big city establishments that played only a small role in their rural lives. And for still others, discrimination, sometimes sanctioned by law and sometimes not, prevented them from fully participating in the experiences of the middle class.[5] Yet even those who were not actively engaged in the struggle to transform how Americans dined were affected by the emergence of a coherent idea of what it meant to be middle class as celebrated in magazines, evidenced in Progressive politics, and displayed in public venues such as colonized immigrant restaurants.[6] By the turn of the century, members of the middle class had established their presence in the public sphere and had come to recognize themselves as a consumer and political cohort with shared aspirations. It was these shared aspirations, including cosmopolitanism, that when championed by an urban middle-class vanguard transformed the aristocratic restaurant in the early twentieth century.

The middle-class vanguard proved to be formidable opponents of ostentation. Collectively, their modest salaries provided considerable economic leverage, and even if their spending habits were not perfectly synchronized, their mutual preferences were consistent enough to create a consumer cohort with the power to transform enterprises—such as restaurants—that relied on mass patronage. Aided by the popular press, especially the newly minted culinary magazines, the middle-class vanguard (which, for simplicity, I generally refer to as middle-class diners, urbanites, or consumers) successfully challenged the gastronomic flamboyance of the upper class and brought about lasting changes in the aristocratic restaurant and the national diet.

The first evidence of the shared aspirations and growing influence of the middle-class diner was the celebration of ethnic food, but cosmopolitanism—as it was practiced by the middle class at the turn of the century—was more than a salute to immigrant cuisines. Cosmopolitanism undermined the hegemony of the French restaurant and the cultural authority of the upper class. It was, as San Franciscan Clarence Edwords explained, "the protest of naturalism against the too rigid, and, oft-times, absurd restrictions established by Society."[7]

In the aristocratic restaurant, there was only one sanctioned way to eat. Diners ordered French food and followed European rules of etiquette, acts that required considerable wealth, specialized language skills, and faith in the supremacy of European cooking and manners. Cosmopolitanism undermined these "rigid" and "absurd restrictions." It maintained that German, or Japanese, or Syrian cooking could be as good as French, and by celebrating these alternatives, it destroyed the monopoly on culinary cultural capital that elites had created. Knowing which imported French wine to order with Chapon à la Bressoise was the pinnacle of expertise for the Francophile gourmet, but for the middle-class cosmopolitan diner it was even more important to know a little about German beers and Japanese rice wines. Suddenly, growing up in a household with a private French chef was no more effective at preparing a diner to eat in a respectable establishment than a life of urban adventures in basement restaurants in Germantown or Little Tokyo. Cosmopolitanism did not eliminate all the barriers to fine dining, but it eroded the foundations of aristocratic privilege, shaped the aspirations of the emerging middle class, and provided a rallying point for the middle-class vanguard.

As a result, cosmopolitanism not only introduced more ethnic dishes to the menus of elite restaurants (a topic explored in chapter 8) but also brought about a total reinvention of the aristocratic restaurant. Cosmopolitanism created an opportunity for the middle class, long chafing under the thumb of elites, to advance a middle-class ideal of dining (examined in this chapter and the three that follow), which not only introduced the plate dinner but also made it easier for women to dine alone, challenged tipping, and ended the use of French-language menus. Yet as important as cosmopolitanism's revaluing of middle-class culture was to the fin-de-siècle revolution in dining, the middle-class vanguard would not have been quite so successful if the economic climate had not favored change.

The middle-class challenge to elite public dining took place at the moment when the modern American consumer economy was born. As brand-name merchandisers and department stores created a "land of desire" through marketing and advertising, middle-class Americans embraced their new role as consumers and became savvy agents of their destiny. Middle-class consumers negotiated the new urban terrain of shops, restaurants, and entertainments, seeking not only bargains but also sway over the shape and culture of consumption. Not every professional or manager rebelled against upper-class pretentions, but for those who rejected the over-elaborate menus and Gallic dishes of the aristocratic restaurant, mass consumption made it possible for the emerging class to remake the culinary cathedrals of highbrow culture.[8]

For much of the late nineteenth century, aristocratic restaurants were located in hotels. These restaurants depended upon the patronage of captive travelers as well as that of cultivated society to support their corps of waiters, well-stocked wine cellars, massive menus, and foreign chefs. In the United States, hotel patrons, including wealthy permanent guests, paid a set fee for both room and board. This arrangement, called the American plan, guaranteed hotel restaurants a steady source of income to supplement the periodic dinners, balls, and extravaganzas of the urban elite and made it possible for restaurants to uphold aristocratic standards.[9]

As improvements in transportation made travel easier in the late nineteenth century, wealthy entrepreneurs built ever-larger hotels to accommodate the new trade in both major cities and minor towns. The thirteen-story Waldorf Hotel opened in 1893 in New York, and four years later the seventeen-story Astoria was added. The St. Regis and the Hotel Astor both opened in 1904, the Gotham in 1905, the Belmont and the Knickerbocker in 1906, and the Plaza in the fall of 1907.[10] Taking advantage of the same technology that made skyscrapers possible, these new hotels were immense, each with a thousand or more rooms and restaurants that could serve hundreds of patrons on the American plan. While hotels such as the Waldorf-Astoria maintained an elite reputation by catering to visiting royalty, hosting annual horse shows, and encouraging wealthy families to take up permanent residence, they also found it increasingly necessary to accommodate middle-class business and vacation travelers in order to subsidize luxury on a grand scale.[11]

As the middle class began to frequent these grand hotels, they began to resent the American plan. Middle-class guests disliked paying a boarding fee to the hotel and wanted the freedom to dine at restaurants of their choice, restaurants that matched their budgets and their cosmopolitan tastes. Large hotels increasingly could not afford to alienate these customers.[12] By the turn of the century, many hotels had capitulated to their guests' wishes and had adopted the European plan of service, which separated the charges for room and board. But while the European plan was more amenable to middle-class guests, it forced hotel restaurants to compete directly with independent restaurants. Hotels managers increasingly worried about "tooth pickers," diners who "pick[ed] their teeth at the [hotel] after eating at some cheap restaurant" and thus deprived the hotel restaurant of the patrons it needed to maintain high standards.[13]

The increased competition changed the economics of running both hotel dining rooms and independent restaurants and eroded the influence of local elites. To keep their restaurants full and viable, restaurant managers had to attract not only the "nobs" and the "swells" but also the casual middle-class patron.[14] As early as 1893, L. J. Vance, writing in *Frank Leslie's Popular Monthly*, acknowledged that while the "cream of what is called 'society' gathers at Delmonico's, the Logerot, and Sherry's," the "skimmed milk is found there, too. . . . If Delmonico's depended upon the 400 or 611 [New York Society] for its income, it would soon be running behind."[15]

This economic shift empowered middle-class diners who found that their patronage and preferences—the same micromotives that had transformed immigrant restaurants in the nineteenth century—could transform aristocratic restaurants. Edward C. Maginn recounted efforts that hotel restaurants had made over the previous ten years to attract local middle-class customers. "A great many hotels have some specialty which features the house—such as special dining facilities for parties, or a lunch room with stools, to attract cheaper business," he told readers of *The Steward* in 1918. "We now find many of the larger hotels have a delicatessen shop as a part of their premises, where fine bakery goods and other delicacies are sold, and it is the general tendency to get patronage from the local field as well as the traveling public, all of which, of course, adds to the volume of business."[16] While some of the most elite hotels attempted the herculean feat of selling luxury to the masses, few restaurants could afford to ignore the middle class.

Less expensive dining venues—bakeries and delicatessens—attracted the noontime crowd and late-night revelers and encouraged urbanites to view hotels as semipublic spaces where the upper and middle classes might mingle. But for luxury dining in hotels to remain profitable in the era of mass consumerism, these institutions needed middle-class urbanites

"Hotel St. Regis Restaurant." From *Town and Country*, April 29, 1905.
Courtesy of the Picture Collection, The New York Public Library,
Astor, Lenox and Tilden Foundations.

to visit the establishment's better restaurants as well as the delicatessens. If a restaurant had a reputation for being too exclusive or too expensive and could not attract middle-class patrons for the occasional Sunday dinner or holiday feast, it risked failure. This was the odd predicament that R. M. Haan, proprietor of the St. Regis Hotel in New York City, faced in 1904.

Since the rise of the aristocratic restaurant in the mid-nineteenth century, independent and hotel restaurants had sought the patronage of what one editorialist referred to as the "Real New York," the rarified elite that "secludes itself in high-class restaurants and takes refuge in clubland, screening and protecting itself from contact with the coarse and vile elements."[17] Built by John Jacob Astor at a cost of $5.5 million, the St. Regis Hotel was designed to cater to these aristocrats. The hotel's public spaces were filled with imported china, tapestries, and furniture intended to re-create the elegance of royal Europe; its spacious restaurants served only the best food; and it employed a massive, carefully trained staff. "One has but to enter the place to be impressed with its magnificence," the newspapers announced.[18]

The St. Regis Beaux Arts building, with its luxurious appointments and its reputation for exclusivity, was soon front-page news across the globe. Hailed as the finest hotel in America, the press harped on the high prices and suggested that the hotel was the most expensive in the world. "You can live nicely at the Hotel St. Regis at $100,000 a year," noted one newspaper.[19] "It is a caravansary whose cachet will be so unmistakable that none save those of the largest means and the most unmistakable social standing will care to be among its patrons, so icy will be the reception to others." Another awestruck paper joked:

RICH MAN: Waiter, bring me a plate of St. Regis ice cream if it does not cost more than $414.

WAITER: I regret that we are out of that, Sir, the cheapest thing is a chocolate eclaire [sic] at $500 per half portion.[20]

Likewise, a newspaper cartoon depicted a regiment of waiters surrounding a single patron with the caption: "What is one tip among so many? It is possible to live on oysters at $126 a day at the Hotel St. Regis."[21]

Restaurant and hotel managers would have encouraged accounts of such luxuries, even if exaggerated, a decade earlier. But the press accounts did not please R. M. Haan. "There are people who would think this mass of advertising worth a million. It works the other way with me. I am one of the few men who have been actually hurt by advertising."[22] Concerned that reports of luxury were driving away customers with moderate incomes, Haan was soon insisting—to any reporter who would listen—that the St. Regis was not the expensive and exclusive bastion of wealth that rumor suggested. He was particularly concerned about reports that the food at the St. Regis was exorbitantly expensive. "We charge the same [as a nice, but not exclusive restaurant], 30 cents, for oysters," Haan told the *New York Times* in excruciating, almost comic, detail:

Caviar is the same—$1.50. They charge 70 cents for consommé. These are my figures. My prices for fish are a little higher, smelts being 90 cents to their 60 cents. Sweetbreads cost $2.50 at the St. Regis and $2.25 in the other place. The prices for game are practically the same. They charge 75 cents for Brussels sprouts. My price is 60 cents. For oyster plant they charge 40 to my 60 cents. The biggest difference is in turkey, my price being $4.50 and theirs $1.00, but the difference I am sure is in the turkey, for there never were such as mine. They charge $3 for duckling, and I charge 50 cents more.[23]

The middle class, Haan's taxonomy of prices implied, was welcome in the dining room of the St. Regis. To that end, Haan had the breakfast menu printed in English, added American dishes "like mother used to make," and instructed the staff that guests who arrived in "business suits and 'tailor mades'" were to be seated.[24]

Haan was not suggesting, of course, that his hotel was a palace for the common man or woman. In fact, one of his concerns was that the false reports of decadent luxury were attracting "crowds of the vulgar to peep in where they could, to wonder how it would feel to sleep in a $10,000 bed after a dinner costing $75." As the proprietor of an eighteen-story hotel with a dining room that sat hundreds, however, Haan could not afford to have his establishment appear so exclusive that the middle class would feel unwelcome. "My hotel is not a place for billionaires only," Haan insisted, "but a hostelry for people of good taste who have the means to live as comfortably as they choose."[25]

Competitive prices, lunchrooms, and delicatessen shops were only the most conspicuous changes that hotel restaurants made to attract middle-class patrons; more subtle changes were also underway, evidence of middle-class urbanites' growing influence on the culture of fine dining. Mass consumption, as well as the break with tradition that the new cosmopolitan creed entailed, created an opportunity for the middle class to offer its preferred way of dining as the correct way to dine. Drawing on a century-old tradition of reform movements that rejected elaborate preparations in favor of simple, wholesome food, the middle-class demanded that restaurants replace their multicourse dinners with simpler, less pretentious fare.

Simplifying the Aristocratic Menu

In the early nineteenth century, the first clarion calls for eating reform drew on a mixture of pseudoscience, practical experience, quackery, and religious fervor to condemn the nation's groaning boards. At stake was the moral fabric of the nation. In the 1830s, Sylvester Graham promoted a diet devoid of meat and spicy foods as a cure for everything from indigestion to sexual license and civic disorder. Writing in 1838 with the certainty of one who had himself found salvation through diet, Graham told the readers of the *Graham Journal of Health and Longevity*, "GLUTTONY and *not starvation* is the greatest cause of all evil. . . . Excessive alimentation is the greatest dietetic error in the United States—and probably the whole civilized world."[26]

Graham attracted as much ridicule as admiration, but his belief in a culinary cure for the nation's ills was rewarded with imitation. Throughout the nineteenth century, diet gurus offered better living through self-denial at the dinner table. Dr. James Salisbury, a nutritional consultant to the U.S. Army during the Civil War, promoted a diet of lean meat and warm water that he claimed would eliminate dyspepsia.[27] A few years later, in 1876, Webster Edgerly founded the Ralston Health Club of America and gained national fame as the spokesman for a simple diet that called for maximizing consumption of the mysterious "glame" (a form of "organic vitality" found in foods such as milk) with the promise that it would lead to "homes full of health and happiness."[28]

That same year, Dr. John Harvey Kellogg became the medical superintendent of the Battle Creek Sanitarium. Kellogg transformed the small Seventh-Day Adventist facility in Michigan into the nation's leading health and fitness center, a haven for upper-class and upper middle-class Americans seeking relief from dyspepsia or severe indigestion—what was then known as the "American disease." Kellogg became a medical luminary who consulted with some of the leading scientists in the United States and Europe. To his patients he offered not only science but also a gospel of self-denial and purging that attracted fervent converts. Thousands attended his clinic, and millions more discovered his simple diets through the books he and his wife, Ella, published. His annual health almanac sold over 200,000 copies a year.[29]

Dietary reform was not the exclusive province of doctors. With the appearance of a growing number of domestic advice manuals in the 1800s, home and health reformers promoted simpler, lighter eating as well.[30] While domestic advice authors in the midcentury fretted more about middle-class households than elite restaurants and generally accepted the supremacy of European cooking over American, they also strongly emphasized the importance of simple, economical meals for both dietary and fiscal well-being. In 1869, Catharine Esther Beecher in *The American Woman's Home* called attention to the importance of self-denial, listing "eating *too much,* eating *too often,*" and "eating *too fast*" as the foremost of a list of American habits that contributed to a "debilitated constitution from the misuse of food."[31] Similarly, although Helen Hunt Jackson was more concerned about the middle-class family's financial inability to "avoid the poisons which are cooked and served in American restaurants" than the rich man's overindulgence, she also advocated meals of "the plain, substantial sort."[32] In doing so, Beecher, Jackson, and dozens of other domestic doyennes defied nineteenth-century fashions that often associated plumpness with wealth and success.[33]

As the field of home management evolved in the late nineteenth century, domestic advice became domestic science, and good eating was more and more associated with the middle-class table. Juliet Corson, founder of the New York School of Cooking and one of the earliest advocates of domestic science, wrote in 1884: "If cookery now commands intelligent investigation, it is because it no longer serves only the purposes of luxury, but has taken its proper place as an important factor in the scheme of social science."[34] The new generation of female domestic scientists—cooking school instructors and cookbook authors—campaigned for lighter, more nutritious menus and were often vocal critics of ostentation.

Leading the crusade against overeating was Sarah Rorer, the most influential cookbook author of the late nineteenth century. In 1882, this middle-class housewife (schooled in chemistry by her pharmacist father) founded the Philadelphia School of Cooking and four years later published her first cookbook. *Mrs. Rorer's Philadelphia Cook Book* and her column in *Table Talk*, a leading culinary magazine of the early 1890s, transformed Rorer from a local celebrity into a national sensation. In 1897, the *Ladies' Home Journal* offered her a column and an audience of nearly a million readers a month.[35]

Sarah Rorer was a prolific writer and a dynamic speaker with a fondness for the flamboyant quip who, like Kellogg and the other scientific reformers, believed that many of the nation's ills could be traced to a poor diet. Over the course of a public career that spanned nearly forty years, Rorer blamed fried food, sweets, and overeating for intemperance, labor strikes, insanity, crime, and Harvard's lack of success in collegiate football games (she was a University of Pennsylvania partisan). But Rorer, more than her predecessors, turned her wit and authority against the excesses of the aristocratic table. "Most people . . . think that they must have about seventeen things on the table if they want to give a dinner," she told a Philadelphia audience, "and must spend two days getting ready for it. Such people should learn for their first lesson that simplicity is elegance."[36] In the bestselling 1902 edition of *Mrs. Rorer's New Cook Book*, Rorer included a "Plea for the Little Dinner" in which she told readers that guests rarely enjoyed the conventional multicourse dinners "served in the homes of the very wealthy." Disputing the advice offered in many etiquette books, Rorer described aristocratic "feedings" as "extravagant, coarse and vulgar." In place of the elaborate course dinner, she recommended simpler repasts (including vegetarian meals) consisting of only one entrée, a soup, and a light dessert.[37]

One should not overestimate Rorer's influence. Although widely read and admired, Rorer was a notorious scold whose audience often took her proselytizing with a grain of salt. More than once her lectures on the evils of dessert or the dangers of fried food ended with her surrendering to requests to demonstrate the recipe she had just condemned as "deadly." But Rorer's critique of aristocratic gluttony gained adherents among the middle class. She noted smugly in her 1902 cookbook that "'simple dinners' are now the correct thing."[38]

Rorer's complaints were bolstered by a growing body of scientific research on nutrition, especially studies of calories and fats. Traditionally, medical doctors' observations of their patients formed the basis for what was known about diet. These casual observations, although sometimes muddled and moralistic, led to condemnations of luxurious foods. An 1882 article in the *New York Daily Tribune*, for example, introduced readers to the scientific work of one Dr. Nicholls who argued that sweet foods suppressed a natural tendency to eat moderately. "With men, as with animals, a natural diet is self-limiting, and we are disposed to stop when we have got enough," the doctor claimed. "The more artificial the food, the more elaborate and luxurious the feast, the more the liability to overload the stomach, over task the digestive powers and overweigh the forces of life."[39] As medical speculation gave way to more disciplined scientific experimentation, the new science confirmed the critique of elite excess and continued to condemn Americans' overindulgence.

In the 1880s, a chemist at Wesleyan University, inspired by pioneering nutritional studies in Germany, began his own pathbreaking research into the American diet.[40] Dr. Wilbur O. Atwater's findings, popularized by five articles published in *Century* magazine in 1887 and 1888, argued that Americans were eating too much food without taking into account the nutritional value.[41] Atwater set about creating formulas for the number of calories and the amount of carbohydrates, proteins, and fats (minerals and water were considered less important but necessary, and vitamins were not yet understood) that Americans should consume. For the Wesleyan chemist, scientific eating primarily offered the working class a standard by which they could better select their food and reduce their food bills, but Atwater was not shy about condemning the bloated diets of the wealthy. "Probably the worse sufferers from this evil [overeating] are the well-to-do people of sedentary occupations—brain workers as distinguished from hand workers," Atwater scolded.[42]

Atwater's research offered a scientific justification for changes in the American diet, and cooking schools soon incorporated his findings into their curricula. In New England, Mary Lincoln at the Boston Cooking School drew on Atwater's nutritional studies (as well as on the work of

Massachusetts Institute of Technology chemist and home economist Ellen Richards) for her classes and cookbooks.[43] Lincoln and her successor Fannie Farmer were never as tough on the wealthy gourmand as Sarah Rorer, but they preached simple cooking and basic nutrition as practical measures that might eliminate some of the cost and bother of preparing dinner.[44]

Some of the strongest condemnations of the aristocratic table appeared in the culinary periodical press. In the late nineteenth century, articles on cooking were frequent in publications from the *Ladies' Home Journal* to the *New York Times*, and these periodicals were soon joined by a spate of new culinary magazines. By 1911, N. W. Ayer and Son, a company that measured the circulation of magazines for potential advertisers, listed eighteen American culinary journals published in five states with a combined circulation of at least 184,000.[45] In Philadelphia, cookbook author Sarah Rorer contributed to Finley Acker's *Table Talk* until she founded her own magazine, *Household News*, in 1893; in New England, the Boston School of Cooking began publishing the popular *New England Kitchen Magazine* in 1894; and other magazines served regional, specialized, or professional interests.[46] *Chef, Steward and Housekeeper* attracted over 4,000 readers in 1911, while *Vegetarian Magazine* found a readership of over 15,000.[47]

Of all the new culinary publications, no magazine took a stronger stand on the need to simplify the American diet or more stalwartly condemned the excesses of wealth than *What to Eat*. In many ways, the Minneapolis-based journal, founded by Paul Pierce in 1896, was an eclectic journal, an open forum where "no school or practice will be slighted."[48] In the inaugural issue, Pierce juxtaposed a laudatory essay on food reformer Dr. James Salisbury with two nine-course "party" menus submitted by Delmonico's famed chef Charles Ranhofer.[49] Yet the catholic nature of the publication did not mean that the magazine lacked an agenda. Along with advocating pure food laws, *What to Eat* led the crusade to end the wasteful, gluttonous dining habits of upper-crust Americans. "There are many theories about living, many cures for disease," an article in the magazine observed in 1897. "But, while this is undeniably true, there are still certain modes of living which will apply beneficially to the whole race, and about which there need be no two opinions. There is no more doubt, for illustration, that plain food is conducive to good health than there is that pure air is good for the respiratory organs."[50]

An essay by H. C. Chatfield-Taylor in the inaugural issue of the journal set the tone for the editorials that would follow. Chatfield-Taylor was not a member of the middle class. The author and publicist, a denizen

Cover of the inaugural issue of *What to Eat*, August 1896. Courtesy of the Art & Architecture Collection, Miriam and Ira D. Wallach Division of Art, Prints and Photographs, The New York Public Library, Astor, Lenox and Tilden Foundations.

of Chicago's gastronomic clubs, was reputed to be a millionaire, and his influence over the social circles of Chicago was compared to Ward Mc-Allister's influence over the Four Hundred in New York.[51] His 1896 essay "The Philosophy of Gastronomy," however, was a stinging attack on aristocratic eating and the prevalence of French cuisine in America. "Nations," Chatfield-Taylor argued, "that live to eat, judging by the world's history, are invariably degenerate."[52] Although the United States was founded by "practical and morose" Puritans (with a penchant for pie, he incongruously noted), recent history demonstrated that the United Sates had turned away from its Puritan culinary heritage. The trouble, he asserted, was that wealthy Americans harbored a fondness for the decadent food of the French:

> Great fortunes began to be amassed and the East, as the center of great fortunes, became the center of luxury. People had both time and money for pleasure and demand for French cooks was incited. With the advent of French cooks came the downfall of Puritanism, for the cities of the East are now given over to the pleasures of France. . . . Slowly but surely the country is coming under the gastronomic sway of the Gaul. To one who surveys the situation, it is full of foreboding. . . . The church social and pie still hold sway over large portions of the country, but when they disappear, as they must before the triumphant march of the French cook, will our nation degenerate? Wealth breeds idleness, idleness begets luxury, and luxury incites vice. . . . Will the modern American, with his brown stone palace and French cook, command as much respect [as the Puritan]? He has money to give perfect dinners and his children may have the taste, but one doubts whether the national character will be as good and sterling as it was in the days when Americans ate to live.[53]

Chatfield-Taylor was not calling for a return to "the swarthy frontiersman who dines on pork and beans off a tin plate." He applauded the man who "stud[ied] the effect of his viands upon the palate," but he lamented the economic inequality that privileged the millionaire's table.[54] In a refrain that also served as the motto for the new magazine, Chatfield-Taylor insisted that Americans must eat to live, not live to eat.

What to Eat's advocacy of simple eating—inspired by Theodore Roosevelt's public endorsement of the "simple life" as well as Chatfield-Taylor's distrust of European influences—reached a fever pitch in the early years of the twentieth century.[55] "The great sin of American life," the editors complained in 1904, is "gormandizing and over-eating."[56] Nine out of ten people, another writer groused, eat too much.[57] In the future, the magazine announced, Americans would have to eat a smaller and a more varied diet if they were to live healthier lives. And to that end, *What to Eat* offered recipes and menus that promoted simpler meals.

Paul Pierce's campaign against overeating in *What to Eat* was not ascribed, as many of the earlier reform movements had been, to "any motive of economy"; instead, it was an explicit "protest against the gastronomic and extravagant ostentation" of the American aristocracy. "The ordering of long and wearisome courses of a dinner is not an American custom," Pierce claimed, "but was borrowed from the Europeans, and represents an effort to imitate the senseless and foolish extravagance of our friends across the water." *What to Eat*, he promised, was committed to "a constant repeating of the laws of hygiene and of rational dietetics" that he hoped would "utimately [sic] bring Americans to a realization of the fact that the greatest health and happiness are to be found in plain living and simple cooking."[58]

Pierce's scorn for the extravagance of the wealthy elites' diet ran deep. When Marila Pemberton, the magazine's New York correspondent, reported in 1905 that "simple fare" had become the "reigning fad" among New York City's wealthy families, the editor of *What to Eat* reacted with skepticism. In the past, Pierce noted, the excesses of the wealthy were imitated in the homes of those less able to afford it. "Champagne revelries in the millionaire's home have their counterpart in the cocktail carousals of the middle classes[,] in the Dutch beer lunches in other classes[,] and in the 'can-rushings' and drunkenness among the laborers' families." "Let us hope," he grudgingly observed, "that our vulgar rich have learned something with their money and that this reversion to the simple life is a real and lasting reform."[59]

What to Eat's crusade against "gastronomic ostentation" coincided with, and may have contributed to, the journal's success. By 1903, the midwestern monthly had an annual readership of 44,000—just less than the combined circulation of its two closest competitors, the Indiana-based *Cooking Club* and Philadelphia's *Table Talk*. Although mass-market magazines such as the *Saturday Evening Post* and the *Ladies' Home Journal* boasted circulations of more than half a million at the turn of the century, *What to Eat*'s readership surpassed that of political staples such as the venerable *Atlantic Monthly* or the muckraking *Survey*.[60] Rival culinary journals would eventually narrow the gap, but *What to Eat* remained the nation's leading source of dietary information throughout the first two decades of the twentieth century.[61]

Although *What to Eat* was the leading advocate of simpler dining, it was not alone in calling for changes in the way America ate. In its inaugural issue in 1906, *Good Food*, a Boston-based culinary journal, observed that the "hearty diets of the fathers" would not address the needs of a sedentary, middle-class nation, and in subsequent issues the journal criticized the equating of "great wealth with culinary perfection."[62] Likewise, the midwestern journal *Cooking Club* condemned those who viewed culinary skill as a "means of pandering to luxurious appetites" rather than as a road to good health.[63] In an article titled "Simplicity," the journal expressed disapproval of "leaders in society, politics, and business" who set fashions that are "oppressive to the masses in purse."[64] A year later, an article in the same magazine on the merits of simplifying and shortening the meal lambasted the hypocrites of "aristocratic society" who claimed they had adopted simpler meals but had only banished the soup course, one of the lightest and healthiest of the regular dinner courses. "There is no accounting for 'sosassity's' fads," the editors quipped, "many of which are strangers to common sense."[65] While not every culinary journal was as steadfast as *What to Eat* or as sassy as *Cooking Club* in its effort to assign blame for the nation's culinary excesses to upper-class aristocrats, almost every mass-circulation culinary magazine agreed that ostentatious gourmandizing was no longer to be tolerated.

What to Eat and its competitors were, to some degree, echoing the views of their middle-class readership. Although domestic scientists continued to urge the middle class to prepare "fewer things simply and perfectly cooked and served," by the turn of the century, many in the middle class ate modestly because simpler meals were more affordable and because they demonstrated moral self-restraint.[66] Household budgets examined by Daniel Horowitz in *The Morality of Spending* indicate that middle-class families spent 15 to 30 percent of their income on food and were unlikely to increase their culinary expenditures significantly even as their incomes rose. While the middle-class family might benefit from eating more salads and less meat, its larder was simpler and often healthier than the elaborate pantries of elite restaurants that catered to the aristocratic class.[67] As one advocate of scientific eating noted: "The middle classes are the well-to-do classes when it comes to the question of the adequate nourishment of the human body to fit it for the daily and mental demands that are made upon it."[68]

The journalistic outcry against excessive eating was not limited to culinary journals. Beginning in the 1890s, a new breed of muckraking reporter—undaunted by wealth—publicized the antics of the irresponsible rich, including the sumptuous dinners, excessive drinking, and illicit trysts that transpired behind the closed doors of restaurants.[69] For members of the middle class who had once looked to the wealthy as a model of respectability, these revelations confirmed their growing suspicion that elites were morally bankrupt and bolstered their confidence in the need for culinary reform.

Lavish dinners served in contrived splendor at unimaginable cost made headlines. Ministers and protesters roundly condemned the Bradley-Martin ball, held at the Waldorf-Astoria during an economic downturn in 1897, even before the full cost—over $350,000—was revealed. Compared to "a stately court function in one of the capitals of Europe," the ball, attended by eight hundred elite families from New York and surrounding cities, stunned many middle-class families who found it difficult to understand how anyone could consume a twenty-three course supper.[70] The Bradley-Martins' next extravaganza, a dinner for eighty-six "intimate friends" at a minimum of $120 a plate, did nothing to assuage the outrage. And the Bradley-Martins were hardly alone in exciting disapproval. In 1903, a fourteen-course dinner held by the "American Horse King" C. K. G. Billings made headlines when it was learned that the feast, held at Sherry's in New York, was served to mounted guests on horseback.[71] Lurid accounts of fetes with guests dressed as French royalty, of tributes to horses that cost more than $100,000, of recreated barnyards with live pigs and lambs, of tables with artificial lakes and squawking swans, of dinners for dogs and chimps, and of floral displays that cost more than the china place settings drew contempt from the middle-class press and occasionally led to retribution. In 1904, James Hazen Hyde's elaborate dinner costing $200,000 resulted in an investigation of his family's firm, Equitable Life Assurance Society, and eventually to his self-imposed exile from the United States.[72]

The most publicized scandals did not necessarily involve the oldest families or the most august names, nor did they necessarily take place in the most staid aristocratic restaurants. In the 1890s, New York gave birth to lobster palaces, restaurants along Broadway that catered to elites, actors, and curious tourists with "bird-and-bottle" dinners, where the "bird" was a female companion and the bottle held champagne.[73] Immortalized in the 1913 song by Hubble and Conn "If a Table at Rector's Could Talk," the lobster palaces were reputedly the site of brazen dalliances:

You would hear what someone's Adam said to someone else's Eve
You would hear that men don't have to wear a moustache to
    deceive . . .

A lot of men would pony up a lot of alimony . . .
Some good old reputations would start off on long vacations,
If a table at Rector's could talk.[74]

But if the antics of wealthy men (and, less often, women) were more likely to make headlines when enacted in the back room of Rector's than in the back room of Delmonico's, restaurant scandals nonetheless inflated the middle class's sense of its own moral superiority on issues of dining, decorum, and respectability and encouraged widespread condemnation.[75] Writing for *Cosmopolitan* in 1904, William Stewart decried the showy banquets of the elite that stood in such sharp contrast to the dour American businessmen's banquet. "Such affairs afford the vain—and there are many of them—an opportunity for rivalry in extravagance which often is carried to such an extent as to bar any but the very well-to-do from attending. They are a development of the play instinct, which, among children, finds its expression in mud pies; among the idle-rich, in luncheons to dogs, with their mistresses as waiters."[76] Echoing the sentiment, Edwin Tarrisse observed in a 1913 article in *Table Talk* that "Freak Dinners" exposed the culinary "eccentricity" of America's "rich faddists" and invited unflattering comparisons with Europe's aristocracies.[77]

Even as simple dining found support in the middle-class press, stewards of elite culture resisted change. Nineteenth-century fashion dictated that both men and women demonstrate their wealth with a stout appearance, and trendsetters and etiquette guides justified the French multicourse dinner (up to thirteen courses) despite the criticism of nutritionists and the culinary community.[78] *The Bazar Book of Decorum*, for example, resisted blaming dyspepsia on overeating and instead attributed it to the "higgledy-piggledy tables of our country cousins." Audaciously, given the emerging criticism of extravagant dinners, the *Bazar Book* recommended the aristocratic multicourse dinner as the height of scientific dietetics. "The experience of good livers, with their regular succession of courses of soup, fish, meat, vegetables, and dessert, has long since settled this matter of variety of food to their own satisfaction, and in accordance with the teaching of science," Robert Tomes wrote. "Our country friends are apt to scorn all lessons from such a quarter, but we assure them that in regard to the manner of eating they may follow the example of the fashionable with advantage."[79] Even more indignant, *The Chef*, a journal whose readership consisted of culinary professionals who catered to the elite, dismissed domestic scientists as "quacks" who offer nothing but their "own dense sense of ignorance and incompetence."[80]

Thus assured that their diets made sense, elites continued (despite the much ballyhooed simplicity campaigns) to eat extravagantly well into the twentieth century. A 1913 article on fashionable New Yorkers observed that with the sole exception of opera season, when dinners were necessarily shorter to accommodate the theater schedule, "fully one-fourth of the diners will order an eight or nine course dinner, with fruit and flowers and coffee afterward."[81] Defenders of the multicourse dinner became less vociferous over time, but etiquette guides for social elites continued to recommend the elaborate seven-, eight-, or nine-course French-style dinner until the 1920s.

Middle-Class Preferences

Backed by the purchasing power of the middle class, the culinary press pressured restaurants to abandon the elaborate aristocratic dinner in favor of simpler fare. In 1885, *The Cook*, a weekly publication for New York "housekeepers" featuring menus and food prices, took exception when Britain's *Pall Mall Gazette* described Delmonico's as one of the "two most remarkable bits of scenery in the States" (the other was the Yosemite Valley). *The Cook*'s editorial, "True Art in Simplicity," argued that "as an advertisement for Delmonico's [the *Gazette*'s article] has undoubted merit, and there is much truth in the statement that our luxuries are toothsome, but the very last place to procure these dainties cooked to perfection is in the average first-class restaurant." What the French cooks "cannot understand," the magazine explained, "is the simplicity with which our dainties should be cooked, in order that they be enjoyed in perfection." To experience American cookery at its best, one had to "taste some of the toothsome dishes unpretentiously and ordinarily prepared . . . for the family table."[82]

The Cook's nationalism developed into a campaign to have restaurants adopt both shorter menus and simpler dishes. In tandem with the midwestern *Daily National Hotel Reporter*, *The Cook* urged restaurants and hotels to embrace "short, sensible, scientifically arranged . . . bill[s] of fare," and some restaurants, eager to attract middle-class patrons, reduced their menus. "At length [the *Daily National Hotel Reporter*'s] persistent hammering seems to have some effect," *The Cook* enthused, "for now some of the best hotels in the country have adopted the new system of restricting the variety of dishes offered to guests and making up for the reduction by the increased excellence of what they put upon the table."[83] The campaign stalled, however, and it would take another fifteen years before the simple dining movement made further progress reforming the aristocratic restaurant.

At the turn of the century, custodians of elite restaurant culture began to praise the simplified menu. In 1898, Oscar Tschirky, the Waldorf-Astoria's famed steward (known to New Yorkers simply as Oscar), commended Americans for ordering fewer courses. "We used to say that the Frenchman was the bon vivant," Oscar added, "but it is getting very hard to please the American, for his way of eating is so perfect."[84] A few years later in another interview with the *New York Times*, Oscar confirmed his impression that "there are a smaller number of courses than were demanded, say, ten years ago."[85] Other leading New York restaurateurs soon joined Tschirky. J. B. Martin, owner of the fashionable Café Martin, declared in 1906 that it was "nonsense" to have on the bill of fare more than "four or five good soups, four or five varieties of strictly fresh fish, four or five entrees, &c." Likewise, the chefs at the St. Regis and the Savoy hotels, Emile Bailly and Xenophon Kuzmier, called for the elimination of the double portion, an extravagant serving that was common in most elite restaurants, as well as a reduction in the number of items on the menu. Noting that some bills of fare included over a thousand items, the two chefs suggested no more than one hundred.[86]

Archival menus offer subtle evidence of the changes that restaurants were undergoing. In 1886, the Brevoort House on Fifth Avenue in New York was among the city's most fashionable dining establishments. An à la carte menu from November 10 featured nine soup, eleven fish, six roast, eight game, seven cold, eight entrée, and twenty-seven vegetable choices. Nineteen years later, the Waldorf-Astoria menu, served during an annual horse show attended by the city's social elite, was noticeably smaller: the November 17, 1905, café and restaurant menu lists five soup, eight fish, four roast, eight game, three cold, eight entrée, and nine vegetable choices. The comparison is only suggestive, but the 1905 menu is about 40 percent smaller than the 1886 menu. In addition, patrons were given more opportunities to order smaller dinners at the Waldorf-Astoria. While the Brevoort offered whole or half portions for the roast beef, the broiled chicken, and the roast chicken, the Waldorf-Astoria allowed patrons the chance to order a small portion of any of its fish dishes and roasts and the majority of its entrées and vegetables.[87]

Campaigns by the *The Cook*, the *Daily National Hotel Reporter*, *What to Eat*, and other culinary journals may have pushed restaurant owners to simplify their menus, but it was the effort to please middle-class customers that ultimately compelled the change. John A. Ewins of the Hotel Savoy in Kansas City urged attendees at the Annual Convention of the Missouri-Kansas-Oklahoma Hotel Men's Association in 1912 to reduce portions in order to honor customers' wishes. "The patron of your café today spends his money for what he eats and for what goes back to the garbage can; and if in some places he attempts to divide one portion to two people," Ewins explained, "he is charged 25 cents for service. Is not that an injustice? . . . Why not serve a guest a reasonable amount—say half the amount he is now getting, and charge him a little less, thereby permitting him to partake of a greater variety, and what is most important, *pleasing him?*"[88]

As more and more restaurateurs followed Ewins, the middle-class consumer came to exercise unprecedented influence over the shape of dining in America, and smaller portions, smaller menus, and simpler dishes became more common. In 1904, *What to Eat*—still in the midst of its campaign against the excesses of the elite table—applauded "restaurant proprietors" who had recognized the "changing tendency" to eat light and healthy meals and had "made efforts to arrange their courses accordingly."[89] More surprisingly, in 1913 Arthur Bensington, the chef de cuisine at the *New York World*, broke with America's tradition of fawning over European cooking and condemned a celebrated effort by British chefs to construct the "perfect dinner," not because the meal was unappetizing but because too many courses were offered.[90]

From Table d'Hôte to Plate Dinner

Even as restaurants embraced middle-class preferences, they struggled to adapt traditional dinner service to the demands of their new clientele. The aristocratic restaurant's traditional table d'hôte service, in contrast to the simple table d'hôte service found at many immigrant restaurants, was a costly affair that provided patrons with a virtually unlimited amount of food for a fixed price. A typical menu might list seven, eight, or nine courses, and each course might include up to five or six options. While most diners selected only one item for each course, custom allowed a person to order more than one item or to request second servings, and middle-class patrons sometimes felt it was necessary to order as much as possible in order to get their money's worth.[91]

In the nineteenth century, when most restaurants were in hotels and hotel patrons were billed for both room and board, table d'hôte service allowed hoteliers to offer gargantuan feasts to a captive audience. In the twentieth century, however, growing competition from independent restaurants as well as advocacy for simple meals from the culinary press forced restaurateurs to seek alternatives. Some adopted a modified table d'hôte dinner—what one culinary expert termed the American-French dinner—featuring fewer options, fewer courses, and fixed portions, while others hoped that à la carte bills of fare might appease middle-class concerns.[92] The largest New York hotels resolved the problem with redundancy: in addition to a hotel dining room featuring table d'hôte service, they opened restaurants offering à la carte menus.

Middle-class patrons benefited from these changes when smaller menus and à la carte service resulted in lower prices. Yet initially, the new menus disappointed many middle-class diners. Customers complained that the smaller table d'hôte menus were not less expensive, and they were dismayed at the alacrity with which individually ordered à la carte dishes added up to a substantial bill.[93] Accounts abounded of young men who, addled by drink and good company, discovered they had run up restaurant bills larger than they could afford and were forced to fill out bank drafts that, if not made good in a timely fashion, could plunge the men into bankruptcy.[94] For some it seemed as if the evil of excessive portions had been replaced by the evil of excessive prices.[95]

À la carte meals, however, not only were prohibitively expensive but also forced the inexperienced diner to make difficult choices when ordering a restaurant dinner. At restaurants that did not simplify and reduce their offerings, middle-class patrons new to elite dining found the dizzying array of dishes on the à la carte menu intimidating. The "Service to Order" menu at the Planter's Hotel in St. Louis, to cite one example, offered customers a choice of ten oyster and clam preparations, twelve soups, twenty-one hors d'oeuvres, twenty-five fish dishes, dozens of steak, lamb, and veal chops, twenty-three miscellaneous entrées, sixteen poultry dishes, twenty-seven vegetables, more than a dozen salads, an equal number of cold meats, and an endless variety of desserts, ice creams, and after-dinner cheeses.[96] The large menu assumed that the diner was skilled at pairing flavors, selecting wines, and judging unfamiliar cuisines, but many novices despaired of ever having the cultural capital to construct a socially acceptable gourmet meal.[97] In 1910, Charles Fellow concluded that "in the higher class restaurants and hotels where the kitchen crews are generally all foreigners, and the waiters also, it is next to impossible to obtain a bill of fare fitted for the American traveling public, or for the business man who cannot get home, or the flat dweller who wishes to entertain, or the pater familieas [sic], who thinks to give family and friends a treat, or to get plain food cooked and served with plain civility."[98]

A 1909 fictional "study" of restaurants in New York vividly portrayed the insecurity of the urban middle-class restaurant-goer. At first, the waiter at the elite French restaurant was, according to the protagonist, as accommodating as a "Numidian slave," but as soon as he placed his order, the waiter's demeanor changed. "In his eyes I was a helpless infant to be taken care of, and guided in the way I ought to go. I tried to order cauliflower. He said, in a tone of infinite pity, 'No you don't want cauliflower when you have potatoes au gratin.' Now how the devil did he know that? What social crime did I commit in ordering cauliflower and potatoes au gratin? I was so hot that for one insane moment I contemplated ordering sauerkraut and ice cream, just to shock that potentate."[99] No waiter would have dared to second-guess an aristocratic patron for fear of losing his tip, but then again, aristocratic patrons were not intimidated by large menus. It was the unsure middle-class patron who cringed at the waiter's disapproval, even at a time when those of the middle class were beginning to collectively exercise influence over restaurant culture.

Lacking the cultural capital accrued by experience, middle-class diners felt vulnerable at restaurants and suspected the waiters of worse than mere pretentiousness. The novice restaurant-goer worried that servers lay in wait to rob inexperienced diners, and not all of these fears were unfounded. Unscrupulous waiters easily exploited the à la carte menu. A waiter might take advantage of the confusion created by the dozen or so orders required to purchase a complete à la carte meal and overcharge a gullible patron and pocket the profit. Some restaurants, such as the Planter's Hotel in St. Louis, were so concerned about such abuses that they printed admonitions on their menus cautioning patrons to verify the charge before paying the bill. Others adopted complex checking systems. But no solution weeded out every abuse.[100]

Although upper-class restaurateurs were eager to dispel the concerns of middle-class diners and win their patronage, restaurants were slow to find a culturally acceptable alternative to the inherently wasteful table d'hôte service and the unduly expensive à la carte service. It was not until the end of the second decade of the twentieth century that they stumbled across a new form of service that seemed especially suited to the most economical and self-conscious in the middle class. The modern plate dinner (also referred to as the selective, individual, or club meal), with entrée, vegetables, and starch served on a single plate, eliminated wasted food and offered a reasonably priced alternative to both table d'hôte and à la carte service. In 1917, with World War I making food rationing a priority, a number of upper-class restaurants experimented by offering the option of ordering composed, preselected dinners (such as the "Liberty Lunch" at the Hotel

Statler), and by November, the U.S. Food Administration was officially recommending "a plan that has never yet been fully tried out by the hotels of this country . . . to serve meals on the club plan, garnishing a portion of fish, poultry, eggs, or a reduced cut of meat, with several vegetables, all on the same plate."[101] In 1918, the Restaurant Royale in Chicago drew national attention in the restaurant trade journals when it introduced what was perhaps the first significant, restaurant-wide adoption of the plate dinner at a fine-dining establishment. For sixty-five, seventy-five, or eighty-five cents, depending on the dish ordered, the Royale offered a dinner featuring "meats, vegetables and side dishes . . . all served together on a compartment plate."[102]

When restaurants adopted the plate dinner, the advantages of breeding and cultural capital that accrued to aristocratic Americans in the nineteenth century evaporated, and public dining became more hospitable to the middle class. Menus that emphasized simple eating and lighter meals more closely reflected how middle-class families dined at home. Likewise, plate dinners demystified ordering. Proportioned and selected, the plate dinner made the well-balanced and well-selected meal the responsibility of the restaurant's chef.[103] For the middle-class customer, that meant he or she could relish the fun of choosing between entrées without the worry of making an inappropriate or unhealthy choice and without a cringeworthy interaction with the waiter. Although elite dining establishments would not fully embrace the plate dinner until the 1930s, its rising popularity demonstrated the growing influence of the middle class.[104]

"A New Declaration of Independence"

As late as 1894, when Chef Charles Ranhofer of Delmonico's published his epic, thousand-page compilation of entertaining advice, bills of fare, and culinary definitions, the elaborate French menu of the aristocratic restaurant was deemed the pinnacle of public dining.[105] But as the middle class coalesced and gained cultural authority in the early twentieth century, the aristocratic restaurant changed. Restaurants that once served heavy multi-course meals to upper-crust society could no longer afford the disapproval of middle-class customers. Increasingly, these restaurants conceded that the future of public dining rested with mass appeal, not aristocratic exclusiveness, and they simplified their menus to attract a broader segment of the dining public. Within twenty-five years, Ranhofer's *Epicurean* was an antique, and fine dining was no longer solely the prerogative of elites.

The decline of the aristocratic restaurant was made possible in part by economic changes at the turn of the century that endowed the middle-class vanguard with considerable influence. In the late nineteenth and early twentieth centuries, restaurant proprietors in New York, Chicago, and San Francisco built massive restaurants and lofty hotels and then reluctantly acknowledged that their businesses could no longer cater only to the rich. Yet the transformation of American restaurant culture, including changes in how food was served at fine dining establishments, was not driven by economic conditions alone. The emergence of a coherent middle class with shared tastes and the celebration of international cuisines not only helped to create competition that forced upper-class restaurants to revisit their business model but also undermined the hegemony that aristocratic manners and French food exercised over dining. For those who had visited a Greek restaurant or a Scandinavian buffet, traditional aristocratic models of service no longer held the same sway. These experiences devalued the elite's cultural capital and created a culinary relativism that opened the door to middle-class demands that the menu be reduced and simplified. Middle-class mores, including ideas about self-denial, frugality, and healthy eating crafted during the nineteenth century, became a rallying cry against the gluttony of the wealthy in the twentieth century. Respectable restaurants responded with simplified menus, plate dinners, and a surfeit of other reforms designed to appeal to the middle class. Dinner jackets, still the norm in cities like London, were abandoned in New York so that harried businessmen could go to dinner without returning home for tails and tie. Music, once considered a distraction to diners engaged in the fine art of eating, was increasingly commonplace in upper-class restaurants, and the dinner cabaret blurred the distinction between the restaurant and the dance hall.[106]

By 1919, the once sacrosanct multicourse meal was the punch line of a joke:

FIRST MAN: The two-dish dinner seems destined to become popular.
SECOND MAN: It's going to be extremely popular with the man who never knows which fork to use at a seven-course dinner.[107]

And within a few years, even etiquette books, once repositories of aristocratic ostentation and bulwarks against change, acknowledged that the multicourse dinner (and, perhaps, the aristocratic culture that defended it) had been supplanted. Although Emily Post attributed the adoption of smaller dinners to World War I shortages and the desire for "svelte figures" rather than to the cultural influence of members of the middle class, she conceded that "the very rich, living in the biggest houses with the most imposing array of servants, sit down to three, or at most four, courses when alone" and "under no circumstances" more than seven courses. In fact, Post hailed the five-course meal as "ultra-fashionable."[108]

Between 1900 and 1920, the emergence of a culinarily influential middle class transformed fine dining. Today, this transformation may seem like some rarified event from the past, but how upper- and middle-class Americans ate at the turn of the century says much about how people would come to value cultural experiences and consumer goods in the early twentieth century. Contemporaries believed that plate dinners and new dress codes heralded a new, more democratic form of consumption and signaled the end of the upper class's domination of the public sphere.[109] They saw these changes as a revolution.

In 1910, in response to efforts by a number of New York restaurants to reinstate dress codes requiring men to wear dinner jackets in the evening, an editorial in the *Washington Post* invoked the American Revolution and demanded that the middle class's preferences be taken seriously:

> Here is a new Declaration of Independence. It may be assumed that the proprietors or the responsible managers of a restaurant have the legal right to make such regulations as they please; but if the regulations offend customers to the extent of diverting trade, that pleasure will find a speedy ending. This is not to decry decorum, nor to disparage the becoming formalities of [formal] attire for both man and woman. But it may be observed that those who would feast are quite qualified to make their own rules of both apparel and conduct, and that their consensus of wholesome opinion will not brook . . . arbitrary censorship.[110]

This "Declaration of Independence" resonated throughout the twentieth century and continues to define middle-class Americans' view of the marketplace.

SATISFYING THEIR HUNGER
Middle-Class Women and Respectability

"I am very sorry, but that is the regulation of the house, and we cannot make any exceptions in its applications," the hotel clerk at the Hoffman House explained to Mrs. Blatch. "We do this for the protection of just such ladies as you are. We do it to keep out objectionable women; women of the type you would not like to have dining in the same room with you." Blatch's reply was piercing. "I have never been bothered by objectionable women; when I have been annoyed it has been by men. I do not suppose you make any effort to keep the objectionable men out."[1]

Harriot Stanton Blatch, daughter of the late Elizabeth Cady Stanton, was coming into her own as a leading voice of women's suffrage in 1907 when hotel clerk James C. Clancy informed her and a female companion that they were not allowed to dine at the Hoffman House.[2] Blatch had spent the day at the Women's University Club. It was a hot July day; she was tired and hungry. Around six o'clock, she and Mrs. Hettie Wright Graham, a friend visiting from Long Island, made their way to the Hoffman House, an elite hotel that featured a fashionable rooftop restaurant. Blatch and Graham, middle-class cosmopolitans, were fully aware that restaurants often barred unaccompanied women from their dining rooms, but they were unfamiliar with the policies of the Hoffman House. In recent years, restaurants and hotels had relaxed their once-strict regulations concerning unescorted women in order to encourage fashionable women to take lunch or an early dinner in the city. Although a sign in the lobby of the Hoffman House advertised a "Ladies['] and Gentlemen's Restaurant Roof Garden," Blatch checked with the front desk before entering the elevator. Presumably the clerk was unaware of the time, because he signaled that the women should go up, although the Hoffman House prohibited unaccompanied women who were not staying in the hotel from dining in the roof garden after six.

At the top floor, the two women checked their parasols and made their way to an empty table—but before they could sit down, an agitated waiter approached. When he learned that they were unescorted, he refused to serve them. A headwaiter was summoned, and he also asked the women to leave. Angered, Blatch insisted on speaking with a manager. It was in the manager's office that James Clancy told Blatch that the hotel's policy was for "the protection of just such ladies as you are."

"Humiliated by the experience," Blatch vowed to take the Hoffman House to court to establish "the right of women to dine in the public restaurants of the city when and how they desired."[3] Her case was one of the first legal challenges to the widespread policy barring women without male escorts from public dining rooms.[4] But Blatch's decision to file suit was not only about a woman's right to dine; it was also about how aristocratic restaurants defined respectability. "It does seem strange that women, *whose respectability is apparent*, may not satisfy their hunger," Blatch explained, "while men, no matter what their characters may be, are admitted anywhere. . . . I do not think that a restaurant owner has the right to refuse a woman a meal at any hour. There are numbers of women working as physicians and in other professions. They should be permitted to eat wherever they choose and whenever they choose."[5] For Blatch and Graham, a court victory would give women the freedom to dine where they chose and, equally important, ensure that the respectability of middle-class women who dined in public could not be called into question. The two women were as intent on forcing the Hoffman House to recognize that they were ladies as they were eager to pursue equal rights with men.

The Hoffman House also viewed the case as having as much to do with decorum and aristocratic mores as it did with rights for women. The hotel's renown rested on its reputation for exclusivity and respectability. When Blatch's case came to court, the Hoffman House's employees turned the trial into a referendum on the right of a restaurant to deny service to women who did not comport themselves as "ladies." Despite James Clancy's earlier claim that he was only interested in protecting Blatch, he and Moritz Weil, the maître d'hôtel of the Hoffman House, asserted at the trial that Blatch and Graham had demonstrated by their actions that they were not respectable and therefore had no right to expect service. The two hotel men testified that they had offered the women the opportunity to move to another of the hotel's dining rooms, but Blatch and Graham (Weil described the latter as the "tail of the dragon") belligerently refused. Weil claimed that Blatch had told him: "This is what I am after. I will sue you, as I will any hotel that refuses to serve me." The defendants, the men told the court, were not ladies but rather activists seeking a fight.[6]

Judge Spiegelberg of the Fifth Municipal Court apparently agreed. With the judge instructing the jury "that the women were entitled to be served when they applied for dinner in some part of the house, but not necessarily on the roof garden," the jury needed only minutes to find in favor of the Hoffman House.[7] Blatch's attorney moved for a new trial, but the case was never pursued. Blatch did not mention the incident in her memoirs.[8]

In their tepid endorsement of the Blatch suit, the editors of the *New York Times* argued that the modern woman was "not only competing with man on his own footing, but teaching him how to do things in new ways."[9] The Blatch trial, however, was less about "new ways" than old. For much of the nineteenth century, aristocratic privilege and gendered ideals of propriety governed public spaces of consumption—including restaurants. While concerns that the commercial, public sphere might corrupt women initially justified restaurant policies that institutionalized separate spheres for all women, in the Gilded Age, aristocratic restaurants applied these policies unequally to women from the upper and middle classes. Restaurants that regularly admitted elite women—women whose reputations they thought were beyond reproach—continued to discourage middle-class women from dining out. Invoking terms such as "respectable" and "ladylike," elite establishments clung to nineteenth-century notions of propriety that equated wealth with respectability.

Nevertheless, by 1907, when Blatch and Graham were denied a table at the Hoffman House, the cultural and class gerrymander that privileged wealth was falling apart. The growing presence of middle-class women on the streets of American cities threatened the aristocracy of public dining, challenging the traditions of exclusivity that the aristocratic restaurant physically represented and discursively defended. Tired of cooking at home, resigned to living in apartments, unable to secure trained "help," and eager to experience the entertainments of the city, middle-class women embraced cosmopolitanism and demanded the same dining privileges that wealthy men and women received. In doing so, they rejected the aristocratic restaurant's claim to be an arbiter of manners and rebuffed the headwaiter's attempt to pass judgment on their character.

Middle-class women lost some of their battles with aristocratic privilege, but they ultimately won the right to dine when, where, and how they pleased regardless of gender or class.

Separate Spheres, Separate Dining Rooms

For much of the nineteenth century, restaurants were male preserves. At a time when "respectable" women kept close to the home, it was rare to see women, particularly unescorted women, dining in the fashionable restaurants and saloons of America's largest cities. As West Coast resident Noah Brooks observed in 1868, "[The gentlemanly Arabs] are the chief patrons of the San Francisco restaurant. . . . Were all the now single men in San Francisco, between the ages of twenty-one and forty-five years, to be married this month, and set up their own household gods, the restaurants would be insolvent, and half the hotels would be forced to close their doors."[10] Like private men's clubs, the early-nineteenth-century restaurant was a place where men enjoyed the company of men, discussed business, drank to excess, and escaped both work and home. Before the Civil War, "a visit to Pfaff's, on Broadway, was the only really satisfactory ending to a young man's day," recalled one observer. "After the theater, after work, after anything and everything, men would saunter in here (and they knew how to saunter in those quieter days) at any hour of the night, drink beer and eat sandwiches, and smoke cigars, and hold comfortable desultory conversations."[11]

As places where young men gathered, restaurants were viewed as dangerous for women, part of the corrupting public sphere that a respectable lady should avoid. Nineteenth-century standards of propriety held that "ladies" did not dine alone, and women who flouted these standards were assumed, as a matter of course, to be prostitutes trolling for men to buy their dinner. "Not unfrequently [sic] one sees in the great restaurants of San Francisco the unaccustomed garb of women gleaming out with startling effect in the long lines of feeding men," Noah Brooks observed. "There are women at some of the most expensive restaurants, or *rotisseries*, habitual customers, whose gay attire marks where they are grouped apart in the long saloon, taking their dinner with great self-possession. These persons have no better name than 'Boston Sal' or the 'Girl in Green.' They constitute almost the only female element in the restaurant life of San Francisco, as the great eating public sees it."[12] Most women did not flout the rules, fearing they might be mistaken for a "Boston Sal." But on the rare occasions when a woman risked her reputation to challenge the gendered boundaries of the restaurants and requested a table in an all-male dining room, the better class of eating establishments usually refused to seat her or ignored her until she left.[13]

While many fashionable restaurants and saloons simply barred all women from the premises, others, particularly in large cities, provided alternative accommodations. Emmeline Stuart Wortley, an Englishwoman who visited the United States in 1849, arrived in New York, traveled to Niagara Falls, returned to New York, and then made her way to Boston before she ever dined in a public dining room. Traveling without a male escort, the hotels and restaurants at which she stopped, to her great displeasure, sequestered her in private rooms.[14] Other restaurants, particularly those located in large urban hotels, provided special dining rooms for women. A year after Wortley visited the United States, Isabella Lucy Bird stopped at the American House in Boston and noted that the hotel had two dining facilities: "a magnificent eating saloon, principally devoted to male guests," located on the first floor, and upstairs, "a large room furnished with a rare combination of splendor and taste, called 'The Ladies' Ordinary,' where families, ladies and their invited guests take their meals."[15]

Although the "Ladies' Ordinary" was the ideal, not all early-nineteenth-century restaurants were able to provide such elaborate accommodations for female guests. In the hinterland and in small cities where public eating houses (and women travelers) were rare, or at less formal restaurants in larger cities, makeshift arrangements were commonplace. Men were sequestered in the bar, and the dining room—often divided by nothing more than a waist-high partition—was reserved for escorted women. In California, although custom encouraged women to order food to be delivered to their homes rather than undergo the hassles of public dining, eating establishments occasionally served women behind a curtain hung in a corner of the dining room.[16]

Even when a restaurant provided a ladies' ordinary or made other arrangements for families, many refused to admit unescorted women, and hotel restaurants often catered only to women who were staying in the establishment. Restaurateurs who admitted "ladies" carefully scrutinized unescorted women even when they were to be seated in a section of the restaurant reserved exclusively for women. "Ladies who may be traveling alone," Tunis G. Campbell wrote in 1848, "should not be left to come to the table without being seen by the proprietor, and brought in and seated."[17] The Race Bros. New England Oyster and Coffee House in Chicago provided a separate floor for women who sought to "visit the institution at all times of the day without their gentlemen escorts," but it was available, according to a report in *Hotel World* in 1876, only to the "elite of the gentler sex."[18]

In the first half of the nineteenth century, restaurants that could not or did not provide a separate dining space for women and their escorts were not considered suitable for upper- or middle-class women. In these restaurants, working-class men and women crowded onto benches and shared a table d'hôte dinner served "family style." When circumstances brought Isabella Bird to a second-rate Chicago hotel in 1850, she gamely joined her male companions in the public dining room, although she immediately felt "rather out of my element" and demurred that "only the fact of not having tasted food for many hours could have made me touch it in such a room."[19]

By the middle of the nineteenth century, however, women, especially elite women living in large coastal cities, could find alternatives to the upper-class restaurants that refused service to unescorted women. An increasing number of establishments—Mallard's in New York was one of the earliest—catered primarily to respectable women.[20] Ice cream parlors and lunchrooms were the most common places for an unescorted woman to dine, but a bakery might also furnish a few tables where a woman could stop and eat. Initially, these restaurants served little more than "ice cream, pastries and oysters, but as the feminine carriage trade became more brazen about lunching out, a broadening fare appeared—beefsteak, boiled ham, sandwiches, poached or boiled eggs, broiled chickens, omelettes, coffee, chocolate, toast and butter."[21] In New York, the two most famous "ice cream palaces," Taylor's and Thompson's, could each seat over seventy-five guests in their marble-floored, vaulted-ceiling dining rooms.[22] Yet restaurants for women were uncommon enough that restaurateurs sometimes found it necessary to advertise—an unusual extravagance in the nineteenth century.[23] Mrs. Sallie E. Seward and Mrs. Fannie A. Palmer placed an advertisement in the *Overland Monthly* for their "Home" Coffee and Lunch Rooms, asserting that the "Home" was "the only quiet, home-like, down-town Restaurant for Ladies and Gentlemen" in San Francisco in 1888. The advertisement noted that ice cream was available, a guarantee in the idiom of the age that the restaurant was respectable and did not serve alcohol.[24]

Gender and Class in the Gilded Age

In the second half of the nineteenth century, elite restaurants began to relax the strict codes that governed dining for upper-class women whose reputations were considered beyond reproach. In the 1850s, historian Cindy R. Lobel observed, the St. Nicholas and Fifth Avenue hotels followed the lead of a number of independent restaurants and opened their main dining rooms to escorted women.[25] A few decades later, aristocratic hotels and restaurants—eager to capture the business of society women—refashioned their rules so that even unaccompanied women might lunch in public (while still insisting that these women have a male escort at night) as long as the women were recognized "ladies." While Delmonico's had always provided a family dining room for escorted women, it modified its policies in the 1880s to allow unescorted women to dine in the main dining room during daylight hours. Eager to accommodate the society fad for afternoon tea, other respected establishments across the country soon followed suit.[26]

The new rules for society women capitalized on the close association between virtue and wealth that governed nineteenth-century American culture. As historian Mary P. Ryan argued in *Women in Public*, public spaces were mapped by gender and class.[27] Women of good breeding, shielded by an ancestral armor of manners and decorum, might enter the corrupt public sphere secure in the knowledge that they would transform it or know when to withdraw. Although Ryan did not distinguish between upper- and middle-class women, these class differences also shaped the urban landscape. Restaurants, among other urban cultural and consumer institutions, treated society women as incorruptible "ladies" but did not automatically extend the same respect to their middle-class counterparts.

The rules that governed aristocratic dining hinged on who was considered a "lady" and who was not. Class-laden and evoking images of the English titled nobility, the word "lady" was understood at the turn of the century to be closely related to wealth. A "lady," the *Century Dictionary* maintained in 1911, was a "woman of good family and established social position" or a "woman of good breeding, education and refinement of mind and manner." Both definitions implicitly acknowledged social status and a command of upper-class cultural capital. Both definitions excluded working-class women and potentially excluded middle-class women. Notably, the dictionary warned that to use the term lady "indiscriminately" as a synonym for "woman" was considered vulgar.[28]

Aristocratic restaurateurs were never vulgar. They used the term "lady" as shorthand for exclusivity even as they occasionally struggled to decide who was and who was not a lady. Since "good breeding, education and refinement of mind and manner" were not always apparent at first glance, restaurants exercised considerable discretion in determining who would be seated at one of the better tables near the door where the diner might be observed by other fashionables and who would be refused service altogether. Clothing, manners, and social recognition usually decided who was admitted and who was not, but restaurateurs took their role as social gatekeepers very seriously. Delmonico's readily admitted that it had once refused to seat Mrs. Cornelius Vanderbilt because the headwaiter failed to recognize the society woman, but few restaurants could afford mistakes of that magnitude without risk to their reputations.[29]

Many middle-class women in the late nineteenth and early twentieth centuries imitated elite respectability and, after purchasing an armful of etiquette manuals and marshalling their disposable income, sought the title "lady" and a table at the Waldorf-Astoria. Many women, after reading in the *New York Times* or *What to Eat* that society women were wearing short "restaurant dresses" in the winter of 1906, scurried to a Fifth Avenue tailor to have one fitted.[30] When successful, these women did, briefly, traverse class lines to have tea in the company of elite society. A late-nineteenth-century account of Delmonico's noted that "New York women, and their imitating sisters from out of town, can collect, eat, drink, and regard each other, without anybody knowing or caring particularly whether it is Mrs. Astorbilt, of Fifth Avenue, Mrs. Snooks, of Newark, or Miss Prettyface, of the Royal Flats," but the account made clear that this level of social mixing was possible only when upper middle-class women disguised their social status by "look[ing] so much [like the wealthy patrons] you cannot tell one from the other."[31] In practice, few middle-class women had the money or the cultural capital to accomplish such a ruse.

Yet there were rewards for those who passed muster with the head-waiter. The elite restaurant's guardianship of aristocratic distinction not only certified one's social standing but also conferred privilege. Once deemed a "lady," a woman might quietly flout the rules of polite society without substantial risk to her reputation. Secluded from the hoi polloi by class (and from disapproving husbands by gender), an upper-class woman could indulge in vices—alcohol, illicit affairs, or gambling—with only a minimal risk of social consequences. Upper-class women were trusted to show discretion even when they did not act with discretion; middle-class women were barred even when their behavior was respectable.

Alcohol was one of the whispered-about vices that wealthy women could find in restaurants. Writing in the early twentieth century, Samuel Paynter Wilson, author of *Chicago by Gaslight*, lamented that "even women of respectability and good social positions are guilty of the vice of intemperance. They all do not frequent barrooms, however, but obtain liquor at the restaurants patronized by them, and it is a common sight to see well-dressed women, married and single, rise from a restaurant table under the influence of intoxicating drink."[32] While Wilson was a self-described "investigator" with a obsessive belief that department stores, ice cream parlors, and the Young Women's Christian Association were dens of iniquity, a few of the more snobbish society women were of the same mind. Gertrude Atherton, a California aristocrat by marriage and a prolific author of gothic and historical fiction, was vitriolic in describing the vices of New York society in 1906. "There is a woman in New York society whose notorious vulgarities of speech and action, to say nothing of her abominable manners, are only condoned on account of her wealth and inherited position," Atherton confided, "and it is also an open secret that certain of her associates have more than once been carried out of fashionable restaurants, or, resisting, have made a scene on the pavement until forced into their carriages. . . . I took 'tea' with five of them one afternoon at the Waldorf, and those that did not order whiskey revived themselves with absinthe."[33] Likewise, a reporter who followed two well-dressed women to a tearoom in 1913 observed a waiter serve the women a "special brand of tea . . . the notable fact about which was that it failed to steam when poured." This "tea" was discreetly served in teapots and teacups.[34] Other reports seemed to confirm suspicions that society women drank and smoked cigarettes behind the closed doors of exclusive restaurants and tea shops.[35] Acknowledging the lesser of the two vices, at least one fashionable New York hotel established a private smoking room for upper-class women in the 1890s.[36]

Restaurants were also excellent places for men and women to meet without attracting undue attention. As early as 1850, George Foster recounted a visit to an upper-class New York "Ice-Creamery" where he suspected at least some of the women were engaged in romantic rendezvous. "Some unsophisticated reader," Foster mused, "may be shocked at this—but it is a very mild form of the hypocrisy that pervades the fashionable ranks of society."[37] Fifty years later, Genie H. Rosenfeld cautioned readers of *What to Eat* of a similar "hypocrisy" at the ice cream parlor's successor, the tearoom. Rosenfeld warned that as "friendly and delightful as [tea times] are it would be a thousand pities if the habit entered so largely into the life of the American woman that she would encourage the establishment of Tea Rooms" since "these rooms . . . have degenerated into places where the undesirable of both sexes meet to idle away an hour or two."[38]

There is no telling how common it was for "respectable" women to sneak a cocktail, a cigarette, or a kiss at a fashionable women's restaurant. At least one gullible investigator, hoping to track down hard evidence of vice, failed to find a single society woman who would admit to drinking! The author concluded that "smokers and wine drinkers are the exception rather than the rule, even among the most fashionable, else such failings would be more conspicuous."[39] Although the reporter's investigatory skills left much to be desired, his conclusions were not necessarily incorrect. Many upper-class women guarded their reputations religiously, fearful of gossip and losing the privileges that "ladies" enjoyed. In 1894, a New York correspondent for the *Los Angeles Times* observed that it was rare to see men and women socializing during noontime meals. "A woman and a man lunching together at Delmonico's, if they are not husband and wife, always creates a little remark. It is not considered quite good form."[40] Yet even if self-restraint from fear of social scrutiny was more common than was secret tippling, clandestine smoking, or covert "lovemaking," the exceptions demonstrated the central role that restaurants played in sanctifying and shielding elite women's social standing.[41] As long as aristocratic women displayed a modicum of discretion, restaurants were willing to overlook their indulgences and conspire to keep nosy reporters from seeing vice. To do otherwise was to admit that restaurants were not citadels of respectability.

Restaurants for Middle-Class Women

Middle-class women's growing role as consumers was a particular source of cultural anxiety at the turn of the century. Historians have charted how reformers, editorialists, and social scientists alike worried about the rise of the department store, raised concerns about middle-class women's ability to control their desire to shop, fretted about the poor consumer decisions they made, and speculated that they might succumb to kleptomania.[42] There was similar unease about the social consequences of women joining the throngs of male restaurant-goers.[43] Dieticians worried about women's uncontrollable desire for sweets, gourmands worried that women were incapable of ordering a sophisticated dinner, husbands worried that wives who dined out would no longer cook at home, and moralists worried about the effects of restaurant vices—alcohol and tobacco—on the purity of American women.[44] Amelia Gere Mason lamented that when women, the "natural arbiters of manners as well as conservators of morals," were driven "into the hustling crowd," aggression would triumph to the detriment of society.[45] Others fretted that women consigned to eating out would forget the "dignity and decency of making their meals attractive by good cooking and economy."[46] And still others, those of a more salacious bent, worried that the dim lighting in restaurants undermined morality and might lead to flirtations and adultery.[47]

Qualms about middle-class women and restaurant dining came from judges, journalists, homemakers, bon vivants, doctors, and scientists (many from the middle classes themselves), but it was restaurateurs who translated these concerns into policies that determined who could dine and who was barred at the door. While restaurateurs were reluctant to question wealthy women's respectability (regardless of their conduct), they treated middle-class women as suspect, carefully scrutinized them, and, as in the case of Harriot Blatch, sometimes refused them service. The upper-class woman had vices, but she knew enough not to flaunt them and was experienced at managing her public image. Middle-class women made no such promises, and restaurateurs guarded their public image too carefully to risk embarrassment. Restaurants that failed to safeguard their reputations for exclusivity and respectability, the whispered history of the restaurant trade suggested, were doomed to failure.[48]

Accounts of middle-class women dining in restaurants prior to the 1870s are uncommon.[49] Middle-class women might accompany their husbands to an upper-class restaurant, but such visits were expensive and rare. While nothing formally barred middle-class women from visiting ice cream parlors and bakeries during daylight hours, many middle-class women, with servants to help with the cooking and convention tying them to the domestic sphere, took their meals at home. As late as 1898, the *New York Times* assumed its middle-class female readers might not know how to handle themselves in a restaurant and thought it necessary to provide women traveling alone with some rudimentary advice about dining in public. "Upon entering the hotel dining room you will be met and escorted to the seat which you are to occupy, by the head waiter. This official, having seen you seated, will hand you the menu and place you in the hands of the waiter, who will proceed to take your order."[50]

The growth of the American city, however, transformed middle-class dining in the closing quarter of the nineteenth century in ways that affected women as well as men. Families increasingly took an occasional

Otto H. Bacher, [Women in Restaurant in High Building], 1903. Courtesy of the
Prints and Photographs Division, Library of Congress, Washington, D.C.

meal in a downtown restaurant or an ethnic eatery, women shoppers no
longer found it convenient to return home for lunch, and young unmar-
ried women workers preferred dining in restaurants to carrying a lunch
pail. As the proprietor of a New York lunchroom told a reporter for the
New York Times in 1885, "Five years ago, the patronage of women in these
restaurants down here was so trifling as practically to amount to nothing,
but to-day we all provide special accommodation and special dishes for
them, and their trade is well worth catering for."[51] In Chicago, the *Daily
Tribune* observed that "many women of a generation or two back—and
well informed ones at that—have lived and died without ever seeing the
inside of a restaurant. . . . But times change, and the sins of yesterday
become the virtues of today. No one would think for a moment of quar-
relling with the woman who skips away from household cares and punctu-
ates her shopping tours with a friendly chat over a cup of tea."[52]

Initially reluctant to challenge the exclusivity of aristocratic restaurants,
middle-class women often frequented a new class of restaurants that catered specifically to them. Schraft's, a candy store chain, opened its first

restaurant in New York in 1898. A middle-class version of the "ice cream palace," with mahogany and silver decor, the restaurant attracted women of all ages. The same year, the Childs brothers opened their namesake cafeteria chain, an inexpensive lunchroom for both middle- and working-class women who shopped and worked in the city.[53] While neither restaurant served only women, both depended on women for their success. Describing New York's shopping district during the noon hour in a 1901 issue of *Munsey's Magazine*, G. Sudley noted that "men are few, and woman rules. . . . They swoop down in swarms when the luncheon hour arrives, and a man wandering into the places may well think himself an intruder."[54]

Along with new restaurants that catered to both sexes, there was an increase in the number of restaurants that served only women, especially restaurants for middle-class women. In 1893, one of the first lunch counters exclusively for women opened in Philadelphia, and restaurants in other cities soon followed.[55] Meanwhile, tearooms, once enclaves of aristocratic women seeking five o'clock tea, expanded their menus and their hours to attract middle-class women looking for a more substantial meal.[56] Yet despite the growing number of urban lunchrooms that catered to women, formal restaurants that offered accommodations for unescorted women, especially at night, remained relatively rare outside of the largest metropolitan centers. As late as 1910, British traveler M. M. Maxwell warned women traveling alone to the United States that they were in for a difficult time. "It will come as a surprise[,] if not as a positive shock, to many Englishwomen to learn that in some respects a lone woman traveling in the United States has much more difficulty in finding hotel and restaurant accommodation than she has in England . . . despite what we have long been accustomed to think of as the American man's chivalry to women."[57]

The Ambiguity of Language

In the early twentieth century, women first challenged the aristocratic conventions of propriety that empowered the headwaiter to pass judgment on respectability. Arguing that character, not arbitrary rules of conduct, hierarchies of social standing, or the ambiguity of terms such as "ladylike," should determine one's eligibility to participate in the public sphere, middle-class women played a central role in democratizing the restaurant.[58] As Richard Barry told readers of the *New York Times* in 1912, the middle-class women's restaurant was not the final answer to the problem of how to accommodate women diners; it was merely the opening salvo in an ongoing battle over class and gender. "A tea room is a woman's institution," Barry reported. "It is run by women, for women. Men enter with diffidence, and seldom alone. . . . On the battlefield of the modern woman's invasion of man's sphere the tea room is the skirmishing line whereby is defined the position of the enemy. It is the last station occupied by those advancing into the battle and the first sought by the wounded returning from the front."[59] Over the course of the next twenty years, more and more women would (as had Blatch and Graham) forgo dinner at a tea shop and brave the unwelcoming but alluring world of the aristocratic restaurant. They sought the right to dine in any restaurant—unaccompanied or not—without anyone questioning their respectability.

In 1898, the Civic and Political Equality League of the City of New York passed a resolution asking "that women be protected in their civil rights in being entitled to food or shelter in any house of public entertainment by day or night, if they are as respectable as men claiming the same privileges."[60] Although the city did not adopt the resolution, it appears that many middle-class, cosmopolitan restaurants in New York began to accommodate unescorted women at the turn of the century, even if they still maintained separate entrances and continued to discourage women from seating themselves in barrooms. Immigrant restaurants, in particular, rarely refused service to women diners. Elite restaurants, however, did not make the same concessions. Upper-class establishments continued to impose restrictions on middle-class women by applying seemingly arbitrary rules grounded in aristocratic ideas about class, gender, and exclusivity.

The unwillingness of fine-dining restaurants to treat middle-class women with the same indulgence they showed elite women was exposed when the Waldorf-Astoria broke ranks with other aristocratic restaurants and revised its long-standing policy preventing women from dining alone. The controversy began with a brief notice on the hotel bulletin board in January 1907: "Ladies without escort will be served in the restaurants hereafter at any hour."[61]

The Waldorf-Astoria was New York City's largest hotel in 1907, and while it was also among its most elegant, the necessity of filling its vast dining rooms encouraged the management to seek out middle-class patrons. Economic necessity, however, was not something that aristocratic restaurants conceded publicly, and after the new policy unleashed a flood of public excitement and a humorous muckraking exposé, the hotel's management was forced to backpedal in order to preserve the establishment's aristocratic reputation.

It was an enterprising reporter for the *New York Times* who turned the Waldorf-Astoria's new policy into a farcical commentary on aristocratic privilege.[62] The *Times* correspondent noted that until the Waldorf-Astoria revised its policy, it had been "an unwritten rule . . . in most hotels and restaurants in the city that a woman without escort was overlooked—to put it gently—by the waiters, so that she would seek some other places where she would be served." The new policy seemingly eliminated these barriers. However, when the reporter began to ask questions of local restaurateurs, he learned that the new policy was nothing more than a written version of the long-standing practice that allowed elite women to bend the rules and held middle-class women up to scrutiny. When he asked a member of the management of the Waldorf-Astoria what he meant when he used the term "ladies," the manager equivocated.

> "It has always been the rule of this house to entertain ladies— real ladies."
> "But what is a lady? Is it determined by dress or manner or— or accent?" asked the reporter.
> "Why, my dear Sir—why, a lady, my good fellow, is a—um— lady, hey?"[63]

"Unfortunately," the reporter observed, the policy "did not seem to be a question of a woman's right to dine when and where she pleased, but rather one of her eligibility and right to the title of lady." He concluded that the new guidelines were not a sign that "the 'new' woman had conquered."[64]

Undeterred, and perhaps engaging in a bit of fun at the expense of the city's aristocratic establishments, the reporter set out to discover who, in the opinion of the city's other hoteliers and restaurateurs, might claim the title "lady." Even before the Waldorf-Astoria's public announcement, most of the city's restaurants had been informally admitting unescorted upper-class women as long as they met some hazy and ill-defined notion of respectability, but when pressed, none of the restaurateurs were able to define what they meant by "lady." At Delmonico's, the manager claimed he "discouraged" unescorted women from dining at the restaurant, but "where the lady is known to us it is all right"; women who were not "known" were asked to bear the cost of a private room.

> "Suppose she doesn't want to [take a private room]?"
> "Then—Well, one must use discretion. If it is a lady—"
> "Yes, but how do you judge a lady?"

"Well, a lady is one you can tell easily," said the night clerk. "You can tell by the way she sits, by the way she orders, by the way. Oh, man, a lady is a lady, don't you see?"[65]

James B. Regan, the outspoken manager of the Knickerbocker Hotel, was no more helpful. "We cater for the public," Regan stated. "If a woman comes in here and sits down she'll be served as long as she is a lady." But when pressed to describe what makes a lady, Regan stammered. "My good Sir, a lady is—is—Now, see here, a woman who may not be a lady comes in here. She sits down and she realizes that there are fine people around her. She immediately sits up and says to herself: 'Hm! This is the place where I've got to behave myself.'"[66] None of the other establishments the reporter visited were any more willing to define respectability. Sherry's admitted unescorted women at any hour "so long as they looked well and behaved well." Rector's repeated the mantra-like refrain "So long as she is a lady." Tom Shanley of Shanley's Restaurant, not the most distinguished of New York's high-class eateries, refused to discuss what made a lady but promised that when a lady "comes in here, it is not for an Irishman to treat her otherwise." Only the Hotel Astor admitted barring all unescorted women in the evening (unless they were guests of the hotel), ladies or not.[67]

The equivocation over the term "lady" may have served the best interests of restaurants keen to attract new middle-class patrons but unwilling to alienate their aristocratic clientele with the suggestion that the exclusivity they once promised had been compromised. However, the vacillation offered little guidance for middle-class women. Although middle-class women viewed themselves as ladylike, they could not be sure that restaurateurs shared their opinion. The term implied a mysterious quality—a form of cultural capital inscribed into one's appearance—that women who were not bred to wealth might not possess. While it is impossible to know how many middle-class women avoided aristocratic establishments out of fear that they might not pass muster, there is no question that women resented restaurateurs' efforts to judge their character. A visitor to the tearoom in the Plaza Hotel vividly recalled how the headwaiter "in an instant glance of steel-blue eyes decides if you are fit" before he took diners to a table.[68]

Despite the scrutiny (and often in spite of it), some middle-class women challenged the seemingly arbitrary standards that restaurants imposed. It may not be a coincidence that Harriot Blatch demanded a seat at the Hoffman House seven months after the Waldorf-Astoria's new policy launched a public debate over the propriety of women dining unescorted. For middle-class women such as Blatch, nineteenth-century ideals of decorum embedded in such terms as "ladylike" were undemocratic and hopelessly out of step with the reality of their lives. Middle-class women shopped, worked, volunteered, and socialized downtown, and they expected the same treatment from restaurants that they received in department stores and other public venues.[69] For these women, archaic rules that they acquire an escort in order to dine at night posed a greater threat to their respectability than dining alone. A *Chicago Daily Tribune* article from 1908 favorably contrasted the "young business girl" who paid for her date's meal because she received a "fair salary" to the "rich widows who [were] willing to pay the expenses of an escort for the sake of being able to dine at the most fashionable places."[70] For young middle-class women, restaurants' escort policies substituted formal etiquette for genuine morality.

In the years following the Waldorf-Astoria's bungled attempt to define who might dine unescorted, restaurants throughout the country became more sensitive to the expectations of female patrons. As hotel steward Federick Fallisse told *The Caterer* around the time of the Waldorf-Astoria controversy: "The average woman objects to being discriminated against—if she finds that she is given a smaller order when dining by herself than her male companion receives when he orders, her mental criticism will be the reverse of complimentary to the establishment so treating her, no matter how good its intentions may be on the subject."[71] Quietly, aristocratic restaurants that were increasingly unwilling to alienate middle-class patrons began to admit unescorted women, although these capitulations left little historical record.[72]

Toward the Gilded Ceiling

One issue continually resurfaced to remind the restaurant-going public that the negotiation between the nineteenth century's standards of gender propriety and the twentieth century's commitment to consumer democracy was ongoing: the lingering debate over whether women should be allowed to smoke in public restaurants. When a restaurant barred a woman, it was usually a hushed affair. Only an activist such as Harriot Blatch would risk the embarrassment of acknowledging publicly that a restaurant had found her reputation wanting. Smoking, however, was never private or inconspicuous; it was a public challenge to the rules of conduct that restaurants inherited from their aristocratic past.

In the nineteenth century, fashionable restaurants prohibited diners from smoking, regardless of gender, in rooms where both men and women dined.[73] Etiquette demanded that women be insulated from all evidence of men's corruption, and even the smell of smoke on a gentleman's coat, as one 1873 guide warned, might be considered offensive.[74] As increasing numbers of aristocratic women won concessions from restaurants, however, these rules were relaxed—if only a little. By the 1890s, few restaurants prohibited men from smoking in their public dining rooms even when they were dining with a female companion, although the smoking ban still applied to women. Even in the lobster palaces where wealthy married men brazenly courted chorus girls and flouted the rules that governed polite society, Henry Collins Brown observed that the chorus girls, "abandoned creatures" as he called them, "did not smoke in those days—for well they knew that an outraged proprietor would have had them unceremoniously escorted to the door, at such an open affront to public decency."[75]

A decade later, the lobster palaces and their more staid competitors—in an effort to keep up appearances—still barred women from smoking, even though smoking had come to represent freedom from antiquated cultural and gender norms in some women's eyes, and more and more women smoked in private.[76] The growing middle-class restaurant trade, however, created pressure for restaurants to become more accommodating to women who wanted to experience all the pleasures that city life allowed. Nonetheless, when elite restaurants lifted their restrictions on women smoking, they sparked a storm of controversy that once again raised questions about who was considered respectable and who had a right to pass judgment.

The first of a decade-long series of restaurant smoking scandals took place in New York City on the eve of 1908.[77] Martin's Café, a fashionable, upscale lobster palace, announced that it would suspend its nonsmoking policy for "ladies" during its New Year's Eve celebration.[78] Only a dozen or so women availed themselves of the new policy, and "they did it modestly, for the most part, and it was very evident that many were beginners, taking advantage of the edict just for the fun of it." Newspaper accounts the next day pointed out that smoking was "only a small part of the fun, for there was plenty to eat and to drink, songs to be sung, jokes to be played, and everyone was a good fellow, worth wishing a Happy New Years to."[79] At first, it seemed the evening had passed without controversy.

Two days later, James Martin declared that the "experiment succeeded splendidly" and announced his intention to lift his ban on women smoking. Martin justified the new policy by arguing that "the most respectable women in the restaurant" had smoked on New Year's Eve; but to reassure doubters, he adopted the hazy standard that guided restaurateurs in their previous efforts to admit unescorted women. Martin promised that he would not tolerate "indiscriminate smoking" by women who were not "ladies."[80] "The truth is, it is all in the way it is done. If a respected woman comes here with her husband and cares to join him in a cigarette, we would not request her to stop, but if a conspicuous young woman started blowing rings of smoke simply for show we would promptly tell her it was not allowed, and ask her to go to the smoking room reserved for women on the second floor."[81] For Martin, the way one puffed a cigarette was merely another indelible indicator of class and respectability. The *New York Times* neatly summarized the new policy: "In every case, it is likely to depend on the sort of woman who wants to smoke."[82]

Rector's, Martin's closest competition for the patronage of the "smart set," quickly joined the famous lobster palace and announced it would also allow women to smoke, but the more staid New York establishments—Delmonico's, Sherry's, the Plaza, the St. Regis, the Gotham, and the other hotels—cautiously waited, enforcing the old rule "for the present." While a few of these aristocratic restaurants were inclined to allow women to smoke, the *New York Times* reported, none was willing to issue a public announcement.[83]

Word of the new smoking policies quickly spread across the country, and local opinion varied. In Washington, D.C., restaurant owners claimed that women were refraining from smoking in public, thus sparing restaurants from having to set formal policies.[84] In Chicago, "Lucy Page Gaston, arch foe of cigarettes, made the rounds of cafés also, but she was unable to find women smoking cigarettes. She expressed herself as much relieved."[85] In contrast, San Franciscan society women "set the seal of their approval" on women smoking and began to smoke "along with their husbands in full view of the public diners."[86]

The lack of national consensus in favor of women's smoking seemed to embolden critics of the ban, resulting in a backlash against Martin's new policy. Within days of James Martin's announcement, New York's city council considered an ordinance introduced by "Little Tim" Sullivan to restore public morality. "Little Tim," the Manhattan borough president and a Tammany Hall man, made the anti-smoking bill the first priority of his new term on city council—undoubtedly motivated by the populist appeal of a law that would forbid upper- and middle-class women from smoking in the city's most fashionable restaurants. The law passed. "After to-day," the front page of the January 21, 1908, edition of the *New York Times* proclaimed, "it will be against the law for a hotel or restaurant proprietor, or any one else managing or owning a 'public place[,]' to allow women to smoke in public."[87] The ordinance imposed a fine of no more than twenty-five dollars or imprisonment for up to ten days on restaurateurs who disregarded the law.[88]

The Sullivan measure would be short-lived. The *New York Times*, although not an advocate of women's smoking, ridiculed the Sullivan Ordinance and its sponsor. "A more valid objection to the proposed ordinance would be that the surest way to make a woman do anything is to forbid her to do it," editors at the paper asserted. "The minor Mr. SULLIVAN's ignorance of that established fact indicates that he has never been what is called a 'ladies man.' But it is not discreditable to his judgment of public policy. . . . To say that such a law would be unavailing and ridiculous in this practical community is only to say that the exiguous Mr. SULLIVAN is morally superior to his time and his environment."[89] Politics being what it was in early-twentieth-century New York, the city's mayor, George B. McClellan Jr., a one-time Tammany candidate who had turned against his former cronies, rescinded the ordinance on February 4 when "Little Tim" was vacationing in Hot Springs, Colorado. The mayor claimed (although the law had not been tested in the courts) that while the "police power of the Government" might be used to regulate "the conduct of individuals or of the owners of private property" in the interest of public morality, he did not believe that it could "be invoked to sustain an ordinance of this kind."[90]

When Sullivan first proposed the ordinance, the *New York Times* observed that the law had been "suggested by the announcement made just before New Year's Eve that in certain restaurants smoking by women would be permitted," yet by the time the aldermen met to vote, James Martin had rescinded his policy.[91] Concerned about his restaurant's reputation, Martin posted a sign in the restaurant that directed women who wished to smoke to a ladies' smoking lounge. "As a rule, smoking by ladies is not allowed in public dining rooms. A ladies' smoking room is reserved for their exclusive use." In practice, however, Martin's new prohibition did not differ much from the original policy that granted "respectable" women privileges. While claiming that "the bulk of the American public is averse" to women smoking in public, he nonetheless pledged only to "stop promiscuous smoking." Once again, upper-class ladies, particularly escorted ladies, could do as they pleased. "If a lady is with her husband and smokes decorously we do not see her, but I must revoke the official privilege."[92]

Martin's change of heart came too late to prevent the Sullivan motion or to quiet the outcry over women's smoking. Members of the Gotham Club in New York, for example, roundly condemned upstart women who smoked in public. Following a musical evening of "banjo solos and Chopin preludes," Mrs. Alfred Arthur Brooks asked the members of the club to censure women who smoked in restaurants. Brooks did not mince words or hide her belief that aristocratic restaurants should remain exclusive retreats. Finding it impossible to believe that respectable women were smoking, she blamed working-class interlopers. "Now, you know," Mrs. Brooks observed, "that in all the Bowery cafes and dance halls they are putting a stop to women smoking. It seems a pity that places of the better class should welcome persons who can't even retain a footing in their own section of the city." The "militant" Brooks seemingly had the support of her fellow clubwomen. Mrs. Imogene King told the assemblage that she thought it necessary to oppose this "crime" because women who smoked threatened "to corrupt our civilization," and when she spoke of restaurants that treated women who smoked as if they were "ladies," the women nodded disapprovingly and the men tittered. But quietly, a number of the women who attended the meeting disagreed. A reporter who was at the gathering claimed that one of the women who had denounced smoking told him privately that she often smoked, "but it would never do to admit it in public."[93]

Watchdogs of public morality continued to condemn women who smoked in public following the early 1908 controversy. Some blamed the new smoking habit on Europe.[94] Others worried about race suicide. J. W. Nigh told the Pythian Temple in Washington, D.C., that "any woman who would express a frank preference for frequenting cafes where smoking is allowed evidences a tendency toward perverted, depraved tastes, and the ultimate end of such desires is physical, moral, and mental degradation."[95] The Reverend Frederick E. Hopkins of the Pilgrim Congregational Church warned congregants: "It may look chic; it may seem smart, it may appear pert for a girl to catch sight of herself in a mirror in a café with her arm thrown over the back of the chair, . . . and a cigaret [sic] between her teeth. . . . But beside that face in the mirror let us place the bloodless, hollow eyed, narrow headed, slope shouldered, consumptive chested, spindle legged future American citizen, and let me tell you that is the son of his mother. That is what nicotine and his mother will do for the stars and stripes."[96]

Despite the heated rhetoric of these debates, however, the class lines that restaurateurs had been trying to reinforce were increasingly blurred. At times, the public held culpable an upper class that had visited Europe.

At other times, the public outcry focused on working women who adopted smoking as a false mark of sophistication. But slowly, as the public struggled to assign blame, restaurant proprietors were rethinking their position and refusing to pass judgment on the character of women who smoked despite formal rules that prohibited smoking in public dining rooms.

Two years after Martin's rescinded its policy, controversy flared when the staff at the Ritz-Carlton in New York failed to ask a woman smoking in their dining room to put her cigarette out. Once again, the event drew the attention of the local press. "The woman leaned back in her chair, tilted her head, and sent a series of rings toward the gilded ceiling," a reporter wrote. "By that time, every diner in the big room had focused his or her eyes on the centre table. The waiter, leaving two of the coffee cups unfilled, scurried away to inform the head waiter that a woman was actually smoking in the main dining room. The head waiter sought the manager, who came in, looked the party over, and went out again. The woman calmly finished her cigarette without interference."[97] Although the Ritz-Carlton Hotel in London already allowed women to smoke in its public dining rooms, its sister hotel shied away from an explicit policy.[98] Instead, the anonymous diner's rebellion was met with studied inaction:

> "The manager of the restaurant rushed into my office on Thursday night," said [Mr. Harris] finally, "and told me very excitedly that a woman was smoking a cigarette in the large dining room. 'I believe you must be mistaken,' I told him. 'In fact, I am perfectly sure you are mistaken.' That was all I said and the matter was dropped right there. You see," continued Mr. Harris, "I can't presume to teach American women anything at all. They know perfectly well what is right and what is wrong. So I have set no rules on the question of smoking. American women know best what is the correct thing to do in a public restaurant, and I would never dream of posing as an arbiter of etiquette."[99]

The Ritz-Carlton's refusal to acknowledge the smoke rings that wafted toward its gilded ceilings marked a significant change in restaurants' attitudes toward women. Not only were women—notice that Harris did not say "ladies"—allowed to smoke in the Ritz-Carlton, but no one presumed to judge whether the women were respectable or not. Harris did not want his hotel to play the policing role that restaurants and hotels had assumed in the nineteenth century. For the first time, an American aristocratic restaurant refused to pose as "an arbiter of etiquette."

Not all New Yorkers were ready to leave women to their own devices.[100] A month after the Ritz-Carlton opened its dining rooms to women smokers, the front page of the *New York Times* reported that the manager of the prestigious Palm Room at the Plaza had asked four women, one with a "gold mounted cigarette holder," to put out their after-dinner cigarettes.[101] The four women stopped, but women throughout the city continued to test the restrictions on smoking in public restaurants, and more and more restaurants capitulated. An account from mid-1911 noted that "smoking among women in New York seems to be on the increase. It is an ordinary sight to see women puffing at dinner parties and to see them smoking occasionally in certain restaurants."[102]

Concerned by the growing tolerance of restaurant managers, city government once again attempted to bar women from smoking in restaurants. In October 1911, New York aldermen unanimously passed a resolution that ordered the city solicitor to investigate whether there were legal means of preventing women from smoking in public, but the legal effort foundered.[103] Meanwhile, most restaurants were following the Ritz-Carlton's lead.[104] R. M. Haan, explaining the new attitude of restaurateurs, conceded that the era in which restaurants served as guardians of aristocratic tradition had ended. "The hotels do not regulate the taste," he told the New York correspondent for *The Southern Hotel Journal*, "but the public regulate us."[105]

As the sight of women smoking in restaurants became commonplace, local newspapers lost interest in the story. It was not until 1919, eight years later, that a feature article in the *New York Times* addressed women smoking, and this time it was to concede that the debate had been resolved decisively in favor of women. "It was not that long ago," the paper declared, "that the woman with a smoking cigarette was a rare sight in the restaurants of our better hotels. . . . Today, despite proper dress committees and prohibition, that individual that takes a definite stand against women's smoking in his dining room is a rare creature instead."[106] The Ritz-Carlton, everyone acknowledged, had ushered in a new era.[107]

The end of prohibitions against women smoking in restaurants received more public scrutiny than the elimination of the escort policy, but both happened simultaneously, and both shifts in etiquette followed the same pattern. In the nineteenth century, restaurants were guardians of an aristocratic culture that restricted women's public roles yet turned a blind eye to upper-class vice. As stewards of this aristocratic culture, restaurants made distinctions between reputable and disreputable women, between ladies and middle-class women. In doing so they built reputations for being exclusive and discriminating—qualities that secured the patronage of the aristocratic class. In the early twentieth century, however, as aristocratic restaurants' dependence on middle-class patronage increased, they abandoned their fidelity to elites and learned to trust the personal morality of middle-class consumers. With each passing year, restaurants demonstrated their growing unease with their role as cultural stewards, and women were freed to exercise their own moral judgment.

Without Finding the Sex Question a
Necessary Topic of Conversation

Cultural revolutions are not singular events with simple causalities. The changing role of women in the public sphere reflected all of the dramatic convulsions that American society experienced in the early twentieth century. The emergence of a large consumer economy—crafted by manufacturers and exploited by department stores—changed the role of women, invading the hermetic domestic sphere to draw women into the "hustling crowd." New jobs for women, political challenges to disenfranchisement, and moral reform crusades all increased women's presence in public life. But the "middle-classing" of urban culture also contributed to the transformation of traditional gender roles. In the nineteenth century, restaurants sequestered women diners in secluded rooms and, as late as 1911, the "Santerer," a regular contributor to *The Steward*, worried that the "question of admitting women without an escort" was a "wretchedly complex question and, so far as this side of the ocean is concerned, seems to be as far from a solution as ever."[108] But a solution was near. In 1925, when the popular New York lunchroom Child's constructed a Fifth Avenue restaurant, "six stories of window rounded a corner, and the multi-tiered display of ladies at lunch was rumored to have inspired Ziegfeld."[109] Men might complain about "chattering women" and the "talk that rings in subdued shrillness over the clatter of silver and chinaware," but women continued to dine out and increasingly did so on their own terms.[110] The suffrage movement and Progressive reformers helped to usher in these changes, but the revolution in women's dining was also due to the emergence of the cosmopolitan restaurant and a revaluing of sociability encouraged by the burgeoning middle class.

Elite nineteenth-century culture rested on a code of etiquette and manners that equated wealth with excellence and social standing with virtue. Writing just before Martin's new policy on smoking sparked the nationwide controversy, the *New York Times* claimed that "no thoroughly sophisticated American woman of good breeding would think of lighting a cigarette in a New York restaurant, because she would know that the men who were puffing cigar smoke in her face would consider the act unladylike."[111] Middle-class women refused to acquiesce to these traditional definitions of what constituted moral behavior, and the men with whom they dined out refused to consider them "unladylike." Instead, both men and women embraced a cosmopolitan standard of virtue that refused to equate the enjoyment of life with unbecoming behavior. While members of the middle class did not stop believing in decorum, etiquette, or the right of a restaurant to turn away a patron, they increasingly held that the restaurant-going public, the consuming public, should be the sole arbiter of what was acceptable and what was not, relegating the restaurateur, once a powerful gatekeeper of morality, to the role of mere merchant. In 1916, hotel and restaurant managers in Pittsburgh agreed to admit men who were not wearing jackets (especially in hot weather), but only if women endorsed the idea. "As far as eating in comfort in hotels and restaurants goes, the women patrons hold the deciding vote. Downtown café managers are unanimous in wishing the campaign all speed to its accomplishment, but sadly acknowledge their allegiance to woman's opinions."[112] And it was with a similar nod to public opinion that restaurants lifted the ban on women's smoking. "Managers of some of the larger and more conservative hotels," the New York Times reported in 1919, "said their rules against smoking had given way before the popular demand of their customers, some of whom, be it said, come from conservative American families."[113]

As restaurateurs accepted their new role, change came to New York, Washington, Chicago, San Francisco, and other major American cities, and the aristocrats' cultural authority declined. When restaurants embraced public opinion over tradition, they implicitly recognized the economic and cultural influence of the urban middle class and the cultural values embedded in cosmopolitanism. "A. Steele Penn" predicted in The Table in 1873 that attitudes toward women smoking after dinner would change when men realized that they were unwilling to forgo the "social enjoyment" of women's company after dinner.[114] "Penn" was a little before his time, but he was essentially right. The freedoms that women won were, in part, the result of restaurants' embrace of cosmopolitanism, including the relaxed sociability that went hand-in-hand with new ideas about companionate marriage.[115] As San Franciscan Clarence Edwords wrote: "In Bohemia men and women mingle in good fellowship and camaraderie without finding the sex question a necessary topic of conversation."[116]

Those of the middle class were not alone in championing new values for the new century. As historian Nan Enstad has observed, working-class women parodied and subverted elite ideas of what it meant to be a lady when they dressed in their finest to go to work in factories or to appear in picket lines. But as Enstad also acknowledged, these protests—while subjectively meaningful—were often "unintelligible" to those outside of the working class.[117] In contrast, members of the middle class had the consumer purchasing power to ensure that their protests were heard. Although restaurants responded with compromise and concession, rather than complete and immediate capitulation, traditional distinctions between "ladies" and "women" evaporated as middle-class patrons invaded the restaurant. By 1919, only the grossest violations of conduct could justify asking a woman to leave a public restaurant. Women's right to dine, smoke, or drink—at least in the major cities of the United States—would no longer be questioned, and the issue faded from public view.[118]

Historians have often looked to the "Roaring Twenties" as the moment when the public life of modern America was born. Flappers, Prohibition, speakeasies, and jazz clutter our historical memory, obscuring the roots of these social upheavals. But by the outbreak of World War I, the ascendancy of the middle class and the new woman were faits accomplis. On March 17, 1918, C. May, the headwaiter at the Park Avenue Hotel, refused to serve cocktails and beer to a party of five that included a woman. May was not, however, enforcing an anachronistic ideal of what women could or could not do in public; he was enforcing wartime law. The woman, a Red Cross doctor awaiting orders to sail for France, was denied her cocktail because she was dressed in khaki. As the manager of the Park Avenue Hotel explained the next day: "The Government's regulation is perfectly plain. A uniform is a uniform, whether worn by a man or a woman. We can't differentiate between them. If a woman is in uniform it is impossible for her or any member of her party to have liquor in any form. It is not up to us to ascertain first if she is regularly enrolled in the United States service—the mere fact that she is in uniform is enough. *We have no discretion in the matter.*"[119]

THE TIPPING EVIL
The Limits of Middle-Class Influence

In the early twentieth century, August J. Bock waited tables at a number of the East Coast's most fashionable restaurants and hotels. Born in Vienna, he apprenticed in Austria, England, and France before immigrating to the United States in 1907. Bock was a consummate waiter whose motto, borrowed from the *Rotarian of the World*, was "He profits most who serves best." His memoir—tellingly titled *Knight of the Napkin*—is peppered with references to the rich and famous, including the Tafts, Goulds, Vanderbilts, Carnegies, Rockefellers, Rices, and Dukes.[1]

August Bock served these kings of industry with the deference of a loyal retainer. Yet during the years in which Bock was waiting on New York's elite, dining in America was undergoing dramatic changes. In the early twentieth century, the burgeoning urban middle class invaded the aristocratic restaurant and successfully challenged the elaborate menu and stodgy rules that had governed public dining. Service, as Bock understood it, was held up for scrutiny and criticism. In waves of discontent, middle-class diners complained about waiters, gratuities, and imagined slights, seeking to level aristocratic privilege and reinvent the restaurant as a more democratic space of cosmopolitan consumption. They organized campaigns against tipping, worried about being labeled "pikers," and, when restaurants failed to accept middle-class remedies, clung wistfully to egalitarian fantasies of mechanical servers and waiterless restaurants.[2] The fight to eliminate the tip demonstrates the middle-class vanguard's deep-rooted commitment to reconciling consumerism and democracy, but it also reveals the limits of middle-class influence. Tipping persisted.

For the most part, Bock seemed blissfully unaware of the revolution that restaurants were undergoing, and only rarely did he acknowledge the new modes of service demanded by the middle class. An event that happened at the Hotel McAlpin sometime around 1913, however, was seared into his memory. A visitor to the massive, new (and decidedly middle-class) hotel took a meal in the restaurant. As was the custom in aristocratic restaurants, Bock offered the man a demitasse of coffee at the end of the meal. He was brazenly rebuffed. "The gentleman, coming from some far-western or southern state, replied, 'Keep your demitasses for the upper classes, a large cup for mine.'"[3] Even though he was writing more than thirty years after the event, Bock's account still echoed his shock.

Gratuities

A hallmark of the aristocratic restaurant was its service. Waiters at elite restaurants were drilled like soldiers, expected to speak French, and trained to pander to the patron's every whim. At many restaurants and hotels, a waiter might be assigned to only one or two tables, and his job (waiters in the best restaurants were almost always men until World War I) was to provide any service the patron wanted. Early in his career, while waiting tables at the Hotel Plaza in New York, August Bock received an order for a "Dog's Head," a popular type of ale. Misunderstanding the order, the young waiter went from cook to cook, seeking someone who could prepare the unusual request for roast canine. The broiler cook eventually agreed, asking for ten minutes to fill the order. Whether the broiler cook was serious or not is unknown since the headwaiter intervened before the beheading, but Bock's dedication to meeting the needs of his patron offers vivid evidence of the service culture in an aristocratic restaurant.[4]

Prior to the Civil War, even such outstanding service was not routinely rewarded with a tip. Patrons expected quality service, and restaurants and hotels ensured that their waiters were attentive through intense training and constant supervision.[5] A tip was seen as unnecessary, a rare reward for truly exceptional service, and, in the eyes of many, a sign of European decadence. In the post–Civil War era, however, wealthy Americans who traveled in Europe, where tipping was de rigueur, brought the continental custom home.[6] Soon the rare, small tip for truly extraordinary service was replaced with the habitual tip for routine service. Over time, aristocratic diners found that tipping especially generously helped to maintain their monopoly on the best service.

The wealthy embraced tipping because it purchased privileged service for those who could afford to be particularly munificent. In most American cities, wealthy aristocrats had few restaurant choices. While

New York was home to more luxurious restaurants and hotels than were most American cities, there were still no more than five or six restaurants in the 1880s that an upper-class family might regularly frequent.[7] Under these circumstances, a diner established a long-term relationship with the staff of a restaurant, and a reputation for large tips guaranteed exceptional service during subsequent visits. Similarly, in an age when traveling was arduous and time-consuming and wealthy travelers might stay at a hotel for months, eating day after day in the same dining room, a generous tip at the start of the stay guaranteed the long-term guest superior service.

In theory, any patron could command the services of a dedicated and conscientious waiter. Waiters' manuals advised new waiters that they "should not be partial to guests, but give each and every one the same good service."[8] But money bought privilege, especially in the rarified environs of the aristocratic restaurant. In 1885, the culinary journal The Cook complained about the "evil system" of gratuities that had "become very common in the hotels and restaurants of this country" and observed that "in this respect the 'first-class' places are the worst."[9] Experienced waiters at aristocratic restaurants relied on the largesse of wealthy aristocrats, and even when they did not know the customer by reputation, they were expert at spotting large tippers. By paying attention to the customer's clothes and manners and by taking note of how much the newly arrived diner tipped the headwaiter, waiters could spot the rich, openhanded customer.[10] This diligence guaranteed that the richest patrons received the best service.

For the wealthy diner, tipping was a familiar and effective expense and an integral part of the rituals by which elites exhibited their influence and wealth. Cultivating the goodwill of a waiter with large gratuities promised tangible benefits. As one headwaiter explained, "In a great many hotels the regular boarders have their regular waiters and pay them a small fee every week for extra good service, and expect to get everything they want whether it is on the bill of fare or not. The waiter, in turn, will break any rule made by the steward or head-waiter in trying to give satisfaction to said guest, and often does things entirely unnecessary in order to keep in favor with the guest he serves."[11] Regular and generous tips to the headwaiter, for example, might secure a favorable table that could enhance the reputation of a wealthy social ingénue—favoritism that other diners noted and gossiped about.[12] Likewise, a well-tipped waiter would be disposed to provide his patron with the best food that the establishment could offer. At a time when most dishes were not prepared to order, the waiter carved the roast and selected the vegetables. If the waiter chose, he could bring the best cuts of meat, the hottest rolls, an extra helping of oysters, or a specially prepared dish. Visiting the United States in 1887, Charles Beadle noted the dramatic effect his tip had on the corps of African American waiters at his hotel. "I found, however, a quarter-dollar was necessary to get attention; but this understood, they would pile plates of food round you until the sight almost made you turn sick."[13] Nor were the extras that a well-compensated waiter could provide limited to food. A grateful waiter was expected to supply a restaurant patron with any luxury he or she might desire—from a cigar or a newspaper to information on the weather, the stock market, or the train schedule—even if that meant running a quick errand.[14]

Beyond securing extra food and service, tips also bought the waiter's discretion. Since waiters were privy to the conversations that took place at the public tables of the restaurant, they were intrinsically dangerous observers who might, although it meant risking their jobs, share overheard business secrets or damage reputations with gossip. In the best restaurants, well-heeled patrons expected the public table to be treated as private space, and they tipped generously to ensure the discretion of their waiter. A turn-of-the-century poem in the voice of a waiter acknowledged the importance of a generous tip:

> I've seen So-and-So with another man's wife,
> I've seen High Society eat with its knife,
> I've heard the worst claret pronounced "nonpareil,"
> I've heard the best Roquefort condemned for its "smell." . . .
> I've bowed and obeyed, and I've always agreed
> My business to serve is, and not to take heed;
> A quarter will cause me to doubt my own mind,
> And after a half I am deaf, dumb and blind.[15]

A half-dollar tip was a small investment if you had the money to spare and secrets to keep.

A generous tip not only purchased privilege and privacy but also was a signifier of status among the upper crust. As Thorstein Veblen wrote in *The Theory of the Leisure Class*, one of the hallmarks of wealth was the "ability unproductively to consume a large amount of service."[16] When Miss Gladys Vanderbilt was engaged to marry Count László Széchenyi in 1907, the *Washington Post*'s society column reported that Newport society was reassured by the fact that the little-known Hungarian "has the American style of tipping lavishly and appears to be a 'good spender.'"[17] Large gratuities, and the deference they purchased, were evidence of social standing and served as a bulwark against the encroachment of middle-class diners.

For the middle class, however, the tip was an elusive passkey to service and status. Frustrated middle-class urbanites vented their anger in newspaper and magazine editorials and demanded that the tip be abolished for the sake of American democracy.

Contrary to American Principles

"What[,] may I ask, is more un-American than tipping?" wrote Alvin Harlow in an essay titled "Our Daily Bribe." "It doesn't belong in American society; it doesn't belong in a democracy. It is a product of lands where for centuries there has been a servile class."[18] From 1880 through 1920, anxiety about tipping filled the pages of newspapers and magazines. Many in the middle class regarded tipping—a legacy of the upper-class European tradition of rewarding household servants when guests were entertained—as anathema in a democratic society. No one, they believed, should have better access to restaurant service merely because he or she had more money. "Class distinctions are being more and more emphasized in this country, and one of the causes of it is the prevalence of tipping," editors of the *Lincoln Daily News* wrote in 1915. "A considerable number of persons to whom money comes easy like to show off by aping the customs of the aristocracy of the old world by giving freely to those who serve them."[19] Expressing the same sentiment, only more starkly, the *Newark Daily Advocate* griped that "the man with the threadbare clothes is slighted and sneered at, while the one with the costly tailored suit is fawned upon. [The tip] is undemocratic and contrary to American principles."[20]

Eagerly trying to establish their place in the highly classed marketplace, self-conscious middle-class urbanites worried that tipping exposed their lack of both cultural and economic capital. At the heart of the middle-class diner's concern was the fear that a small tip might subject the upstart diner to the disapproval of the waiter—who, although he did not earn as much as his patron, nonetheless served as one of the gatekeepers of elite dining.[21] "If you'd offer a New York waiter in a first-rate place a quarter tip nowadays," an article in the *Washington Post* warned, "[the waiter will] probably hand it back to you together with two bits of his own, and advise you to go and have your shoes half-soled with the money."[22] The *Post* exaggerated (waiters never returned tips), but while the upper-class diner's generous tip never failed to command deference from waiters, the middle-class patron's more modest offering risked the waiter's scorn and the possibility of being publicly exposed as a cheapskate. Typical was a story in *What to Eat* of a Chicago gentleman, "accustomed to tipping in a moderate way, [who] was scowled at and almost rudely treated by a waiter to whom but ten cents was given where a quarter was evidently expected."[23]

Less typical, but often repeated, were stories of waiters taking revenge on patrons who did not tip. Chief among the middle-class diner's many concerns was that a spurned waiter might spit in one's soup. In 1897, the editor of *Life and Health* demanded that the city of New York "make a searching investigation into the tricks and manners prevailing in the first class restaurants" because he had heard "on the best authority" that a disgruntled waiter at the Manhattan Beach Hotel had spit in the soup of a musician who "was not popular among the waiters because he never tipped them." The editor suggested that the "blackguards" should be imprisoned for their offense.[24] In Chicago, Illinois state's attorney Maclay Hoyne had one hundred waiters arrested in 1918 after hearing reports that they had doctored the food of "known opponents to the tipping system."[25] In most cases, the public outcry was unfounded, but fears of sullied soup and doctored dinners exacted a psychological toll. A Harvard professor of German, H. C. Bierwirth, bemoaned "the trouble, the vexation, the agony that the traveler suffers in the uncertainty as to the amount of the compensation expected! The meanness for which he reproaches himself when he has given too little, and the self-disgust he feels at having been duped when he suspects that in his generosity he has given too much!"[26] This feeling of insecurity invariably discouraged some middle-class diners from seeking a table at the best restaurants and helped to secure the aristocratic restaurant's reputation for exclusivity.

The social and psychological cost of the gratuity was only one part of the tipping evil. Many anti-tipping advocates also worried about the financial toll that ever-increasing tips imposed upon the budget-conscious middle-class diner. Ultimately, tipping reformers and concerned citizens warned, competing for the best service was an impossible game of brinksmanship that the middle-class patron could not win. The more the middling folk tipped, it seemed, the more they were out-tipped by wealthier restaurant patrons. *The Southern Hotel Journal* expressed alarm about the inflated cost of providing gratuities in 1912. "The public alone is responsible and especially the 'newly rich,' who, in their eager desire to show off the acquired wealth, stoop for the envy or admiration of their servants by lavishing tips," the journal reported. "Such people who come after them and offer but the reasonable tips are grossly insulted."[27] Already, anti-tipping campaigners warned, high tips were making it nearly impossible for the middle class fully to enjoy restaurant life. "If the pernicious practice of forcing up the scale of tips were to continue much further than the point it is said to have reached now," cautioned an article in the *Living Age*, "only the rich would be able to purchase in certain restaurants the brief gratification of the waiter's smile or immunity from the terrible look."[28] In the near future, still others warned, the middle class may no longer be able to avail themselves of the best restaurants. A joke, vintage 1903, unfavorably compared the cost of tipping to the cost of the meal.

> WIFE TO HUSBAND: Let us have supper at Dary & Anthony's
> after the theater.
> HUSBAND: Why, my dear, I have only a dollar and ten cents.
> WIFE: That is more than enough.
> HUSBAND: Why no. One dollar for the waiter and ten cents
> for supper?[29]

Eustace Williams, a *Washington Post* subscriber who could recall a time in the 1850s and 1860s when waiters and bellhops refused tips, likewise suggested in a 1905 letter to the editor that the size and uncertainty of the modern tip discouraged middle-class urbanites from going to restaurants. "This tipping nuisance has now become so extortionate that many persons of moderate fortune are deterred from going to the best hotels and restaurants, not so much by the prices charged there—and they are high enough in all conscience—but on account of the blackmail levied by waiters and other servants, who appear to be insatiate and whose avarice grows by what it feeds upon."[30] Another writer worried that if tipping was not curtailed, "unfortunate citizens will have to leave, and seek a cheaper country."[31]

Complaints about tips and waiters were not the rantings of a few disgruntled diners but the view of a broad spectrum of the urban middle class who resented the power that waiters exercised and the privilege that tips purchased. "It is not the question of us upper class profligates," William Dean Howells wrote as editor of *Harper's Monthly Magazine* in 1913, "but of the middle, the bourgeois, the citizen class, who by mere dint of their numbers do most of the tipping, and the grudging that goes with it."[32] In 1908, the *New York Times* held a contest in which readers were asked to complete the caption for a cartoon in which a "reformer" asks his dinner companion, "Why don't you refuse to tip waiters?" In dozens of responses, the newspaper's readers expressed their anxieties about their social standing and their resentment of the waiter's tyranny. J. S. Markam wrote, "Because I'm afraid of what the waiters will think of me," and won a prize in the contest.[33] H. Dummer, a New Jersey resident, admitted, "One scornful look makes cowards of us all." In his entry, A. Kuntz suggested, "Don't you know I'm the under dog? Why rub it in?" And J. Russell weighed in with "Because I would rather be considered a coward by the reformer than a tightwad by the supercilious waiter." Other readers feared more direct reprisals from their waiters. F. Bain humorously conceded, "[The waiters] hold too much over my head." Similarly, W. Robbins wrote, "Because Tipping is a game that two can work at and this is my only suit." Charles Barton punned, "Because I will not feed well if he is not fee'd." And G. Livingston of Washington, D.C., penned, "Because I believe in civil service." Only a few of the nearly one hundred replies demonstrated any support for tipping. Emile Yunker of Newark voiced the middle class's despair best: "We're living in Gotham, not Utopia," she wrote.[34]

Deep anxieties about tipping reflected the middle-class diner's uncertainty about the emerging consumer economy. The "grudge-stained middle-class tip"—as William Dean Howells referred to gratuities—was a barrier to the best tables and the most attentive service, offering unequivocal evidence that the marketplace was not equally accessible to all.[35] Reflecting these concerns, anti-tipping diatribes regularly evoked political language in order to equate the threat of unfettered tipping with a threat to democracy. Terms such as "discrimination" and "bribe" were used to stir patriotic outrage. H. C. Bierwirth, writing in the *Andover Review* in 1886, complained about the "few guests or travelers of wealth who secure the waiter's service by bribes" as well as the "selfishness of the demoralized waiter who exacts a like bribe from all guests."[36] Three decades later, Richard Barry reminded readers of *Everybody's Magazine*: "If the tip were only a reward for good service, or even only a means of averting bad service, it might not be so complete in its destructive effect on the elements of character. But a tip is more. It is a bribe for discriminatory service."[37] And dozens of newspaper editorials in the early twentieth century condemned tipping for its antidemocratic elitism. "What is a particularly lavish tip," the editors of the *Syracuse Herald* wrote, "but a bribe for special favors? And are not special favors to one man usually given at the expense of someone else?"[38] Likewise, when one of the more progressive restaurants in New York substituted a service charge for gratuities, they implored their patrons to respect the new policy and not to tip the waiters because tipping was a "relic of Old Europe," was "essentially un-American," and "place[d] the stamp of servitude upon the Waiters' Profession."[39] All of these anti-tipping efforts echoed late-nineteenth-century claims (most often made by trade unionists and Populists) that the democratic promise of the American Revolution was threatened by moneyed interests who manipulated the political system to their own advantage.

To argue that tipping posed a risk to American democracy was hyperbolic. Middle-class opponents of gratuities and graft regularly conflated concerns about the inequality of the consumer marketplace with more fundamental fears about how industrialization was chipping away at political rights. But for the newly minted, modern middle class, the outcome of the debate over tipping mattered. Extravagant gratuities reinforced class hierarchies, limited consumer choice, emptied wallets, and, most important, undermined the growing influence of the middle class. For a class whose existence owed everything to the bonds formed in the marketplace and whose influence stemmed from its members' roles as consumers, the unruliness and unpredictability of waiters extorting high tips for better service threatened their status and identity. No one should suffer the humiliation of a sneer or shy away from taking a date to a nice restaurant simply for want of a ten-cent tip. Yet even some anti-tipping advocates admitted that until the tipping vice was banned outright, they would continue to leave generous tips so as to avoid confrontations with waiters and public exposure as a cheapskate.

Editorial diatribes about the dangers of tipping may have curtailed some of the worst abuses, but they did not eliminate the "tipping evil."[40] More concrete action would be required. Some in the middle-class vanguard advocated voluntary reforms ranging from consumer boycotts to percentage-based tips, but these efforts were largely ignored. For example, a widely reprinted 1905 defense of tipping in *Town and Country* claimed that the "ten per cent rule is generally followed in all first class places," and subsequent etiquette guides universally endorsed the practice.[41] The 10 percent tip, however, depended upon the cooperation of wealthy restaurant-goers who could pay more for extra services—and aristocratic diners often flouted the rules in order to command the full attention of a waiter. As a result, the middle-class diner who tipped 10 percent felt that there was little he could do to "insure himself against the impertinence of the waiter who, with the tip of a millionaire in his pocket, holds him up to the public gaze when he has paid the logical tribute which common sense pleads as enough."[42] Moreover, the 10 percent tip did not eliminate the familiarity that regular restaurant-goers might have with a waiter, and in fact, some of the same guides that endorsed the percentage tip recommended that regular guests provide a full week's gratuity in advance to guarantee the best service.[43]

Anti-tipping sentiment was strong enough by the second decade of the twentieth century to attract the attention of both federal and state legislators. In 1910, the U.S. Congress banned waiters in the District of Columbia (notably, almost all of Washington's waiters were African American) from accepting tips, although they failed to pass a national law against tipping and Capitol Hill reporters noticed that senators openly flouted their own rules in the Senate restaurant.[44] Meanwhile, statewide anti-tipping legislation was passed in Washington in 1909, in Mississippi in 1912, in Arkansas in 1913, and in Iowa, South Carolina, and Tennessee in 1915, and at least four other states considered similar laws.[45] But despite the outrage that tipping engendered, state anti-tipping laws, like their congressional counterpart, were generally ignored and only sporadically enforced.

In a national column that appeared in the *Elyria Chronicle-Telegram* in 1920, Roy K. Moulton observed that reports of the demise of tipping were greatly exaggerated. "It has been a very interesting piece of news to us that the tipping system has been abolished," Moulton wrote. "The papers tell us of hungry waiters and bartenders standing about the streets waiting for a meal. In view of this news we took a chance the other night on Broadway and escorted the missus to a restaurant. We were privileged to pay the hat girl 25 cents for depositing our hat. The head waiter got 50 cents for showing us to a table. The waiter got $1 and, going out, the hall boy got 35 cents. The meal cost $2.50 and the help got $2.10. Yes, tipping is abolished, if you know where to go."[46] Conceding that the laws had been ineffective, every state that had passed anti-tipping legislation had repealed it by the mid-1920s.[47]

The persistence of tipping in American restaurants suggests the limits of the middle-class urbanite's influence in the public sphere. Opponents of anti-tipping initiatives argued, with some justification, that if tipping was wrong, people should just stop tipping. "By the exercise of a little moral courage in ignoring the scorn of those whom he has the best of right to consider his inferiors he can instantly and forever free himself from the tip hunter's tyranny," one reporter noted. "[Tips] would disappear as soon as all, or even a majority of those who share his dislike for tipping acquired the courage to imitate his example."[48] Similarly, George Brunswick, one of the few hoteliers to argue that hotels and restaurants might play a role in ending the tipping plague, nonetheless felt that restaurant patrons were ultimately responsible for the practice. "The greater share of this shameful condition is due to a hypocritical bribe-giving public, who, in spite of independence and equality spouting Americanism, meekly submitted to this constant growth of Oriental servility as well as blackmail. A determined stand by means of boycott would have nipped that imported abuse in the bud."[49] But no such concerted action materialized, and it soon became apparent that the middle-class diner's cultural authority had limits. Fear of acting alone and losing prestige prevented the middle class from participating in the self-conscious collective protest needed to eliminate tipping.

The failure to end tipping also suggests the limits of the middle class's influence over restaurateurs. For the most part, the economic interests of restaurant owners coincided with the demands of their growing middle-class clientele. Eager to woo those of the burgeoning middle class and to win their business, twentieth-century restaurant proprietors modernized and simplified menus and accepted women diners.[50] But when the restaurants' economic interests and the middle class's cultural and economic interests did not coincide, as in the case of tipping, restaurateurs were reluctant to make changes. As long as the tipping system allowed restaurants to hide the cost of service, tipping endured.[51]

"Mr. Man! Do You Know You Are Spending a Fortune Every Year in Tips in Indianapolis So You Won't Be Called a Piker?" a headline in the *Indianapolis Sunday Star* screamed in 1912.[52] "Mr. Man" knew, but it seemed he had few options. He could withhold his tip and be called a "piker," tip sensibly and find himself ignored by waiters searching for bigger rewards, or tip lavishly and dine out rarely. Acknowledging the likelihood that tipping was not going away in the near future, *Harper's Monthly Magazine* referred to a hotel rumored to have banned tipping as the "Hotel Utopia."[53]

Was utopia really unattainable? As it became increasingly clear that political and economic efforts to eliminate tipping held little promise of success, middle-class visionaries put their faith in progress and science, staples of middle-class Progressive thinking. Frustrated by the failure of reform movements to end the "tipping evil," some in the middle class came to believe that technology offered the only genuine promise of a consumer democracy.

Technological Utopia

Mrs. Bobs, a character in George R. Chester's story "The Millennium in Dining," asks the protagonist: "I wonder what you will do when we reach the promised millennium in dining."

"Continue to eat, I suppose. But what is this millennium? A glorious period when every family will be able to secure the services of a good cook, by marriage or otherwise?"

"That's a Utopian dream we shall never be able to realize," she said. "But science holds out the hope of solving at least part of the servant problem by doing without cooks. By and by the food specialists will do away with all the waste material in our provender and give us all the sustenance of a seven course dinner, for instance, in half a dozen tiny capsules."[54]

Mrs. Bobs's turn-of-the-century faith in technology was neither entirely unfounded nor unshared, although the meal-in-a-pill was not forthcoming.[55] In the late nineteenth century, middle-class idealists turned to technology to eliminate the drudgework of domestic labor. Prepared foods, household appliances, and the application of scientific management principles transformed housework and reduced some of the arduousness of cooking. By 1900, the food processing industry made up one-fifth of American manufacturing, and local markets now offered goods—butchered meats, canned vegetables, and pancake mixes—once produced or processed at home. Meanwhile, new technologies made household appliances—mechanical mixers and improved stoves—more affordable for middle-class families. Maria Parola, one of the most popular cookbook authors of the 1880s, recommended ninety-three "essential" utensils for the well-stocked kitchen, and by 1912, the *Delineator* was extolling the virtues of such "modern labor-saving inventions" as the dumbwaiter, the lazy Susan, and papier-mâché plates.[56] While packaged foods and domestic appliances did not necessarily decrease the time women spent cooking and caring for their families, scientific management made it possible for middle-class families to maintain a respectable home with fewer servants.[57] Domestic technologies had addressed, if not solved, Mrs. Bobs's "servant problem," and some hoped it would do the same for the beleaguered middle-class restaurant patron.

Faith in technology came easy for many in the middle classes. In less than forty years, spurred by an unprecedented explosion in patents, the development of new industrial techniques, and the creation of a business culture free of regulation, the United States rose from the fourth-largest manufacturing nation in the world to the single largest producer of consumable goods.[58] Many in the middle class owed their livelihood to the new technologies that streamlined American industry after the Civil War. The modern business enterprise created a growing demand for managers, clerks, lawyers, and other professionals, and the new professionals were disposed to believe that just as technology had offered them solvency and stability, it could do away with social problems. Soon the technology that made industrialization possible was being used to eliminate social interactions that might pit class against class. Vending machines, traffic lights, escalators, and coin-operated turnstiles replaced personal exchanges.[59] "In a period torn by class struggle, violence in the workplace, cultural diversity, and general social unrest," historian Carroll W. Pursell wrote in *The Machine in America*, "'science' seemed to hold the promise not only of efficiency but also of impartiality."[60]

Could technology eliminate the awkward exchange between restaurant patron and waiter? Middle-class visionaries promised that the technology that had solved the "servant problem" and leveled class differences in the public sphere would soon eliminate the "tipping evil."[61] Entrepreneurs and inventors, restaurateurs and mechanics envisioned restaurants where food would be served with the touch of a button and the middle class would be spared the humiliation, discomfort, and expense of ordering dinner from a waiter. In the eyes of these quixotic visionaries, technology would replace waiters, lowering the cultural barriers to middle-class dining and thereby creating a democracy of consumption free from stodgy nineteenth-century aristocratic codes of conduct. At least twenty inventors filed patents for "waiterless restaurants" in the late nineteenth and early twentieth centuries.[62] From Josephine Doriat's "Means for Serving Guests in Restaurants" in 1887 to Yan Phou Lee's "Combined Table and Dumb-Waiter" in 1900 to Charles P. Paul's "Waiterless Restaurant" in 1921, these visions of restaurants without servers gave hope to the middle-class diner that a consumer democracy might yet be realized by eliminating the waiter and the tip, two of the most galling vestiges of the aristocratic past.[63]

While the new technology was never as successful as promised, the popular discourse about the "waiterless" restaurant reveals the pivotal role that many in the middle-class public expected technology would play in their re-envisioning of American culture. Technological innovation seemed to promise a consumer utopia, an opening up of the public space to mass consumption based on money and choice, not hereditary status.[64]

Restaurant historians generally regard the Exchange Buffet as the first waiterless restaurant in the United States. Opened in 1885 in New York's financial district, the restaurant featured an innovative new form of counter service. Men—the restaurant was a male preserve—ordered and paid for their food at a window and then ate standing up.[65] The success of the Exchange Buffet encouraged imitation, and when in 1898 the fledgling Child's restaurant chain in New York added trays to its self-service restaurants, the modern cafeteria was born.[66] Featuring consistent and relatively inexpensive food, cafeterias offered the growing number of urban white-collar workers a place to get a quick bite to eat during the lunch hour. But despite efforts to glamorize the cafeteria with marble tables and oak-paneled walls, most people regarded cafeterias as lunch counters or late-night coffeehouses. Long lines, impersonal mass seating, and entrées that had been kept warm for hours undermined any attempts to attract the middle-class diner seeking a romantic or luxurious meal. The Exchange Buffet and the cafeteria were, after all, not that different from the lunch wagons, street vendors, and notorious free-lunch saloons that made self-service dining a commonplace (but not necessarily respectable) practice through much of the nineteenth century.

Technological visionaries demanded more than basic self-service and dreamed of eliminating waiters without compromising the dining experience. A year after Americans first heard about the German Quisiana Café, a self-service, automated restaurant in Berlin that critics claimed "compared favorably in point of variety with a first-class restaurant of the common type," there was already talk of building a mechanical restaurant in the United States.[67] An 1897 editorial in *What to Eat* promised a future in which "guests will be served automatically with a complete dinner on pushing a button."[68]

Five years passed before Joseph Horn and Frank Hardart, a successful team of coffee shop proprietors, imported the technology used in the Quisiana Café, made a few modifications, and opened a mechanized restaurant in Philadelphia they dubbed the "Automat." Patrons of the first Automat purchased a token and then deposited it in a labeled slot representing the hot item they desired. The token signaled the basement kitchen, the food was prepared, and a dumbwaiter delivered the meal to the waiting customer, who carried it to a table to eat. Offering freshly prepared food in a lavish setting, a "glittering . . . combination of plate glass, marble tiling, weathered oak, wainscoting and hammered brass trimming," Horn and Hardart's first restaurant was an automated alternative to the less formal middle-class restaurants that were popular in cities like New York, Boston, and Chicago.[69] From the customer's perspective, there was only one important distinction: no waiter.[70] As one pundit observed with glee, "There will be no waiting, no swearing at the waiter, and no tipping."[71]

Horn and Hardart's automatic restaurant was heralded as one of the great technological feats of the era. "The horseless carriage, the wireless telephone and the playerless piano have been surpassed," claimed one local newspaper. "Philadelphia will have Monday next a waiterless restaurant. After this the millennium!"[72] But as the novelty wore off, the restaurant foundered. Middle-class customers seeking an elegant if affordable dinner became impatient with standing around, waiting for their orders.[73] Recognizing the limitations of the new technology, Horn and Hardart modified their restaurant over the next ten years, abandoning luxury for speed.[74] By 1912, they had replaced the dumbwaiters with a postal box system of heated and cooled cabinets and were using a central commissary to supply their restaurants. The new Automat catered to the teeming masses of shop girls and office workers looking for a quick lunch and was immensely successful in both Philadelphia and New York. Yet as popular as it was for lunch, the Automat, like the cafeteria, lacked the formality and fresh cooking that the middle-class diner demanded in a first-class waiterless restaurant.

Constructing an automated white-tablecloth restaurant turned out to be a more ambitious project than Horn and Hardart were prepared to undertake, but the formal waiterless restaurant remained a preoccupation of idealistic restaurant entrepreneurs. Throughout the first two decades of the twentieth century, newspapers and magazines routinely featured stories on restaurants where food would move from kitchen to table without touching human hands. These tales included detailed descriptions of restaurants with hydraulically lowered tables and machines that sent meals "zimmering" through tubes directly to the home.[75] A 1901 article in the *Lima Times-Democrat* announced the patenting of a "slot-machine restaurant" that would deliver hot dinners to the restaurant table with "no more tipping of restaurant waiters."[76] A 1921 *Literary Digest* article meticulously described—with detailed diagrams—an innovative lunchroom fitted with a serpentine conveyor that moved the seated guests past a serving counter and then a cashier.[77] Many of these articles implied that the first waiterless restaurants were no more than a year away.[78]

The two most detailed plans for an American waiterless restaurant were not only the most luxurious but also, if press accounts are to be believed, the closest to being realized.[79] In 1908, Henry Erkins, architect of the popular Murray's Roman Gardens restaurant, and John L. Murray, the owner, announced plans to build an eight-story restaurant in Times Square. The planned restaurant would seat five thousand, making it the largest restaurant in the world.

Erkins and Murray were successful showmen who hoped the novelty of the establishment would attract patrons.[80] Erkins vowed that "there will be so many surprises that New York will be astounded," and while he refused to divulge most of his "cherished notions . . . lest imitators steal our thunder," he promised that the new restaurant would be elegant (featuring a marble staircase with winged lions and "one of the largest and most famous paintings in the world") and, at least in part, waiterless.[81]

There would be many dining rooms in the eight-story establishment, but the highlight of the building's design was to be a grand hall featuring a "wonderful waiterless restaurant." Erkins clarified his plan for "invisible waiters" for the *New York Times*. "The idea of automatic tables which can be operated by invisible waiters is my invention," Erkins told the paper. "Guests will not give verbal orders to waiters, but will write on automatic pads what they want, and instantaneously the orders will be reproduced in the kitchen. . . . Not the entire table but the inner part of the table will be lowered, leaving the rim before the guests. The segment of the table will then be spread with the desired food and ascend to the guests." Noting that the waiter's "presence is not desirable," Erkins explained that the restaurant would employ "captains" and "omnibuses" to handle complaints and remove dirty dishes, but in the new restaurant, as the headlines screamed, "YOU NEEDN'T SEE A WAITER."[82] The technological magic wand might eliminate the tipping evil once and for all.

Contemporary newspaper and magazine accounts celebrated Erkins's restaurant and suggested that the future of dining was at hand. The *National Food Magazine* declared "the waiterless restaurant has arrived"; readers were told that a company had been formed, the land had been rented, and Erkins's restaurant, not yet named, would open shortly.[83] Erkins claimed the company had already raised $800,000, and the *New York Times* suggested, despite denials, that J. B. Duke and J. B. Cobb of the United Tobacco Company were financial backers.[84] But New York's waiterless restaurant never became a reality.

In 1913, John F. Daschner, a well-known maître d'hôtel at the Hotel Statler in Cleveland, Ohio, and a former president of the Elite Headwaiters Association, resurrected the idea of a waiterless white-tablecloth restaurant. Although Daschner may not have been aware of Erkins's earlier efforts, the restaurant Daschner described was similar in design.

> Here is a picture that will be a reality within the near future: You enter a beautiful restaurant. The tables and table-cloths are the same as in any other first-class place. . . . You look over the bill of fare, mark your selections with a pencil, and then press the button, as directed, having attached your menu card to the menu holder on the table. Lo, the centre part of the table with the bill of fare goes down; you look into the opening, but you see nothing as a screen automatically closes like a Kodak shutter. . . . Before you are over your surprise—in less

than a minute—the dish ordered appears on the table. . . . You dined comfortably, were served with dispatch, the food was hot, wholesome and nicely prepared. You were well pleased. You dined in a waiterless dining-room.[85]

Daschner intended his restaurant for the "middle class" and cited a host of benefits that would flow from the waiterless restaurant.[86] It would eliminate noise, minimize error, do away with unsightly piles of dirty dishes, lower prices, and guarantee that food arrived at the table hot. But as with previous ventures, no justification for the waiterless restaurant was heralded more than the elimination of the awkward, unequal, and discriminating exchanges between waiter and patrons. Daschner bragged that his new restaurant took ordering out of the hands of the "careless waiter" who invariably "disappoint[s] the guest" and reminded diners that eliminating the waiter meant there was "no one to overhear your conversation, whether it be on business or of a confidential nature." Most important, Daschner promised an end to tipping:

> Many people now eat at restaurants to avoid the trouble at home with inexperienced cooks and other servants; but how many more people would dine out regularly if the price were not so high and were they not confronted at each meal with the necessity for giving the everlasting tip. . . . There is a solution near. . . . Experts on the tipping question for waiters claim that it can never be abolished; but everybody will agree that by this method the tipping question is absolutely solved . . . and the prices are not raised. . . . Is this not a question worth considering, when the expense of tips for eating and drinking amounts to about $300,000 each year?[87]

Daschner's model of the waiterless restaurant was a middle-class utopia, a place where the individual diner could order dinner heedless of social censure and the waiter's condemnation. One "funny man" allegedly described it as "Hell below and Heaven above."[88] Aided by technology, the public "servant problem" would disappear, and middle-class diners, freed of their discomfort, would flock to the restaurant.

Daschner announced his venture in an open letter to *The Steward* in 1913. He claimed that he had secured a lawyer and was seeking a patent for his waiterless restaurant.[89] Three years later, editors at *The Caterer* reported that Daschner had opened a waiterless restaurant in Detroit and quoted the inventor as saying that business was booming and that he soon planned to open similar restaurants in New York, Philadelphia, San

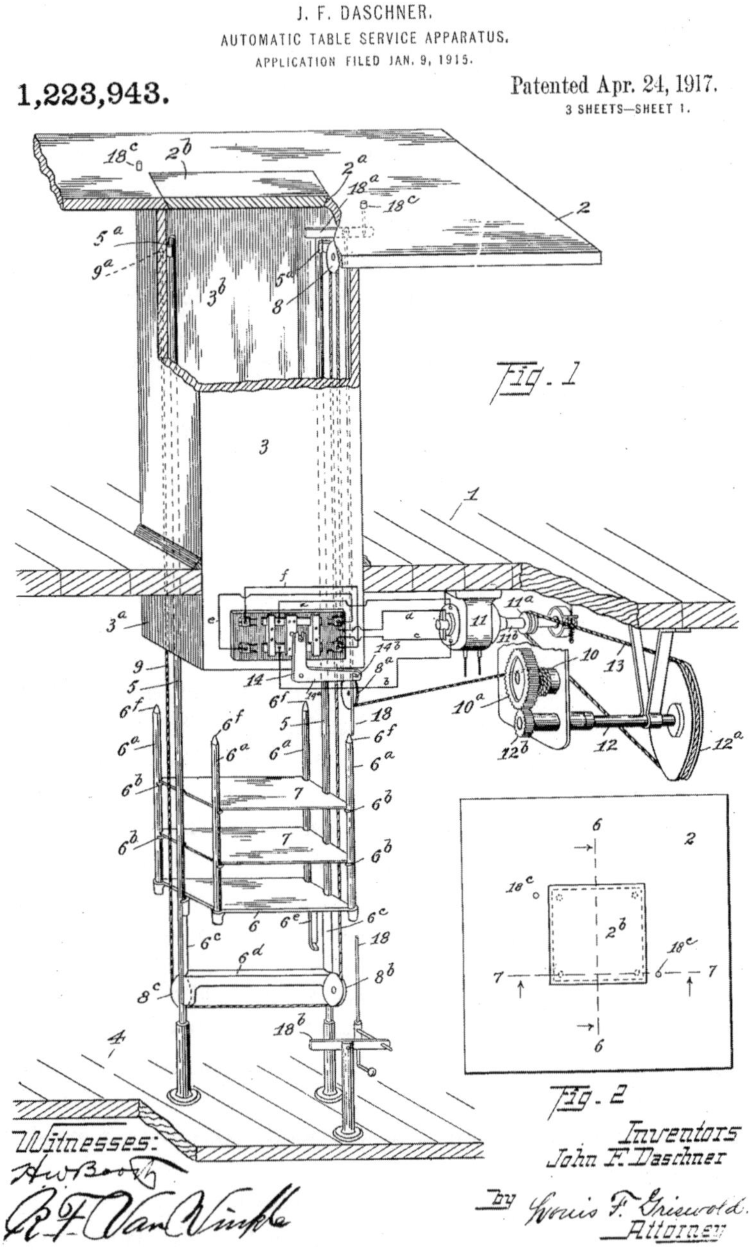

1,223,943.

Fig. 1

Fig. 2

Witnesses:

Inventors
John F. Daschner

By Louis F. Griswold.
Attorney

Patent, J. F. Daschner, "Automatic Table Service Apparatus," 1917.
Courtesy of the U.S. Patent and Trademark Office, Alexandria, Va.

Francisco, and Chicago. But Daschner was no more successful than the other quixotic inventors who dreamed of waiterless restaurants. Despite the brash claims and grand designs, there is little verifiable evidence that Daschner's Detroit restaurant ever opened; it appears that the cost of installing the dumbwaiters bankrupted the venture.[90]

Republican Tables, Technological Tables

Intricate rules about how to dine—from which spoon to use to the level of deference that waiters should show—governed the aristocratic table of the Gilded Age. These rules, published in etiquette books and inculcated in the children of the wealthy, were justified by the claim that manners promoted the civil discourse required by a democracy.[91] It was a peculiar argument. Since well-mannered men and women of the upper classes were instructed not to discuss anything as potentially divisive as politics at dinner, the formal dinner's contribution to the vitality of the national discourse was indirect. Aristocrats and their apologists credited the long, slow meal "freed from grossness by a graceful ceremony" with promoting sociability and civility and with nurturing the discipline and manners that made politics without rancor possible. Good comportment at the dinner table offered evidence of the moral fitness required of republican politics, and advocates for the aristocratic table predicted disaster if gustatory codes of conduct were ignored. "Universal cleanliness and good manners," Robert Tomes, author of *The Bazar Book of Decorum*, wrote in 1870, "are essential of a democracy. This must be generally recognized and acted upon, or the refined will seek in other countries the exclusiveness which will secure for them that nicety of life essential to its enjoyment, and we shall be left alone to wallow in our brutality and foulness."[92] Waiters were especially important to these interactions because they freed diners to focus on witty conversation and conviviality.[93]

For the middle class, however, the rules that governed the formal dinner created nearly insurmountable barriers to full participation in public dining culture that undermined the grandiose claims that the upper class made about the importance of good manners in a "democracy."[94] Codes of manners and behavior—at least the foppish conventions of the aristocratic restaurant—may have preserved decorum, the middle class conceded, but they accomplished this feat by excluding all those who lacked the cultural capital that the blue books of behavior required. The aristocratic table was civil but substanceless, a sterile space achieved by barring those who by their dress, demeanor, and inability to tip were regarded as less worthy and potentially disruptive.[95]

The middle-class diner did not propose to replace the aristocratic table with an alternative discursive space grounded in a new code of civility; political discourse was best left to electioneering newspapers and political lackeys. Instead, the middle class offered an alternative vision of equality, one that prioritized equal access to consumer goods above polite conversation. Deeply distrustful of plutocracy and inclined to place their faith in the competitive marketplace, those of the middle class argued for a cosmopolitan table without unnecessarily burdensome rules or restraints, a place where those of modest wealth and commonsense manners would be welcomed. The effort to end tipping, no less than the turn-of-the-century fight to dismantle monopolies and trusts, demonstrated the middle class's belief that a disciplined and regulated economy could guarantee equality, both economic and political. Historian Lizabeth Cohen, describing the "yoking of free choice as consumers with political freedom" and the belief that American abundance could secure equality in the post–World War II era, called this idealization of the consumer marketplace the "consumer's republic." The struggle to restrain tipping suggests that this middle-class vision of consumer equality had its roots in turn-of-the-century efforts to democratize consumption.[96]

When it came to tipping, however, the middle-class diner's faith in the marketplace was misplaced. The waiter's "toadyism" shielded restaurateurs from the accusation that they were pandering to the wealthy, and tips helped disguise the real cost of dinner. As long as restaurateurs reaped benefits from the tipping system, they were reluctant to join middle-class campaigns to end gratuities, and without their cooperation, efforts to bar tipping faltered. The market, even the regulated market, offered no solution to the "tipping evil."

When the marketplace failed to deliver equality, the middle class turned to technology. The utopian dreamers who envisioned the waiterless, mechanical restaurant understood that the desire for impartial service was a uniquely middle-class reimagining of a democratic marketplace. Daschner observed that his invention held no appeal for the "wealthy or well-to-do people" who "will continue to patronize the elegant restaurants, and always will."[97] Technology that promised equality of exchange even at the expense of human interaction spoke to middle-class diners' most deeply held insecurities and their most desperate re-envisioning of the commercial sphere.[98]

While the American waiterless restaurant was never widely realized, twentieth-century entrepreneurs' tenacious efforts to develop a mechanical dining room—and the way in which the middle-class press applauded their idealism—demonstrate how far members of the middle class were willing to go to promote equality in the new consumer economy that flourished in the early twentieth century. The waiterless restaurant was an uncomplicated, impersonal public space. The lone diner did not have to speak to anyone: he or she could order dinner on an electric tablet, have food magically appear on the table, and then pay the bill in silence. There would be no tip, no scrutiny, and no need for elaborate codes of civility. When dining was stripped of the inherently dangerous human elements, advantages of birth and breeding disappeared.

The waiterless restaurant's promise that technology could secure equal access to consumer goods by eliminating the messiness of human interaction was not an anomaly. Magazines and newspapers promoted idealistic innovations like the meal-in-a-pill that, as food historian Warren Belasco observed, served as explicit rejections of the "conspicuous consumption of upper-class banquets."[99] Likewise, utopian novels published in the late nineteenth and early twentieth centuries envisioned a future where technology would overcome human corruptibility.[100] In these imaginings of the future, as in the middle-class diner's idealization of the waiterless restaurant, technological progress leveled class differences.

The social costs imposed by these advancements were potentially high. The technological utopia that many turn-of-the-century visionaries wanted was not a place of endless abundance but instead a world in which machines managed scarcity. In their novels and essays, as in accounts of the waiterless restaurant, technology did not facilitate equality but enforced it. Yet for some middle-class diners, this trade-off was acceptable. Cosmopolitan diners were willing to sacrifice the rough-and-tumble of a participatory marketplace for the simple fairness of technocratic equality. The waiterless restaurant was a fantastic, impersonal, and unrealized vision of a true consumer democracy.

ENDING LINGUISTIC DISGUISES
The Decline of French Cuisine

In 1936, the Ohio Society of New York reenacted a banquet first held at Delmonico's fifty years earlier.[1] The event was intended to be a faithful reproduction of the original fete, which had featured a multicourse French meal, but the twentieth-century dinner differed from its nineteenth-century prototype. The banquet was held at the Hotel Pennsylvania because Delmonico's had closed in 1923. Unable to reconcile the "leisurely affair" and long-winded speeches of 1886 with the schedule imposed by radio-broadcasted speeches, the dinner was shorter and the food was served earlier. Two courses were eliminated, only one soup was offered, and the elaborate European pastries of 1886 were "telescoped into the dual items of fancy ice cream and little cakes." But the most significant change involved the language of the menu. Since diners in the 1930s could not be expected to understand a nineteenth-century French-language menu, the bill of fare was in English. As a local newspaper reported: "For the diner the function became less of a guessing game if his French was a bit rusty. The oysters, soup, fish and duckling of the old menu all came out from behind their linguistic disguises."[2]

The Ohio Society's decision to accommodate its largely middle-class guest list by eliminating courses and substituting English for French acknowledged that the era of the aristocratic restaurant had come to an end. As elite restaurants in the twentieth century translated French-language menus into English and replaced French cuisine with American and international dishes, they substituted the middle class's cosmopolitan sensibility for nineteenth-century aristocratic conventions. The modern restaurant patron, observed restaurateur Alice Foote MacDougall in 1929, may "go at times to the hotel *de luxe*" for a French meal but prefers restaurants that offer "home conditions and home produce"—and, she might have added, Chinese chop suey and Mexican chili.[3]

The authority that nineteenth-century aristocrats exercised over how Americans ate was not unassailable. It required that restaurateurs continually reaffirm an elite cultural hierarchy that celebrated obscure French dishes by offering French-language menus, serving sauced entrées, and hiring foreign chefs. In the late nineteenth century, an increasingly self-aware middle class challenged the aristocrats' monopoly on dining culture and restaurateurs capitulated.

As with most cultural upheavals, the rise of the cosmopolitan restaurant was unpredictable, uneven, and unhurried. French cuisine remained one of the world's great cuisines, and formal barriers to participation in upper-crust restaurants, including high prices and dress codes, did not disappear entirely. Yet eager to win the patronage of middle-class cosmopolitans, elite restaurateurs rejected the idea that French cuisine, and only French cuisine, could be served at upscale restaurants and embraced middle-class tastes. While the marketplace sorted out these contradictions, critics from the middle class were often vocal and impatient, demanding that immediate steps be taken to ban the French-language menu and replace French cuisine with cosmopolitan fare. These critics, no less than the disgruntled middle-class diner, demonstrated the ultimate effectiveness of the middle class's negotiation of the new consumer economy. Marshalling nationalism while simultaneously exploiting the exoticism of foreign cuisines, the middle class created a new cosmopolitan restaurant culture. Not only did English-language menus replace French-language menus, but elite restaurants also began to serve American and international dishes.

By the time America entered World War I, the cultural capital that was most valued in the world of dining no longer belonged to the aristocratic class. Once restaurants embraced cosmopolitanism, the urban middle class replaced the aristocrats as arbiters of the nation's taste.

The Language of Dining

"Waiter, these dishes are all in French," the secretary of the Geneva White Cross Society, Gaston G. Netter, complained in 1912. "Yes, sir," the waiter stammered, "but the prices are in English. Most people go by them."[4] The same year, in an article reprinted in *The Southern Hotel Journal*, novelist Constance Cary Harrison joked about a nouveau riche man who pointed to a line in a menu and told the waiter, "I'll have some of that please," only to have the waiter retort, "I am sorry, sir, but the band is playing that."[5] Five years later, the fashion editor for the *Washington Post* summarized middle-class Americans' consternation over the use of French on the bill of fare. "Why, oh, why do we insist on using French names on our American menus? . . . Half of us can't read them and those of us who can very often have difficulty in translating them, and when an American with an admittedly poor taste for languages struggles over a French phrase with an Irish waiter, the result is almost tragic."[6]

Lacking the linguistic proficiency in French that breeding and education granted the American aristocrat, the middle-class restaurant-goer found language, as often as tipping or prices, a barrier to full participation in aristocratic restaurant culture. The French menu with its hundreds of linguistic conventions confused the novice, undermined his or her cultural authority, and kept many from dining in the best restaurants. During the closing decades of the nineteenth century and the first two decades of the twentieth century, a strident, increasingly outspoken middle class openly rejected the French-language menu and waged a public campaign against the use of French culinary terms. By 1920, although adoption of English-language menus was not universal, the middle class had once again demonstrated its ability to shape the culture of dining.

The first complaints about the use of the French menu were more aristocratic than middle-class. In 1875, Gail Hamilton warned readers of *Scribner's Monthly* about restaurants where "the table-cloth is spotted and the coffee is mud . . . but the bill of fare lies by your plate with all its French and fearful viands as mysteriously formulated as if you were at the Fifth Avenue or the Sherman."[7] Upper-class diners sought to protect their monopoly on French pretension and complained when restaurants appropriated French terms for everyday fare. But as the number of middle-class diners increased, complaints about the use of French terms and French dishes were less about the affectations of greasy spoons and more about the exclusivity of fine dining.

In 1885, the *Scranton Truth* challenged the New York culinary journal *The Cook* to abandon the use of French terms in its recipes and menus. The editors of *The Cook* initially defended French as the language of good cooking. "You might as well expect a scientist to write intelligently about electricity without mentioning 'volts,' 'ohms,' or 'webers,'" *The Cook* responded, "as require a cook to write about his art without calling things by their proper names."[8] But this chauvinistic defense of French culinary conventions was short-lived. Within months, the journal reversed its policy of printing French bills of fare after its avowed readership, middle-class housewives, "protest[ed] . . . against the use of French words in our columns." Humbly, *The Cook* pledged to use English where it could be "effectually, clearly and succinctly" substituted, and then, to deflect criticism, it attacked the deplorable conduct of America's restaurants. "The thing that would be protested against is the useless and unnecessary jamming in of French words among English, for no other purpose than mere affectation, as in the case of the [restaurant] cook who puts upon his bill of fare 'calf's liver au jus,' when he might better, for English speaking patrons, write it 'calf's liver with gravy.' Ignorant people, those who want all things done as they are done 'in Yurrup,' are most likely to be the offenders in this direction."[9] Cowed by the public outcry over its own use of French terms, *The Cook* eventually became a leading advocate for the use of "short, sensible, scientifically arranged and English worded bill[s] of fare" in restaurants.[10]

Behind the barbs levied at the pretension of French menus was a growing concern, expressed in journals and newspapers read by the middle class, that the use of French was a conspiratorial effort to exclude those of modest incomes and limited cultural experience from the bounty of restaurant culture.[11] A joke from the mid-1880s that first appeared in the *Philadelphia Call* expressed these concerns as clearly as any editorial. A mother and daughter are dining in a table d'hôte restaurant, which charges a set price no matter how much food is ordered. The daughter cannot read the menu and asks her mother what language the bill of fare is printed in. The mother, a bit embarrassed, tells her daughter that the menu is in French and admits that she can read only a little of it. Confused, the daughter asks, "Why does the hotel man put the names in French?" The mother answers, "Because most people can't pronounce the names without making themselves ridiculous and they therefore order just as little as possible."[12]

Middle-class advocates of English-language menus became more strident in the early twentieth century.[13] As middle-class restaurant-going increased, the indecipherable French bill of fare was seen as evidence that elites had abandoned American values. In a fiery December 1897 article in *What to Eat*, Donald G. Ross lambasted the "privileged class who have been abroad" and "the imitators of foreign habits and appetites who have not been 'abroad'" for preferring the "'a la mode' preparations" of the French to the plainer, more flavorful food of the American. Ross went on to argue for both English-language menus and American cookery. "We find such delicate [American] foods disturbed by all manner of harrowing [European] seasonings and 'patois' titles, that not only successfully disguise the plain American name, but their first virtue—the flavor." "It probably looks well to see broiled pompano on a Boston bill of fare,"

Ross complained, "but when a faded taste has to be made up by using artificial flavoring and presented under a foreign alias, we should draw the line."[14]

Stronger polemics soon followed. In 1907, August E. Gans, a European émigré living in Chicago and the business manager at the Chicago Cooking College, argued that the French-language menu pandered to the "patrician" class and undermined America's democratic traditions. "Are we getting to be more Europeanized from year to year, and, are we quietly losing some of our distinctively American ways? Is the use of high sounding, although mostly atrociously misspelled[,] French terms on the ordinary bills of fare of even our ordinary restaurants in smaller cities a sign of this 'catering' to 'classes'?"[15] Gans and others thought so. *Keeler's Hotel Weekly*, with the same blend of nationalism and frustration, agreed. "Why quarrel? Let those who like to eat in French go to France, while those who like to eat in English stay right here and enjoy themselves."[16]

The debate over the French menu eventually spilled out of the culinary and hotel journals and into the mainstream press. Max Bloch, a New Yorker, launched an extraordinary public debate over the use of French-language menus when he complained to the editors of the *New York Times* in 1909, "What sense is there in calling potatoes 'Pommes de terre,' oysters 'huitres,' soups 'pottages,' and so on through a lot of lingual fol-de-rol, when plain everyday English would tell the story comprehensively?"[17] French-language menus, Bloch felt, represented "humbug and snobbery." Other frustrated diners seconded Bloch's protest in the weeks that followed. A. H. La Mont, despite his French surname, called for a "scrimmage" not only against the use of French terms for dishes but also against the word "menu," another Parisian import. "Banish it and return to the good old understandable 'bill of fare,'" wrote La Mont. "I want to eat in English—not French."[18] Bloch and La Mont were hardly exceptional. As middle-class urbanites dined out en masse, they increasingly expected restaurants to cater to their language preference, eating habits, and national pride. They believed the bill of fare should not, as a *New York Globe* humorist penned, be primarily a means of learning a foreign language.[19]

Growing ire over French-language menus appeared in newspapers and magazines across the country, including some unlikely publications. In 1910, Colonel Henry Watterson's flamboyant, widely read newspaper, the *Louisville Courier-Journal*, popularized the concerns of Gaston G. Netter. Netter, an international spokesperson for unadulterated foods, was dismayed that the Pure Food and Drug Act of 1906 did not prevent restaurants from disguising what they served with French names. In Watterson's populist paper, Netter's concerns were transformed into an attack on American elites. Netter (as paraphrased by the paper) argued that "restaurants in the United States are patronized chiefly by persons who speak English only. The label should tell on the bill of fare [what is being served] as well as on the bottle of catsup where the federal law compels frankness." Like Gans, Bloch, and La Mont in the *New York Times*, Netter draped his argument with contempt for those who would imitate European manners. "The confusion resulting from the use of a foreign language upon a home-use of a foreign bill of fare," he observed, "is negligible in comparison with the implied toadyism. If we are to have opera in English for patriotic reasons, by all means let us reform the bill of fare similarly."[20]

Reflecting widespread disdain for French-language menus, similar complaints about French "naims" and "fashuns" appeared in even the unlikeliest of forums, the hunting and fishing magazine *Field and Stream*. Employing a stock character, "Unkel David," who spoke in a countrified black dialect, the magazine criticized women who were easily beguiled by European fads and fancy-sounding French dishes. "When in the coarse of hooman events a man's troo & belovid wife gits so she can tawk nothing but fashuns & soshul affares & will eet only things with French naims to them, like sharlot roozes & blum mong & demmy tasses," Unkel David lamented, "then it is hi time to taik her away from the bizzy hants of welth & bild a tent big enuff for two (2) in the loansum forrist, whare . . . the only tabel dellykisses are fried poark & sody biskits."[21]

From *The Cook* to Unkel David, the outcry over French cuisine and French-language menus was remarkable, not only because it defied the established hegemony that held French culinary achievements in high regard but also because the condemnations of aristocratic pretensions were accompanied by calls for immediate action. Members of the middle class may have been willing to let market forces champion smaller, simpler menus and plate dinners, but they were less sanguine about the language of dining. French-language menus were viewed as ostentatious evidence of the corrupting influence of elites, and they were explicitly condemned on those grounds. Anger at the custom of printing menus in French was so widely shared that it served as a common trope in jokes and stories.[22]

Still, not everyone was ready to abandon French menus. When the editors of the *New York Times* eventually responded to the letter-writing campaign against foreign language menus that appeared in the paper in April 1909, they endorsed the use of "cook's French." Admitting that their "own blood . . . doesn't boil very hotly at this outrage," the editors focused on the practical need for a special language for dining:

As the best French cooking is generally held to be the best in the world, it is not remarkable that the proprietors of the more ambitious hotels and restaurants like to hint in this cheap and convenient way that the rulers of their kitchens belong to the favored race. When such is the case—and perhaps it is in about one out of twenty establishments using French food names—there is an excuse for the habit, since those names are the only ones there are for many of the dishes set before the diner. And when cooks of other nationalities make the same or approximate dishes, why shouldn't they, too, apply to them the same or approximate appellations?[23]

The *Times*, in other words, endorsed the restaurant tradition of using extravagant, high-sounding names to enhance their reputations for exclusivity, what some referred to as the "$5 a syllable" rationale for the French menu. A month later, the paper published a *New York Times Sunday Magazine* feature that included a lexicon of "cook's French" that would-be diners could memorize.[24]

The *Times'* glossary was not the first effort that newspapers and magazines had made to provide dictionaries, pronunciation guides, and other forms of advice to middle-class restaurant-goers. *What to Eat*'s Parisian correspondent, Frank Tryon Charles, penned a long-running series of articles in the 1890s that defined hundreds of restaurant terms and provided a pronunciation key. His comprehensive list of soups and consommés, for example, included *potage à la bisque d'écrevisses (beeske-day-crev-eese)—crawfish soup; bouillon gras—gravy soup; potage à la Chantilly (chaan-tee-e)—purée of lentils; consomme à la Colbert (colebear)—clear soup with garnish of cos lettuce, celery, button onions;* and *potage à la Conde—purée of red haricots.*[25] Other magazines offered similar, if not quite so comprehensive, guides to "cook's French."[26] These guides may have been well-intentioned, but they were never very practical. Brave was the diner who memorized Frank Tryon Charles's massive list of culinary terms and ordered his dinner in French. As Charles himself warned, phonetic renderings of French were tricky, and a misplaced accent could be a disaster (turning "peach" into "sin," for example).[27] Furthermore, "cook's French" was so idiosyncratic that no guide could account for all the variations that diners encountered. Diners complained that even when they memorized the name of a favorite dish at one restaurant, they got "stung" when they tried to order the same dish at another restaurant.[28] One had to be fluent in the language of dining to understand fully a turn-of-the-century French menu.

As with the anti-tipping campaign and other middle-class efforts to remake dining, an outspoken vanguard led the attempt to eliminate the French menu, but the effort enjoyed support among many middle-class diners. Middle-class urbanites recognized that the paternalistic guides written by Europhiles like Frank Tryon Charles represented the upper class's social dominance, and they largely ignored them. Perhaps the *Times* editors were, in some small way, acknowledging the increasing influence of these middle-class consumers when they predicted, despite their endorsement of "cook's French," that "widespread hostility for French menus in this or any other country" would eventually bring about reform.[29] In fact, by 1909, public pressure was already having an effect on the language that restaurants used to describe the food they served.

Until the early twentieth century, hotels and restaurants were deaf to middle-class concerns about the language of the bill of fare. Jessup Whitehead, author of the 1899 *Steward's Handbook*, encouraged restaurateurs to write clear, explanatory menus but equivocated when it came to language. Whitehead acknowledged that "perhaps not one in ten thousand in this country understands French, as applied to dishes in a menu," but he held that a restaurant menu should pose a challenge to readers. A challenging menu, Jessup wrote, "implies a compliment to the guests by the supposition that they are 'gastronomically educated.'"[30] J. A. Pinard, one of New York's most prominent Gilded Age caterers, took a similar stance. Asked in 1890 by the *New York Daily Tribune* why he still printed his menus in French, he cobbled together a novel defense. After offering the obligatory justification for French cooking by calling it "the perfection of culinary art," he boldly asserted that "one of the delights of a dinner is its surprises. It is not well to anticipate, and by concealing the precise character of what is coming, the pleasures of the table are greatly enhanced. Many of the beauties of a dinner are hidden behind some curious French word or phrase, only to be revealed at the proper moment."[31]

Others found weightier arguments to justify French names on menus. Both food historian George Ellwanger and the outspoken proprietor of the Hotel Knickerbocker, James B. Regan, maintained that French names for French dishes were indispensable. Writing in 1902, Ellwanger, the son and namesake of the Rochester horticulturalist, claimed that it was impossible to translate French dishes into English without sounding silly. "'Les quenelles de levraut saucees d'une espagnolle au fumet,' 'les amourettes de boeuf marinees frites,' 'Vepaule de veau en musette champetre,' 'un coq vierge en petit deuil,'" Ellwanger observed, "while natural and comprehensible in French, would sound somewhat bizarre as 'Forcemeat balls of leverets sauced with a racy Spanish woman,' 'the love-affairs of soused beef fried,' 'a shoulder of veal in rural bagpipes,' and 'a virgin rooster in half-mourning.'"[32] James Regan, although more sensitive to critics (some of whom were potential customers), also argued for the naturalness of the French-language menu. "French is the language of the table," Regan told an interviewer in 1911, "and while it might be possible to use English here and there, so many terms uppermost in our dietaries are of French origin without an English equivalent, that I think our reformers have quite a task before them."[33]

Despite the cultural elites' continued support of French-language menus, restaurants grudgingly began to address middle-class protests in the early twentieth century. *The Caterer* printed the story of a businessman who spent the summer at a "prominent resort hotel on the Atlantic coast" and, with the aid of other middle-class guests, forced the resort to abandon its French-language menus. "At the beginning of the season," he told the restaurant industry journal, "à la's were all the rage, but they were more than the guests could stand, and there was such a general kicking that the proprietor was obliged to take them off the bill of fare."[34] This experience was not unique. When middle-class diners complained, restaurants were faced with the prospect of losing valuable customers or making changes, and most opted to make changes. As a result, even the most upscale restaurants in New York City reconsidered the use of French at the turn of the century. The Waldorf Hotel, predecessor of the Waldorf-Astoria, appears to have used French menus exclusively until the mid-1890s. Around 1895, however, the hotel adopted a bilingual dinner menu (although French was still used on the menus of catered events). On the left side of the menu card, the elaborate à la carte menu listed such items as *roast beef, red head duck,* and *fresh strawberries with cream*; on the right, it listed *rôti de boeuf, canard tête rouge,* and *fraises fraîches, à la crème*.[35] Other elite hotels and restaurants in New York followed suit. The St. Regis Hotel, considered the bastion of old Knickerbocker wealth, offered patrons an English translation of its French menu in 1905 as part of its campaign to dispel rumors that it catered only to the upper class.[36]

While a few stodgy, old-school restaurants such as Delmonico's remained wedded to their French menus, more progressive restaurants abandoned French entirely in the following two decades. The Waldorf-Astoria, for example, shifted to a mostly English-language menu by 1914. Using a standard that is still common, the hotel employed English whenever possible and convenient, although it retained a few foreign flourishes. The halibut with lobster sauce was simply *Halibut, Lobster Sauce*. The duck was listed as *Duckling (half)*. The clams with Newburg sauce, however, were described as *Soft Clams à la Newburg*. Although the Waldorf-Astoria did have an alternative bilingual menu, possibly for foreign visitors, the hotel increasingly saw the merit of using English rather than French.[37]

The Waldorf-Astoria's new menus were not unusual. Restaurants throughout the country adopted English-language menus. In 1885, The Antlers in Colorado Springs was so committed to gallicizing its menu that it created French terms for dishes named after American presidents. When the restaurant hosted the Fifteenth Annual Meeting of the Colorado Bar Association in 1912, however, the menu paid tribute to French culinary expertise only when strictly necessary. The trout made an appearance as *mountain trout, Meuniére*, but the chicken was simply *roast spring chicken* and the salad was simply *lettuce and tomato*.[38] Likewise, the Hotel Cadillac in Detroit avoided French culinary preparations and used simple English cognates on its extensive September 29, 1911, menu. The menu included over fifty main dishes and salads, of which only seventeen used any form of "cook's French"—and in most of these cases, middle-class patrons would have easily understood the term either because the French could be straightforwardly translated (*crab flake a l'Epicure*) or because the dish was so common as to defy linguistic disguise (*chicken a la King*). Even menu items that one might have expected to be described in French did not necessarily receive a French title. Frog legs, a dish that urban Americans did not widely accept until after World War I, appeared on the menu as *frog legs roadhouse style*.[39] At restaurants and hotels in rural areas, such as the vacation resorts of New Hampshire that had once been fashionable with wealthy tourists, the erosion of the French menu was even more precipitous.[40]

French did not fully disappear from the menus of eating establishments. It still commanded enough respect that it was used on occasion to describe a restaurant or a menu item, even when the menu itself included few French dishes. Schraft's Fifth Avenue lunchroom called itself a "Petit Salon," although the menu, mostly sandwiches, was generic and in English.[41] Likewise, Macy's, a bastion of middle-class consumerism, included a few French terms on a laundry-list menu that featured nearly sixty variations of steaks and roasts (including *planked sirloin steak, Rochambeau* and *calf's head, Poulette*).[42] Nevertheless, while a few French names lingered, public demand for more accessible bills of fare won out in the early twentieth century.

Experiments in English-language menus gained permanence with the outbreak of World War I in Europe. The war increased America's suspicion of everything European, and restaurateurs joined in the patriotic fervor to

Dinner.

Oysters 25 Lynn Haven 35

Canapé Anchovies 50   Pin-Money Pickles 20   Olives 25   Radishes 20
Canapé Sardines 50   Lyon Sausages 35   Pitted Queen Olives 30
Canapé Caviar 50   Anchovy Salad 50   Salted Nuts 20   Salted Almonds 20   Celery 50

Consommé Adelina 40   Vermicelli 30
Cream of Turnips, Jussienne 50   Bisque of Shrimps. Nantaise 50
Strained Okra 75   Green Turtle 1 00   Mock Turtle 50
Petites Marmites 50   Okra, Créole 60   Pea Soup 35
Croûte-au-Pot 40   Julienne 40   Mongol 40
Chicken Broth à la Bellevue 80   per cup 40   Clam Broth per cup 25

Timbale of Ham 75

BROOK TROUT 1 00

Fresh Mackerel, Maître d'Hôtel 50   Striped Bass, Corse 80
Perch, Polonais 70   Trout au Bleu 90
Frog's Legs 1 00   Whitebait 50
Shad Roe 50   Planked Shad 2 50   Half 1 25   Shad 50   Soft Shell Crabs 85

FROGS LEGS IN SHELLS WITH FRESH MUSHROOMS 1 00   CHICKEN, TUNISIENNE 1 25
SPRING LAMB STEW WITH TURNIPS 80   LOIN OF BEEF, SPORTSMAN 1 00
MUTTON CHOPS, GARIBALDI 80   FILET MIGNON, RISTEIN 1 25
SWEETBREAD, HENRY VIII 1 25   REED BIRDS, COLUMBUS 1 00

Roast Turkey 1 00   Roast Spring Lamb, Mint Sauce 1 00
Roast Lamb 65   Roast Mutton 50   Roast Beef 60   Roast Duck 2 00   half 1 00
Roast Chicken 2 00   half 1 00

Chicken Squab, Whole 1 50   Spring Turkey 2 50 half 1 25   Squab 80   Chicken 2 00 half 1 00

Fresh Mushrooms 1 00   Terrapin 2 50

— GAME --

Canvas Back Duck 4 00   Imported Plover 75   Ruddy Duck 1 50   English Snipe 75
Red-Head Duck 3 25   English Partridge 75   Partridge 1 50   Quail 75
Philadelphia Reed Birds 1 00   English Pheasant 3 00   Grouse 1 50

Potatoes Bibi 30   Artichokes with fresh mushrooms 50
Celery braisé 50   New Asparagus 80   French Asparagus 1 25   Cauliflower 60
French String Beans 50   Oyster Bay Asparagus 60   Sweet Potatoes 30   Stuffed Peppers 60
French Peas 50   New String Beans 50   New Peas 60   Cêpes 60   New White Squash 50
Spinach 50   Cardons 40   Fresh Artichoke 60   New Beets 30   Stuffed Egg Plant 60
Stuffed Hothouse Tomatoes 75   Bermuda Onions 30   Bermuda Potatoes 25
Rice Croquettes with Maraschino 50

— COLD —

SALAD { Lettuce and Tomato 60   Hot-house Tomato 60   Mayonnaise 70
Celery Mayonnaise 60   Lettuce 50   Waldorf 60
Hot-house Cucumbers 75   Dandelion 40   Romaine 50

CHEESE { Gruyère 25   Port Salut 30   Pont l'Evêque 30
Edam 30   Philadelphia Cream 25   Roquefort 30   Camembert 30
Gorgonzola 30   Cream Gervaise 25   American 50   English 25

FRUITS { Pears 40   Pineapple 35   Grapes 75   Apples 20
Bananas 20   Figs 35   Oranges 25   Fresh Strawberries with Cream 60

Cupola Madison 40   Cream Yvette Eclairs 25
Tunisian Jelly 30   Strawberry Soufflé 60   Macédoine Flan with Rice 25
Fruit Compote with Maraschino 40   Strawberry Short Cake 50
Bar-le-Duc Jelly 40   Sweet Limes 40   Apple Pie 20
Benedictine Sorbet 30   Duchesse Pudding 50   Vanilla Mousse 30
Biscuit Tortoni 30   Chestnut Plombières 40   Tutti Frutti 40
Nesselrode Pudding 40   Lalla Rookh 40   Roman Punch 30
Orange, Lemon and Raspberry Water Ice 25
Fresh Strawberry Ice Cream 35
Turkish Coffee 20   French Coffee 15

The Waldorf   Thursday, April 23rd, 1896.
☞ Special Arrangements made for Theatre Parties.

Bilingual dinner menu (English and French), The Waldorf, New York, N.Y., April 23, 1896. Courtesy of the Buttolph Menu Collection, Rare Books Division, The New York Public Library, Astor, Lenox and Tilden Foundations.

Diner.

Huîtres 25
Lynn Haven 35

Canapé d'Anchois 50　　Cornichons Petit-Poucet 20　　Olives farcies Reine 30　　Radis 20
Canapé de Sardines 50　　Saucisson de Lyon 35　　Noix Salées 20　　Olives 25
Canapé de Caviar 50　　Salade d'Anchois 50　　Amandes Salées 20　　Celeri 50

Consommé Adelina 40　　　　　　　　　　　　　　　　　　　　Vermicelle 30
　Crême de Navets, Jussienne 50　　　　　　　Bisque de Crevette, Nantaise 50
　　Consommé de Volaille à la Bellevue 80　par tasse 40　　Clam Broth par tasse 25
　　　Tortue verte claire 1 00　　Gombaut passée 75　　Gombaut Créole 60
　　　　Petites Marmites 50　　Croûte au Pot 40　　Purée de Pois 35
　　　　　Julienne 40　　Fausse Tortue 50　　Mongol 40

Timbale de Jambon 75

TRUITE DE RIVIERE 1 00

Maquereau Frais, Maître d'Hôtel 50　　　　　　　Bass Rayée à la Corse 80
　Perche, Polonais 70　　　　　　　　　　　　　　　　Truite au Bleu 90
　　Grenouilles 1 00　　　　　　　　　　　　　　　　　Blanchaille 50
　　Oeufs d'Alose 50　　Alose sur planche 2 50　Demi 1 25　　Alose 50　　Crabes Moux 85

RAGOUT D'AGNEAU DU PRINTEMPS AUX NAVETS 80　　**FILET MIGNON, RISTEIN 1 25**
COTELETTE DE MOUTON, GARIBALDI 80　　**CONTREFILET, SPORTSMAN 1 00**
COQUILLE DE GRENOUILLES AU CHAMPIGNONS FRAIS 1 00　　**ORTOLANS, COLUMBUS 1 00**
POULET, TUNISIENNE 1 25　　**RIS-DE-VEAU, HENRY VIII 1 25**

Rôti d'Agneau, du printemps, sauce Menthe 1 00
Rôti de Mouton 50　　Rôti de Boeuf 60　　Agneau rôti 65
Poulet rôti 2 00　Demi 1 00　　Rôti de Dinde 1 00　　Canard rôti 2 00　Demi 1 00
Poulet de serre 1 50　Pigeonneau 80　Dindonneau 2 50　Demi 1 25　Poulet 2 00　Demi 1 00

Champignons frais 1 00
Terrapin 2 50

— GIBIER —

Canard Canvasback 4 00　　Canard Tête Rouge 3 25
Canard Ruddy 1 50　　　　　Faisan Anglais 3 00
Grouse 1 50　Bécassine Anglaise 75　Caille 75　Pluvier Importé 1 00
Perdreau 1 50　　　　Ortolans 1 00　　　　Perdreau Anglais 75
Pommes de terre, Bibi 30　　　　Fonds d'Artichaut au champignons frais 60
Pommes Nouvelles 25　Pois Nouveaux 60　Betteraves nouvelles 30　Oignons Bermuda 30
Choux-fleurs 60　Haricots verts Français 50　Aubergines farcies 60　Cêpes 60
Haricots verts nouveaux 50　　Artichaut frais 60　　Epinards 50
Piments verts 60　Petits Pois Français 50　Courge blanche nouveaux 50
Tomates de serre farcies 75　Celeri braisé 50　Cardons 40　Patates 30
Asperges nouvelles 80　　Asperges Française 1 25　Asperges Oyster Bay 60
Croquettes de Riz au Marasquin 50

— FROID —

Salade	Laitue et Tomate 60	Tomate de serre 60	Mayonnaise 70
	Céleri Mayonnaise 60	Waldorf 60	Laitue 50
	Romaine 50	Dent-de-lion 40	Concombres de serre 75

Fromage	Pont l'Evêque 30	Port Salut 30	Gorgonzola 30
	Roquefort 30	Camembert 30	Americain 20
	Edam 30　Crême Gervais 25	Gruyère 25　Crême Philadelphie 25	Anglais 25

Fruits	Poires 40	Fraises fraîches 60	Figues 35	Oranges 25
	Bananes 20	Ananas 35	Raisins 75	Pommes 20

Coupole Madison 40　　Eclairs Crême Yvette 25
Gelée Tunisienne 30　Soufflé aux Fraises 50　Flan Macédoine au Riz 25
Gateâux de fraises 50　　Compote de fruits au Marasquin 40
Flan aux Pommes 20　　Chinois au Jus 40　　Confitures de Bar-le-Duc 40
Sorbet Bénédéctine 30　　Mousse à la Vanille 30　　Pouding Duchesse 30
Biscuit Tortoni 30　　Plombières aux Marrons 40　　Tutti Frutti 40
Pouding Nesselrode 40　　Lalla Rookh 40　　Punch Romain 30
Glaces à l'Eau, Orange, Citron et Framboise 25　Glace aux fraises fraîches 25
Café Turc 20　　Demi Tasse 15

The Waldorf　　　　　　　　　　　　　　　　Jeudi le 23 Avril 1896.
☞ Arrangements Speciaux pour des Parties aprés le Théatres.

eliminate foreign entanglements. In 1914, the *Literary Digest* applauded the resolution of Chicago restaurants to abandon the use of French and German in menus. "We at home must take foreign names as they come," the magazine observed, "but already the war has moved us, tho [*sic*] quite in the spirit of neutrality, to alter a few names in our own land. As evidence of this, from Chicago comes news of a change that may sweep like a fury of flame over the whole country, avenging in one instantaneous reversion to common sense an abuse of years' standing. Briefly, it is this: Chicago restaurateurs are deciding to call the dishes they serve by American names instead of German or French."[43]

A few years later, as America prepared to enter the European conflict, New York joined Chicago in the jingoistic call for an end to the French-language menu. The regular meeting of the Manhattan Waiters' Association (held in April 1917) unanimously endorsed a resolution by John Bowman, manager of the Biltmore Hotel, urging restaurants to eliminate foreign-language menus. As might be expected of a waiters' association eager to protect American jobs, the waiters condemned the foreign-language menu because it encouraged the hiring of immigrant waiters, "rendering us more and more dependent on Europeans in conducting the greatest industry in America today." Members of the Waiters' Association, however, also felt that foreign-language menus were hurting their industry at a time when restaurants were eager to attract a middle-class public nervous about wartime inflation and willing to sacrifice luxuries. "The enormous growth in the last ten years of the number of people who . . . are compelled to eat in hotels and restaurants," the waiters observed, required change. Noting—without explanation—that French-language menus had served a purpose in the past, they argued that in recent years the "unintelligible foreign menus have become[,] in many cases, the basic reason for poor service, unsatisfied appetites, and dissatisfied patrons."[44]

By the end of the war, English-language menus at fine-dining restaurants were common. But as French-language menus became rarer, the debate over the language of dining was often shriller. In 1923, a government contract with the Ritz-Carlton to operate a restaurant on the captured German ocean liner *Leviathan* provoked a heated public outburst by Chicago-area congressman Fred A. Britten. Contending that no more than a "portion of the waiters and not 2 per cent of the passengers can read [French menus]," Britten wondered why "we should follow a silly fashion of printing menus in French when Americans are quite generally a one-language people?"[45] Britten won public support with his populist rhetoric. "Let those that will have their quail a la Mirepoix or pate de foi gras," he opined. "Personally I favor baked Virginia ham and sweet potatoes." Yet despite his fervor, Britten's crusade faded from the headlines and no legislative action was taken, at least in part because so many restaurants had already replaced the once ubiquitous French menu with bills of fare that accommodated English-language speakers. The "Ooo la la la a la LaLa" of "cook's French" had already largely disappeared from the American bill of fare.[46]

The Cosmopolitan Menu

As French-language menus disappeared, French culinary preparations also became less common. Menus from the first two decades of the twentieth century showed their creators' willingness to experiment with a variety of cuisines; they increasingly featured American ingredients and preparations as well as Italian, German, and other foreign dishes. French cuisine remained on many upscale restaurant menus, but French food was now viewed as one among many equally worthy culinary choices.

When the Bar Association of the City of Boston met in 1914 at the city's very fashionable Copley Plaza Hotel, the menu was in English and featured an American bouillabaisse, *green turtle and chicken gumbo with tapioca*, as well as more typical French preparations such as *filet of sea bass a l'Ancienne*.[47] Likewise, at a slightly more pretentious dinner for Chicago seedsmen held at the Hotel Sherman in 1912, the menu included an idiosyncratic mix of French and English terms paired with a mix of French and American delicacies. The dinner started with *strained gumbo en tasse* and ended with *roast stuffed jumbo squab on toast*.[48]

Even at fashionable restaurants in New York, evidence of the middle class's influence was apparent in the increasing number of dishes from countries other than France. In 1912, the St. Denis Hotel continued to serve a few French dishes, but the menu used English-language titles liberally, and the chef introduced a variety of continental European dishes. Of the twelve entrées on the December 15 menu, only five employed formal French techniques or sauces (*Flamande, Bordelaise, Polonaise, Parisienne, Bearnaise*), and the daily specials were international. French *bouillabaise a la Marseillaise* was served on Fridays, but *paprika schnitzel with homemade noodles* was available on Mondays, *corned beef and cabbage, Irish style* on Wednesdays, and *Hungarian goulash* on Saturdays.[49] And the St. Denis was not exceptional. One of the premier French restaurants in New York prior to World War I was Louis Bustanoby's Café des Beaux-Arts, described as "a bit of Paris transplanted in the midst of this great Metropolis."[50] A July

1912 dinner menu featured the cold consommés, grouse with truffles, larded tenderloins, and boar's head that one might expect to find in a French restaurant, but while the menu employed French terms liberally, not all of the dishes were French. The menu included a plain, unsauced *leg of lamb* and American-style *Philadelphia chicken*.[51]

These small but significant changes were evidence of a dramatic shift in restaurant dining. Not only were menus increasingly written in English, but French cuisine, the hallmark of aristocratic taste in the nineteenth century, had lost its hegemonic sway.[52] Once restaurateurs discovered middle-class customers' enthusiasm for diverse cuisines, fine dining no longer had to feature only French dishes, and restaurants could experiment with cosmopolitan offerings. Yet there was one factor that prevented restaurants from adopting alternatives to French cuisine in the early twentieth century: the lack of alternatives. Efforts to unseat French cuisine were hindered by the failure of the United States to develop a widely accepted "American" restaurant cuisine.[53]

AMERICAN FOOD

"There seems to be no especial school of American cooking," Fannie C. W. Barber complained to readers of the *Chautauquan* in May 1897, "although we have cook-books innumerable, and there is no end to the cooking lessons given at present, to both rich and poor, all over the country."[54] Others concurred. George Ellwanger observed that despite the emergence of some local favorites, the United States lacked a "high-class" cuisine.

> STRICTLY speaking, there exists as yet no general high-class English or American cuisine, beyond the natural alimentary resources of these countries, supplemented by the efforts of foreign cooks. There are certain native dishes of merit in England, to be sure, and there is a so-termed Southern and Eastern kitchen in the United States where not a few dishes are admirably prepared. But the art of baking bread and of pastry-making, as well as that of frying, is, alas! lacking to a great extent in both countries, while the entree is still largely an uncertain quantity with the housewife.[55]

A widely reprinted 1910 article from the *Chicago Tribune* came to the same conclusion. "The art of cooking in the United States is, relatively speaking, a primitive affair," the newspaper observed. "Compared to French cooking, it is as a string quartet to a full orchestra. It is good at its best, but its range is narrow."[56] A headline in the *Chicago Daily Tribune* simply declared: "Discovered, American Restaurant; Chances Are It's the Only One Alive."[57]

The sorry state of American cuisine marked the failure of a nationalist project that dated to the early years of the Republic.[58] Despite occasional efforts to distinguish American cooking from its British and French antecedents, America—most commentators agreed—had developed no recognized cuisine that was served nationally and acknowledged universally. Particularly frustrating for advocates of an American cuisine was the fact that the nation's culinary providence—game, fish, fowl, and produce—was of unequaled variety and abundance but so far had yielded only regional dishes.[59] Ross Hasbrouck, writing in the *New York Times* in 1909, complained that cooking magazines—*Gourmet* and *Jigot*—"have cast aspersions on American cooking, and have claimed unapproachable superiority for the French kind." In rebuttal, Hasbrouck offered an impressive list of American foods that "make your mouth water": "thick, rare beefsteak, Southern fried chicken, . . . planked shad, Connecticut stewed eel, Maryland terrapin, Virginia ham, Boston brown bread[,] . . . Southern butter beans cooked with pork, scrapple and Philadelphia ice cream."[60] Yet the list—little more than a hodgepodge of celebrated ingredients and favorite local dishes—only confirmed the regional nature of American cooking. New England had a distinctive set of dishes, and so did the South, but the United States, it seemed, lacked a central city comparable to Paris, where regional dishes were transformed and incorporated into a national cuisine. In an essay on cooking rice in *Table Talk* in 1905, Mary E. Parmelee despaired: "Can't the Western woman learn to bake her pot of beans after the Boston method, and the Northerner to boil rice as light and as snowy white as on the plantation?"[61]

Observers offered a host of reasons for America's failure to achieve gustatory greatness. Some held the Puritans and their legacy of joylessness responsible.[62] Others joined the *Chicago Tribune* in claiming that the nation's agricultural abundance "has wrought [culinary] scarcity" by discouraging creative cooking.[63] Many blamed the hustle and bustle of modern commerce. Writing in 1905, Aubrey Fullerton described the "feverish waiting," "hurried order," and "rapid eating" at a typical large urban restaurant and concluded that eating in the United States had become "a mechanical thing and a business."[64] Still others made scapegoats of aristocrats, corporations, restaurants, and housewives. One group of pessimists maintained that it was elites' promotion of French food and French culinary techniques that prevented the emergence of an American cuisine.[65] Another group, the pure food advocates, blamed adulteration for ruining Americans' taste for good food. Temperance advocates, meanwhile, worried that the free lunches offered by saloons dulled the senses and stifled the creativity necessary to create truly American dishes. And anti-suffragists blamed women's colleges since education drew housewives out of their kitchens and stunted the development of domestic resourcefulness.

If there was little agreement about the underlying cause of the culinary crisis, however, there was general consensus among critics about the national tragedy that had ensued. Despite the rich abundance of the nation's farms and stockyards, Americans were content to eat whatever dyspepsia-inducing dishes immigrant cooks and foreign chefs served, and the situation would continue to get worse before it got better. Having failed to develop an appreciation for healthy, well-cooked American foods, young men believed cooking was a lowly pursuit, and few became chefs. "The young American has no love for pots and pans," wrote John Ferguson in 1909. "He seldom dons the cap and apron of a cook; in fact, he rather despises the calling. . . . And this is unfortunate, for who could better understand American likes and dislikes than Americans themselves?"[66]

Nonetheless, some believed that a culinary renaissance was still possible. "The day is not yet, but its dawn is breaking," the New York Times predicted in 1896, "when an American dinner will be recognized as the best on earth."[67] This optimism inspired advocates of a national cuisine to engage in a frantic effort to describe, catalog, and publicize America's elusive regional culinary accomplishments in the hope that they might assemble them into a recognizable national cuisine. As early as 1885, Juliet Corson of the New York Cooking School joined with John Eaton, the United States Commissioner of Education, to solicit recipes from across the United States in order to correct for the "fact that the cookery of Europe, and especially of France, enter[ed] so largely into the author's scheme of teaching, and of constructing her books already published."[68] Corson's new cookbook, a mix of French and regional American preparations, did not end the clamor for a national cuisine, and other efforts to discover and celebrate American cooking soon followed.

In the early twentieth century, American culinary magazines regularly featured articles on regional dishes. The Boston Cooking School, exercising its considerable influence as the most prolific institute for training domestic economy instructors, did its best to suggest that baked beans and brown bread, New England favorites, might serve as the basis for the national cuisine.[69] But much like other nationalist projects initiated at the turn of the century (including the search for the Great American novel and attempts to develop a single, distinctive style of American painting), movements to win public recognition of a national cuisine foundered. Reflecting the growing desperation among advocates of American cooking, editors of *The Steward* called for federal authorities to conduct a "census of distinctive American dishes" in 1909, and a decade later Charles J. Rosebault, the *New York Times*' most prominent food writer, facetiously claimed he was forming a "Society for the Exposition, Development and Glorification of American Cookery" to raise awareness about Americans' contributions to dining.[70]

Despite the lack of consensus on what constituted "American cuisine," some aristocratic restaurants took notice of the culinary nationalism of their middle-class customers. Beginning in the early twentieth century, they experimented with distinctly American dishes, including regional favorites. A few respectable establishments, such as the dining room at the Cosmopolitan Hotel, even made an extra effort to highlight American ingredients and preparations. Although the January 15, 1905, menu at the Cosmopolitan included *Turkey Livers en Brouchette on Toast* and *Sweetbread Cutlets [with] Sauce Périgueux*, the hotel also served a *Half Fried Spring Chicken, Maryland*, a *Roast Half Philadelphia Spring Chicken*, a *Roast Half Long Island Duckling [with] Apple Sauce*, and a *Roast Yarmouth Turkey [with] Cranberry Sauce*.[71] The New Grand Hotel in New York likewise offered a curious mix of entrées on its June 14, 1905, menu, including *Fresh mushrooms sans cloche*; *Calf's head a la Poulette*; *Cromesquis of crab flakes a la Manhattan*; *Croustade of terrapin, Baltimore style*; and *Fried spring chicken with corn fritters and bacon, half*.[72] It was in this spirit that George C. Howe, the proprietor of New York's Hotel Lorraine, made sure his "French pastry chef [was] taught how to make all kinds of New England pastry, including our national apple pie."[73]

While many old-guard establishments were reluctant to embrace the middle-class diner's demand for a more patriotic menu, competition from independent restaurants and simple, respectable tearooms (featuring home-style cooking) created a ripple of concern among the chefs and managers at aristocratic restaurants. In an unprecedented act, the Société Culinaire Philanthropique, the nation's oldest and most prestigious culinary association and steadfast defender of French cuisine, surrendered to popular protests and launched a well-publicized contest to nominate an "all-American" restaurant menu in 1923. The "All-American Restaurant Competition" invited housewives to submit "dishes the names of which are in everyday English and adaptable to hotels and restaurants. Soup, relish, entrée, fish, meat, salad and dessert are to be included."[74] American cooking did not always win the praise that French cuisine did, but it would nonetheless become an increasingly important part of the menus of fine dining establishments.

FOREIGN FOOD

Even as some of the most staid restaurants continued to struggle to accommodate demands for American dishes, they began to offer dishes that showcased the international culinary diversity of America's more cosmopolitan cities. Cosmopolitan menus at upper-class restaurants had been unthinkable in the nineteenth century. Restaurant menus rarely included foreign dishes, and the few dishes with an international flavor that made an appearance were prepared according to French tradition and given French names. The Arlington Hotel's menu on May 10, 1871, for example, included *Macaroni a la Milanaise, Fromage de Parmesan*, a staple dish on many French menus consisting of boiled pasta with grated cheese and butter. But while *Macaroni a la Milanaise* (and its many linguistic variants) was a tribute to the Italian influence on French cooking, French chefs prepared it as a French dish following French recipes. Likewise, the *Kuri des Volailles, a l'Indienne* that appeared on the Arlington's menu referred to a French poultry dish incorporating curry powder and not to an authentic dish from the Indian subcontinent.[75]

The failed efforts to enshrine a national cuisine seemed to encourage beleaguered aristocratic restaurateurs to offer ethnic dishes in a bid to bolster their reputations with the middle class. Middle-class diners had embraced international cuisines with patriotic fervor at the turn of the century. Italian restaurants, German beer gardens, and Chinese chop suey houses were all widely patronized, and many viewed America's embrace of cosmopolitan cuisine as evidence that the United States was one of the great culinary nations of the world. Henry T. Finck, a Harvard-trained psychologist and one of America's more prolific food writers, argued half seriously in a 1911 article in *The Century* magazine that "the [German] Kaiserschmarren and the Apfelstrudel ought to be made national American dishes by special act of Congress."[76]

In the twentieth century, international dishes, while still only a small part of the offerings of most restaurants, began to appear on the menus of non-ethnic restaurants with some regularity—including at some of the most firmly entrenched aristocratic institutions. In 1905, the Hotel Astor had a French-language menu and served only French preparations. By 1927, however, the menu, with the exception of a few "à las," was written entirely in English, and the "Carte du Jour" featured two "créole" preparations, a *Manhattan Clam Chowder*, and an eclectic mix of entrées that included *Wiener Schnitzel with noodles* and *Sicilian Spaghetti with Tunnyfish*.[77] In fact, the demand for cosmopolitan menus was great enough that even some decidedly French restaurants experimented with a more assorted mix of dishes. The Fifth Avenue Restaurant in New York described itself as "Le Restaurant Français par Excellence" in 1912, and at night the restaurant was indeed the formal French establishment its advertising promised.[78] During the day, however, the Fifth Avenue Restaurant offered a broad variety of dishes drawn from French, American, and international cuisines. On the restaurant's noontime menu, predominantly written in English, *sausage with wine sauce and mashed potatoes* and *deviled beef bones and chips* complemented dishes dressed with specifically French sauces such as *quail in casserole Liegeoise*. Lunch was when the middle-class businessperson, briefly released from work, joined the midday shopper looking for a meal, and the Fifth Avenue's more cosmopolitan offerings were apparently an effort to attract this noontime patronage. French cuisine and French sauces still appeared on the menu, but the menu was not decisively French.[79]

The transformation of spaghetti from a "French" side dish to an Italian entrée tells the tale of the evolution of cosmopolitan cuisine and elite dining. In the nineteenth century, American restaurants most often served *macaroni à l'Italienne*, a French version of the Italian pasta dish, usually with a Gallic brown or white sauce. Although it only infrequently appeared on American menus, when it did, it was the first and smallest course (the sauced entrée) in the series of courses that made up the substantive portion of a dinner in Franco-American service. Over time, however, as the middle-class cosmopolitan diner ventured into finer restaurants, the ways in which spaghetti was prepared and its place on the menu shifted. By the turn of the century, the dish had been rechristened *Spaghetti l'Italienne* (suggesting a growing American familiarity with Italian pasta styles), was more often found on elite restaurant menus than in the past, and was served with a southern Italian tomato sauce. It was now considered a side dish and was usually listed on à la carte menus as a vegetable.[80] A decade later, the dish returned to the list of main courses but this time as an unambiguously cosmopolitan dish. In imitation of how Italian restaurants in the United States routinely served spaghetti, *italian spaghetti with tomato sauce* (sometimes with the reassurance that the dish was "real native Italian style") often appeared on American menus as a main course.[81] Diners now regarded spaghetti (and occasionally other pastas) as Italian and as a meal, and restaurateurs embraced these new attitudes. Italian cuisine was so well established by the second decade of the twentieth century that at least one upper-class establishment completely overhauled its menu. In

1912, the fashionable restaurant at the Hotel La Salle in Chicago "[left] the French cuisine era" and reinvented itself as an Italian restaurant. "I don't know if the guests notice the change," Frank Cucco, the new Italian chef stated, "but everybody seems pleased. They should be, for I am a culinary artist and know how to please the stomach."[82]

German dishes and other international cuisines were also becoming more common on upscale menus at the turn of the century. In 1905, patrons of the respectable restaurant at the New Grand Hotel in New York were offered a sidebar menu attached to the standard French-styled supper menu. The sidebar featured a long list of "Our German Specialties." Three years later, the Hotel Majestic, another respectable New York hotel and restaurant, offered its patrons a menu that included "Viennese specialties."[83] Restaurants in other cities were also beginning to offer German dishes in addition to more traditional French and American preparations. On April 13, 1913, for example, the daily specials at the New Washington Hotel in Seattle included wiener schnitzel.[84] These cosmopolitan offerings were necessary if upscale restaurants that had once served only French cuisine were to compete with fashionable establishments that specialized in German, Austrian, and Hungarian cuisine like New York's HofBräu Haus, Café Boulevard, and Lüchow's.[85]

More exotic foreign cuisines were rarer, but they also occasionally appeared on restaurant menus in the first two decades of the twentieth century. While it is not surprising that the middle-class Levy's Restaurant in Los Angeles, reflecting local familiarity with Hispanic cuisine, featured *Chicken Tamales* for twenty cents a serving, Mexican food was also winning a national following at the turn of the century and began to appear on the menus of upper-class establishments.[86] In 1895, the Christmas menu for the Windsor in New York City—an upper-class hotel restaurant whose 1870s menus were decidedly French—featured *Fried Bananas, Mexican Style*. In 1912, at the Gunter Hotel in San Antonio, advertising executives hosted by the *San Antonio Express* dined on a "purely Mexican dinner, cooked by Mexican people, [and] served by Mexicans" while they were "entertained . . . by a Mexican orchestra and Mexican entertainers whom the Express had procured from a local Mexican theater."[87] A few years later, three men, none Hispanic, opened a "first class Mexican Restaurant" in Detroit.[88]

Likewise, elite restaurants occasionally served Chinese cuisine. The Capital City Club in Atlanta held a Chinese dinner for five hundred on its roof garden in 1915, and the Hotel Seminole in Jacksonville sponsored an "oriental evening" featuring *hop ho gai din* and *mushi kugira* in 1916.[89] The

Pekin, a white-owned Chinese restaurant that marketed itself as an upper-class establishment, opened in New York in 1915, and the Hotel McAlpin, one of New York's largest and most respected hotels, went so far as to convert its tearoom into a Chinese restaurant in 1919.[90]

Increasingly, creative restaurateurs drew inspiration from across the globe. In Chicago in 1913, patrons of the Hotel LaSalle could dine in a re-creation of a "gypsy camp" ("with chickens roosting in the trees") and order from a themed menu, while those who visited the Grand Pacific could choose their repast from a menu titled "Bohemian dinners of all nations," featuring a dish from a different country every night of the week.[91] Citing the "international culinary triumphs" and "cosmopolitan taste[s]" that regularly appeared on American menus late in the second decade of the twentieth century (including "goulas [sic], the schnitzel, the bortsch [sic], caviar, spaghettis, olla podrida, bouillabaisse, haggis, hasenpfeffers and our Irish stew"), the chef at the Hotel Gotham, Xenophon Kuzmier, predicted that America would soon develop a new "international conglomerate" cuisine that combined the best of every culture.[92] But perhaps the most vivid demonstration of the growing popularity of foreign dishes in upper-class restaurants was an advertisement by the manufacturer of a tonic for the "bilious, malarious [sic], and persons with weak kidneys." Hostetter's Stomach Bitters advertised in 1898 that "[whether] the engrafting of French and German dishes upon the bills of fare of the better class of American restaurants is or is not an improvement," Hostetter's would cure the resulting dyspepsia.[93]

Restaurants eager to capitalize on the growing interest in foreign cuisine also employed foreign culture as a means of establishing an exotic atmosphere in their dining rooms. When the luxurious, aristocratic Hotel Astor in Times Square opened in 1904, the new hotel featured a Spanish lounging room, a Chinese tearoom, and (inexplicably) an "Indian rathskeller."[94] The Savery Hotel in Des Moines, Iowa, boasted a Chinese Tea Room, an Italian Room, and a French Patisserie when it opened in 1919.[95] Likewise, the Hotel Seville in New York offered guests the opportunity to visit its Spanish Café, the "Bodega," decorated with glazed Spanish tiles, dark oak furniture, and red, stamped leather ceilings.[96] Themed dining rooms did not necessarily indicate that the establishment had embraced international culinary fare, but it did signal growing interest in the exoticism of foreign cultures. In 1915, the Homestead Restaurant in the upper-class vacation community of Hot Springs, Virginia, served a diet menu typical for a spa but advertised that a "Colored Cabaret" performed every night in the Japanese Room from 10:00 to 11:30 P.M.[97] Similarly, the famous

"Italian Garden" at the St. Charles Hotel in New Orleans—a vine-covered Romanesque lounge described as a "dream in hotel architecture"—did not mean the dining room had abandoned its New Orleanian French menu.[98]

Exotic restaurant atmospheres appealed to cosmopolitan sensibilities, and middle-class urbanites regularly dined in restaurants featuring Roman gardens or Spanish tiles. In 1904, Rupert Hughes commented on the role that internationally themed restaurants played in the daily life of middle-class New Yorkers.

> Some astute New York caterer found that, while few people will go to a basement restaurant, great crowds will throng to the same place if it is called a rathskeller, and furnished in a pseudo-German style. The rathskeller, which, as you know, means "council-cellar," is well named, being the favorite resort for those who are most in need of good advice. In the spume of beer, the broth of society finds its counterpart. Here the chorus girl and the woman-about-town meet the sporting salesman and the roué who is a shoe clerk by day. Gradually the more discreet code of foot-flirtation leads to the open holding of hands, and finally to embraces and bibulous love-making.[99]

Even the music played at these fashionable restaurants catering to middle-class patrons added to the construction of an ethnic pastiche. "Here, in an uptown place," an article in the *New York Times* observed, "you find Irish waiters serving German beer to American diners-out, while a polyglot orchestra, dressed in Spanish costume, plays negro ragtime, or wants to know in voices that rise above the sound of their instruments has anybody here seen Kelly, which, you may be sure, they haven't, as it is a Teutonic assemblage."[100]

Admiration of foreign cultures was not a uniquely middle-class trait. In imitation of European aristocrats, American elites in the late nineteenth century purchased "oriental" art, bric-a-brac, and clothing. Upper-class restaurants and hotels covered their floors with imported Persian rugs and decorated their interiors with Chinese vases and Japanese silk screens. The cover art of upper-class restaurant menus often evoked Asian, mythical, and vaguely international pastoral themes.[101] Wealthy Americans, however, did not seek to experience foreign cultures as they were lived. Instead, as an act of conspicuous consumption, they amassed symbols of elegance, luxury, and sophistication that had served as evidence of privilege in faraway places. In this, they looked to and imitated Europe.[102] Elite Americans bought kimonos and went to fancy balls dressed as Cleopatra because that was the fashion in Paris and London, where appropriating the luxuries of the East bolstered the aristocracy's sense that they were part of a timeless tradition of refinement. Notably, these appropriations did not extend to the food served. There was no reason. Just as the Persians made the best rugs and the Chinese the most prized porcelain, the French had mastered cookery. In the aristocratic restaurant, decor and design might invoke world cultures, but the dinner itself remained tenaciously French.

At the turn of the century, America's growing presence in the global economy, the invocation of the primitive "other" at the World's Columbian Exposition of 1893, journalistic forays into burgeoning immigrant neighborhoods, and the imperialism of the Spanish-American War created an increased awareness of foreign cultures at home and abroad. Depictions of the exotic flourished in commercial culture, and middle-class Americans purchased mass-marketed clothing, prints, and home decor from distant lands.[103] These middle-class ventures into the "consumers' imperium" (as Kristin L. Hoganson has aptly named it) served as antidotes to the ennui of the modern urban experience, as collecting Turkish and Asian antiquities had for the elites.[104] "The Orient provided metaphors and models for greater sensuality and liberated passions," art historian Holly Edwards has written, "relaxing enforcement of strict propriety."[105]

Middle-class consumers, however, experienced these invocations of the exotic differently from their elite counterparts. The ubiquity of exotic images in advertisements for electric lights and cigars robbed these symbols of some of their power to invoke luxury.[106] Moreover, middle-class diners' previous experiences with immigrant and foreign cultures colored their encounters with international cuisine. Cosmopolitan diners, some not more than one generation removed from their Irish, German, or Italian forebears, often experienced ethnic food for the first time at home or in the little basement restaurants of ethnic enclaves.[107] While these previous encounters did not render the middle-class cosmopolitans immune to the romanticism of the exotic—especially to the naive belief that culinary adventurism could lead to a meaningful understanding of strange new cultures—their prior experiences invariably shaped their understanding of the exotic.[108] Middle-class cosmopolitanism was not orientalism, even if some of the emotional responses it invoked were the same. It had its roots in trips to Chinatown to tour the joss house, in traveling lecture series about far-away places, and in trips to German, Italian, and Chinese restaurants in ethnic enclaves. And while cosmopolitanism did not guarantee racial tolerance toward foreign or immigrant populations, it did invest America's culinary diversity with nationalistic pride. For many in the United States, enthusiasm for international cuisines was less about how the United States viewed "less civilized" or poorer societies and more about how America was perceived abroad. Cosmopolitans celebrated culinary diversity as evidence that America's largest cities ranked among the great cities of the world.

When Italian, German, and Chinese food eventually appeared on the menus of elite restaurants and German and Hungarian restaurants joined the pantheon of respectable aristocratic establishments in restaurant guides, it marked a triumph of the middle-class cosmopolitan sensibility. But for restaurateurs, culinary diversity was about money. They embraced exotic cuisines because cosmopolitan and American offerings attracted a larger clientele and gave their restaurants a competitive advantage. In 1911, the editors of *The Steward* warned restaurateurs that to be profitable in future years, they would have to provide variety:

> Notwithstanding the fact that almost every nationality on the face of the earth finds representation to a greater or less extent in the metropolis of [New York], it is amazing after all what an element of sameness there is in the cuisine of those places which are mostly in the lime-light. This may not be much of a factor in a solution of this question [of profits] which most people seem to think is supply in excess of demand, but nevertheless on the principle that "variety is the spice of life" it might be well to consider if the present number of high-class restaurants could not be made profitable by striking differenciation [sic] and the adoption of distinct features, for instance, as have made Luchow's a place of international renown for German food and cooking. . . . The opportunity seems to be equally good for any kind of distinctive dish and service.[109]

For *The Steward*, a New York-based journal for restaurant professionals, culinary diversity—be it orientalism or cosmopolitanism—simply made good business sense in the new, middle-class-dominated marketplace. The elite restaurant could adapt its menu to the middle-class taste for international foods and decorate with faux grape vines and Greek columns without necessarily driving away the wealthy aristocrats, since foreign cultures enchanted both the middle and upper classes.

Prior to the 1920s, restaurant menus were not multicultural, but in their slow and quiet embrace of American dishes and international cuisines, they signaled that the era of the French-only restaurant had come to an end. French cuisine had been both a symbol and a vehicle of elite culture in the nineteenth century, not only reflecting the upper class's admiration of European aristocracy but also displaying the elite's cultural power. When restaurants acknowledged that excellence could come in more than one flavor, they accepted cosmopolitanism and recognized the influence of the middle class in the consumer economy.

At the turn of the century, French chefs were still men of prestige to be admired and indulged. When Adrein Tenu, the Paris-born chef at the Waldorf-Astoria, died unexpectedly in 1901, the front page of the *New York Times* described the former private chef of railroad magnate Jay Gould as an "artist."[110] By the 1920s, these tributes were rare. The devaluing of French cuisine, and with it the elite aristocracy's loss of cultural authority in the culinary marketplace, was dramatically illustrated by a story that appeared under the heading "Foreign News" in *Time* magazine in July 1926. The article opened by belittling the French culinary tradition with the snide claim that "[i]n France, *and perhaps in France alone*, the traditions of la haute cuisine survive from the days of the great gastronomes."[111] The article closed by recounting the strange tale of Parisian chef Berthelin. Berthelin, "one of the greatest of French chefs," had been brought before the Paris Court of Assize after he killed his dishwasher, Davillard, for disparaging his sauces. The story seemed absurd, but it was made all the more ridiculous by the inclusion of a long quote from Chef Berthelin:

> This creature . . . what did he do that I should stab him in the chest with my carving skewer? Ha! Nom de Dieu! Standing at his filthy sink, he declared that my sauces stink, that they engender colic in delicate stomachs. My sauces! Sacre bleu! The pride of my cuisine. The pride of France. . . . Mes amis, the sensibilities, the temperament of a great chef cannot be thus baited with impunity! Blood swam before my eyes. . . . I skewered him it is true. . . . But it was to avenge my art, my sauces, my honor![112]

Following this impassioned speech, according to *Time*, "the court, overcome, sentenced . . . chef Berthelin to but one year in jail."

The news item was probably fabricated.[113] But the offhanded dismissal of French cuisine and the bizarre story that followed were telling not only because the melodramatic tale illustrated the degree to which French chefs were no longer admired but also because the article marked the first time (according to the *Oxford English Dictionary*) that "haute cuisine" was used as an English-language loanword.[114] No longer synonymous with fine dining, French cuisine was now merely one foreign cuisine among many, and as such it required its own designation. Yet, while the term allowed French food to retain its distinction as "high" (haute) culture, its first use in English was draped in mockery.[115]

Catering to the Classes

Delmonico's shuttered its doors in 1923. While the deleterious effect of World War I on the lucrative business of banquets and balls and the passage of national Prohibition in 1919 are often cited as leading factors in Delmonico's decline, there are compelling reasons to believe that the great aristocratic restaurant was eclipsed by the rise of the middle class. Delmonico's went into receivership in 1917, well before the United States experienced the full impact of the war in Europe and years before the constitutional amendment banning alcohol went into effect.[116] The Delmonico family's chief chronicler, Lately Thomas, concluded that while "prohibition, the deterioration of dining habits, upward spiraling costs, a hurried, oblivious generation, the breakup of social distinctions, the disintegration of society as it had once flourished," and "internal decay" had led to Delmonico's closing, it was the "enormous expansion of the city and the changing customs" that had finally "outmoded" Delmonico's.[117] Thomas did not identify the source of this change, but the fall of Delmonico's coincided with the rise of the middle-class cosmopolitan consumer.

The reasons behind the decline of the French aristocratic restaurant were both economic and cultural. French cuisine had bolstered the status of elites, and, in turn, elites had celebrated French cuisine. But in the economically competitive dining climate of the early twentieth century, the patronage of elites was not enough to keep an aristocratic restaurant open. New ideas about what constituted good food made French cuisine seem dated, and elite restaurants found it increasingly hard to justify the aristocratic standards they once celebrated. The turn-of-the-century challenge to French-language menus, the introduction of American and international dishes at fine dining establishments, and the growing importance of middle-class consumers undermined the cultural legitimacy and economic viability of aristocratic culinary culture.

Cosmopolitanism was not merely the substitution of one dish for another or of one language for another but a shift in how cultural experiences were valued. Cosmopolitan diners did not always have the money to dine out at the best restaurants night after night, but they had the expertise necessary to enjoy a good meal at a nice restaurant when their budgets allowed. They had visited Chinatown and spoke knowingly about Hungarian dining customs. They were not reluctant to try new, exotic foods, even if they had to hold their noses to get down the first bite. They did not endorse a restaurant simply because others viewed it as good but rather visited it themselves and made their own judgment. They had discriminating tastes and preferred the German food at the HofBräu Haus to that at the Flat Iron Restaurant, but while their preferences were personal, they were not arbitrary, and they did not shy away from debating the relative merits of various restaurants and cuisines.[118] Cosmopolitanism was a rejection of hidebound tradition and the embrace of the experiential.

Not everyone could participate in the new cosmopolitan culture. While the ecumenical nature of cosmopolitan dining made it more accessible than the aristocratic restaurant, not everyone had the resources or wherewithal to become a cosmopolitan. The worldliness of the cosmopolitan ethos was a luxury of time, money, and education, and the middle class, much more than the working class, had access to these luxuries. Moreover, formal as well as cultural barriers to fine dining remained. The best restaurants were still expensive, and while they often simplified their dress codes, they did not eliminate them. Thus the cosmopolitan restaurant, although open to all, remained uniquely, if not exclusively, middle class. A good meal at one of the better of these restaurants communicated status, only now the fine-dining restaurant served to distinguish the new middle class from both the upper class and the working class.

As small, shared preferences structured the consumer market around ideas like cosmopolitanism and these aspirations were recognized and even celebrated, class happened. Cosmopolitanism made it possible for the middle class, to paraphrase E. P. Thompson, to feel and articulate an identity of interests that stood in opposition to the aristocratic ideals of the nineteenth century.[119] Slowly, members of the professional and managerial occupations as well as shopkeepers, clerks, and schoolteachers came to identify with each other and, even if they never actually visited a Hungarian wine cellar, vicariously embraced a shared view of life.

The decline of the aristocratic restaurant did not go uncontested. Viewing themselves not only as purveyors of food but also as guardians of a legacy, some restaurateurs—in the face of falling profits—resisted change. Culinary industry spokesmen such as Adolphe Meyer of the International Mutual Cooks and Pastry Cooks Association of New York urged "high-class restaurants" not to abandon their aristocratic fare despite World War I shortages and wartime conservation programs. "The less expensive foods should be left to the poorer classes," Meyer wrote in 1918, "and those blessed with a swelled pocketbook can best serve their country by eating the more costly foods or table luxuries."[120] Some restaurants took heed.

The Plaza, the St. Charles, and many elite establishments in New York and throughout the country continued to serve French dishes with French titles—particularly on special occasions like New Year's Day.[121] But in the larger culinary marketplace, the elaborate French menu was no longer the exclusive mark of civility. Restaurants experimented with American and international dishes, and French cuisine came to be seen as just one of dozens of cosmopolitan cuisines forced to compete for space on the upper-class restaurant's menu.

Restaurateurs who tenaciously preserved the aristocratic tradition did so at the peril of the institutions they guarded. Not every aristocratic restaurant that resisted change suffered the same fate as Delmonico's, but many lost customers and suffered financially.[122] By the late 1930s, having survived both Prohibition and the Great Depression, the last of the aristocratic restaurateurs gathered in New York for an extraordinary "culinary congress." The 1939 meeting was called to address dwindling sales and what a columnist for the *Washington Post* described as the "halt-who-goes-there?" atmosphere in many elite dining rooms. Speaking to members of the congress assembled at the hotel he managed, the Waldorf-Astoria's president, Lucius Boomer, urged immediate action to lure back "the vanquished throngs" who had abandoned the aristocratic restaurant. Endorsing what the middle class had been demanding for more than fifty years, Boomer called for simplifying the menu and adopting the plate dinner. "The vogue for the selective meal [plate dinner], which is growing very rapidly, has much merit," he conceded. "It started outside hotels, has largely killed a la carte in hotel restaurants, and hotels have been forced to follow suit. It meets the economic necessities of the patron. It makes variety possible at popular prices."[123]

The audience applauded Boomer's suggested reforms warmly, but for many of the restaurant owners, managers, and chefs who gathered in New York, Boomer had not gone far enough. Some restaurateurs had already broadened their menus to include American and international dishes, and many others were prepared to adopt simplified service, but as a last testament to the aristocratic past, many continued to describe their dishes in French. The Philadelphia contingent, headed by William Sprinzing of the International Cooks Association, called for more extensive reforms than Boomer had endorsed, including menus that were not only smaller but also "printed in English." In the report that accompanied his proposal, Sprinzing blamed the "many fancy names" used on menus as "perhaps one of the main causes for the inappreciation [sic] of fine cuisine by the American public."[124] But it was a newspaper columnist covering the congress, H. I. Phillips, who best recognized the difficulties that the aristocratic restaurant faced. "Not so many years ago the hotel restaurants were the right places to dine. That was in the era when dining out was quite a lark anyhow and before so many small restaurants and lunch rooms blossomed on the streets of any city that it became quite an adventure to eat at home," Phillips wrote. But in recent years, the "small restaurant [had] swept the country," providing "the hungry man plenty of meat and potato at cut rates and in simple English."

> The hotel restaurant men should have staged a counter-attack by the mere process of making it less involved to eat with them. But they stuck to the table d'hôte which made $1.80 the bottom rate for a midget dinner, clung to the French language and continued to regard rolls and butter as extra equipment. They have been slow to realize that nothing drives the trade away like the association of a square meal with a Federal loan.

Phillips concluded that the expensive hotel restaurant, unwilling or unable to change, was on its "last frog legs."[125]

"Each one to his taste and according to his bank account," *The Steward* acknowledged in 1920.[126] English-language menus demystified ordering, and American and international dishes made public dining more accessible. While that did not necessarily mean fine-dining restaurants were democratic public spaces open to all, it did indicate that by the early twentieth century, a leveling had taken place that allowed the middle-class cosmopolitan to exercise his or her own cultural capital, a new standard of taste that was open to diverse culinary experiences. As a result, in the twentieth century, more Americans than at any previous time in the nation's history would be able to muster the knowledge and financial resources necessary to dine out. Restaurants, even the best restaurants, were no longer exclusive fraternities, and the middle class was no longer a pale imitation of the elite.

INDIFFERENT GULLETS

The Middle Class and the Cosmopolitan Restaurant

Charles J. Rosebault, a former assistant city editor at the *New York Sun*, occasionally wrote about restaurants for the *New York Times*. In "The Lost Tribe of New York," published in 1921, Rosebault lamented the death of epicureanism. "Nothing is so conducive to dulling the initiative of your real chef as evidence that those for whom he expends his efforts have no discrimination," Rosebault grieved. "Why prepare a soigné repast for barbarians? Can there be a greater grief for a thorough gastronome than to see a masterpiece of his art disappeared in an indifferent gullet? What is there to hope for from a people who demand jazz with dinner?"[1] For Rosebault, the decline of the aristocratic restaurant—and the retreat of the aristocratic class from the public sphere—guaranteed mediocrity. Fondly recalling the 1890s when "every fourth man in our best clubs was a valiant defender of the canons of food taste, and stood firmly for principles which today are not even understood," Rosebault was contemptuous of the culinary changes that cosmopolitanism had wrought. In less than forty years, the dining culture of the nation's culinary capital, New York, had undergone a startling transformation that reverberated through the nation. French cuisine, once the unquestioned hallmark of culinary excellence, no longer set the tone for American dining, and debates over the relative merits of saucing terrapin had given way to arguments over whether to eat Chinese or Italian.

In the following decades, other melancholy old men would echo Rosebault's wistful recollections of the golden age of dining.[2] And yet the cosmopolitan restaurant was increasingly a fact of life. More and more Americans were eating out, and as they experimented with an ever-expanding variety of cuisines, they embraced a new standard of taste—more diverse and complex, more personal and idiosyncratic, than the old aristocratic code that held that everything French was good and everything else was not. By the end of World War I, restaurants that had once catered exclusively to the upper class were trying out plate dinners, banishing French words from the menu, and hiring Chinese chefs. They rescinded policies that kept middle-class women from dining alone and even occasionally offered tipless service. The aristocratic restaurant had succumbed to the cosmopolitan, and the middle class now set the nation's table.

Restaurant Reviews

The turn-of-the-century revolution in dining was, more broadly, a revolution in consumerism. Not only had the marketplace expanded to include more, and more diverse, consumers, but the old conventions of taste and etiquette had been undermined and new standards were emerging. French cuisine had been such a certain marker of excellence that the upper class had, in considerable part, staked their claim to aristocracy upon the art of dining. Now the rules were less clear. Bohemian epicures insisted that the best Italian food could be found in little places with checkered tablecloths, but why should their idiosyncratic preferences be trusted? For cosmopolitanism to have meaning, its loose and inclusive standards had to be recognizable and transferable.

Even for those who benefited from the new era in public dining, the dramatic changes that restaurants underwent were disconcerting. There was no cosmopolitan Delmonico's, no restaurant that set culinary benchmarks. Cosmopolitanism replaced the singularity of aristocratic French meals with a hodgepodge of restaurants, competing models of service, and a diversity of cuisines.[3] Americans were not "indifferent," as Rosebault claimed, but many were perplexed by the multitude of choices that the new consumer culture offered. The author of an early restaurant guide recalled that acquaintances provided "friendly remonstrance" when he first proposed the idea of codifying dining in New York. "'How can it be done?' they asked. 'We are in such a state of flux, not to say chaos.'"[4]

The "state of flux" was inherent in the middle-class envisioning of the cosmopolitan restaurant. In a study of gourmet food magazines that were published in 2004, Josée Johnston and Shyon Baumann observed that "omnivorousness" (or cosmopolitanism) is a constant negotiation of a "fundamental ideological tension between democracy and distinction."[5] Cosmopolitanism celebrated democracy. It championed culinary cultures—American and ethnic cuisines—that had not been "sacralized" (as Lawrence Levine described high culture) by association with Europe, myth, and tradition. Eliminating French-language menus, ending character judgments about which customers were "ladies" and which were not, and banishing the multicourse meal made restaurant dining more accessible. Yet for cosmopolitanism to bind potential members of the middle class to each other, it also needed to be able to draw distinctions between middle-class dining and both the upper- and working-class culinary cultures.

Small, individual consumer choices brought middle-class urbanites together, and as they discovered themselves in the culinary (and broader consumer) marketplace, those choices became a part of what it meant to be middle class. A central part of this identity was cosmopolitanism, "a measure of the breadth of taste and cultural consumption."[6] Cosmopolitanism was not only democratic and individualistic but also the middle class's claim to a distinctive class identity. But as more diners from all walks of life dined at restaurants that were cosmopolitan and embraced the new culinary standard, the middle-class diner's claim to distinctiveness, and cultural power, was threatened.

This hazard to the middle class's growing influence over dining culture was mitigated by the emergence of restaurant reviewing. Employing the tools of the Progressive middle class—expertise and investigative journalism—restaurant reviewing was a search for order and distinctiveness that would not undermine the democratization of restaurant dining. "Reading and evaluating," Priscilla Parkhurst Ferguson writes, "like eating and cooking, are so many 'taste acts' by which individuals 'perform' their connections to a taste community."[7] The restaurant review could not sanctify a cuisine the way that the mythic origins of French cooking had sanctified the aristocratic restaurant, but reviews could provide ephemeral snapshots of trends, sustaining distinction not as a timeless and unquestioned standard but as a specific and immediate recommendation about where a middle-class diner might like to eat. Reviews helped demarcate the boundaries of the middle-class cosmopolitan's taste community. Yet reviews, influential as they sometimes were, did not exclude. Reviews were widely accessible and personal, and despite some pretention, the information they conveyed was never as daunting as the long lists of French terms aristocratic guides had offered novice diners. Reviews made middle-class cosmopolitanism available to those with a minimum of cultural literacy while still validating those who through their extra investment in the new dining experiences saw themselves as part of the middle class.

In the nineteenth century, little guidance was available to diners in search of a place to eat. Word of mouth and the occasional advertisement in a newspaper or city directory might steer the traveler to a decent restaurant, but the hegemony of French cuisine did not encourage discussions about taste, and the choice of where to eat was more often about the size of one's purse than the quality of the food. At the top of the culinary hierarchy in most large cities was a hotel with a French chef. If diners had the money, the cultural knowledge, and the time, they chose the restaurant with the French menu. If they did not, there was a clutter of restaurants at the bottom of the scale that served the masses.

Appleton's Hand-book of American Travel: Northern and Eastern Tour, published in 1876, offered readers a directory of nondescript restaurants in various American cities. Insisting that New York was "filled with restaurants, and the ordinary traveler requires no guide to find them; for wherever he may turn, a short walk will bring him to one," the guidebook provided few aids for the hungry traveler. No attempt was made to include comprehensive listings, no attention was paid to the quality of the dinner served at the few restaurants mentioned, no information was offered for those looking for ethnic cuisine, and no prices, hours, or dress codes were mentioned. The New York guide listed only fifteen restaurants (including all four Delmonico establishments) in no apparent order. The only detail that was offered with any regularity was information on whether the restaurant catered to respectable women:

> In the Astor House is a fine restaurant.
>
> Bigot, 42 Fourteenth Street, between Fifth Avenue and Broadway, keeps a ladies' restaurant, which is quiet and respectable.
>
> Iaunch keeps a well-known and popular place at 804 Broadway, a short distance above Union Square.
>
> Delmonico's, in Fifth Avenue, corner of Fourteenth street, is the largest and most elegantly-appointed restaurant in New York.
>
> The Café Brunswick, at the corner of Fifth Ave. and Twenty-sixth Street, is sumptuously appointed and admirably kept.
>
> E. Solari's, in University Place, corner of Eleventh Street, is noted for its dinners and suppers.
>
> "Overton & Blair's," Tenth Street, near Broadway, is among the cheap and popular eating-houses for both sexes.[8]

Lippincott's General Guide to the United States and Canada, issued the same year as *Appleton's* (each an attempt to capitalize on the increased tourism expected for the Centennial celebration in Philadelphia), provided even less information, and both were typical of the era.[9] At the turn of the century, Karl Baedeker's guides offered insight into American eating habits for foreign visitors to the United States but provided no specific suggestions on where to secure a meal. "In New York and other large cities the traveler will find many excellent restaurants," the 1909 Baedeker guide observed, "but in other places he will do well to take his meals at his hotel or boarding-house. . . . Soup, fish, poultry, game, and sweet dishes are generally good; but beef and mutton are often inferior to those of England." The most helpful observation the Baedeker guide offered was to warn travelers away from "restaurants which solicit the patronage of 'gents'" and those found in railway terminals.[10]

Perhaps it is not surprising that travel guides, chock-full of information on tourist sites, hotels, and rail schedules, had little room left to discuss restaurants, but the rare guide specifically dedicated to public dining was seldom more informative. One of the first book-length guidebooks to describe restaurant dining in the United States was issued in 1903. The author of *Where and How to Dine in New York* is unknown, but the book published by Lewis and Scribner was wedded to the conventions of aristocratic dining, and for more than two hundred pages it waxed poetic about decor and clientele, largely ignoring food.[11] At the highly regarded Café des Beaux-Arts, for example, could be found "beautiful women who are smart and smart women who are not so beautiful, all in handsome dinner gowns," as well as "the sparkle of diamonds and the sparkle of champagne." Women, diamonds, and champagne, the author insisted, "all mingling in a scene of vivacity . . . makes the enjoyment of the dinner itself a sort of subconscious, though none the less real[,] pleasure."[12]

The description of the Café des Beaux-Arts was not unusual. Even when the guidebook embraced the growing interest in cosmopolitanism by including three well-established restaurants featuring foreign cuisine—The HofBräu Haus (German), the Café Boulevard (Hungarian), and Lüchow's (German)—it provided few details about the restaurants' potentially unfamiliar bills of fare. The guide described the venerable Hof-Bräu Haus as "famous" with "German dishes . . . that tempt the epicure," but it lavished more attention on the "Nürnberg architecture" and the museum-like decorations (a museum "without the tiresome, scientific, classified regularity that is deadening") than on the food.[13] Despite the author's promise that the book would "stand as guide, counselor and friend to the ever increasing army of New Yorkers who practice the gentle art of dining," it was apparently written for visiting elites who wanted to know where to go to be seen by society.[14] The "guide" included only the best-known restaurants, did not discuss prices or dress, and provided only the most fleeting clues as to what was served at New York's restaurants.

For the middle-class diner, the lack of a comprehensive and genuinely informative guide to dining in urban America was frustrating. Seeking affordable restaurants that catered to their idiosyncratic tastes, middle-class diners demanded more information. An 1896 article in the *New York Daily Tribune* expressed the growing irritation many felt at the trial-and-error approach to picking a restaurant:

> There is no surer way to get a bad dinner than to go to the wrong place for it. It does not follow that because a place is the wrong place for you to get your dinner it is the wrong place for anybody else to get his. You may not want just the same dinner that somebody else wants. It would be a good thing if all the leading New-York restaurants were to advertise in the newspapers, the advertisements being grouped and each one setting forth the character of the restaurant and kind of breakfasts, luncheons, dinners and suppers that it could serve best. All the restaurants would profit by such an arrangement, because even a stranger could then pick out the right place and get what he wanted, instead of getting what he did not want, and then going away and telling all his friends never to go there because he was disappointed, when perhaps it would be the very place that they would want.[15]

Initially, however, such complaints fell on deaf ears. Although more comprehensive lists of restaurants than were offered by *Appleton's* or *Where and How to Dine* were published in the second decade of the twentieth century, it was not until the middle class's influence over restaurant dining was well established—after World War I—that restaurant reviewing emerged as a new genre of nonfiction writing.[16]

In 1924, George S. Chappell, an architectural critic for the *New Yorker*, published *The Restaurants of New York*. Acknowledging the rapid changes that dining in the United States was undergoing, Chappell "essay[ed] the difficult task of fixing, if only for a moment, some of the remaining restaurants of the old régime and a number of the new ones."[17] *The Restaurants of New York* did not rate restaurants—Chappell felt that his taste in food was "necessarily personal" and was reluctant to impose his opinion on his readers—but the book did take into account "the excellence of the food" as well as the "interest of the place itself" in choosing which restaurants to include.[18] While Chappell buried his broad-stroke descriptions of the culinary offerings in passages dedicated to the history, decor, and clientele of each restaurant, he was more explicit about food than were his predecessors. "The menu" at Ye Olde Chop House "is surprisingly extensive, and it seems impossible that it can all come out of the little center kitchen," he noted. "Chops, steaks and all manner of grilled foods are the specialties, and the old house also prides itself on Cape Cods and Lynnhavens and Woods Hole clams which really come from the waters whose names they bear, genuine, autographed shellfish, so to speak, the name blown in the shell."[19] *The Restaurants of New York*'s most significant contribution to the emerging art of restaurant reviewing, however, was not the brief description of favorite dishes but the scale of the undertaking. Chappell did not claim to discuss every restaurant—not every restaurant in New York was worthy of inclusion—but he marched through Manhattan recording not only the well-known establishments patronized by elite society but also the "little restaurants" on "side streets" as well as "foreign feeding grounds." He even included a chapter that described some of the restaurants available to motorists.[20]

On the West Coast, innovations in restaurant reviewing were also underway. Clarence Edwords's 1914 *Bohemian San Francisco* and Jack L. Dodd and Hazel Blair Dodd's 1925 *Bohemian Eats of San Francisco* broke new ground in introducing restaurants to the middle-class diner.[21] Edwords's opinionated, gossipy account of San Francisco's restaurants, like Chappell's guide to New York, included descriptions of both food and decor at restaurants past and present and dedicated ample attention to ethnic fare. While Edwords did not review the food at these restaurants, he did include something that most guides at the time did not: recipes. The recipes not only provided San Franciscans the opportunity to experience restaurant dishes at home but also let readers know in advance what to expect when they ordered *Terrapin a la Maryland* or *Chili Reinas*. Edwords also made it easier for middle-class diners to venture into strange new restaurants by providing generic menus from which meals might be ordered at various restaurants in the city, depending upon the desired cost of the meal. The Dodds' *Bohemian Eats of San Francisco*, based on newspaper articles from the magazine section of the *San Francisco Bulletin*, provided an even more practical guide to public dining. Each review included the usual, ample descriptions of the restaurant's atmosphere, but the articles also discussed the service, hours, prices, and food. And the Dodds used each review to introduce a favorite, often novel, dish. Bigin's Bologna Restaurant, for example, served *green tagliarini*, a spinach pasta with a meat and tomato sauce. Jacinto's Real Mexican Restaurant, the couple wrote, sold favorites such as chile con carne, enchiladas, and tamales as well as less familiar dishes such as *chorizo con huevo* (sausage and eggs) and *posole* (soup made with pig's head and hominy).[22]

Chappell, Edwords, and the Dodds did not rank restaurants, although restaurant guides that rated culinary excellence were being introduced in Europe at about the same time these guides were being published in the United States. In 1900, the French tire manufacturer Michelin offered complimentary guides to wealthy motorists seeking information on hotels, and in 1926, *Le Guide Michelin* began to assign a single-star rating to restaurants it considered notable. By the early 1930s, the ratings had evolved into a three-star system designed to distinguish the finest restaurant cuisine from the less exceptional.[23] But through the 1930s, restaurant reviewing in the United States lagged behind that of France. Although the women's pages and Sunday supplements of newspapers sometimes discussed trends in restaurant dining, neither routinely reviewed restaurants. In fact, newspapers generally opted for objectivity by not naming the restaurants they discussed unless the establishment was especially well-known.

The first thorough American dining guide that discriminated between the good and the bad was published in the mid-1930s. Duncan Hines, a traveling salesman who had amassed a collection of "reviews" based on his business travels, returned to his home in Bowling Green, Kentucky, in 1936 to publish *Adventures in Good Eating*. This book had none of the pretensions of its forerunners. It was published by a middle-class salesman for a middle-class audience. Although the national restaurant guide included some of the finer restaurants in America, Hines did not reserve his highest praise for the most expensive and well-established eating places. He often saved the nicest comments for chain restaurants that catered consistently and efficiently to the needs of hungry diners seeking a good meal at a reasonable price. Nonetheless, Hines discussed food, and his guidebook provided clear recommendations for both locals and travelers seeking a good restaurant meal. Most entries recommended a dish or two to try when visiting the establishment. As a result, for the thousands who purchased the guide, public dining was transformed from a hit-or-miss adventure into a professionally managed evening on the town where private tastes could be matched with public restaurants.[24]

The success of Hines's guide set the stage for the first newspaper restaurant reviews. Clementine Paddleford at the *New York Herald Tribune* occasionally profiled restaurants in her syndicated columns of the late 1930s and

1940s, but it was Craig Claiborne, hired in 1957 by the *New York Times*, who pioneered the modern American restaurant review. Claiborne established strict standards for reviewing: he visited a restaurant repeatedly, sampled a variety of offerings, remained anonymous, and used a system of stars to rate the restaurants he reviewed.[25] While Claiborne, Mississippi-born but Swiss-trained, could hardly be described as a champion of the middle class, by establishing standards for restaurant reviewing he made it possible for middle-class readers to find restaurants they would like. After Claiborne revolutionized the genre, other reviewers imitated his technique. By 1979, when Lawrence Van Gelder observed that "restaurant reviewing, next to the destruction of subway car doors, is New York's principal industry," reviews could be found in most large urban newspapers (and many smaller ones), and the majority of the restaurants profiled catered to the middle class.[26]

The cosmopolitan ideal of public dining required restaurant reviews. Reviews provided restaurant-goers with guidance, exposing diners to new restaurant cuisines and rationalizing the complex world of consumption without championing an absolute ideal of taste. Whereas the first restaurant guides did little more than create lists of the most exclusive restaurants, operating under the assumption that every diner wanted a French meal, the reviewers of the mid-twentieth century described the food and offered advice, not dictates. Reviewers presented their opinions, generally including the worst as well as the best, and diners made their own decisions.[27] By consulting a review, cosmopolitan diners—middle class or not—were empowered to match their personal preferences to the available restaurant offerings.

Like other turn-of-the-century middle-class campaigns to manage the complexities of industrial, urban, and consumer transformations (most notably efforts to Americanize immigrants), the restaurant review established high standards for what it meant to be middle class and then (somewhat naively) encouraged everyone to embrace those values.[28] Unlike the aristocratic restaurant, whose conventions were designed to maintain exclusivity, the middle-class cosmopolitan restaurant's standards were an invitation to conform. Upper- and working-class Americans were encouraged to take a seat at the table, to adopt cosmopolitanism, and to become middle class. Not everyone, even those with the occupation and income necessary to claim membership in the middle class, sought to identify themselves as such. But as more Americans accepted cosmopolitan consumer values as their own, the middle class "transformed the tang and feel of the American experience."[29]

The Middle Class and the
Transformation of Restaurant Dining

Many of the changes in public dining that took place at the turn of the century were rooted in broad economic changes as well as in the subtle preferences of the burgeoning middle class. The tale that emerged was not always simple. The industrial expansion that America experienced in the late nineteenth century churned out inexpensive consumer goods and drew an ever-increasing number of Americans to urban centers where department stores and other consumer emporia tempted even the most frugal. Restaurants were a part of this growth. Technological innovations made it possible to raise, package, preserve, and transport food more cheaply and quickly than in the past. The lower food prices that resulted, coupled with rising demand fueled by the managerial revolution, helped to bring about an increase in restaurants and restaurant-going. Given their stable incomes and ample leisure time, it is not surprising that middle-class urbanites flocked to public dining rooms.

Yet the patronage of the fledgling middle class did not mean that the "middle-classing" of American restaurant culture and the emergence of cosmopolitan restaurant dining was inevitable. Aristocratic traditions were well entrenched. Etiquette guides defended the status quo, and restaurateurs clung stubbornly to the patronage of the wealthy whose incomes and numbers, not unlike those of the middle class, were growing at the turn of the century. Accustomed to earning their livings from the balls and banquets of the very rich, many restaurateurs were personally flattered by their association with those of high status and continued to cater deferentially to upper-class society's whims. At the turn of the century, pandering restaurateurs in New York and Philadelphia turned away men dressed only in "shirt waists," even during stifling East Coast summers, until society mavens gave their explicit approval.[30] Expressing a view shared by many in the restaurant business, Thomas Hilliard of the Waldorf-Astoria told readers of *The Caterer* in 1912 that it was the "moneyed class of wealthy people of leisure," those who knew how to "live from an aesthetic and culinary standpoint," who were responsible for improvements in the restaurant industry, and it was these patrons who would guarantee the industry's future success.[31] For restaurateurs who were accustomed to taking their every fashion cue from the wealthy, accommodating middle-class patrons was not easy or inevitable.

Nor was it certain that the fledgling middle class would discover a sense of itself and demand changes in elite dining. Initially, many in the nascent middle class seemed more interested in imitating the wealthy than in challenging aristocratic cultural authority. Even as vocal middle-class critics of aristocratic dining appeared, members of the middle class still had to embrace these criticisms and wrest control of dining from the upper class. Despite their growing numbers and collective purchasing power, members of the middle class initially lacked a collective identity. They occasionally organized as professionals, political activists, or, on very rare occasions, consumers, but at first they lacked a shared sense of themselves as a class. Thus, no national or local group spoke for the middle-class diner, and few concerted efforts emerged to coordinate demands for something as mundane as simpler menus. It is not difficult to imagine middle-class consumers accommodating themselves to a bifurcated consumer economy, high and low, where elite values remained the signifiers of status. In the late nineteenth century, however, members of the middle class became aware of their shared interests as consumers.[32] As they sat in what were once businessmen's lunchrooms and immigrant restaurants, they came to recognize that collectively they were making similar decisions about how to value the emerging market of consumer and culinary goods. More and more they embraced this new, shared identity and demanded that restaurateurs respect their cosmopolitan values. Restaurateurs—at first, only those who ran common restaurants, but later, those who governed fine dining—yielded, recognizing the potential economic importance of the growing class.

Even as some members of the middle class became aware of their shared interests and joined the chorus demanding restaurant reform, such a diverse group of people (divided by occupation, income, ethnicity, and race) did not march in unison. The "middle-classing" of the American restaurant was a process in which disparate decisions produced collective results. This process was akin to guessing the number of jellybeans in a jar at the county fair. Individual guesses will vary substantially, but the average guess is generally close to accurate.[33] Likewise, not every member of the middle class envisioned his or her ideal restaurant experience in exactly the same way, but collectively, members of the middle class could recognize themselves in the cosmopolitan ethos that emerged.[34]

Historians have long acknowledged the importance of middle-class consumption at the turn of the century, although most studies have focused more on how consumption transformed the middle class than on how the middle class transformed consumption. The turn-of-the-century history of restaurants corrects that record. Material changes in restaurant culture demonstrate that the concerns of middle-class critics of the aristocratic restaurant were heard, and the dining culture that emerged in the early twentieth century was especially friendly to middle-class consumers. Unstated preferences, repeated thousands of times each day and reinforced through small revolts and journalistic diatribes, refashioned public dining. Restaurants that had once catered to the rich increasingly catered to the tastes of the middle class—cosmopolitan tastes that were shaped in opposition to the culture of aristocracy. These changes and the belief that the modern consumer economy should reflect democratic principles are evidence of what E. P. Thompson referred to as a moral economy, the point where cultural attitudes and social mores shape economic marketplaces.[35]

The material changes that the restaurant underwent were also an essential part of creating the modern, urban middle class. The shared values and collective action the cosmopolitan restaurant represented were not limited to efforts to get dinner. The nascent middle class's commitment to democracy, tempered by experts and experience, not only shaped attitudes toward dining but also influenced decisions made in voting booths and at charity board meetings. Repeatedly, members of the emerging middle class expressed opinions, made small choices, and undertook individual actions that demonstrated these shared commitments. The consumer marketplace played a critical role in making manifest to those of the nascent middle class their shared interests and in forging a sense of collective purpose. As professionals and managers realized their common commitments, they began to act as a class in myriad venues, both public and private. While the making of a class is never complete, in the early years of the twentieth century, members of the professional and managerial cohort claimed a collective class identity. And with each additional choice they made, they asserted the power of that class to transform the urban landscape.

The power of the middle-class consumer was not without limits. Middle-class opposition to the rarified culture of elites never succeeded in eliminating all of the cultural barriers to formal dining (in fact, the middle class did not want to eliminate barriers that distinguished the citizen consumer from the uncultivated masses), but it did democratize dining. Cultural snobs might bemoan the dumbing-down of dining epitomized by English-language menus and the ubiquitous "continental" restaurant, but the middle-class restaurant opened a gateway to fine dining for millions and continued to shape dining culture for years to come. If some of the reforms that the middle class demanded, including plate dinners and acceptance of business attire, were not fully realized by 1920, the battle for cultural authority had nonetheless been fought and won, and those changes soon followed. By the 1940s, the phrase "where the elite meet to eat" was ripe for parody.[36]

Neither elite society nor French cuisine completely disappeared. Although many of the old-guard aristocrats retreated to private clubs and country estates, younger socialites continued to dine out and to exert an influence on the life of their communities. But after 1920, restaurateurs rarely viewed "café society" (as the young bluebloods were called) as the cornerstone of their industry, and French cuisine (despite a number of celebrated revivals in the twentieth century) survived as only one cuisine among many.[37] As early as 1918, one industry journal estimated that there were fifty different types of "cooked food dispensing" businesses in New York, including everything from chop-suey restaurants and five-and-dime stores to private restaurants, bakeries, and lunch wagons.[38] The vast majority of these establishments, even the majority of the fine dining restaurants, did not serve French food exclusively.

Nonetheless, the persistence of elite restaurants and French cuisine serves as an important reminder that the transformation of restaurant culture championed by the middle class was never strictly about the rejection of a specific restaurant, cuisine, or custom. The "middle-classing" of public eating was about cultural power, access, and choice. It was grounded in the premise that the individual preferences of consumers could be given consideration and respect and that collectively these preferences should shape the marketplace. For the middle-class diner, a good meal could be as bland as Howard Johnson's macaroni and cheese or as spicy as the local Mexican restaurant's chili rellenos. Cosmopolitanism was the freedom to choose to be middle class.

Over the course of the twentieth century and into the twenty-first, restaurants have become increasingly democratic spaces ungoverned by formal codes of behavior and accessible to anyone with a little money. Specialized cultural knowledge, although helpful, is now no longer a prerequisite. To accommodate more and more diners, restaurants have added descriptions of dishes to their menus—and sometimes even pictures and glossaries. Maître d's, once practiced in the art of discriminating between the elite and the hoi polloi, have been replaced with hosts and hostesses who are charged with welcoming patrons and encouraging them to stay and spend their money. Tables are now more private, dress codes are more relaxed (to the point that shirts and shoes are often the only requirement), and servers occasionally sit at the table with customers as they discuss the dinner specials. In the largest American cities today, only a few restaurants are beyond the reach of the middle class. They charge high prices, and it takes months to get a reservation unless one has the right connections. But these establishments are rare, and even in the most exclusive, the menus would not be all that unfamiliar to the majority of diners. Most of the best restaurants in New York and Chicago, as well as in Kansas City and Denver, are priced to be affordable to the middle-class couple celebrating a wedding anniversary, and they serve food that one does not have to be a devotee of the Food Channel to order and appreciate.

Democratizing consumption has had consequences. Americans never fully developed, and probably never will, a distinctive national cuisine, although our stores are filled with cookbooks that claim otherwise. Instead, we have (at least since the 1920s) celebrated the efficiency and diversity of our restaurants as our contribution to the culinary world. Most restaurants today barely disguise their reliance on national distributers (rather than local markets), and even the freshest ingredients have been processed and cryovacked.[39] Slow-cooked dishes, despite the occasional Crock-Pot fad, are not a part of public dining. Speed has replaced craftsmanship, stainless steel has replaced silver, and luxury now amounts to little more than white tablecloths and cloth napkins, even at the better establishments. Television shows that purport to uphold culinary excellence are often little more than high-speed races to a gustatory finish line. Today, classical luxury, measured in courses and draped in linen, is so far beyond our grasp that most of us could not even imagine a three-hour dinner, floral displays that stretch from one side of the table to the other, servers who never leave your side unless it is to secure you a theater reservation, and dishes that cannot be reproduced in home kitchens. Now we define luxury as an elaborate recipe for chocolate chip cookies.[40] And all of this, to some degree or another, is a legacy of the triumph of the cosmopolitan restaurant in the first two decades of the twentieth century.

But is that so bad? We may not have a national cuisine, but we have foregone nationalism in favor of cosmopolitanism, and every modestly sized city in America has an Italian restaurant (if only an Olive Garden), a Chinese restaurant, and often a Thai restaurant. Few foods are made entirely from scratch, but that does not keep us from loving the Alfredo sauce at our local mom-and-pop restaurant (where the sign claims that everything is homemade, although the sauce, with a dash of pepper added, was probably purchased from the culinary-supply goliath Sysco). Are we not better off as a society when our tendency to emphasize class distinction (or as Robert Frost insisted, build fences) is mitigated by the occasional trip to McDonald's or Waffle House, Applebee's or Red Lobster? Restaurants remain among the few shared spaces where differences of race, ethnicity, and class are confronted and sometimes transcended. Cosmopolitan dining has provided us with a common experience.

By 1920, the tables had turned, and increasingly the middle class, not the upper class, determined what would be served in America's restaurants. This revolution in dining is now over a hundred years old, and in a world of increasing shortages and growing disparities between the rich and poor, its prospects are in question.[41] Yet it is possible that future historians, looking back at this era of democratic gluttony unlike any that preceded it, will declare: "Verily, they lived in the period of the Restauration."

NOTES

NOTE ON LANGUAGE

1 Matthew M. Trumbull, "Aristocracy in America," *The Nineteenth Century* 18, no. 102 (1888): 210.

INTRODUCTION

1 "Flock to Inspect the Biggest Hotel," *New York Times*, December 30, 1912, 18; Christopher Gray, "Streetscapes: The McAlpin Marine Grill," *New York Times*, July 23, 1989, sec. 10, 6; P. C. Jennings, "New York Letter," *The Southern Hotel Journal* 2, no. 5 (1912): 35.

2 "Chinese Dishes Served Daily at a Big New York Hotel," *The Steward*, March 1919, 16–17.

3 Ibid.

4 Louis H. Chu, "The Chinese Restaurants in New York City" (master's thesis, New York University, 1939); Andrew P. Haley, "The Chop Suey Craze in American Popular Culture" (paper presented at the American Culture Association/ Popular Culture Association National Conference, Atlanta, Ga., April 2006). See also Andrew Coe, *Chop Suey: A Cultural History of Chinese Food in the United States* (New York: Oxford University Press, 2009), esp. 144–79.

5 George G. Foster and Stuart M. Blumin, *New York by Gas-Light and Other Urban Sketches* (Berkeley: University of California Press, 1990), 219.

6 The term "aristocratic" is used throughout this work to refer to wealthy Americans with leading positions in "society." In the United States, the aristocracy was not a product of noble lineage but rather of wealth, especially hereditary wealth, and social jockeying. I have used the term for three reasons. First, as argued in this chapter and throughout the book, America's elites intentionally modeled themselves after Europe's aristocrats. They not only embraced French food but also bought European clothes and art, paid genealogists to trace their lineages to Europe's first families, sought marriages with European nobilities, and emulated European manners. As Susan Williams has observed, "The model for etiquette conventions has in fact traditionally been the aristocracy, and reference to an aristocracy among Americans meant reference to Europe." Susan Williams, *Savory Suppers and Fashionable Feasts: Dining in Victorian America* (New York: Pantheon Books, 1985), 24. Second, I use the term because it was regularly employed in contemporary accounts of the wealthy in the United States. In 1831,

a Tocqueville acquaintance was circumspect about the use of the term to describe "an ever-changing class which makes its pretensions but has no power," but contemporaries used the term without apology, and it remained in wide circulation throughout the nineteenth century and into the early twentieth century. See Francis J. Grund, *Aristocracy in America* (London: R. Bentley, 1839); Matthew M. Trumbull, "Aristocracy in America," *The Nineteenth Century* 18, no. 102 (1888): 209–17; Foster and Blumin, *New York by Gas-Light*, 219; William Dean Howells, *A Modern Instance* (Harmondsworth, U.K.: Penguin Books, 1984), 178; Ethel Spencer et al., *The Spencers of Amberson Avenue: A Turn-of-the Century Memoir* (Pittsburgh: University of Pittsburgh Press, 1983); and Edmund Wrigley, *The Workingman's Way to Wealth: A Practical Treatise on Building Associations* (Philadelphia: James K. Simon, 1869) (with thanks to Elaine Lewinnek at Yale University for calling attention to this work). Although the term is less commonly applied to wealthy Americans today, it was still in common use in the 1930s. For an example, see Jeanette MacDonald's description of a wealthy San Francisco family in the 1936 film *San Francisco*. Anita Loos, *San Francisco, Film*, directed by W. S. Van Dyke (Los Angeles: Metro-Goldwyn-Mayer, 1936). Finally, some scholars of the American elite have already embraced the term. Eric Homberger defines aristocracy as "a group of high status possessing a conscious sense of shared rituals, identity, and organization." Eric Homberger, *Mrs. Astor's New York: Money and Social Power in a Gilded Age* (New Haven: Yale University Press, 2002), 3. Admittedly, however, the practice is not universal. For an opposing view (and an argument for using the term "bourgeoisie"), cf. Sven Beckert, *The Monied Metropolis: New York City and the Consolidation of the American Bourgeoisie, 1850–1896* (Cambridge: Cambridge University Press, 2001), 6.

7 "The Hotel McAlpin N.Y. City," *The Southern Hotel Journal* 2, no. 6 (1912): 58.

8 "Chinese Dishes Served Daily at a Big New York Hotel," 16–17.

9 C. Wright Mills, *White Collar: The American Middle Classes* (London: Oxford University Press, 1951; reprint, 1981), ix.

10 "Exploring Democracy in America," C-Span, http://www.tocqueville.org/ny3 .htm#0607a (accessed December 12, 2007). "Mr. Livingston" was probably Secretary of State Edward Livingston's nephew John, but he might have been the secretary himself. See Donna Greene, "Renewing Tocqueville's America Tour," *New York Times* (1997), http://query.nytimes.com/gst/fullpage.html?res=9B0CE0 D9153FF933A15757C0A961958260 (accessed April 19, 2008).

11 On the lifestyle of European aristocracy, see Amy Milne-Smith, "Clubland: Masculinity, Status, and Community in the Gentlemen's Clubs of London, c. 1880–1914" (PhD diss., University of Toronto, 2006); Maria Malatesta, "The Landed Aristocracy during the Nineteenth and Early Twentieth Centuries," in *The European Way: European Societies during the Nineteenth and Twentieth Centuries*, ed. Hartmut Kaelble (New York: Berghahn Books, 2004), 44–67; and J. Mordaunt Crook, *The Rise of the Nouveaux Riches: Style and Status in Victorian and Edwardian Architecture* (London: John Murray, 1999).

12　Beckert, *Monied Metropolis*, 267, 273.

13　"The Fool Congressman," *The Caterer* 29, no. 11 (1918): 45; Research Department of the American Restaurant Magazine, *A Market Analysis of the Restaurant Industry* (Chicago: Patterson Publishing, 1930), 11; William Foote Whyte, *Human Relations in the Restaurant Industry* (New York: McGraw-Hill, 1948), 5.

14　E. P. Thompson, *The Making of the English Working Class* (New York: Pantheon Books, 1964), 9–10.

15　D. A. Bethea, *Colored People's Blue-Book and Business Directory of Chicago, Ill., 1905* (Chicago: Celerity Print, 1905), 136–37. The *Colored People's Blue Book* listed fifty-seven African American–owned restaurants and dozens of bakeries, ice cream parlors, and caterers.

16　Lawrence W. Levine, *Highbrow/Lowbrow: The Emergence of Cultural Hierarchy in America* (Cambridge: Harvard University Press, 1988), esp. 144–46.

17　Cindy R. Lobel, "Consuming Classes: Changing Food Consumption Patterns in New York City, 1790–1860" (PhD diss., City University of New York, 2003), 110.

18　For more on efforts to define the middle class, see Burton J. Bledstein and Robert D. Johnston, eds., *The Middling Sorts: Explorations in the History of the American Middle Class* (New York: Routledge, 2001), especially the introduction. See also Burton J. Bledstein, *The Culture of Professionalism: The Middle Class and the Development of Higher Education in America* (New York: Norton, 1976); Melanie Archer and Judith R. Blau, "Class Formation in Nineteenth-Century America: The Case of the Middle Class," *Annual Review of Sociology* 19 (1993): 17–41; Walter Nugent, "Tocqueville, Marx and American Class Structure," *Social Science History* 12, no. 4 (1988): 327–47; Peter N. Stearns, "The Middle Class: Toward a Precise Definition," *Comparative Studies in Society and History* 21, no. 3 (1979): 377–96; Cindy Sondik Aron, *Working at Play: A History of Vacations in the United States* (New York: Oxford University Press, 1999); and Cindy Sondik Aron, *Ladies and Gentlemen of the Civil Service: Middle-Class Workers in Victorian America* (New York: Oxford University Press, 1987).

19　Mills, *White Collar*, 65–66.

20　Michael E. McGerr, *A Fierce Discontent: The Rise and Fall of the Progressive Movement in America, 1870–1920* (New York: Free Press, 2003), esp. 91.

21　Torill Strand, "Introduction: Cosmopolitanism in the Making," *Studies in Philosophy and Education* 29, no. 2 (2010): 103–5; Leszek Koczanowicz, "Cosmopolitanism and Its Predicaments," *Studies in Philosophy and Education* 29, no. 2 (2010): 148; Anthony Appiah, *Cosmopolitanism: Ethics in a World of Strangers* (New York: W. W. Norton, 2006), esp. v–xiv, 31. As Appiah and others have demonstrated, the first use of "cosmopolitanism" was paradoxical, and the term continues to straddle tensions between respecting difference and believing there are universal values. Nonetheless, modern theorists have called on the term in their quest to find moral clarity in the modern, global world. This work does not address the contemporary debate, but it does contend that the term's instability opened the door to individual, relativistic ideas about taste that made possible the unseating of French cuisine. My approach, in effect, mimics recent scholarly examinations of cosmopolitanism as practiced (especially cosmopolitanism "from below"). See, for example, Loren B. Landau and Iriann Freemantle, "Tactical Cosmopolitanism and Idioms of Belonging: Insertion and Self-Exclusion in Johannesburg," *Journal of Ethnic and Migration Studies* 36, no. 3 (2010): 375–90.

22 David Chaney, "Cosmopolitan Art and Cultural Citizenship," *Theory, Culture and Society* 19, no. 1–2 (2002): 158.

23 My ideas about late-nineteenth-century cosmopolitanism owe much to recent sociological work on omnivorism. In 1992, sociologists Richard A. Peterson and Albert Simkus coined the term "omnivorism" to describe the investment elites (primarily upper- and upper-middle-class Americans) made in a broad swath of culture drawn from both traditionally high and traditionally low sources. Peterson and Simkus cited late-twentieth-century survey data that demonstrated that while the upper class continued to patronize opera, they were also interested in rock and country music. Richard A. Peterson and Albert Simkus, "How Musical Tastes Mark Occupational Status Groups," in *Cultivating Differences: Symbolic Boundaries and the Making of Inequality*, ed. Michèle Lamont and Marcel Fournier (Chicago: University of Chicago Press, 1992), 152–86. Subsequent works have described "omnivorism" in relation to other cultural preferences including cuisine: Gerry Veenstra, "Can Taste Illumine Class? Cultural Knowledge and Forms of Inequality," *Canadian Journal of Sociology/Cahiers canadiens de sociologie* 30, no. 3 (2005): 247–79; Jane Zavisca, "The Status of Cultural Omnivorism: A Case Study of Reading in Russia," *Social Forces* 84, no. 2 (2005): 1233–55; and Josée Johnston and Shyon Baumann, "Democracy versus Distinction: A Study of Omnivorousness in Gourmet Food Writing," *American Journal of Sociology* 113, no. 1 (2007): 165–204. Although his conclusions were never intended to be more than suggestive, Peterson later speculated that the emergence of omnivorism was a post–World War II response to structural changes in education and media access, new trends in high art, generational shifts, greater tolerance for ethnic and racial differences, and globalization. Richard A. Peterson and Roger M. Kern, "Changing Highbrow Taste: From Snob to Omnivore," *American Sociological Review* 61, no. 5 (1996): 900–907. Although these shifts are instructive, I believe that Peterson was mistaken in dating these changes, at least in the case of the middle class, to the postwar era and that many of these changes were underway at the turn of the century.

24 Although initially the middle class appropriated working-class restaurants and transformed them, the emerging model of dining was supple enough to eventually accommodate working-class preferences and trends. It is outside the scope of this study to fully examine the relationship between middle-class and working-class cultures of public dining; however, in the second and third decades of the twentieth century, the middle class often embraced and incorporated working-class culinary traditions. For example, the middle-class cosmopolitan restaurant began serving sandwiches early in the twentieth century, and sandwiches be-

came popular in the 1920s. On sandwiches, see "The Sandwich of Commerce," *Cooking Club Magazine* 9, no. 2 (1907): 120.

25 Alexis de Toqueville, "Of the Taste for Physical Well-Being in America," American Studies Programs at the University of Virginia, http://xroads.virginia .edu/~HYPER/DETOC/ch2_10.htm (accessed December 1, 2004).

26 William Leach, *Land of Desire: Merchants, Power, and the Rise of a New American Culture* (New York: Pantheon Books, 1993), 36–37; Richard M. Ohmann, *Selling Culture: Magazines, Markets, and Class at the Turn of the Century* (London: Verso, 1996); Richard L. Bushman, *The Refinement of America: Persons, Houses, Cities* (New York: Vintage Books, 1992).

27 Aron, *Working at Play*; Leigh Eric Schmidt, *Consumer Rites: The Buying and Selling of American Holidays* (Princeton: Princeton University Press, 1995); Katherine C. Grier, *Culture and Comfort: Parlor Making and Middle-Class Identity, 1850–1930* (Washington, D.C.: Smithsonian Institution Press, 1997). See also Elaine S. Abelson, *When Ladies Go a-Thieving: Middle-Class Shoplifters in the Victorian Department Store* (New York: Oxford University Press, 1989); Ellen Gruber Garvey, *The Adman in the Parlor: Magazines and the Gendering of Consumer Culture* (New York: Oxford University Press, 1996); Williams, *Savory Suppers and Fashionable Feasts*; and Louise L. Stevenson, *The Victorian Homefront: American Thought and Culture, 1860–1880* (New York: Twayne Publishers, 1991).

28 Leach, *Land of Desire*, 36–37.

29 Daniel Horowitz, *The Morality of Spending: Attitudes toward the Consumer Society in America, 1875–1940* (Baltimore: Johns Hopkins University Press, 1985). For members of the working class seeking to construct a middle-class lifestyle, see John Model, "Patterns of Consumption, Acculturation, and Family Income Strategies in Late Nineteenth-Century America," in *Family and Population in Nineteenth-Century America*, ed. Tamara K. Hareven and Maris Vinovskis (Princeton: Princeton University Press, 1978), 213–14.

30 Gilbert Seldes, "Bourgeois Not Meant as Term of Contempt," *Denton (Md.) Journal*, December 17, 1927, 1.

31 Thompson's contention that "class happens" has not been overlooked by those who study the American middle class in the late nineteenth century, but the process by which class takes shape and then shapes culture is not fully resolved in the existing literature. Scholars agree that the modern middle class is a product of the Industrial Revolution and the rise of corporate America, but few historians argue that those transformations *made* the American middle class. Most researchers have emphasized the role that class anxiety, professionalization, and/or the acquisition of consumer goods has played in middle-class formation. Yet there is no single definitive work on the post–Civil War middle class, and the existing literature is subject to critique. Studies of class anxiety have been challenged for attributing a simple psychological state to a diverse class. Studies of professionalization often make class formation appear to be an almost accidental byproduct of doctors, members of fraternities, and vacationers seeking simpler

rules to govern themselves and leave questions about class-consciousness unanswered. Studies of consumer goods too often skip over issues of class formation, in effect attributing a coherent "middle-class" identity to middling folks without explaining how everyone mysteriously seems to know which soap to buy. On efforts to describe middle-class politics and class anxiety, see Richard Hofstadter, *The Age of Reform from Bryan to F.D.R.* (New York: Knopf, 1955); and McGerr, *Fierce Discontent*, 40–74. For criticism of this approach, see Michael P. Rogan, "Progressivism and the California Electorate," in *Political Change in California: Critical Elections and Social Movements, 1890–1966*, ed. Michael Paul Rogin and John L. Shover (Westport, Conn.: Greenwood, 1970), 35–61; Roger E. Wyman, "Middle-Class Voters and Progressive Reform: The Conflict of Class and Culture," *American Political Science Review* 68, no. 2 (1974): 488–504; and David F. Labaree, "Curriculum, Credentials, and the Middle Class: A Case Study of a Nineteenth Century High School," *Sociology of Education* 29, no. 1 (1986): 56. On associations, see Lynn Dumenil, *Freemasonry and American Culture, 1880–1930* (Princeton: Princeton University Press, 1984). In addition, Bledstein offers a narrow but convincing argument that college-inspired professionalism helped form the middle class. Bledstein, *Culture of Professionalism.*

32 On the nineteenth century, see Stuart M. Blumin, *The Emergence of the Middle Class: Social Experience in the American City, 1760–1900* (Cambridge: Cambridge University Press, 1989); Mary P. Ryan, *Cradle of the Middle Class: The Family in Oneida County, New York, 1790–1865* (Cambridge: Cambridge University Press, 1981).

33 Stuart Ewen, *All Consuming Images: The Politics of Style in Contemporary Culture* (New York: Basic Books, 1988), 66–70.

34 Roy Rosenzweig, *Eight Hours for What We Will: Workers and Leisure in an Industrial City, 1870–1920* (Cambridge: Cambridge University Press, 1983), 223; Nan Enstad, *Ladies of Labor, Girls of Adventure: Working Women, Popular Culture, and Labor Politics at the Turn of the Twentieth Century* (New York: Columbia University Press, 1999), 6–7.

35 Stearns, "Middle Class," 381–82.

36 For example, Aron, *Working at Play.* Aron argues that growth of vacationing came as the middle class shed puritanical loyalties to work. This approach sheds light on how the middle class thought about pleasure, but not on how this new middle-class attitude toward pleasure shaped the dominant culture except in the narrowest possible terms. *Working at Play* and other similar works are important, but they leave questions unanswered. Although *Turning the Tables* is about food, it is also about a shift in cultural authority.

37 Lobel, "Consuming Classes," 88–130.

38 Lesley Poling-Kempes, *The Harvey Girls: Women Who Opened the West* (New York: Paragon House, 1989).

39 See, for example, "Daniel Sweeny—May 9, 1884," New York, Vol. 267, p. 500A36, R. G. Dun & Co. Collection, Baker Library, Harvard Business School, Cam-

bridge; Ralph C. Epstein, "Industrial Profits in 1917," *Quarterly Journal of Economics* 39, no. 2 (1925): 241–66.

40 These numbers are based on occupational data in the U.S. Census. A full explanation appears in chapter 3.

41 Typical of the simple publicity that nineteenth-century restaurants depended upon, *The Table* listed the names of recommended restaurants in New York in 1873. The list begins: "Adler, Louis, No. 42 Bowery; Alton, Alvin, 754 Sixth Avenue; Atwood, Rufus, M., 411 Broadway and 68 Lispenard . . ." "Restaurant Directory," *The Table* 1, no. 2 (1873): 43. An early and exceptional article on restaurant advertising highlights how rarely restaurants advertised. See "Restaurant Advertising," *The Caterer* 11, no. 1 (1900): 26.

42 "Chefs," *The Chef* 8, no. 6 (1898): 254; "Chicago News," *Restaurant Bulletin* 2, no. 13 (1904): 25–26.

43 "Menus and Their Manufacture," *The Caterer* 3, no. 6 (1885): 205.

44 See for example, "New York Restaurants," *The Dining Room Magazine* 2, no. 11 (1877): 262; Marila Pemberton, "New York Adopts Simple Life," *What to Eat*, October 1905; "The World's Greatest Kitchen," *Cooking Club* 6, no. 11 (1904); and Jennings, "New York Letter," 35. *The Southern Hotel Journal* later added a "Chicago Letter." "Chicago Letter," *The Southern Hotel Journal* 2, no. 11 (1913): 31.

45 "Orange Juice Is Served Now," *The Southern Hotel Journal* 1, no. 1 (1911): 14. See also Editors, *Restaurant Bulletin* 2, no. 18 (1905): 11.

46 Industry journals kept even rural restaurants informed of changes in the restaurant business and reported on the widespread movement of chefs, stewards, and waiters from city to city, resort to resort, and small town to small town. See, for example, "Restaurant Notes," *The Caterer* 19, no. 9 (1903): 44–45.

47 *Printer's Ink*, "The 'Standard of Taste,' " *The Caterer* 11, no. 5 (1900): 21. Late-nineteenth- and early-twentieth-century journals and newspapers, especially culinary magazines, borrowed material from competitors, stole stories from foreign journals, and reprinted articles year after year in order to fill space. Because I was interested in reading these newspapers and journals as fledgling members of the middle class would have, I did not find it necessary to identify the original source in most cases. Thus, when the original source was cited as the author (as it was in the case of this article republished in *The Caterer*), I treated the original source as the author. In addition, if the article was originally intended for a foreign audience, I usually excluded it from my study, and when on occasion I used a work that was originally published outside the United States, I made it clear in the text or note where the article was first published. Finally, when the same article was printed more than once and I was aware of it, I cited the original article.

48 J. Elliott Lane, "My Advice on Hotel Keeping," *The Caterer* 11, no. 8 (1901): 14. Even rural restaurants were not entirely isolated from national trends, however, and the most out-of-the-way establishment considered it a compliment to be compared, if only wistfully, to the Waldorf-Astoria or Delmonico's in New York. "How to Make Money in a Small Country Hotel," *The Caterer* 11, no. 2 (1900): 11.

49 John F. Mariani, *America Eats Out: An Illustrated History of Restaurants, Taverns, Coffee Shops, Speakeasies, and Other Establishments That Have Fed Us for 350 Years* (New York: Morrow, 1991); Richard Pillsbury, *From Boarding House to Bistro: The American Restaurant Then and Now* (Boston: Unwin Hyman, 1990); Harvey A. Levenstein, *Revolution at the Table: The Transformation of the American Diet* (New York: Oxford University Press, 1988). See also Warren Belasco, "Future Notes: The Meal-in-a-Pill," in *Food in the USA: A Reader*, ed. Carole Counihan (New York: Routledge, 2002); Warren James Belasco and Philip Scranton, eds., *Food Nations: Selling Taste in Consumer Societies* (New York: Routledge, 2002); Frances de Talavera Berger and John Parke Custis, *Sumptuous Dining in Gaslight San Francisco* (Garden City, N.Y.: Doubleday, 1985); Michael Batterberry and Ariane Ruskin Batterberry, *On the Town in New York: The Landmark History of Eating, Drinking, and Entertainments from the American Revolution to the Food Revolution* (New York: Routledge, 1999); Donna Gabaccia, *We Are What We Eat: Ethnic Food and the Making of Americans* (Cambridge: Harvard University Press, 2000); Kathryn Grover, ed., *Dining in America, 1850–1900* (Amherst and Rochester: University of Massachusetts Press and the Margaret Woodbury Strong Museum, 1987); John L. Hess and Karen Hess, *The Taste of America* (New York: Penguin Books, 1977); Kristin L. Hoganson, *Consumers' Imperium: The Global Production of American Domesticity, 1865–1920* (Chapel Hill: University of North Carolina Press, 2007); Stephen Mennell, *All Manners of Food: Eating and Taste in England and France from the Middle Ages to the Present* (Oxford: B. Blackwell, 1985); Lawrence R. Schehr and Allen S. Weiss, eds., *French Food: On the Table, on the Page, and in French Culture* (New York: Routledge, 2001); Hillel Schwartz, *Never Satisfied: A Cultural History of Diets, Fantasies, and Fat* (New York: Free Press, 1986); Kerry Segrave, *Tipping: An American Social History of Gratuities* (Jefferson, N.C.: McFarland, 1998); Laura Shapiro, *Perfection Salad: Women and Cooking at the Turn of the Century* (New York: Farrar Straus and Giroux, 1986); Laura Shapiro, *Something from the Oven: Reinventing Dinner in 1950's America* (New York: Viking, 2004); Rebecca L. Spang, *The Invention of the Restaurant: Paris and Modern Gastronomic Culture* (Cambridge: Harvard University Press, 2000); Peter N. Stearns, *Fat History: Bodies and Beauty in the Modern West* (New York: New York University Press, 1997); and Jan Whitaker, *Tea at the Blue Lantern Inn: A Social History of the Tea Room Craze in America* (New York: St. Martin's Press, 2002).

50 Levenstein's account makes sense if his time line makes sense. If, as Levenstein contends, the restaurant industry did not grow dramatically until the 1920s, then the cultural shifts of the Roaring Twenties, science, and Prohibition may explain the changes that dining underwent in the early twentieth century. However, my statistical study of restaurant growth demonstrates that the restaurant industry had been expanding at a dramatic rate (faster than population growth and faster than similar service industries) since at least the 1880s. The shift in the time line is important; it reveals a more tumultuous history driven by class conflict and debates about ethnic cuisine, the size of the meal, women's roles,

and a host of other culinary concerns that first emerged in the late nineteenth century and then came to fruition in the first two decades of the twentieth century.

51 Edward R. J. Fischel, "Fischel Says Commercialism Is Playing Havoc with the Culinary Art," *The Caterer* 23, no. 3 (1911): 25.

52 Related arguments can be found in Hoganson, *Consumers' Imperium*; and Lizabeth Cohen, *A Consumer's Republic: The Politics of Mass Consumption in Postwar America* (New York: Vintage Books, 2003).

CHAPTER 1

1 Quoted in Sidney Phil Moss, *Charles Dickens' Quarrel with America* (Troy, N.Y.: Whitston, 1984), 2.

2 Charles Dickens, *Life and Adventures of Martin Chuzzlewit* (London: Educational Book, 1910), 282–83.

3 Quoted in S. Moss, *Charles Dickens' Quarrel with America*, 134.

4 Charles Dickens, "Preface to the First Cheap Edition of 'American Notes,' London, June 22, 1850," in *American Notes for General Circulation and Pictures from Italy* (London: Chapman & Hall, 1914), unnumbered page.

5 S. Moss, *Charles Dickens' Quarrel with America*, 280, 306–10. City elders in New York arranged for a French meal at the City Hotel during Dickens's first visit to the United States, but the hodgepodge menu of over sixty dishes was more impressive for its size than for the cuisine offered. During his second visit, New York dignitaries prudently decided to have Delmonico's (where Dickens regularly ate during his stay in the city) cater the event. See also Lately Thomas, *Delmonico's: A Century of Splendor* (Boston: Houghton Mifflin, 1967), 108–16.

6 Charles Dickens, *American Notes for General Circulation and Pictures from Italy* (London: Chapman & Hall, 1914), 211.

7 Ibid., 210. The culinary failures of Dickens's first visit left a lasting scar on the American psyche and in subsequent years served as a reference point for how much dining in America had improved. See "The Hotel of the Past and the Coming Century," *The Caterer* 11, no. 5 (1900): 11.

8 On the status of French cuisine, see C. de Lutèce, "Our Paris Letter," *The Caterer* 2, no. 12 (1884): 485. On food and elite status in general, see Carmen Sarasúa, "Upholding Status: The Diet of a Noble Family in Early Nineteenth-Century La Mancha," in *Food, Drink and Identity: Cooking, Eating and Drinking in Europe since the Middle Ages*, ed. Peter Scholliers (Oxford: Berg, 2001), 37–61; and Stephen Mennell, *All Manners of Food: Eating and Taste in England and France from the Middle Ages to the Present* (Oxford: Blackwell, 1985).

9 Michael E. McGerr, *A Fierce Discontent: The Rise and Fall of the Progressive Movement in America, 1870–1920* (New York: Free Press, 2003), 7. Although the wealthy were sometimes referred to as the "upper ten" (as in the top 10 percent) during the Gilded Age, McGerr argues that only 1 or 2 percent of the population had the resources necessary to be considered extremely wealthy. See also James L.

Huston, *Securing the Fruits of Labor: The American Concept of Wealth Distribution, 1765–1900* (Baton Rouge: Louisiana State University Press, 1998), 84 (Table 1).

10 The widespread belief that wealth was increasingly concentrated in the hands of the owners of trusts energized diverse social movements ranging from the Populists to the Progressives to the labor movement. Historians, however, have debated whether there was a significant increase in economic disparity or a leveling off in the post–Civil War era (although most agree that disparities did increase in the early twentieth century). Some innovative recent scholarship has suggested that the distance between classes was increasing. Richard Steckel and Carolyn Moehling's examination of property tax records in Massachusetts demonstrate that the distribution of taxable wealth in Massachusetts was becoming more concentrated. In 1870, the wealthiest 20 percent of male household heads held 90.1 percent of the sampled wealth; by 1910, they held 98.3 percent of the wealth. Likewise, the top 1 percent's holdings rose from 27.2 to 35 percent. Richard H. Steckel and Carolyn M. Moehling, "Rising Inequality: Trends in the Distribution of Wealth in Industrializing New England," *Journal of Economic History* 61, no. 1 (2001): 160–83. For an overview of historical debates, see Carole Shammas, "A New Look at Long-Term Trends in Wealth Inequality in the United States," *American Historical Review* 98, no. 2 (1993): 412–31.

11 McGerr, *Fierce Discontent*, 7.

12 Sven Beckert, *The Monied Metropolis: New York City and the Consolidation of the American Bourgeoisie, 1850–1896* (Cambridge: Cambridge University Press, 2001), 211.

13 Thorstein Veblen, *The Theory of the Leisure Class: An Economic Study of Institutions* (New York: Modern Library, 1934), 68–75.

14 Sven Beckert argues that while new wealth constituted an important part of society (particularly in New York), two-thirds of elites acquired their fortunes through inheritance. Similarly, Steckel and Moehling have demonstrated that in Massachusetts, land, more than entrepreneurial innovation, was the source of late-nineteenth-century riches. Beckert, *Monied Metropolis*, 238; Steckel and Moehling, "Rising Inequality," 180–81. The terms "nobs" and "swells" were coined by Ward McAllister. Ward McAllister, *Society as I Have Found It* (New York: Cassell, 1890), 246.

15 See, for example, Albin Pasteur Dearing, *The Elegant Inn: The Waldorf-Astoria Hotel, 1893–1929* (Secaucus, N.J.: L. Stuart, 1986); and Beckert, *Monied Metropolis*, 246–56.

16 Dixon Wecter, *The Saga of American Society: A Record of Social Aspiration, 1607–1937* (New York: Scribner, 1970), 183.

17 For a comparison with Europe, see Mennell, *All Manners of Food*.

18 Beckert, *Monied Metropolis*, 258.

19 Paul Bourget, *Outre-Mer: Impressions of America* (New York: C. Scribner's Sons, 1895), 54. Bourget's comments sparked outrage among America's elites and a humorous rebuttal from Mark Twain. However, not everyone disagreed with

his assessment. The *New York Times* argued that Bourget's description of the "American spirit" should not be taken to represent all Americans but conceded that "M. Bourget's picture of society, as it exists at Newport and similar localities, is a fairly correct one." Mark Twain, *Essays on Paul Bourget* (1895), http://www.gutenberg.org/etext/3173 (accessed March 7, 2005); "Gossip about Gotham," *Washington Post*, January 28, 1894; "New Publications: Paul Bourget's Book About Us," *New York Times*, May 19, 1895, 31. See also "Women Who Smoke Rare," *New York Times*, December 9, 1894, 18.

20 Wecter, *Saga of American Society*, 306–7; Howard Mumford Jones, *America and French Culture, 1750–1848* (Chapel Hill: University of North Carolina Press, 1927), 301, 307. Jones noted, however, that many early American notables, from John Adams to Thomas Jefferson, were admirers of French cuisine and that French cuisine, imported by way of England, probably exerted a greater influence in the early nineteenth century than contemporary accounts indicate.

21 Eric Homberger, *Mrs. Astor's New York: Money and Social Power in a Gilded Age* (New Haven: Yale University Press, 2002), 5. See also Barry Gray, "As We Journey through Life: Bohemian Days and a Word About Them," *The Caterer* 2, no. 9 (1884): 337–41.

22 Jones, *America and French Culture*, 309 n. 72. For a general discussion of the role of French food in France and in European society, see Mennell, *All Manners of Food*, 134–35; and Susan Pinkard, *A Revolution in Taste: The Rise of French Cuisine, 1650–1800* (Cambridge: Cambridge University Press, 2009).

23 Homberger, *Mrs. Astor's New York*, 176; "Blot's Cooking Academy," *New York Times*, October 3, 1865; "A New School of Art," *New York Times*, February 9, 1865. Some contemporaries dismissed Blot's efforts, noting that his pupils did not necessarily put his teaching into practice. Nonetheless, Blot's fleeting popularity gives evidence of a changing attitude toward French food among America's elites. For a positive account of Blot's influence from a food reformer, see Dio Lewis, *Talks about People's Stomachs* (Boston: Fields, Osgood and Company, 1870), 180. See also Jan Longone, "Professor Blot and the First French Cooking School in New York, Part 1," *Gastronomica* 1, no. 2 (2001): 65–71; and Jan Longone, "Professor Blot and the First French Cooking School in New York, Part 2," *Gastronomica* 1, no. 3 (2001): 53–59.

24 On travel, see Harvey A. Levenstein, *Seductive Journey: American Tourists in France from Jefferson to the Jazz Age* (Chicago: University of Chicago Press, 1998), 81; "Passing of French Cookery," *Washington Post*, September 18, 1912, 6; McAllister, *Society as I Have Found It*, 126–27 (italics in original). McAllister's chronology is unclear, but it appears he is talking about the period between 1860 and 1870.

25 Delmonico's was one of the first American restaurants to have an all-French menu. There were, however, a number of other restaurants with French chefs that opened at about the same time in both New York and Philadelphia. For a discussion of American hotels, for example, see Sexagenarian, "New York City: Its Ancient Taverns and Modern Hotels," *The Caterer* 3, no. 5 (1885): 182.

26 Quoted in Thomas, *Delmonico's*, 15.

27 Ibid., frontispiece. A salmi is a spiced dish consisting of game bird and wine.

28 Quoted in George G. Foster and Stuart M. Blumin, *New York by Gas-Light and Other Urban Sketches* (Berkeley: University of California Press, 1990).

29 George Augustus Sala, "Chats About Cookery: The American Cuisine," *Table Talk*, February 1908, 85.

30 "Delmonico's New Restaurant," *New York Times*, April 7, 1862, 5; Henry Collins Brown, *Delmonico's: A Story of Old New York* (New York: Valentine's Manual, 1928), 60; Editors, *The Chef* 8, no. 1 (1898): 22.

31 Ranhofer was born in 1836 in S. Denis, France, and began his study of cooking in Paris at the age of twelve. In 1856, he traveled to the United States, but he returned to France in 1860 to work at the court of Napoleon III. In 1861, he again traveled to the United States and worked at the Maison Doree in New York until Lorenzo Delmonico acquired his services in 1862. Ranhofer briefly left Delmonico's in the late 1870s but returned and stayed with the restaurant until his retirement in 1898. He died a year later.

32 Thomas, *Delmonico's*, 90. See also Brown, *Delmonico's*, 49.

33 Brown, *Delmonico's*, 59.

34 Menu, "Menu," Delmonico's, New York, N.Y., March 17, 1884, Box 3 (1884-55a [a-b]), Buttolph Menu Collection, New York Public Library, New York (spelling in original; hereafter cited as Buttolph Menu).

35 Menu, "Complimentary Banquet to the National Board of Trade by the Commercial Associations of the City of New York," Delmonico's, New York, N.Y., June 29, 1876, Box 1 (1876-77-30), Buttolph Menu.

36 It is impossible to know how often Delmonico's menus were copied. However, recipes from Delmonico's appeared in two influential turn-of-the-century culinary magazines, *What to Eat* and *Table Talk*, as well as the New York–based restaurant journal *The Steward*. In 1889, Alessandro Filippini published *The Table*, a collection of Delmonico's recipes intended for home use. In 1894, Charles Ranhofer published his encyclopedic *The Epicurean*, a nearly complete list of his recipes and menus. Alexander Filippini, *The Table: How to Buy Food, How to Cook It, and How to Serve It* (New York: Baker & Taylor, 1895); Charles Ranhofer, *The Epicurean: A Complete Treatise of Analytical and Practical Studies on the Culinary Art* (New York: C. Ranhofer, 1894). For a discussion, see Thomas, *Delmonico's*, 261.

37 The United States did not have a trademark law until 1881 and then only for foreign commerce. The first domestic trademark legislation was approved in 1905. The Delmonico family tried to control the use of the family name and sued a restaurateur named Gailliard in 1889 after a number of patrons visiting France claimed they had gone to a Parisian restaurant named "Delmonico" mistakenly thinking it was run by the New York family. "The Paris 'Delmonico,'" *New York Times*, November 8, 1889, 8.

38 Thomas, *Delmonico's*, 149; Editors, *Hotel World*, September 21, 1876, 6. "Delmon-

ican" was sometimes used as an adjective to indicate a particularly elaborate meal. For an example, see Miriam Leslie, *California: A Pleasure Trip from Gotham to the Golden Gate* (New York: G. W. Carleton, 1877), 36.

39 On the influence of Delmonico's in New York, see Thomas, *Delmonico's*, 279; and Henry Collins Brown, *Brownstone Fronts and Saratoga Trunks* (New York: E. P. Dutton, 1935), 397. On the other "Delmonico" restaurants, see Perry Duis, *Challenging Chicago: Coping with Everyday Life, 1837–1920* (Urbana: University of Illinois Press, 1998), 147; and Frances de Talavera Berger and John Parke Custis, *Sumptuous Dining in Gaslight San Francisco* (Garden City, N.Y.: Doubleday, 1985), 132–33. Delmonico's in New Orleans is still in business. None of these "Delmonico's" was owned by the Delmonico family of New York. Jeannette Young, "The Famous 'Yiddish Delmonico's,'" *Table Talk*, January 1911, 23–25; Jessup Whitehead, *The Steward's Handbook and Guide to Party Catering* (Chicago: J. Anderson, 1889), 379.

40 Quoted in Thomas, *Delmonico's*, 175.

41 Gene Bourg, "New Orleans Foodways," in *New Encyclopedia of Southern Culture*, ed. John T. Edge (Chapel Hill: University of North Carolina Press, 2007), 85; Berger and Custis, *Sumptuous Dining in Gaslight San Francisco*, 83; "Brillat Savarin," *The Table* 1, no. 1 (1873): 13–14.

42 Menu, "Dinner on Friday, November 21, 1873," Fifth Avenue Hotel, New York, N.Y., November 21, 1873, Box 1 (1871-73-27), Buttolph Menu. On a French menu and on most American menus of the nineteenth century, items served during the entrée course were "prepared" dishes served as a side or as a light course. Since simply cooked meat, chicken, or fish were typically served as the other main courses, the entrée course was often a crafted French dish. Americans began to refer to the daily special—and eventually any main dish—as an entrée only in the early twentieth century.

43 Menu, "Gardner House," Gardner House, Chicago, Ill., May 6, 1873, Box 2 (1871-73-42), Buttolph Menu.

44 Menu, "Dinner, Friday, September 9, 1870," Fifth Avenue Restaurant, New York, N.Y., September 9, 1870, Box 1 (1870-38), Buttolph Menu.

45 Menu, "The Oceanic," The Oceanic, Star Island, N.H., August 19, 1874, Box 2 (1875-80-35), Buttolph Menu. Although the French-derived term "fricassee" was used, it was used without an accent.

46 Menu, various, Boxes 1–20, Buttolph Menu. There were exceptions. Dixon Wecter exempted "conservative Boston, threadbare Charleston, and a few other cities." Wecter, *Saga of American Society*, 182.

47 Noah Brooks, "Restaurant Life of San Francisco," *Overland Monthly*, November 1868, 467.

48 Menu, "Carte du Jour," Brevoort House, New York, N.Y., November 10, 1886, Box 4 (1886-76a [a-b]), Buttolph Menu.

49 Menu, "Dinner," West Hotel, Minneapolis, Minn., February 21, 1886, Box 4 (1886-09 or 1886-24), Buttolph Menu.

50 Menu, "The Oceanic," The Oceanic, Star Island, N.H., August 30, 1884, Box 4 (1884-27 or 1884-16), Buttolph Menu.

51 Menu, "Banquet, Annual Dinner by the Association of American Physicians," New Willard Hotel, Washington, D.C., May 16, 1905, Box 124 (1905-399), Buttolph Menu; Menu, "Banquet for the Commercial Clubs of Boston, Chicago and St. Louis," St. Nicholas Hotel, St. Louis, Mo., October 24, 1895, Box 22 (1895-170) or (1895-171), Buttolph Menu; Menu, "St. Charles Hotel," St. Charles Hotel, New Orleans, La., April 11, 1875, Box 2 (1875-80-16), Buttolph Menu; Menu, "The Annual Meeting Merchant Tailors National Exchange Banquet given at the Hotel Iroquois," Hotel Iroquois, Buffalo, N.Y., February 7, 1895, Box 20 (1895-243 or 1895-032), Buttolph Menu.

52 As late as 1933, the Waldorf-Astoria's Oscar Tschirky wrote to French chef Escoffier expressing relief that he had been able to find a French chef to staff the famous hotel's dining room. "It saved us much trouble, because here in America chefs are very rare; I don't know where to find them." Quoted in Amanda Watson Schnetzer, "The Golden Age of Cooking," Policy Review 97 (October/November 1999): 57.

53 Menu, "The Antlers," The Antlers, Colorado Springs, Colo., March 4, 1885, Box 4 (1885-58b [a-b] or 1885-010), Buttolph Menu. Note that the pudding, an English dish, was also described in French.

54 Menu, "Dinner," United States Hotel, Saratoga Springs, N.Y., August 15, 1880, Box 4 (1880-5), Buttolph Menu.

55 Emmett Dedmon, Fabulous Chicago (New York: Random House, 1953), 223–24. Although, as we shall see, the French restaurant's influence declined in the twentieth century, celebrations of French cooking continued. See F. Reichenbach, "French Cuisine," The Caterer 27, no. 8 (1916): 64–66.

56 Helen S. Conant, "Kitchen and Dining Room," Harper's New Monthly Magazine, February 1877, 427.

57 Lucy Langdon Wilson, Handbook of Domestic Science and Household Arts for Use in Elementary Schools: A Manual for Teachers (New York: Macmillan, 1900), 70. See also Lutèce, "Our Paris Letter," 360. The myth of the French Revolution serving as a spark for restaurants remained popular into the twentieth century. See Barbara Ketcham Wheaton, Savoring the Past: The French Kitchen and Table from 1300 to 1789 (Philadelphia: University of Pennsylvania Press, 1983); and Henri Gault and Christian Millau, A Parisian's Guide to Paris (New York: Random House, 1969).

58 Rebecca L. Spang, The Invention of the Restaurant: Paris and Modern Gastronomic Culture (Cambridge: Harvard University Press, 2000). Jean-Robert Pitte, in a work first published in French in 1991, continues to maintain that French restaurants are the legacy of out-of-work chefs who once worked for nobles. While that is not true, French gastronomy benefited from the support of the aristocracy in ways that suggest there is a grain of truth to American's assumptions that the food served at French restaurants owed its origins to the French aristocracy. Jean-

Robert Pitte, *French Gastronomy: The History and Geography of a Passion*, trans. Jody Gladding (New York: Columbia University Press, 2002), 102–9, 118–19.

59 Nicholas M. Kiefer, "Economics and the Origins of the Restaurant," *Cornell Hotel and Restaurant Administration Quarterly* 43, no. 4 (2002): 58–65.

60 Tales of the aristocratic origins of dining regularly appeared at the turn of the century. The story of Vatel, the loyal cook who fell on his sword when the fish did not arrive on time, appeared in dozens of nineteenth-century food writings. In 1907, George Ellwanger, in his painstaking review of the origins of French cooking (an account that correctly distinguishes between the aristocratic and bourgeois origins of the restaurants), declined to retell the story of Vatel because he was so sure his audience already knew it. George H. Ellwanger, *The Pleasures of the Table: An Account of Gastronomy from Ancient Days to Present Times* (New York: Doubleday Page, 1902), 59. While stories of chefs displaced by the Revolution and Vatel's sacrifice were the most often repeated tales, the story of the Chevalier d'Albignac, as reported in *What to Eat*, demonstrates the ubiquity of the genre. According to *What to Eat*, "In the evil days of the French Revolution, the Chevalier d'Albignac escaped from Paris to London, where he subsisted painfully, if not miserably, on a small pittance allowed him by the English government until accident afforded him a field for the profitable exercise of the only art which he could turn to money." The "accident," an invitation at a London hotel to prepare a salad in the "French fashion," led to a profitable business making salads for wealthy Londoners. In time, he became known as the "Gentleman Salad Maker." "The Gentleman Salad Maker," *What to Eat*, October 1896, 69.

61 Veblen, *Theory of the Leisure Class*, 127–29. This idea is echoed and complicated by Pierre Bourdieu. See Pierre Bourdieu, *Distinction: A Social Critique of the Judgment of Taste* (Cambridge: Harvard University Press, 1984), 177–78.

62 Ellwanger, *Pleasures of the Table*, 259.

63 On nineteenth-century French culinary standards, see Priscilla Parkhurst Ferguson, "A Cultural Field in the Making: Gastronomy in Nineteenth-Century France," in *French Food: On the Table, on the Page, and in French Culture*, ed. Lawrence R. Schehr and Allen S. Weiss (New York: Routledge, 2001), esp. 26–31.

64 "Gotham's Chefs," *The Caterer* 3, no. 7 (1885): 268.

65 Felix L. Oswald, "International Food Studies: France," *What to Eat*, May 1901, 145. See also A. Kenney-Herbert, "The Art of Cooking," *Nineteenth Century*, November 1892, 764.

66 M. E. Carter, "The Chef," *What to Eat*, January 1901, 19. See also Adolphe Meyer, "Letter," *The Caterer* 23, no. 3 (1911): 24. For a comparison of French and American chefs, see "Running a 'Smart' New York Restaurant—Parisian Methods," *Restaurant Bulletin* 2, no. 14 (1904): 22. On apprenticeship, see Amy B. Trubek, *Haute Cuisine: How the French Invented the Culinary Profession* (Philadelphia: University of Pennsylvania Press, 2000), esp. 70–76. For an example of the French system of apprenticeship, see Ian Kelly, *Cooking for Kings: The Life of Antonin Carême, the First Celebrity Chef* (New York: Walker and Co., 2003), 33–38. Although the French ap-

prenticeship was thorough, Americans often overestimated the degree to which chefs received formal schooling in the nineteenth century. The École Profession-nelle de Cuisine et des Sciences Alimentaires, organized in the 1890s, survived only two years despite a government stamp of approval. Trubek, *Haute Cuisine*, 104–7. Alain Drouard, "Escoffier, Bocuse et (Surtout) Les Autres . . . : Towards a History of Cooks in France in the Nineteenth and Twentieth Centuries," in *Eating out in Europe: Picnics, Gourmet Dining, and Snacks since the Late Eighteenth Century*, ed. Marc Jacobs and Peter Scholliers (Oxford: Berg, 2003), 218–19.

67 On American marriages to Europeans, see Kristin L. Hoganson, *Consumers' Imperium: The Global Production of American Domesticity, 1865–1920* (Chapel Hill: University of North Carolina Press, 2007), 79.

68 "Dishes for the Million: Good Things to Tempt Hungry Men at Hotels and Clubs, Elaborate Menus for New Year's," *New York Times*, January 1, 1895, 6; Frank G. Carpenter, "Washington Dinners," *Los Angeles Times*, July 10, 1887.

69 "Dishes for the Million," 6.

70 R. Burns, "Art of the Paris Cook," *Current Literature*, December 1900, 688. Origi-nally published in the *New York Sun*. The reference appears to be to the Académie Culinaire de France.

71 Carter, "The Chef," 19, 21.

72 McAllister, *Society as I Have Found It*, 101.

73 "Cooking as a Fine Art: Beautiful Exhibits by Dexterous French Chefs," *New York Times*, February 4, 1891, 8.

74 Carolyn Korsmeyer, *Making Sense of Taste: Food and Philosophy* (Ithaca: Cornell University Press, 1999), 125.

75 Herbert M. Kliebard, *Forging the American Curriculum: Essays in Curriculum History and Theory* (New York: Routledge, 1992), 10, 22. See also H. Jones, *America and French Culture*, 214–16.

76 Levenstein, *Seductive Journey*, 99–100. Levenstein notes that in the post-1850s, in-creasing numbers of parvenus joined the upper class in Europe.

77 Alfred Hennequin, "Do Americans Need to Speak French?" *Education* 15 (1895): 171.

78 Alan Davidson, "A La," in *Oxford Companion to Food* (Oxford: Oxford University Press, 1999), 8–9.

79 Minnie E. Leo, "Jests for the Table," *What to Eat*, February 1902, 65.

80 As the nineteenth century closed, French menus in the United States were gener-ally standardized. In part, these reforms followed the emigration of more French chefs at the turn of the century and the influence of a generation of American-born chefs trained in kitchens run by French chefs, but it also reflected reforms in French cooking, particularly the system of classification promoted by Auguste Escoffier in his *Le Guide Culinaire* (1903). A. Escoffier, *Le Guide Culinaire: The First Complete Translation into English* (New York: Mayflower Books, 1979).

81 Knowledge of cook's French was passed on to children at an early age. Since menus were printed daily and wealthy Americans often brought their menus

home as souvenirs, upper-class children were slowly exposed to French menus as they grew up. Then, when they were old enough, they could take the grand tour of Europe and, with the help of tutors and guides, finish their culinary education.

82 "Eating in American," *Literary Digest*, October 10, 1914, 702–3.

83 Whitehead, *Steward's Handbook*, 186. A similar idea was expressed by W. F. Cozart: "Never seat a poorly dressed and 'seedy' looking person or persons at the same table with a well dressed, aristocratic person and yet this maneuvering must be so artistically done that it will not be detected, and consequently there will be no offense given." Winfield Forrest Cozart, *A Technical Treatise on Dining-Room Service: The Waiters' Manual* (Chicago: H. J. Bohn and Brother, 1898), 84. As time passed, middle-class patrons became increasing aware of the discrimination restaurateurs showed.

84 The Brunswick Hotel, once a rival to Delmonico's, suffered irreparable damage to its reputation in 1882 when concert hall owner Billy McGlory, posing as a "Mr. Thompson," booked a private room and arrived that night with forty-seven female concert hall girls and three male guests. The guests created havoc, and the Brunswick Hotel never recovered. It closed in 1896. Michael Batterberry and Ariane Ruskin Batterberry, *On the Town in New York: The Landmark History of Eating, Drinking, and Entertainments from the American Revolution to the Food Revolution* (New York: Routledge, 1999), 156–58.

85 Cozart, *Technical Treatise*, 61. One guide even suggested that height should be a concern when selecting waiters in order to maintain discipline. "In the army there is a rule which shuts out all men below a certain standard height, and if it is bad for the little men, the rule is good for the appearance of the ranks on parade. Small waiters may do well enough, but if they run large it comes hard for a stumpy headwaiter to play the peremptory colonel over them." Whitehead, *Steward's Handbook*, 187.

86 Cozart, *Technical Treatise*, 58. See also Whitehead, *Steward's Handbook*, 191.

87 Cozart, *Technical Treatise*, 62, 15.

88 E. A. Maccannon, *Commanders of the Dining Room: Biographic Sketches and Portraits of Successful Head Waiters* (New York: Gwendolyn, 1904), 11. Although the proximate source of the preference for black waiters in the nineteenth century was slavery, the practice may have been influenced by the use of "court moors" as servants in European aristocratic homes. Jan Nederveen Pieterse, *White on Black: Images of Africa and Blacks in Western Popular Culture* (New Haven: Yale University Press, 1992), 124–28.

89 Maccannon, *Commanders of the Dining Room*, 11. Maccannon felt confident that the recent trend away from hiring African American waiters had been reversed. However, no evidence supports this claim and, in fact, the growth of the restaurant trade was quickly outstripping the number of available black waiters in cities like New York. See Mary White Ovington, *Half a Man: The Status of the Negro in New York* (New York: Longmans, Green, 1911), 78–79. Alternatively, the *Restaurant Bulletin* suggested the black waiters were abandoning the profession

for less menial work. "Negroes as Waiters," *Restaurant Bulletin* 2, no. 18 (1905): 27. Not everyone appreciated the African American waiter. Rudyard Kipling in his 1891 account of American life commented: "Now let me draw breath and curse the negro waiter and through him the negro in service generally." Kipling felt that African American waiters were manipulative and not genuinely subservient. This widespread attitude also may have contributed to the shift away from black waiters in the early twentieth century. Rudyard Kipling, *American Notes* (New York: Arcadia House, 1950), 41.

90 African American waiters continued to dominate the serving profession in the South, where they were considered appropriately subservient. See the comments of W. R. Lucus, Secretary of the Southern Hotel Association, in "New York Letter," *The Southern Hotel Journal* 2, no. 12 (1913): 31.

91 Elenor Blissford, "Fads and Fancies of Gotham," *What to Eat*, September 1907, 114.

92 Tunis G. Campbell, *Hotel Keepers, Head Waiters, and Housekeepers' Guide* (Boston: Coolidge and Wiley, 1848), 11, 34–35.

93 Cozart, *Technical Treatise*, 61.

94 Ibid., 13, 83.

95 While most hotel dining rooms used the table d'hôte method of service, some hotels and many independent establishments provided a "restaurant" where food was served à la carte. In either case, the dedicated waiter could secure preferential servings for a favored patron.

96 Campbell, *Hotel Keepers, Head Waiters, and Housekeepers' Guide*, 59.

97 Frank W. Doolittle, "A Waiter's Mission," *The Caterer* 11, no. 8 (1901): 26.

98 McAllister, *Society as I Have Found It*, 257.

99 Homberger, *Mrs. Astor's New York*, 217.

100 Dearing, *Elegant Inn*, 78. The public association between the rich and restaurants occasionally made dining establishments sites of violent clashes. In 1893, Delmonico's windows were shattered when a disgruntled laborer, George Roeth, stood outside the restaurant and fired his revolver at diners in the restaurant while screaming, "Curse the rich! Curse them now and for all time." M. H. Dunlop, *Gilded City: Scandal and Sensation in Turn-of-the-Century New York* (New York: W. Morrow, 2000), 201–3. And in 1897, the Bradley-Martin ball at the Waldorf-Astoria, held in the midst of an economic downturn, attracted so much negative publicity that 250 policemen had to form a protective cordon around the hotel. McGerr, *Fierce Discontent*, 5.

101 "Delmonico's Restaurant," *New York Times*, September 14, 1876, 8.

102 "Passing of the Fifth Avenue Hotel About to Remove One of New York's Noted Landmarks," *New York Times*, July 7, 1907, sec. Sunday Magazine, 2.

103 "Stevens House," *The Steward* 13, no. 1 (1918): 33. The Delmonico family owned the Stevens House for a time. For another example of the restaurant obituary, see Sexagenarian, "New York City: Its Ancient Taverns and Modern Hotels," 311.

104 Veblen, *Theory of the Leisure Class*, 128.

105 This "American" attitude might be contrasted with the French approach to their own cuisine. According to Priscilla Parkhurst Ferguson, by the late nineteenth century, French cuisine was identified with the nation and had lost its aristocratic associations. Priscilla Parkhurst Ferguson, *Accounting for Taste: The Triumph of French Cuisine* (Chicago: University of Chicago Press, 2004), 7–9.

106 Bourdieu, *Distinction*, 66.

107 "How to Make Money in a Small Country Hotel," *The Caterer* 11, no. 2 (1900): 11.

108 Abraham Hayward, "The Art of Dining," *Current Literature*, May 1900, 219. Abraham Hayward's *The Art of Dining* was first published in 1843 before Darwin's *On the Origin of Species* and before the advent of social Darwinism. However, the influential work was reprinted in both 1883 and 1899 (and the 1899 version was widely reviewed in the American press) at a time when Herbert Spencer's ideas about natural selection were being widely discussed. As the excerpt reprinted in *Current Literature* suggests, the passages on heredity were particularly interesting to Americans in the late nineteenth century. See also Ferguson, *Accounting for Taste*, 31.

109 Irvin Wyllie and Robert Bannister have demonstrated that late-nineteenth-century businessmen were less likely to invoke social Darwinist explanations in debates over social and political policy than their critics. And, of course, the laissez-faire economy had roots that predate social Darwinism. Robert C. Bannister, *Social Darwinism: Science and Myth in Anglo-American Social Thought* (Philadelphia: Temple University Press, 1979); Irvin G. Wyllie, "Social Darwinism and the Businessman," *Proceedings of the American Philosophical Society* 103, no. 5 (1959): 629–35. The emphasis on political and economic discourse, however, has distracted historians from noticing how often social Darwinist ideas, especially the belief that biology determines one's status and that economic accomplishment is proof of superiority, appeared in popular works. See, for example, debates over women's role in popular science monthlies in Louise Michele Newman, *Men's Ideas/Women's Realities: Popular Science, 1870–1915* (New York: Pergamon Press, 1985). More generally, see Herbert Spencer, *The Principles of Sociology* (Westport, Conn.: Greenwood Press, 1975); Richard Hofstadter, *Social Darwinism in American Thought* (Boston: Beacon Press, 1992); and Mike Hawkins, *Social Darwinism in European and American Thought, 1860–1945* (Cambridge: Cambridge University Press, 1997).

110 A. H. Gouraud, "The Cultured Palate," *Current Literature*, October 1900, 452.

111 M. O. Warren, "The Basis of Dietetics," *The Steward* 3, no. 7 (1903): 23. Warren went on to argue that the development of Japanese society had been severely retarded by vegetarianism.

112 For a related discussion of civilization and nutrition, see Deborah Neill, "Finding the 'Ideal Diet': Nutrition, Culture, and Dietary Practices in France and French Equatorial Africa, c. 1890s to 1920s," *Food and Foodways* 17, no. 1 (2009): 1–28.

113 Albert J. Bellows, *Philosophy of Eating* (Boston: Houghton Mifflin, 1870); "A Curious Experiment," *What to Eat*, August 1897, 44.

114 Carl Benson, "French Cooking," *New York Times*, April 24, 1873, 4.

115 Dedmon, *Fabulous Chicago*, 225.

116 Quoted in William Griffith, "The New Yorker and His Dinner," *New York Times*, March 26, 1905, sec. 3, 1.

117 The biological argument was about quality, not quantity. Although the rich were said to suffer disproportionately from dyspepsia and some argued that the wealthy needed to demonstrate more discipline at the table, the quantity one ate was a moral choice whereas the quality of the food was a biological necessity.

118 Not every spokesperson for the hereditary nature of the culinary arts was as clear or as absolute as Dr. Burt. See "Carver Like Poets, Born and Not Made," *New York Times*, December 13, 1908, sec. 6, VI6.

119 "Kings of the Kitchen: When Chef Explodes Even His Employees Tremble," *Washington Post*, September 15, 1901, 17.

CHAPTER 2

1 "Dishes for the Million: Good Things to Tempt Hungry Men at Hotels and Clubs, Elaborate Menus for New Year's," *New York Times*, January 1, 1895, 6.

2 "The Tourney of the Chefs: Artistic New Year Feasts Spread by the Big Hotels," *New York Times*, January 3, 1893, 2.

3 Ibid. (emphasis added).

4 Michael Batterberry and Ariane Ruskin Batterberry, *On the Town in New York: The Landmark History of Eating, Drinking, and Entertainments from the American Revolution to the Food Revolution* (New York: Routledge, 1999), 144.

5 "Tourney of the Chefs," 2.

6 "Dishes for the Million," 6.

7 "Tourney of the Chefs," 2.

8 For a much more nuanced description than is provided here, see Stuart M. Blumin, *The Emergence of the Middle Class: Social Experience in the American City, 1760– 1900* (Cambridge: Cambridge University Press, 1989), 68–78.

9 Ibid., 290.

10 Alfred Dupont Chandler, *The Visible Hand: The Managerial Revolution in American Business* (Cambridge, Mass.: Belknap Press, 1977); Olivier Zunz, *Making America Corporate, 1870–1920* (Chicago: University of Chicago Press, 1990); Burton J. Bledstein and Robert D. Johnston, eds., *The Middling Sorts: Explorations in the History of the American Middle Class* (New York: Routledge, 2001).

11 Mansel G. Blackford, *A History of Small Business in America* (Chapel Hill: University of North Carolina Press, 2003), 43–44.

12 Bledstein and Johnston, *Middling Sorts*, 18; Peter N. Stearns, "The Middle Class: Toward a Precise Definition," *Comparative Studies in Society and History* 21, no. 3 (1979): 384–85. See also Melanie Archer and Judith R. Blau, "Class Formation in Nineteenth-Century America: The Case of the Middle Class," *Annual Review of Sociology* 19 (1993): 17–41; Richard M. Ohmann, *Selling Culture: Magazines, Markets, and Class at the Turn of the Century* (London: Verso, 1996); and Walter Nu-

gent, "Tocqueville, Marx and American Class Structure," *Social Science History* 12, no. 4 (1988): 327–47. Even if income analysis for the late nineteenth century could offer an accurate picture of the middle class, there is a limited amount of data available.

13 Scott Derks, *The Value of a Dollar: Prices and Incomes in the United States, 1860–1999* (Lakeville, Conn.: Grey House, 1999), 63.

14 John Model, "Patterns of Consumption, Acculturation, and Family Income Strategies in Late Nineteenth-Century America," in *Family and Population in Nineteenth-Century America*, ed. Tamara K. Hareven and Maris Vinovskis (Princeton: Princeton University Press, 1978), 206–40.

15 Archer and Blau, "Class Formation in Nineteenth-Century America," 22.

16 Ohmann, *Selling Culture*, 119.

17 Booth Tarkington, *Alice Adams* (Garden City, N.Y.: Doubleday, Page & Company, 1921).

18 Frank Norris, *McTeague: A Story of San Francisco* (Mineola, N.Y.: Dover Publications, 2004). Lines between middle-class and working-class Americans were not the only distinctions that occupation blurred. Although the practice decreased in the early twentieth century, wealthy capitalists often held white-collar jobs as lawyers and brokers managing family estates. See also Richard H. Steckel and Carolyn M. Moehling, "Rising Inequality: Trends in the Distribution of Wealth in Industrializing New England," *Journal of Economic History* 61, no. 1 (2001): 160–83.

19 Survey data not only suggest the weakness of income and occupation as predictors of class identity but also argue against using work and wage as factors in determining class identity. Richard Hamilton's examination of survey data on white-collar workers in the 1950s, for example, found that more than half viewed themselves as working class. Other studies, most notably a widely cited 1940 *Fortune* magazine poll, suggest that Americans described themselves as middle class regardless of occupation and income. Richard F. Hamilton, "The Marginal Middle Class: A Reconsideration," *American Sociological Review* 31, no. 2 (1966): 195 n. 14; "The Fortune Survey," *Fortune*, February 1940, 14. See also Norval D. Glenn and Jon P. Alston, "Cultural Distances among Occupational Categories," *American Sociological Review* 33, no. 3 (1968): 365–82.

20 Post–Civil War industrial growth was accompanied by a change in management and a restructuring of the labor force. By 1917, four-fifths of the largest 236 manufacturing firms in the United States employed some form of "management system based upon departmentalized corporate offices." Blackford, *History of Small Business in America*, 46. See also Chandler, *Visible Hand*.

21 These studies are based primarily on manufacturing industry incomes. Clarence Dickinson Long and the National Bureau of Economic Research, *Wages and Earnings in the United States, 1860–1890* (Princeton: Princeton University Press, 1960), 60–61; Albert Rees, *Real Wages in Manufacturing, 1890–1914* (Princeton: Princeton University Press, 1961), 5.

22 P. K. Whelpton, "Occupational Groups in the United States, 1820–1920," *Journal*

of the American Statistical Association 21, no. 155 (1926): 336. Whelpton reclassified jobs according to commonsense categories in order to match twentieth-century categories with earlier census reports.

23 On managerial increases, see Blackford, *History of Small Business in America*, 46–47. On the number of clerks, see Cindy Sondik Aron, *Ladies and Gentlemen of the Civil Service: Middle-Class Workers in Victorian America* (New York: Oxford University Press, 1987), 18–19. For additional figures on the size of the middle class, see Ohmann, *Selling Culture*, 119; David Montgomery, *The Fall of the House of Labor: The Workplace, the State, and American Labor Activism, 1865–1925* (Cambridge: Cambridge University Press, 1987), 216; Burton J. Bledstein, *The Culture of Professionalism: The Middle Class and the Development of Higher Education in America* (New York: Norton, 1976), 35–39, 45; Thomas J. Schlereth, *Victorian America: Transformations in Everyday Life, 1876–1915* (New York: HarperPerennial, 1992), 29, 64; and Jacob Benjamin Salutsky Hardman, *American Labor Dynamics in the Light of Post-War Developments* (New York: Harcourt, 1928), 60.

24 On suburbs, see Kenneth T. Jackson, *Crabgrass Frontier: The Suburbanization of the United States* (New York: Oxford University Press, 1985). On consumption, see Susan Strasser, *Satisfaction Guaranteed: The Making of the American Mass Market* (New York: Pantheon Books, 1989). On government jobs, see Aron, *Ladies and Gentlemen of the Civil Service*. On leisure, see John S. Gilkeson, *Middle-Class Providence, 1820–1940* (Princeton: Princeton University Press, 1986), 109. In general, see Maury Klein, *The Flowering of the Third America: The Making of an Organizational Society, 1850–1920* (Chicago: Ivan R. Dee, 1993), esp. 107–11.

25 Richard Ohmann estimates that the middle class constituted about 12 percent of the population in 1910. Ohmann, *Selling Culture*, 119. Michael McGerr, drawing on a 1932 study by F. W. Taussig and C. S. Joslyn, as well as on U.S. Bureau of the Census figures, estimates that the middle class made up 20 percent of the population at the turn of the century. Michael E. McGerr, *A Fierce Discontent: The Rise and Fall of the Progressive Movement in America, 1870–1920* (New York: Free Press, 2003), 43.

26 Scott A. Sandage, *Born Losers: A History of Failure in America* (Cambridge: Harvard University Press, 2005).

27 Cindy R. Lobel, "Consuming Classes: Changing Food Consumption Patterns in New York City, 1790–1860" (PhD diss., City University of New York, 2003), 87.

28 In her dissertation on the "consuming classes" in New York City in the first half of the nineteenth century, Cindy Lobel argues that there were opportunities for members of the upper middle class to rub shoulders with the elite in antebellum hotels and restaurants. These opportunities were, however, always somewhat limited and not equally shared with all members of the nascent middle class. See ibid., esp. 101–4.

29 Blumin, *Emergence of the Middle Class*, 26–27.

30 "Ocean Table d'Hote-Rie," *The Caterer* 3, no. 3 (1884): 85.

31 Dixon Wecter, *The Saga of American Society: A Record of Social Aspiration, 1607–1937* (New York: Scribner, 1970), 108–9.

32 "Appearances Are Everything," *Washington Post*, July 9, 1888, 7. A single man living in New York with a salary of over $1,000 was comfortably middle class.

33 Ward McAllister, *Society as I Have Found It* (New York: Cassell, 1890), 78.

34 "Eating on Trust," *New York Daily Tribune*, December 10, 1899, sec. Illustrated Supplement, 1.

35 Arthur M. Schlesinger, *Learning How to Behave: A Historical Study of Social Etiquette Books* (New York: Macmillan, 1946), 18, 34; and Mary Reed Bobbit, "A Bibliography of Etiquette Books Published in America before 1900," *Bulletin of the New York Public Library* 51 (1947): 687–720, both quoted in John F. Kasson, *Rudeness and Civility: Manners in Nineteenth-Century Urban America* (New York: Hill and Wang, 1990), 44, 265. Kasson notes that Schlesinger's numbers are probably too low (although he defined the genre liberally by including all advice manuals).

36 Ohmann, *Selling Culture*, 231–33.

37 Wecter, *Saga of American Society*, 108–9. John Kasson argues that etiquette guides promised that "with the proper drive, knowledge, and success, an individual or family might climb the social ladder to new heights. Though the path to the summit rose precipitously and was guarded by jealous watchdogs of the upper class, middle-class members might nonetheless emulate some of its forms and manners." However, Kasson's assessment of these etiquette guides is rather inconsistent. In places, he argues that the guides offered the middle class a means of accessing upper-class culture (43); in other places, he suggests that advice manuals popularized middle-class notions of behavior and dress (121); and in still other places, he suggests that civility leveled class differences (210). In part, these varying interpretations may hinge on the sources, especially on who was writing the advice. Overall, however, Kasson's work suggests that etiquette guides evolved from instructions to the middle class from the wealthy to instructions to the middle class from the middle class. Kasson, *Rudeness and Civility*, 43.

38 Abby Buchanan Longstreet, *Social Etiquette of New York* (New York: D. Appleton, 1883), 8.

39 Kasson, *Rudeness and Civility*, 43.

40 Robert Tomes, *The Bazar Book of Decorum* (New York: Harper and Brothers, 1870), 206, 216–17.

41 Readers of etiquette books were sometimes reminded that public expediencies were not acceptable at private gatherings. In an 1869 guide, Sarah Annie Frost warned against treating the home waiter as one would a restaurant waiter. "If you want anything, take the occasion of a waiter being near to you, to ask for it in an undertone. To shout out 'Waiter!' or order one about, as if you were in a restaurant, is a certain mark of ill-breeding." S. Annie Frost, *Frost's Laws and By-Laws of American Society: A Condensed but Thorough Treatise on Etiquette and Its Usages in America* (New York: Dick and Fitzgerald, 1869), 59.

42 Tomes, *Bazar Book of Decorum*, 227.

43 Longstreet, *Social Etiquette of New York*, 119.

44 Ibid., 121.

45 Frank Tryon Charles, "Don'ts for the Table," *What to Eat*, February 1897, 164. Charles's celebrations of Parisian culture were often at odds with the journal's general hostility to aristocratic dining. See also Frank Tryon Charles, "Why I Prefer Paris," *What to Eat*, June 1901, 203; and Frank Tryon Charles, "Paris vs. New York," *What to Eat*, June 1899, 14.

46 In addition to the articles discussed, see "Restaurant Dinners: How to Make the Best of Them," *New York Daily Tribune*, November 15, 1896, sec. 3, 4.

47 "Cheap and Dainty Feast," *New York Times*, October 17, 1897, sec. 10, 6.

48 Ibid.

49 "'Covers for Two': A Gastronomic Study," *New York Times*, September 2, 1906, sec. Sunday Magazine, 2.

50 Ibid.

51 Ibid.

52 James L. Huston, *Securing the Fruits of Labor: The American Concept of Wealth Distribution, 1765–1900* (Baton Rouge: Louisiana State University Press, 1998), 83 (Table 1). Since income taxes were not collected, data on the distribution of wealth in the late nineteenth century is scarce. Jeffrey G. Williamson and Peter H. Lindert (whose work is one of Huston's sources for the data cited above) argue that inequality probably increased around 1900 after a period of relative "quiescence." Notably, they also argue (by examining payroll changes) that the urban middle class started to distance itself from skilled labor around 1896. However, comparisons of the consolidation of wealth by the top 1 percent and by the top 10 percent suggest that even as the middle class made progress, its members did so at a slower rate than the wealthy. Overall, the sketchy data available suggest the importance of taking a cultural rather than an economic approach when looking at wealth in the late nineteenth and early twentieth century. Jeffrey G. Williamson and Peter H. Lindert, *American Inequality: A Macroeconomic History* (New York: Academic Press, 1980), 77.

53 Michael G. Kammen, *American Culture, American Tastes: Social Change and the 20th Century* (New York: Alfred A. Knopf, 1999), 29. See also Lawrence W. Levine, *Highbrow/Lowbrow: The Emergence of Cultural Hierarchy in America* (Cambridge: Harvard University Press, 1988), 234; and Richard L. Bushman, *The Refinement of America: Persons, Houses, Cities* (New York: Vintage Books, 1992), 419–20.

54 In an 1888 interview with the *New York Tribune*, McAllister claimed that New York "Society" consisted of four hundred individuals. The number (often attributed to the size of Mrs. Caroline Astor's ballroom) represented the optimal number of guests Delmonico's could accommodate and appears to have been set as early as 1880. "Fashion at Delmonico's: The Gay Season Opened by the Patriarchs," *New York Times*, December 21, 1880, 2. See also Stuyvesant Fish's

comments in Eric Homberger, *Mrs. Astor's New York: Money and Social Power in a Gilded Age* (New Haven: Yale University Press, 2002), 215.

55 The Social Register had precursors in *American Queen* (1879), *The List* (1880), and *The Season* (1883). Homberger, *Mrs. Astor's New York*, 11.

56 Although food prices generally fell during the nineteenth century, the disparity between first-class and second-class meals seems to have widened. An article in *Hotel World* in 1876 observed that the difference between the top two tiers of restaurants in New York was fifty cents (although it also stated that tables d'hôte were served for as little as one dollar). *New York World*, "Restaurant Prices," *Hotel World*, September 21, 1876, 7. The *Times'* "frugal" dinner for six, priced at $20 in 1897, cost $326 ($54 per person) in 1990 dollars. The dinner proposed in "'Covers for Two'" in 1906 would cost $276 ($138 a person). "Cheap and Dainty Feast," 6; "'Covers for Two,'" 2. Calculations utilize John J. McCusker's historical price index. The index is constructed from commodity prices and, as McCusker warns, "is better considered as hypothetical rather than as definitive." The commodity index McCusker uses is not based on restaurant prices either and therefore can serve only as a rough approximation of the effects of price inflation on public dining. It is useful to remember that food prices, a product of agricultural, transportation, storage, and preparation costs, are volatile and fluctuate according to weather, technological innovation, and world demand. John J. McCusker and American Antiquarian Society, *How Much Is That in Real Money? A Historical Price Index for Use as a Deflator of Money Values in the Economy of the United States* (Worcester, Mass.: American Antiquarian Society, 1992), 313. Other "inflation calculators" produce similar results. S. Morgan Friedman's online "Inflation Calculator" calculates that "what cost $20 in 1897 would cost $297.92 in 1990." This site uses the Consumer Price Index statistics from *Historical Statistics of the United States* (USGPO, 1975) and the annual *Statistical Abstracts of the United States* as the basis of its calculations. S. Morgan Friedman, "Inflation Calculator," http://www.westegg.com/inflation/ (accessed August 8, 2001).

57 Derks, *Value of a Dollar*, 53. Annual salaries were divided by fifty-two to produce weekly salaries. In some cases, most notably school teachers, this assumes the annual pay was for fifty-two weeks of work when it may have been for less and there would have been opportunities for additional income. Derks provides "selected incomes" for some occupations based on newspaper advertisements. These are consistent with the national data quoted. For example, a "business representative" position was advertised in the *New York Times* in 1903 for eighteen dollars a week; a bookkeeper/stenographer position was advertised in the *Chicago Tribune* in 1902 for twenty dollars a week.

58 H. Schuyler, "Home Versus Restaurant Dining," *New York Times*, February 10, 1908, 8.

59 Adolph Klauber, "Woes of the Well-to-Do," *New York Times*, June 5, 1904, sec. Sunday Magazine, 5.

60 "Restaurant Prices," *New York Times*, February 1, 1908, 8.

61 The *New York Daily Tribune* suggested that "if you go to the same place often try to find a good waiter and always sit at one of his tables when you can" to guarantee good service. "Restaurant Dinners," 4.

62 Charles Fellows, *The Menu Maker: Suggestions for Selecting and Arranging Menus for Hotels and Restaurants* (Chicago: Hotel Monthly Press, 1910), 57 (punctuation in original).

63 Mary F. Henderson, "Cooking as an Accomplishment," *The Dining Room Magazine* 2, no. 2 (1877): 36–37.

64 Elizabeth Tompkins, "A Dinner with Wine: Scenes in the Popular Public Eating Places of New York," *Washington Post*, September 15, 1889, 9.

65 Wecter, *Saga of American Society*, 7.

66 Longstreet, *Social Etiquette of New York*, 7–8.

67 Clara L. Cousine, *The Columbia Ideal Account Book* (Chicago: Columbia Publisher, 1894), 44.

68 Elizabeth Fries Lummis Ellet, *The Practical Housekeeper: A Cyclopaedia of Domestic Economy* (New York: Stringer and Townsend, 1857), 37.

69 William Dean Howells, *The Rise of Silas Lapham* (Boston: Ticknor and Company, 1885); Edith Wharton, *The House of Mirth* (New York: Macmillan, 1905); David Graham Phillips, *Susan Lenox: Her Fall and Rise*, 2 vols. (New York: D. Appleton, 1917); Tarkington, *Alice Adams*; Theodore Dreiser, *An American Tragedy*, 2 vols. (New York: Boni and Liveright, 1925).

70 T. S. Winslow, "When We Get In with Nice People," *American Mercury*, October 1925, 173.

71 Ibid., 182.

72 Hilda Richmond, "One Amusing Feature of Journeying," *Table Talk*, September 1910, 478. In another of her stories, the protagonist's bluff is immediately recognized. "Recently a young woman in a dining car complained loudly that there were no salads on the bill of fare. After making various remarks to her husband loud enough to include the people at three tables about the stupidity of having no salads, and how impossible it was for her to make a meal without this necessary dish, she called the busy waiter and inquired if he could not get up one for her especial benefit. . . . It is safe to say that the young woman who could not exist without salad . . . [is] not quite so important in the [town] in which [she lives], as [she] would like others to imagine" (478).

73 Helen Bruce Wallace, "The Summer Gadder and Her Ways," *Table Talk*, July 1911, 385.

74 Ibid.

75 "Cheap and Dainty Feast," 6. Dinner portions were large, and it was not unusual to share orders. However, one imagines it must have been considerably easier to share three portions of beef fritadelles than three orders of larded quail.

76 Ibid.

77 "Restaurant Dinners," 4.

78 Kasson, *Rudeness and Civility*, 48.

79 Huston, *Securing the Fruits of Labor*, 344. See also McGerr, *Fierce Discontent*, 39.

80 Dio Lewis, *Talks about People's Stomachs* (Boston: Fields, Osgood and Company, 1870), 18–19.

81 "German Restaurants," *New York Times*, January 19, 1873, 5.

82 "The Romance and Reality of New York's Restaurants," *New York Times*, November 23, 1913, sec. Sunday Magazine, 9.

83 Bushman, *Refinement of America*; Mary P. Ryan, *Cradle of the Middle Class: The Family in Oneida County, New York, 1790–1865* (Cambridge: Cambridge University Press, 1981); Susan Williams, *Savory Suppers and Fashionable Feasts: Dining in Victorian America* (New York: Pantheon Books, 1985).

84 A. T. Stewart's is a possible exception, but department store chronicler William Leach dismissed Stewart's as a dry goods store and contends that the department store did not exist before 1880 and really gained a foothold only in the 1890s. William Leach, *Land of Desire: Merchants, Power, and the Rise of a New American Culture* (New York: Pantheon Books, 1993), 22–24.

85 The Harvey House chain opened its first restaurant on the Atchison, Topeka and Santa Fe Railway in 1876, but its influence was limited to the Far West. Lesley Poling-Kempes, *The Harvey Girls: Women Who Opened the West* (New York: Paragon House, 1989).

86 Contemporary studies have similarly demonstrated that restaurant patrons avoid eating in places where they feel "uncomfortable." See Alan Warde and Linda Martens, "The Prawn Cocktail Ritual," in *Consuming Passions: Food in the Age of Anxiety*, ed. Sian Griffiths and Jennifer Wallace (Manchester: Manchester University Press, 1998), 121. For a discussion of the public sphere in the United States, see David Scobey, "Anatomy of the Promenade: The Politics of Bourgeois Sociability in Nineteenth-Century New York," *Social History* 17, no. 2 (1992): 203–27. For a discussion of how groups excluded from full participation in the political public sphere form "alternative public spheres," see Jürgen Habermas, *The Structural Transformation of the Public Sphere: An Inquiry into a Category of Bourgeois Society* (Cambridge: MIT Press, 1989), 54; and John A. Guidry and Mark Q. Sawyer, "Contentious Pluralism: The Public Sphere and Democracy," *Perspectives on Politics* 1, no. 2 (2003): 273–89. For a comparable discussion of the development of black counterpublics, see Houston A. Baker, "Critical Memory and the Black Public Sphere," in *The Black Public Sphere: A Public Culture Book*, ed. Black Public Sphere Collective (Chicago: University of Chicago Press, 1995), 7–37; and Joanna Brooks, "The Early American Public Sphere and the Emergence of a Black Print Counterpublic," *William and Mary Quarterly* 62, no. 1 (2005): 67–92.

CHAPTER 3

1 Junius Henri Browne, *The Great Metropolis: A Mirror of New York* (Hartford: American Publishing, 1869), 260–61.

2 "Restaurants," in *Appleton's Dictionary of Greater New York and Its Neighborhood* (New York: D. Appleton, 1892), 220.

3 Historian Cindy Lobel argues that while culinary venues were not diverse in the early nineteenth century, the middle class had access to elite establishments. Lobel describes a city in which taverns were slowly giving way to elite hotels and independent restaurants (including a few that primarily accommodated women). Most of these public dining facilities were restaurants of convenience, establishments for hurried businessmen. However, hotels did provide service to both the upper class and, according to Lobel, upper middle-class society. I don't question Lobel's findings, but I maintain that whatever access the middle class had to public dining establishments in the early days of the Republic was lost when aristocratic Americans consolidated their control over dining in the mid-century. Cindy R. Lobel, "Consuming Classes: Changing Food Consumption Patterns in New York City, 1790–1860" (PhD diss., City University of New York, 2003), 90–130.

4 George G. Foster and Stuart M. Blumin, *New York by Gas-Light and Other Urban Sketches* (Berkeley: University of California Press, 1990), 216–17. The original Foster compilation was titled *New York in Slices*.

5 Edgar Fawcett, "Old New York Restaurants," *Lippincott's Monthly Magazine* 54 (1894): 709.

6 Foster and Blumin, *New York by Gas-Light*, 219 (emphasis in original).

7 Browne, *Great Metropolis*, 265.

8 On the growth of apartments, see Perry Duis, *Challenging Chicago: Coping with Everyday Life, 1837–1920* (Urbana: University of Illinois Press, 1998), 83–84; and Paul Erling Groth, *Living Downtown: The History of Residential Hotels in the United States* (Berkeley: University of California Press, 1994), 57. On kitchenless dining, see "The Mania for Apartment Hotels," *New York Times*, May 18, 1902, 6. See also Thomas J. Schlereth, *Victorian America: Transformations in Everyday Life, 1876–1915* (New York: HarperPerennial, 1992), 110.

9 "A Few Hints to Boarding House-Keepers," *The Table*, May 1873, 99; Howard P. Chudacoff, *The Age of the Bachelor: Creating an American Subculture* (Princeton: Princeton University Press, 1999), 92, 126–31.

10 "Fair Women at Lunch," *New York Times*, December 20, 1885, 4. See also Kathy Lee Peiss, *Cheap Amusements: Working Women and Leisure in Turn-of-the-Century New York* (Philadelphia: Temple University Press, 1986), 53.

11 On shopping, see the advertisement for Shanley's Restaurants in "Interior Views of One of Shanley's Restaurants," *New York Daily Tribune*, December 24, 1898, sec. Metropolitan Supplement, 10. On sweethearts and the theater, see "15,000 Chicago Girls Who Work at Night," *Chicago Daily Tribune*, June 16, 1912, sec. F, 5.

12 On etiquette, see Robert Tomes, *The Bazar Book of Decorum* (New York: Harper and Brothers, 1870); and Abby Buchanan Longstreet, *Social Etiquette of New York* (New York: D. Appleton, 1883). On economics of domestic service, see Faye E. Dudden, *Serving Women: Household Service in Nineteenth-Century America* (Middle-

town, Conn.: Wesleyan University Press, 1983), 127, 240; Ruth Schwartz Cowan, *More Work for Mother: The Ironies of Household Technology from the Open Hearth to the Microwave* (New York: Basic Books, 1983), 122; and Sarah Tyson Heston Rorer, *Mrs. Rorer's New Cook Book: A Manual of Housekeeping* (Philadelphia: Arnold, 1902), 653, 667–68.

13 Cowan, *More Work for Mother*, 122.

14 Mrs. Alec Tweedie, "Mrs. Alec Tweedie Mourns Our Disappearing Home Life," *New York Times*, March 23, 1913, sec. Sunday Magazine, 5. See also "Some of the Mysteries of the Servant Question," *Chicago Daily Tribune*, March 29, 1903, sec. A, 5; and Harvey A. Levenstein, *Revolution at the Table: The Transformation of the American Diet* (New York: Oxford University Press, 1988).

15 Fawcett, "Old New York Restaurants," 711. In the Gilded Age, three to four meals a day were common. Breakfast was followed by lunch and then a substantial dinner. Among fashionable urbanites, a fourth meal, a late evening supper, was often taken after the theater.

16 Occupational data are not without their weaknesses as a measure of restaurant growth. Census categories changed, census reporting was notoriously inaccurate, and occupational census classifications do not represent a one-to-one relationship to the number of restaurants. Census groups such as "restaurant, café and lunch room keepers" included both owners and managers of restaurants. For example, the Nixon Restaurant in Pittsburgh was probably counted more than once. Thomas Griffith, its owner, would have been counted in the occupational classification, but so would his partners (if he had any) and possibly his lunch, dinner, and supper managers. However, as a measure of expansion, occupational figures represent a general trend in restaurant dining. Higher numbers of keepers are evidence of more restaurants and illustrate the expansion of existing establishments. (Data is available for 1870, but the number of restaurant keepers listed in the 1870 census appears inflated and probably included all restaurant employees [excluding cooks and waiters] and not just restaurant owners and managers. As a result, comparisons with 1870 are not included here.)

17 Data for 1870–1900, U.S. Bureau of the Census, *Special Reports. Occupations at the Twelfth Census* (Washington, D.C.: Government Printing Office, 1904), Table 3, "Number of Persons Credited to the Various Occupation Designations Used at the Census of 1870, 1880, 1890, and 1900." Data for 1910–30, U.S. Bureau of the Census, *Fifteenth Census of the United States, 1930, Population* (Washington, D.C.: Government Printing Office, 1933), Table 3, "Gainful Workers 10 Years and Over, by Occupation and Sex, for the United States: 1930, 1920, and 1910."

18 Boston's decrease may have reflected the declining status of the city. San Francisco's decrease probably represented a disruption of growth patterns following the earthquake of 1906. But even an industrial city such as Pittsburgh witnessed substantial, if delayed, growth in the number of restaurants. In 1870, the city directory listed only 32 eating houses, eating saloons, oyster houses, and restaurants. For the next twenty years, the number of eating establishments remained small.

However, from 1890 to 1905, Pittsburghers saw the number of restaurants in their city double, and this substantial rate of growth was surpassed in subsequent years. By 1930, the city boasted 818 restaurants (and an overall rate of change remarkably similar to the national growth rate). Adjusting for increases in the city's population, the increase in the number of restaurants serving the city of Pittsburgh is no less phenomenal. Although per capita growth was erratic in the nineteenth century, apparently responding to downturns in the economy, by the early twentieth century, restaurant growth substantially outstripped population growth. From 1870 to 1930, the number of Pittsburgh restaurants per capita rose over 400 percent. *Polk's Pittsburgh City Directory* (Pittsburgh: R. L. Polk, 1869–70, 1874–75, 1879–80, 1885, 1890, 1895, 1900, 1905, 1910, 1915, 1920, 1925, 1930).

19 The rise of modern hotels and apartments depressed the expansion of boarding-houses. New technologies in the hotel industry reduced the number of employees required to run a hotel even as more rooms became available for tourists. And, although the decline started long before national Prohibition, anti-alcohol leagues probably had an effect on the number of men and women who operated and worked in saloons (the census continued to list saloonkeepers in 1920, but by 1930, aggregate tables no longer listed them). Yet many of these trends might have affected the growth of the restaurant industry as well. Although the popularity of modern apartment complexes probably helped to spur restaurant growth, economic consolidation and the development of larger restaurants very likely drove small restaurants as well as hotels out of business. Similarly, restaurants might have been adversely affected by Prohibition as one profitable line of income, alcohol, was eliminated.

20 C. W. Gesner, "Concerning Restaurants," *Harper's New Monthly Magazine*, April 1866, 593; "Reduction in Restaurant Rates: Great Success of Cheap Eating-Houses and General Lowering of Prices among All Except the Most Fashionable," *New York Daily Tribune*, January 29, 1877, 8. See also "The Restaurant System: Choice Cuisine at Reasonable Figures; How Foreign Fashions Are Acclimatized in New-York," *New York Times*, May 24, 1885, 3; *New York World*, "Restaurant Prices," *Hotel World*, September 21, 1876, 7. Importantly, these articles suggest that one of the reasons for the emergence of the middle-class restaurant was that the cost of dining out dropped in the mid-1870s as the inflationary pressures of the Civil War subsided.

21 Noah Brooks, "Restaurant Life of San Francisco," *Overland Monthly*, November 1868, 471. See also Samuel Williams, "The City of the Golden Gate," *Scribner's Monthly*, July 1875, 274.

22 Alessandro, "Los Angeles Restaurants," *Los Angeles Times*, April 30, 1892, 11.

23 On proliferation of terms, see Richard Pillsbury, *From Boarding House to Bistro: The American Restaurant Then and Now* (Boston: Unwin Hyman, 1990), 23. See also *Polk's Pittsburgh City Directory*, 1879–80, 1885, 1890, 1895, 1900, 1905, 1910, 1915, 1920, 1925, and 1930. As late as 1921, H. L. Mencken noted in *American Language* that "a common *public-house*" might be called "a *café, a restaurant,* an *exchange,* a *buffet*

or a *hotel.*" H. L. Mencken, "Euphemisms," in *The American Language: An Inquiry into the Development of English in the United States* (New York: A. A. Knopf, 1921). Typical of the long lists of meaningless names is the "Restaurant Directory" published in *The Table* in 1873. It began "Adler, Louis, No. 42 Bowery; Althon, Alvin, 754 Sixth Street" and continued on in a similar vein for two pages. "Restaurant Directory," *The Table*, 1, no. 2 (1873): 43–44.

24 Restaurants occasionally advertised in city directories in the nineteenth century, but the ads were seldom descriptive, typically displaying little more than the restaurant's name and address. In 1912, D. F. Pride noted that restaurants were just beginning to advertise but that their advertising was seldom effective. "Some of this publicity work is fairly well put together, but the greater portion of it is exceedingly crude with little chance of getting any adequate returns from the cost of the space used in absurd and meaningless statements. In short, about the poorest kind of advertising put out in New York to-day is that pertaining to restaurants." D. F. Pride, "Restaurant Advertising," *The Steward*, March 1912, 11.

25 The *New York Mail* maintained that the first restaurant/hotel to offer meals without interruption from early morning to midnight was the Metropolitan in New York in 1852. *New York World*, "Restaurant Prices," 7.

26 L. J. Vance, "New York Restaurant Life," *Frank Leslie's Popular Monthly*, January 1893, 102.

27 William Dean Howells, *A Modern Instance* (Harmondsworth, U.K.: Penguin Books, 1984), 152–53.

28 Ibid.

29 "Men Who Live Down Town," *New York Times*, December 4, 1881, 3.

30 Ibid.

31 Alessandro, "Los Angeles Restaurants," 11.

32 Charles S. Greene, "The Restaurants of San Francisco," *Overland Monthly*, December 1892, 565. See also Williams, "City of the Golden Gate," 274.

33 Brooks, "Restaurant Life of San Francisco," 467. See also Frank Norris, *McTeague: A Story of San Francisco* (Mineola, N.Y.: Dover Publications, 2004), 5.

34 "Restaurants of New York," *Washington Post*, February 20, 1898, 13.

35 American, "A Table d'Hote Dinner," *New York Times*, August 2, 1899, 6. The author's choice of the pseudonym "American" suggests, in part, that his complaint was that most table d'hôte restaurants were foreign-owned and served ethnic foods.

36 H. S. H., "As to Table d'Hote Dinners," *New York Times*, August 4, 1899, 6; Housekeeper, "Table d'Hote Dinners," *New York Times*, August 4, 1899, 6.

37 Housekeeper, "Table d'Hote Dinners," 6.

38 Bab, "Restaurants of Gotham: Meals Served on American and Several Other Plans," *Washington Post*, August 21, 1892, 12. Even those who were sympathetic toward table d'hôte dining worried about the effects of the restaurant, particularly the table d'hôte restaurant, on the family. "Bab the epicure," a food writer whose work appeared in both the *Washington Post* and the *Los Angeles Times* in

the 1890s, fretted about the neglect that home life suffered when women did not cook. See also Tweedie, "Mrs. Alec Tweedie Mourns Our Disappearing Home Life," 5.

39 "German Restaurants," *New York Times*, January 19, 1873, 5.

40 "Men Who Live Down Town," 8.

41 Alessandro, "Los Angeles Restaurants," 11.

42 Duis, *Challenging Chicago*, 148.

43 "German Restaurants," 5. The term "American restaurant," although not universally used to describe these restaurants, stemmed from the fact that these à la carte restaurants, "although based upon the European plan, [have] certain distinguishing features all their own." At least one article distinguished these restaurants from family restaurants, but I have grouped them together. "The Economy of New York Dining-Rooms," *The Table*, April 1873, 79.

44 "Men Who Live Down Town," 8.

45 For a favorable reminiscence about the American restaurant, see "How New York Eats," *The Steward*, November 1920, 22–23.

46 "Boston Women Well Fed," *Washington Post*, November 22, 1908, sec. Sunday Magazine, 8; Duis, *Challenging Chicago*, 148.

47 John F. Mariani, *America Eats Out: An Illustrated History of Restaurants, Taverns, Coffee Shops, Speakeasies, and Other Establishments That Have Fed Us for 350 Years* (New York: Morrow, 1991), 116–18; Alec Tristin Shuldiner, "Trapped behind the Automat: Technological Systems and the American Restaurant, 1902–1991" (PhD diss., Cornell University, 2001), 78–85; J. MacDonald, "Eastern Menus," *Overland Monthly*, November 1904, 529; "How New York Eats," 24.

48 MacDonald, "Eastern Menus," 529. On origins, see Ina Marie Hamlin and Arthur Harry Winakor, *Department Store Food Service* (Urbana: University of Illinois, 1933), 6; and Jan Whitaker, *Service and Style: How the American Department Store Fashioned the Middle Class* (New York: St. Martin's Press, 2006), 225–26. Department store restaurants did not always have a reputation for good food, but as their quality improved at the turn of the century, tearooms and cafés intended mostly for women began to attract men.

49 On various American cuisines, see Duis, *Challenging Chicago*, 150.

50 "Men Who Live Down Town," 8.

51 "The Cost of Living," *Washington Post*, December 24, 1877, 1.

52 On beaneries, see "How New York Eats," 24. On vegetarian eating, see "Boston Women Well Fed," 8.

53 "Chicago Topics: Gastronomical and Otherwise," *New York Times*, May 11, 1876, 4. The German *conditorei* or *konditorei* is a pastry shop; the French *cremeries*, or more accurately *crémeries*, were teashops. Perry Duis dates the emergence of coffeehouses, gentlemen's restaurants, and ice cream saloons in Chicago to the 1850s. Like Chicago's elite restaurants, these were often imitations of restaurants in New York and other eastern cities. See Duis, *Challenging Chicago*, 147.

54 Alessandro, "Los Angeles Restaurants," 11.

55 "Cost of Living," 1. "Of course it cannot be expected that a man who is limited in his expenditures can have cut-glass and damask on the table, but there are scores of places where, although the prices are ridiculously low, the service is good and neatness and cleanliness prevail. The dairy lunch is peculiarly a Washington institution, and its popularity is ever on the increase." Many dairy lunchrooms started out serving cold food but by the turn of the century were serving hot, simple, course meals similar to New York's lunchrooms. "Diet Costing a Dime: Local Dairy Lunch Rooms Sell Meals at Small Cost," *Washington Post*, February 15, 1897, 8.

56 Greene, "Restaurants of San Francisco," 561.

57 Edwin Bates, *The San Francisco Restaurant Industry*, ed. U.S. Bureau of Foreign and Domestic Commerce (Washington, D.C.: Government Printing Office, 1930), 1.

58 Pillsbury, *From Boarding House to Bistro*, 28. No comprehensive study of the restaurant industry in the nineteenth century exists, and census data on restaurants were not collected until the late 1920s. In general, however, small businesses did not fare well in the nineteenth century. For example, of 1,530 businesses in Poughkeepsie, New York, monitored by the credit agency R. G. Dun and Company between 1845 and 1880, 30 percent closed in three years or less, and only 14 percent survived more than twenty years. Mansel G. Blackford, *A History of Small Business in America* (Chapel Hill: University of North Carolina Press, 2003), 70. In 1917, however, the U.S. Congress, apparently concerned about war profiteering, called for a study of industrial profits. Eight years later, Ralph C. Epstein of Harvard University used the income and excess profits tax data assembled in 1917 to calculate the relative profitability of various American industries. In Epstein's analysis, restaurants fared well. Of the 108 business enterprises that Epstein examined, restaurants—while requiring very low capital investments—produced a net income relative to capitalization in the top 50 percent of the industries he examined. In fact, compared to other service businesses, restaurants were a bullish investment in 1917. While hotels mustered only a 19.24 percent net return to invested capital and laundries only a 16.52 percent return, restaurants demonstrated a 27.96 percent rate of return. The restaurant industry's success in 1917, however, cannot be taken as evidence that the industry was stable or profitable in the nineteenth century. First, World War I offered an exceptional opportunity for the service industry. Demand for services rose, and, unlike other industries that found it difficult to expand during the war, restaurants could easily add a few tables. Second, by 1917, the restaurant industry had matured, with advertising, trade organizations, and a stable middle-class restaurant-going public. Ralph C. Epstein, "Industrial Profits in 1917," *Quarterly Journal of Economics* 39, no. 2 (1925): 241–66. Nonetheless, at least one casual observer in the nineteenth century felt that restaurants were making their proprietors rich. See Browne, *Great Metropolis*, 261.

59 New York, vol. 278, p. 600A47, R. G. Dun & Company Collection, Baker Library, Harvard Business School, Cambridge.

60 Ibid., vol. 272, pp. 930, 1000BB.

61 H. S. H., "As to Table d'Hote Dinners," 6. On the low profits of Italian restaurants in the nineteenth century, see "Restaurant System," 3.

62 J. Fanning O'Reilly, "James B. Regan—Evolutionist," *The Steward* 5, no. 5 (1910).

63 "One Way to Get Trade," *New York Times*, January 18, 1885, 4.

64 "Kinds of Restaurants: How They Vary According to Place and Purpose," *New York Daily Tribune*, November 1, 1896, sec. 3, 6.

65 "Culinary Lore," *The Steward* 12, no. 1 (1917): 50. The middle-class chef was expected to take his customers' wishes into consideration. "Although no one has ever succeeded in pleasing all palates, because the tastes are as different as the faces, yet the palates must be studied by the cook, and if he be industrious and energetic, he will, with tact and observation, soon acquire a knowledge of the particular tastes of his patrons." For an earlier discussion of the restaurant industry's willingness to cater to middle-class patrons' tastes, see "New York Restaurants," *The Dining Room Magazine* 2, no. 11 (1877): 262.

66 "Dime Dinners," *The Cook*, July 27, 1885, 8. Arguing that the modern restaurant emerged under specific economic conditions, Nicholas M. Kiefer has more recently noted: "Competition forces suppliers to pay attention to consumers' desires. As dining establishments proliferate within a town or city, they will find that they must compete with each other for customers. . . . The supply-side and demand-side forces are thus reinforced by competitive pressures." Nicholas M. Kiefer, "Economics and the Origins of the Restaurant," *Cornell Hotel and Restaurant Administration Quarterly* 43, no. 4 (2002): 58–65.

67 Thomas C. Schelling, "Models of Segregation," *American Economic Review* 59, no. 2 (1969): 488–93. See also Jonathan Rauch, "Seeing around Corners," *Atlantic Monthly*, April 2002, 35; Michael Hechter and Christine Horne, *Theories of Social Order: A Reader* (Stanford: Stanford Social Sciences, 2003); and Richard Zeckhauser, "Distinguished Fellow: Reflections on Thomas Schelling," *Journal of Economic Perspectives* 3, no. 2 (1989): 153–64.

68 "Kinds of Restaurants," 6.

69 The origins of individual choices—the source of these micromotives—is beyond the scope of this work. As a historian, I believe that they may be rooted in the development of the nineteenth-century middle class, but Jason Read's provocative rereading of Karl Marx suggests another possibility. Just as capitalism produces goods and classes, Read argues, it produces subjectivities (in urban centers), including the social valorization of goods. If that is true, than potentially the same economic forces that were producing the middle class might also have created opportunities for the nascent middle class to value goods in ways that could have produced a self-conscious middle class. Jason Read, *The Micro-Politics of Capital: Marx and the Prehistory of the Present* (Albany: State University of New York Press, 2003), esp. 122–35.

70 An article in the *New York Daily Tribune* referred to a three-story restaurant that catered to a different clientele on each floor. "Kinds of Restaurants," 6.

71 "Economy of New York Dining-Rooms," 78.

72 "Restaurant System," 3.

73 Alessandro, "Los Angeles Restaurants," 11. Although restaurants responded to their clientele, few restaurateurs described their establishments as middle-class restaurants. Class, after all, was just one of the many factors that determined clientele, hours, type of service, or decorations. In the late nineteenth century, for example, a group of New York restaurateurs organized the Association of Licensed Restaurant Keepers Closing Sundays and Nights. The group wanted licenses for restaurants that were open only eight hours a day to be less expensive than those of restaurants that stayed open late into the night. To a degree, this pitted downtown restaurants that served businessmen and their families against uptown aristocratic restaurants that served the aristocracy, but it would be inaccurate to suggest that the restaurateurs saw their campaign in those terms. "Restaurants Want Lower Licenses," *New York Daily Tribune*, December 8, 1898, 3; "Day Restaurant Keepers Organize," *New York Daily Tribune*, December 15, 1898, 4.

74 On the middle class and cleanliness, see Suellen M. Hoy, *Chasing Dirt: The American Pursuit of Cleanliness* (New York: Oxford University Press, 1995), 88; "Twinkles [the Bostonian's Last Request]," *New York Daily Tribune*, November 15, 1896, sec. Comics, 5.

75 "Many Fine Restaurants: West Siders Favored in This Regard," *New York Daily Tribune*, May 12, 1899, 4.

76 "The Chicago Rusher," *New York Daily Tribune*, December 29, 1901, sec. Illustrated Supplement, 5; "Outdoor Dining: Many Persons Take Their Meals in the Open Air in the Heated Term," *New York Daily Tribune*, August 4, 1901, sec. Illustrated Supplement, 6.

77 Charles J. Rosebault, "Where New York Dines Out," *New York Times*, May 27, 1923, sec. Sunday Magazine, 8.

78 "Kinds of Restaurants," 6.

79 Ibid.

80 "Why People Go to a Restaurant," *New York Daily Tribune*, July 7, 1901, sec. Illustrated Supplement, 1. Music and other entertainments grew in importance in the years before World War I and remained a central part of dining well into the 1920s. A long, well-illustrated article in the *New York Times Sunday Magazine* in 1910 ascribed the trend to a desire for uplift and to the popular support of an unspecified public. Both imply the influence of the middle class. "Where Music Soothes While Lobsters Broil," *New York Times*, April 24, 1910, sec. Sunday Magazine, 7. See also Lewis A. Erenberg, *Steppin' Out: New York Nightlife and the Transformation of American Culture, 1890–1930* (Westport, Conn.: Greenwood Press, 1981).

81 "Economy of New York Dining-Rooms," 78.

82 "Music Versus Digestion," *Atlantic Monthly*, June 1907, 869, 870.

83 "Where Music Soothes While Lobsters Broil," 7.

84 "Comments," *The Chef* 8, no. 3 (1898): 118.

85 James Remington McCarthy and John Rutherford, *Peacock Alley: The Romance of the Waldorf-Astoria* (New York: Harper and Brothers, 1931), 61–62. Aristocratic hotels and restaurants did offer entertainments in the nineteenth century but not usually during dinner.

86 Chicago restaurateurs attempted an experiment in 1905 and stopped providing entertainment. "The verdict was that the public demands music with its food." Editors, *Restaurant Bulletin* 2, no. 16 (1905): 11.

87 Pride, "Restaurant Advertising," 11.

88 "New York Restaurant Prices," *The Steward*, December 1911, 15. The original reads "chucking a bluff." The colloquial phrase used by sailors may mean, roughly, to fire pointlessly or to act without expecting results.

89 Ibid.

90 Research Department of *The American Restaurant Magazine, A Market Analysis of the Restaurant Industry* (Chicago: Patterson Publishing, 1930), 8.

91 John R. Thompson, *Where We Foregather* (Chicago: n.d., c. 1922), 1–2.

92 Pierre Bourdieu, *Distinction: A Social Critique of the Judgment of Taste* (Cambridge: Harvard University Press, 1984), 375. The development of highbrow and lowbrow culture, a prerequisite to the type of remapping I am discussing, is treated extensively by Lawrence Levine. Levine also recognizes that in the twentieth century, lowbrow has often won the day. Lawrence W. Levine, *Highbrow/Lowbrow: The Emergence of Cultural Hierarchy in America* (Cambridge: Harvard University Press, 1988), esp. 171–256.

93 Bourdieu, *Distinction*, 372.

94 For alternatives to Bourdieu's model of cultural exchange that allows for up-heavals, see T. J. Jackson Lears, "The Concept of Cultural Hegemony: Problems and Possibilities," *American Historical Review* 90, no. 3 (1985): 567–93; and John A. Guidry and Mark Q. Sawyer, "Contentious Pluralism: The Public Sphere and Democracy," *Perspectives on Politics* 1, no. 2 (2003): 273–89. Political scientists and social historians have also begun to explore the effects of small preferences on behavior and events. See Patricia S. Mann, *Micro-Politics: Agency in a Postfeminist Era* (Minneapolis: University of Minnesota Press, 1994), esp. 156–63; and Mona Domosh, "Those 'Gorgeous Incongruities': Polite Politics and Public Space on the Streets of Nineteenth-Century New York City," *Annals of the Association of American Geographers* 88, no. 2 (1998): 209–26.

CHAPTER 4

1 Walter F. Brown, "Our Artist's Dream of the Centennial Restaurants," *Harper's Weekly*, July 1, 1876, 541.

2 The restaurant La Fayette appears to have been the more Americanized of the two and also the more affordable. Of the other, Trois Frères Provençaux, William Dean Howells wrote: The restaurant is "so called because each of the Brothers

makes out his bill of Three Prices, and you pay the sum total." William Dean Howells, "A Sinnight of the Centennial," *Atlantic Monthly*, July 1876, 94.

3 On eating in hotels, see "My Trip to Philadelphia in 1876,"Frank L. Thomas Diary, July 12–July 26, 1876, Prints and Pictures Department, C070000, Free Library of Philadelphia, Philadelphia, Pennsylvania, http://libwww.library.phila .gov/CenCol/ (accessed February 28, 2004). The seventeen-year-old Thomas barely mentions eating. Except for one dinner listed in his account of expenses (90 cents), he purchased only soda water, cream mead, and ice cream (which in the diary are referred to as lunch). Given his late daily arrival at the fair (typically around 10:30) and the lack of food-related expenses, it would appear that he took most of his meals in his hotel. This was typical of the Victorian-era traveler. On comfort stations, see Café Leland menu, Centennial Exhibition 1876 Philadelphia Scrapbook, Centennial Exhibition Digital Collection, Free Library of Philadelphia, Philadelphia, Pennsylvania, http://libwww.library.phila.gov/CenCol/ exh-food.htm (accessed February 28, 2004).

4 Donald G. Mitchell, "In and About the Fair," *Scribner's Monthly*, November 1876, 116.

5 Hasia R. Diner, *Hungering for America: Italian, Irish, and Jewish Foodways in the Age of Migration* (Cambridge: Harvard University Press, 2001), 65–68, 200–204; Donna Gabaccia, *We Are What We Eat: Ethnic Food and the Making of Americans* (Cambridge: Harvard University Press, 2000), 64–92.

6 "Middle-Age Cookery," *New York Times*, October 25, 1872, 4.

7 Ibid.

8 C. W. Gesner, "Concerning Restaurants," *Harper's New Monthly Magazine*, April 1866, 593.

9 Noah Brooks, "Restaurant Life of San Francisco," *Overland Monthly*, November 1868, 467.

10 Ibid., 471–72.

11 Ibid., 472.

12 "Polish Dishes," *The Cook*, July 20, 1885, 9.

13 "Barbaric Feeding," *The Cook*, April 13, 1885, 7.

14 "A Nightmare of Gastronomic Horrors," *The Cook*, June 15, 1885, 9. *Lippincott's Magazine* seemed to take a perverse pleasure in disparaging national cuisine. An 1898 article on German cooking, widely reprinted in the newspapers of the era, claimed that in the German restaurant "the cuisine is on the whole monotonous and the food singularly insipid." "Teutonic Cookery," *New York Times*, June 5, 1898, 17. See also "German Dinners," *Boston Daily Globe*, September 26, 1873, 3.

15 E. Lyell Earle, "Foreign Types of New York Life," *New York Times*, August 28, 1898, sec. Illustrated Magazine, 14. French cuisine was the exception, and the wide appeal of French cuisine was further evidence of the French chef's skill.

16 "The Restaurant System: Choice Cuisine at Reasonable Figures; How Foreign Fashions Are Acclimatized in New-York," *New York Times*, May 24, 1885, 3.

17 "Cheap Restaurants," *New York Times*, August 6, 1871, 5.

18 For a thorough treatment of immigrant communities (especially Irish, Jewish, and Italian communities) and their attitude toward food and restaurants, see Diner, *Hungering for America*. Diner, however, does not discuss the patronage of these restaurants by non-immigrant Americans.

19 "German Restaurants," *New York Times*, January 19, 1873, 5. Compare to descriptions of only moderately patronized Italian restaurants in "Cheap Restaurants," 5.

20 "Cheap Restaurants," 5. See "German Restaurants," 5.

21 "Cheap Restaurants," 5.

22 Ibid.

23 "German Restaurants," 5.

24 "Cheap Restaurants," 5.

25 Charles S. Greene, "The Restaurants of San Francisco," *Overland Monthly*, December 1892, 566.

26 "Cheap Restaurants," 5. Even before they began to attract large numbers of non-immigrant patrons, Italian restaurants modified their menus and image to create a "unified Italian community in America." Diner, *Hungering for America*, 66–67.

27 "Restaurant System," 3; *New York Sun*, "The Italian's Cookery," *Current Literature*, July 1901, 67. Italian food was still quite new in 1885, and the paper felt it judicious to define "spaghetti—by which title the vermicelli-like form of macaroni is known." But Italian cuisine had received the approval of the late Charles Delmonico of New York's most famous restaurant, and the middle class was not yet so thoroughly disabused of the elite's influence in matters of taste that such things did not matter. A number of newspaper articles in the nineteenth century made reference to Delmonico's penchant for the risotto and ravioli at Café Moretti. See, for example, *New York Daily Tribune*, "Delmonico's Delights," *Washington Post*, February 24, 1884, 3. Nonetheless, a number of recent accounts have dated acceptance of Italian food, especially in fine dining establishments, to much later in the twentieth century. See Harvey Levenstein, "Immigration, Travel, and the Internationalization of the American Diet," in *Food Selection: From Genes to Culture*, ed. Harvey Anderson, John Blundell, and Matty Chiva (Levallois-Perret, France: Danone Institute, 2002), 153–73; and Krishnendu Ray, "Ethnic Succession and the New American Restaurant Cuisine," in *The Restaurants Book: Ethnographies of Where to Eat*, ed. David Beriss and David Sutton (New York: Berg, 2007), 97–114.

28 *New York Daily Tribune*, "Delmonico's Delights," *Washington Post*, February 24, 1884, 3.

29 Greene, "Restaurants of San Francisco," 567. Wealthy Americans of the nineteenth century took their "Grand Tour" in Europe. The Grand Tour almost always included stops in France and Italy.

30 Ibid., 567–69.

31 Ibid., 570.

32 Alessandro, "Los Angeles Restaurants," *Los Angeles Times*, April 30, 1892, 11.

33 Ibid.

34 "All Palates Pleased: Cosmopolitan Variety in the Washington Restaurants," *Washington Post*, July 14, 1901, 20.

35 Rosa Belle Holt, "Bohemian House-Keeping in New York," *What to Eat*, June 1897, 251–52.

36 "The Italian Cook's Best," *Washington Post*, June 20, 1909, sec. M, 7. Although some early reports of ethnic eating encouraged cautious experimentation with ethnic food, they conceded biological limits. The 1871 *Times* article discussed previously, "Cheap Restaurants," noted that a bottle of cheap claret "will go far to remove the unpleasant taste that any of the foreign-flavored viands may have left in the mouth." "Cheap Restaurants," 5.

37 The new standards of taste were only one factor that attracted middle-class consumers to new restaurants. Members of the middle class were also concerned about cleanliness, safety, and health. Notably, food writers always made an effort to point out that uptown ethnic restaurants were clean. They also stressed the health benefits of ethnic food. As a *New York Sun* reporter remarked: "Besides the flavor that distinguishes Italian cookery it has the merit of being extremely nourishing and healthful. While it may not tempt the over-delicate palate it will never injure the digestion or the nerves. The foods most in favor are the farinaceous sort, all of which possess much nutriment." *New York Sun*, "The Italian's Cookery," 67.

38 Ibid. The reference is to Charles Delmonico.

39 Lucien Adkins, "A General View," in *New York's Chinatown: An Historical Presentation of Its People and Places*, ed. Louis J. Beck (New York: Bohemia Publishing, 1898), 297. See also "Strange Chinese Dinner Customs," *Cooking Club Magazine* 9, no. 5 (1907): 295; and Andrew Coe, *Chop Suey: A Cultural History of Chinese Food in the United States* (New York: Oxford University Press, 2009).

40 Reprinted from the *Milwaukee Sentinel*, "The German Palate," *Current Literature*, July 1901, 67. The piece was widely reprinted. A 1907 printing credits it to Clinton Rogers Hayes. Clinton Rogers Hayes, "German Cookery and the Delicatessen," *Cooking Club Magazine* 9, no. 3 (1907): 144–45, 153.

41 The rise of cosmopolitanism and the concurrent explosion of scientific studies on nutrition undermined the earlier, aristocratic efforts to justify the upper-class diet in terms of science. Proteins and fats were increasingly seen as more helpful for laborers and lighter fare better for office workers. See, for example, "Food and Its Uses," *Cooking Club* 10, no. 5 (1904): 224.

42 See "A Highly Spiced Spanish Restaurant," *Washington Post*, August 20, 1905, sec. G, 12; "For German Palates," *Washington Post*, April 26, 1903, sec. B, 2; "Food a La Scandinavia," *Washington Post*, January 12, 1903, 9; and "Italian Cook's Best," 7.

43 For example, Felix L. Oswald, "International Food Studies: France," *What to Eat*, May 1901, 145; Felix L. Oswald, "International Food Studies: Germany," *What to Eat*, June 1901, 183; Felix L. Oswald, "International Food Studies: China," *What to Eat*, July 1902, 1; Pansy Viola Viner, "Excellent Dishes Found Abroad," *Table*

Talk, January 1907, 30–31; Marion Harris Neil, "Curries as They Should Be Made," *Table Talk*, February 1908, 95–96; Marion Harris Neil, "Recipes from Over the Seas," *Table Talk*, June 1908, 242–43; and May Henry and Kate Halford, "Jewish Cookery for Gentiles," *Cooking Club* 8, no. 10 (1902): 10–11. An early example of the genre can be found in *The Dining Room Magazine* in 1877. Giuseppe Rudmanii, "Foods of Southern Europe," *The Dining Room Magazine* 2, no. 10 (1877): 235. See also Kristin L. Hoganson, *Consumers' Imperium: The Global Production of American Domesticity, 1865–1920* (Chapel Hill: University of North Carolina Press, 2007), 106–7.

44 "Exotic Bits for Gourmets," *The Steward*, September 1909, 66. For other examples, see snails at M. P. Handy, "A Dish of Snails," *What to Eat*, January 1897, 139; and "An Invasion of Snails: They Are of the Edible Variety," *New York Times*, September 28, 1902. See macaroni at Theodore Tracy, "Macaroni: Italian Cooking of the Toothsome Vegetable," *Los Angeles Times*, November 27, 1892, 16; William Gilbert Irwin, "Macaroni: How and Where It Is Made," *What to Eat*, October 1898, 97; and "Italian Macaroni in Italy," *New York Times*, July 16, 1893, 11. See Chinese and Italian at Wong Ching Too, "The Chinese Cuisine," *Washington Post*, July 13, 1884, 6; and *New York Star*, "What Is 'Zabaglione'?" *Washington Post*, April 19, 1890, 4.

45 "Don't Snub the Spaghetti," *Washington Post*, December 8, 1903, 10. See Jane Eddington, "Economical Housekeeping: Macaroni," *Chicago Daily Tribune*, March 8, 1910, 8.

46 Rosa Belle Holt, "An Armenian Dinner," *What to Eat*, November 1897, 116.

47 "Cheap Restaurants," 5.

48 Philosopher Lisa Heldke argues in *Exotic Appetites* that "food adventurers" are engaged in a selfish act that values the "colonized culture" solely because of the novelty of the experience, an approach to dining that is grounded in "an incidental fact" about themselves. Colonial acts of culinary appropriation and refinement, Heldke maintains, "mine" the exotic other's culture and undermine the original cultural meanings embedded in food and food rituals. Lisa M. Heldke, *Exotic Appetites: Ruminations of a Food Adventurer* (New York: Routledge, 2003), 15, 45–59. Historically, I contend that members of the middle class appropriated ethnic cuisines to advance their class interests. This approach differs from many recent works on ethnic food in the United States in which the emphasis is on the multicultural gains achieved by culinary exchange. Thus, Donna Gabaccia in *We Are What We Eat* describes the development of a market for uniquely ethnic cuisine neutrally as "cross-over eating." Richard Pillsbury in *No Foreign Food* uses a melting pot metaphor and is soberly triumphant. And while Harvey Levenstein understates the role of ethnic food in American life prior to the 1960s, he views the exception, Italian food, as having been "internationalized." These accounts reflect the perspective of their authors who view the success or failure of ethnic food largely from the standpoint of immigrants (even if Levenstein claims otherwise). While fully acknowledging that Americans did not adopt ethnic cuisines

without demanding changes, they nevertheless see the increase in ethnic food consumption in the United States as a triumph of ethnic integration. Gabaccia, *We Are What We Eat*, 117–21; Richard Pillsbury, *No Foreign Food: The American Diet in Time and Place* (Boulder, Colo.: Westview Press, 1998); Levenstein, "Immigration, Travel, and the Internationalization of the American Diet," 154. I do not take issue with that argument (except to emphasize the importance of ethnic cuisines at an earlier date), but from the vantage point of those of the middle class, the foreign restaurant was as much a product of their patronage as it was an immigrant achievement.

49 "Restaurant System," 3. The article also notes that by 1885, fashionable "swells" were patronizing downtown restaurants.

50 Ibid.

51 Ibid.

52 "Business Changes in Times Square," *New York Times*, December 26, 1920, 82.

53 Michael Batterberry and Ariane Ruskin Batterberry, *On the Town in New York: The Landmark History of Eating, Drinking, and Entertainments from the American Revolution to the Food Revolution* (New York: Routledge, 1999), 222; Jie Zhang, "Transplanting Identity: A Study of Chinese Immigrants and the Chinese Restaurant Business" (PhD diss., Southern Illinois University at Carbondale, 1998), 127, 135–36. See Gabaccia, *We Are What We Eat*, 102. Ting-chiu Fan, "Chinese Residents in Chicago" (master's thesis, University of Chicago, 1926) as cited in Xinyang Wang, *Surviving the City: The Chinese Immigrant Experience in New York City, 1890–1970* (Lanham, Md.: Rowman and Littlefield, 2001), 76.

54 "Increase in Chinese Restaurants," *New York Daily Tribune*, May 27, 1901, 4.

55 "German Restaurants," 5. Hybridization should be understood as a continuum that sometimes favors the ethnic cuisine and sometimes the more generic national or international cuisine. See, for example, Eve Jochnowitz, "Dining out and Spectacle in Russian Jewish New York," in *The Restaurants Book: Ethnographies of Where to Eat*, ed. David Beriss and David E. Sutton (New York: Berg, 2007), 115–32.

56 "Restaurant System," 3.

57 "Chop Suey Resorts," *New York Times*, November 15, 1903, 20.

58 Menu, "Menu," HofBräu Haus, New York, N.Y., December 29, 1915, Box 292 (not numbered), Buttolph Menu. The only other two German items on a menu that featured a choice of three soups, three vegetables, a salad, and five desserts were the *Deutsch Linsen Suppe mit Wurstschnitten* (Lentil and Sausage Soup) and *Sauerkraut*.

59 Menu, "Special Sunday Course Dinner," Chin Lee Company's First Class Chop Sooy and American Restaurant, Providence, R.I., December 28, 1914, Box 284 (1914-1056), Buttolph Menu. See "Pek-in Cafe," *Los Angeles Times*, September 3, 1911, 14.

60 Menu, "Ye Olde Dutch Tavern," Ye Olde Dutch Tavern, New York, N.Y., September 1, 1914, Box 281 (1914-0891), Buttolph Menu.

61 Charles J. Rosebault, "Where New York Dines Out," *New York Times*, May 27, 1923, sec. Sunday Magazine, 8.

62 Louis J. Beck, ed., *New York's Chinatown: An Historical Presentation of Its People and Places* (New York: Bohemia Publishing, 1898), 47–48; "A Dinner in Disguise," *Washington Post*, October 16, 1894, 10; "The Enterprising Chinese," *Washington Post*, December 13, 1903, sec. T, 2. Anthropologist E. N. Anderson notes that "salt, expensive and hard to get in much of old China, was usually used only in the form of soy sauce and pickles." In the United States, however, salt began to appear on Chinese restaurant tables in the 1890s. "Salt is now served on the tables in some restaurants, but formerly the sal shí yau, or soy, was expected to supply its place." E. N. Anderson, *The Food of China* (New Haven: Yale University Press, 1988), 155, 173; Stewart Culin, "Customs of the Chinese in America," *Journal of American Folk-Lore* 3, no. 10 (1890): 197; Haiming Liu, "Chop Suey as Imagined Authentic Chinese Food: The Culinary Identity of Chinese Restaurants in the United States," *Journal of Transnational American Studies* 1, no. 1 (2009), http://escholarship.org/uc/item/2bc4k55r (accessed May 10, 2010).

63 Marty, "Supposedly Foreign Restaurant" illustration for "The Romance and Reality of New York's Restaurants," *New York Times*, November 23, 1913, sec. Sunday Magazine, 9.

64 Ibid. See Clarence E. Edwords, *Bohemian San Francisco: Its Restaurants and Their Most Famous Recipes* (San Francisco: P. Elder, 1914), 48. Edwords made similar comments about Chinatown: "But with the changed conditions there has come a change in the restaurant life of the quarter, and now a number of places have been opened to cater to Americans, and on every hand one sees 'chop suey' signs, and 'Chinese noodles.' It goes without saying that one seldom sees a Chinaman eating in the restaurants that are most attractive to Americans. Some serve both white and yellow and others serve but the Chinese, and a few favored white friends." Edwords, *Bohemian San Francisco*, 54–55; Rosebault, "Where New York Dines Out," 8.

65 Alessandro, "Los Angeles Restaurants," 11. The article does not specifically attribute this exclusiveness to immigrant restaurants but rather to middle-class establishments.

66 Hoganson, *Consumers' Imperium*, 11; Robert W. Rydell and Rob Kroes, *Buffalo Bill in Bologna: The Americanization of the World, 1869–1922* (Chicago: University of Chicago Press, 2005), 6, 11–12; Mark Lamster, *Spalding's World Tour: The Epic Adventure That Took Baseball around the Globe—and Made It America's Game* (New York: Public Affairs, 2006).

67 Dale Carter, "A Bridge Too Far? Cosmopolitanism and the Anglo-American Folk Music Revival," *European Journal of American Culture* 29, no. 1 (2010): 47.

68 L. J. Vance, "New York Restaurant Life," *Frank Leslie's Popular Monthly*, January 1893, 102.

69 "Dining in Eleven Languages," *What to Eat*, October 1896, 71.

70 "New York's Restaurants," *The Steward*, December 1910, 50.

71 D. F. Pride, "Restaurant Advertising," *The Steward*, March 1912, 11.

72 *Where and How to Dine in New York: The Principal Hotels, Restaurants and Cafes of Various Kinds and Nationalities Which Have Added to the Gastronomic Fame of New York and Its Suburbs* (New York: Lewis, Scribner, 1903); Rupert Hughes, *The Real New York* (New York: Smart Set, 1904). *Where and How to Dine*'s discussion of ethnic restaurants is limited to a few fashionable establishments, but it is notable that the book is subtitled "The Principal Hotels, Restaurants and Cafes of Various Kinds and Nationalities Which Have Added to the Gastronomic Fame of New York and Its Suburbs." The reference to "nationalities" sets the guide apart from similar guides to European capitals published at the same time. See Nathaniel Newnham-Davis, *Dinners and Diners: Where and How to Dine in London* (London: G. Richards, Pall Mall Publications, 1899); and Roland Strong, *Where and How to Dine in Paris, with Notes on Paris Hotels, Waiters and Their Tips* (London: G. Richards, 1900).

73 George S. Chappell, *The Restaurants of New York* (New York: Greenberg, 1925), 5.

74 Charles Multerer, "Modern Hotel Service: Part 6, Gastronomy," *The Steward*, December 1911, 15–16. Biographical information taken from the 14th Census of the United States.

75 La Billie, *The Steward*, February 1909, 17.

76 Hughes, *Real New York*, 252.

77 Hoganson, *Consumers' Imperium*, 117.

78 Brooks, "Restaurant Life of San Francisco," 472–73.

79 Greene, "Restaurants of San Francisco," 561–66.

80 R. Whittle, "Humbler Restaurants of San Francisco," *Overland Monthly*, May 1903, 362–64. The quote is set next to a discussion of the French table d'hôte, but in the context of the article as a whole it is clear that the city's "pride" was its cosmopolitan cuisine.

81 Ibid., 364–65.

82 Writing in 1914, Edwords used the term "bohemian" to refer to a cultured middle-class vanguard. The term had evolved significantly during the previous fifty years from a word used to refer to elites who rejected their birthright and slummed in ethnic neighborhoods to a term with salacious, free-love connotations. Edwords was adamant that the term had another meaning, one grounded in middle-class cosmopolitanism. "To us Bohemianism means the naturalism of refined people." Edwords, *Bohemian San Francisco*, 6.

83 Ibid., 3.

84 Ibid., 4.

85 Edwin Bates, "The San Francisco Restaurant Industry," ed. U.S. Bureau of Foreign and Domestic Commerce (Washington, D.C.: Government Printing Office, 1930), 1.

86 Otis M. Wiles, "All Nation's Food Served Here," *Los Angeles Times*, January 15, 1922, sec. 2, 1.

87 "All Palates Pleased," 20.

88 "Like Oriental Cuisine," *Washington Post*, November 30, 1902, 28.

89 "Boston Women Well Fed," *Washington Post*, November 22, 1908, sec. Sunday Magazine, 8.

90 For additional examples of cities claiming to be cosmopolitan, see Hoganson, *Consumers' Imperium*, 116–17.

91 E. C. Bishop, *Twenty-First Biennial Report of the State Superintendent of Public Instruction to the Governor of the State of Nebraska* (Lincoln, Nebraska: Department of Public Instruction, 1911), 387.

92 Ibid., 387–88.

93 "The Romance and Reality of New York's Restaurants," 9.

94 Kwame Anthony Appiah, "Cosmopolitan Patriots," in *For Love of Country: Debating the Limits of Patriotism*, ed. Martha Craven Nussbaum and Joshua Cohen (Boston: Beacon Press, 1996), 22.

95 J. Torrey Connor, "A Western View of the Chinese in the United States," *Chautauquan*, January 1901, 374. See also Hoganson, *Consumers' Imperium*, 128–31.

96 M. Lane Griffin, "Two Mexican Recipes from San Antonio," *What to Eat*, February 1898, 201. See L. W., "Mexican Kitchens and Cooks," *Table Talk*, October 1913, 545–50; and Felix Koch, "On Juarez Market," *Table Talk* 27, no. 4 (1912): 184. Embracing ethnic food did not necessarily lead diners to accept immigrants, and likewise, expecting that immigrant restaurants would modify their food to suit local tastes was not necessarily evidence of racism. For an opposing view, cf. Sherrie A. Inness, *Dinner Roles: American Women and Culinary Culture* (Iowa City: University of Iowa Press, 2001), 88–108.

97 Richard Peterson and Albert Simkus examined music preferences across occupational status groups (based on a 1982 survey) and concluded that high occupational status corresponded to diverse tastes, or omnivorism, and lower occupational status corresponded to less diverse tastes, univorism. More recent work by Josée Johnston and Shyon Baumann has demonstrated the role of omnivorism in gourmet food magazines in the twenty-first century.

Peterson and Simkus, and later Peterson and Roger Kern, speculated that omnivorism was a late-twentieth-century phenomenon and contrasted this new approach to cultural expertise to the nineteenth-century monopolizing of high culture by elites documented by Lawrence Levine in *Highbrow/Lowbrow*. However, the celebration of cosmopolitanism at the turn of the century suggests that while elites were marshalling high culture as a mark of distinction, members of the middle class were embracing omnivorism as a counterpoint in the late nineteenth century. Richard A. Peterson and Albert Simkus, "How Musical Tastes Mark Occupational Status Groups," in *Cultivating Differences: Symbolic Boundaries and the Making of Inequality*, ed. Michèle Lamont and Marcel Fournier (Chicago: University of Chicago Press, 1992), 152–86; Michèle Lamont, *Money, Morals, and Manners: The Culture of the French and American Upper-Middle Class* (Chicago: University of Chicago Press, 1992); David Halle, "The Audience for Abstract Art: Class, Culture, and Power," in *Cultivating Differences: Symbolic Boundaries and the Making of Inequality*, ed. Michèle Lamont and Marcel Fournier (Chicago: University of Chicago Press, 1992), 131–51; Josée Johnston and Shyon Baumann, "Democracy versus Distinction: A Study of Omnivorousness in Gourmet Food Writing," *American Journal of Sociology* 113, no. 1 (2007): 165–204; Richard A. Peterson and Roger M. Kern, "Changing Highbrow Taste: From Snob to Omnivore," *American Sociological Review* 61, no. 5 (1996): 900–907; Lawrence W. Levine, *Highbrow/Lowbrow: The Emergence of Cultural Hierarchy in America* (Cambridge: Harvard University Press, 1988).

98 Cosmopolitanism not only rejected French cuisine's claim to superiority but also acknowledged that American dining habits seemed better than those in the rest of the world only because they were familiar. For early expressions of these ideas, see Georgiana Sherburne Hull, "'What Shall We Eat?'" *The Dining Room Magazine* 2, no. 7 (1877): 156. See also Lara, "Gastonomic Chat," *The Dining Room Magazine* 2, no. 1 (1877): 11.

99 Peterson and Kern, "Changing Highbrow Taste," 904.

CHAPTER 5

1 Julian Street, *Abroad at Home: American Ramblings, Observations and Adventures of Julian Street* (New York: Century, 1915), 37–39.

2 "'Bread and Milk' for Society," *The Caterer* 11, no. 3 (1900): 34; "Mrs. Astor Adopts Simple Life," *What to Eat*, September 1905, 105; "Business Dishes," *The Cook*, April 20, 1885, 1.

3 For a historical overview of the food reform movements of the nineteenth century, see Hillel Schwartz, *Never Satisfied: A Cultural History of Diets, Fantasies, and Fat* (New York: Free Press, 1986); Emma Seifrit Weigley, *Sarah Tyson Rorer: The Nation's Instructress in Dietetics and Cookery* (Philadelphia: American Philosophical Society, 1977); Harvey A. Levenstein, *Revolution at the Table: The Transformation of the American Diet* (New York: Oxford University Press, 1988); Laura Shapiro, *Perfection Salad: Women and Cooking at the Turn of the Century* (New York: Farrar Straus and Giroux, 1986); and Sarah Abigail Leavitt, *From Catharine Beecher to Martha Stewart: A Cultural History of Domestic Advice* (Chapel Hill: University of North Carolina Press, 2002).

4 Twelve percent is Richard Ohmann's rough estimate based on data from the 1910 census. Richard M. Ohmann, *Selling Culture: Magazines, Markets, and Class at the Turn of the Century* (London: Verso, 1996), 119.

5 "New Hotel Laws for New York State," *The Steward* 8, no. 7 (1913): 14–15; Elizabeth Dale, "'Social Equality Does Not Exist among Themselves, nor among Us': Baylies vs. Curry and Civil Rights in Chicago, 1888," *American Historical Review* 102, no. 2 (1997): esp. 335–36. After the Supreme Court overturned the Civil Rights Act of 1875, a number of northern states passed their own civil rights acts. Yet even in places where the law allowed African Americans equal access to restaurants, the sight of a black man dining in a restaurant usually frequented by whites was rare enough to attract complaints and media atten-

tion as late as 1907. See "Heard at the Capitol," *Washington Post*, January 16, 1907, 4.

6 For example, studies on progressivism, consumerism, and housing in the late nineteenth and early twentieth centuries demonstrate that members of the black middle class viewed themselves as part of a national middle class (both black and white) with whom they shared values. On progressivism, see Glenda Elizabeth Gilmore, *Gender and Jim Crow: Women and the Politics of White Supremacy in North Carolina, 1896–1920* (Chapel Hill: University of North Carolina Press, 1996), 3–4; Robert D. Johnston, "Re-democratizing the Progressive Era: The Politics of Progressive Era Political Historiography," *Journal of the Gilded Age and Progressive Era* 1, no. 1 (2002): 84; on shared consumer aspirations, see Robert E. Weems, *Desegregating the Dollar: African American Consumerism in the Twentieth Century* (New York: New York University Press, 1998), esp. 27; on housing, see Andrew Wiese, "The House I Live In: Race, Class, and African American Suburban Dreams in the Postwar United States," in *The New Suburban History*, ed. Kevin Michael Kruse and Thomas J. Sugrue (Chicago: University of Chicago Press, 2006), esp. 106. In fact, a shared sense of middle-class identity was occasionally strong enough to motivate efforts to fight segregation. The nineteenth-century black newspaper *The Western Appeal* based its arguments against segregation on the contention that racial restrictions forced middle-class blacks into segregated public spaces with working-class blacks with whom they felt they had little in common. Dale, "'Social Equality Does Not Exist among Themselves, nor among Us,'" 318.

7 Clarence E. Edwords, *Bohemian San Francisco: Its Restaurants and Their Most Famous Recipes* (San Francisco: P. Elder, 1914), 6. Edwords used the word "bohemianism," but at the turn of the century, "bohemian" and "cosmopolitan" were often used interchangeably. For example, "That little Bohemian restaurant where I've been going for the cosmopolitan flavor will never be the same." "Wrecked by Cleanliness," *The Southern Hotel Journal* 1, no. 10 (1912): 24.

8 Since the cultural authority of the aristocratic restaurant stemmed from repeated rituals of obsequiousness, even small acts of transgression helped to undermine the cultural authority of aristocrats. For case studies and theory, see Mona Domosh, "Those 'Gorgeous Incongruities': Polite Politics and Public Space on the Streets of Nineteenth-Century New York City," *Annals of the Association of American Geographers* 88, no. 2 (1998): 209–26; Patricia S. Mann, *Micro-Politics: Agency in a Postfeminist Era* (Minneapolis: University of Minnesota Press, 1994); and Jason Read, *The Micro-Politics of Capital: Marx and the Prehistory of the Present* (Albany: State University of New York Press, 2003).

9 On the appeal of the American plan to restaurateurs, see "Editorial," *The Steward* 8, no. 6 (1913): 15.

10 Albin Pasteur Dearing, *The Elegant Inn: The Waldorf-Astoria Hotel, 1893–1929* (Secaucus, N.J.: L. Stuart, 1986), 196, 197, 211. See also Paul Erling Groth, *Living Downtown: The History of Residential Hotels in the United States* (Berkeley: University of California Press, 1994), 42.

11 James Remington McCarthy and John Rutherford, *Peacock Alley: The Romance of the Waldorf-Astoria* (New York: Harper and Brothers, 1931), 59.

12 Middle-class resentment of the American plan was observed as early as 1876. The *Boston Journal* reported that travelers to the centennial celebration in Philadelphia "take a room at a hotel on the European plan and dine at a restaurant. . . . A plate of bread or a dish of potatoes and cup of tea suffice [for the whole family]." *Boston Journal*, "Hotels and the Centennial," *Hotel World*, August 24, 1876.

13 "An Oriental Evening," *The Caterer* 27, no. 8 (1916): 59; "Don't Pick Their Teeth at the McAlpin," *The Caterer* 28, no. 4 (1916): 42.

14 On competition, see for example "Hotels against Cafeterias," *The Caterer* 27, no. 8 (1916): 19.

15 L. J. Vance, "New York Restaurant Life," *Frank Leslie's Popular Monthly*, January 1893, 108.

16 Edward C. Maginn, "Building Patronage and Good Will: Learning from Competitors," *The Steward* 13, no. 9 (1918): 21.

17 "The Misunderstood Metropolis Explains," *New York Times*, September 15, 1907, sec. Sunday Magazine, 3.

18 "Palatial St. Regis to Open Its Doors to-Day," *New York Times*, September 4, 1904, 5.

19 "Too Well Advertised, St. Regis Man Laments," *New York Times*, November 6, 1904, 12.

20 "Those St. Regis Stories," *New York Times*, October 25, 1904, 6.

21 "Too Well Advertised," 12.

22 Ibid.

23 Ibid.

24 "Representative American as Well as French Cookery at the St. Regis," *The Caterer* 20, no. 4 (1908): 21.

25 "Too Well Advertised," 12.

26 Sylvester Graham, "Excessive Alimentation," *Graham Journal of Health and Longevity* 2 (1838): 161 as quoted in Schwartz, *Never Satisfied*, 25.

27 Ibid., 101–2.

28 Frank J. Jungen, "Ralstonism in General," *What to Eat*, August 1896, 6–7; Edmund Shaftesbury, *Book of General Membership of the Ralston Health Club* (Washington, D.C.: Martyn College Press Association, 1896).

29 John Harvey Kellogg, *Plain Facts for Old and Young; Embracing the Natural History and Hygiene of Organic Life* (Burlington, Iowa: I. F. Segner, 1890), preface, 115; E. E. Kellogg, *Science in the Kitchen: A Scientific Treatise on Food Substances and Their Dietetic Properties* (Battle Creek, Mich.: Health Publishing, 1892), 28, 42; Schwartz, *Never Satisfied*, 187; Andrew F. Smith, *Eating History: 30 Turning Points in the Making of American Cuisine* (New York: Columbia University Press, 2009), 144.

30 Leavitt, *From Catharine Beecher to Martha Stewart*, 9–10.

31 Catharine Esther Beecher and Harriet Beecher Stowe, *The American Woman's Home; or, Principles of Domestic Science* (New York: J. B. Ford, 1869), 190, 137.

32 Helen Hunt Jackson, *Bits of Talk about Home Matters* (Boston: Roberts Brothers, 1873), 139. On acceptance of French cuisine, see also Elizabeth Fries Lummis Ellet, *The Practical Housekeeper: A Cyclopaedia of Domestic Economy* (New York: Stringer and Townsend, 1857), 126.

33 Simple eating emphasized less food rather than less fat and should not be confused with dieting. For more on dieting, see Peter N. Stearns, *Fat History: Bodies and Beauty in the Modern West* (New York: New York University Press, 1997), 3–24.

34 Juliet Corson, *Every-Day Cookery and Hints for the Laundry* (Chicago: Adams and Westlake Manufacturing, 1884), 42.

35 Fannie Farmer's cookbook would have a longer shelf life than Rorer's, but a part of her longevity stems from the kind treatment of historians. Historians have generally ignored culinary movements outside of New England, conflated them with their New England counterparts, or dismissed them as quackery. This is understandable. In New England, food reform had the blessing of both Boston's progressive women (the Women's Education Association) and New England's preeminent educational institutions (notably the Massachusetts Institute of Technology and Wesleyan University). However, as we will see, mid-Atlantic and midwestern culinary journals played a substantial role in culinary reform at the turn of the century.

36 Quoted in Weigley, *Sarah Tyson Rorer*, 37, 63, 69.

37 Sarah Tyson Heston Rorer, *Mrs. Rorer's New Cook Book: A Manual of Housekeeping* (Philadelphia: Arnold, 1902), 664–65. Like many late-nineteenth-century culinary progressives, Rorer's contempt for the rich stemmed, at least in part, from concern for the poor. In the first installment of a series of articles for *Table Talk* titled "How to Live on a Thousand Dollars a Year," Rorer blamed the liberal diets of the wealthy for the meager diets of the poor. "By this wonderful American extravagance we are making the poor poorer, by keeping the demand beyond the supply; consequently, keeping the price of good food above their reach. A little economy, on the part of our housewives, would bring some of the luxuries to the doors of our smallest wage earners." *Table Talk* (October 1898) as quoted in Weigley, *Sarah Tyson Rorer*, 46.

38 Weigley, *Sarah Tyson Rorer*, 61; Rorer, *Mrs. Rorer's New Cook Book*, 664.

39 "How Much Should We Eat?" *New York Daily Tribune*, October 22, 1882, 9. For a more extensive treatment of the self-regulating diet, see Albert J. Bellows, *Philosophy of Eating* (Boston: Houghton Mifflin, 1870).

40 Harvey A. Levenstein, *Seductive Journey: American Tourists in France from Jefferson to the Jazz Age* (Chicago: University of Chicago Press, 1998), 45–46.

41 For a sample, see Wilber O. Atwater, "The Chemistry of Foods and Nutrition," *Century* 34, no. 1 (1887): 59–74; Smith, *Eating History*, 115.

42 Wilber Olin Atwater, "Food Wastes in American Households," *Forum* 16 (1893): 116.

43 Atwater's research buttressed the work of Kellogg and Rorer and the emerging home economics movement. Inspired by—if not always true to—Atwater's

charts and graphs, food reformers sought to remake the American diet, empha-
sizing balance over excess and quality over quantity. At the Massachusetts Institute of Technology, Ellen Richards, with the support of the Boston-based progressive Women's Education Association, established the first "home economics"
laboratory in 1876. Richards brought chemistry to bear on home management
and home cooking with the goal of "help[ing] the housewife to regain control
over her kingdom." Although Richards wrote that the "well-to-do classes are
being eliminated by their diet, to the detriment of social progress, and *they* and
not the poor are the most in need of missionary work," in practice, her proselytizing was often among poor immigrants. Shapiro, *Perfection Salad*, 38–40.

44 Lincoln, for example, included "the richest and most elaborately prepared" recipes in her 1884 cookbook for "those who can afford [them] physically as well as
pecuniarily [*sic*]." Mary J. Lincoln, *Mrs. Lincoln's Boston Cook Book: What to Do and
What Not to Do in Cooking* (Boston: Roberts Brothers, 1884), vi.

45 *N. W. Ayer and Son's American Newspaper Annual and Directory* (Philadelphia: N. W.
Ayer and Son, 1911), 1165–66.

46 Shapiro, *Perfection Salad*, 57.

47 *N. W. Ayer and Son's American Newspaper Annual and Directory* (1911), 1165.

48 The journal's lengthy subtitle promised it would provide "information about
What to Eat, How to Eat, When to Eat, How to Cook, How to Serve, How to
Give Up-to-Date Dinners, How to Give *Recherche* Luncheons, How to Set Tables
a la Mode, The Latest Thing in Tableware, Table Furnishings and Novel Effects."
Masthead, *What to Eat*, June 1897, 264.

49 "The Salisbury Treatment," *What to Eat*, August 1896, 21; Charles Renhofer [Ran-
hofer], "Dinner Giving at Delmonico's," *What to Eat*, August 1896, 20. See also
Paul Pierce, "Our Magazine and Its Mission," *What to Eat*, August 1896, 18; "Ralstonism," *What to Eat*, August 1896, 4–6; Jungen, "Ralstonism in General," 6–7.

50 "Avoid Temptation," *What to Eat*, August 1897, 43. Paul Pierce used *What to Eat*
to promote the pure food movement and eventually organized the St. Louis Exposition's pure food booth, one of the first events to bring together the diverse
forces fighting for quality controls on food sales. Before that he seems to have
been involved in various "pure food shows" in Minneapolis and Buffalo. However, Pierce's influence over the restaurant industry was severely tarnished in
1917 when he embraced Prohibition. "The Pure Food Show," *What to Eat*, April
1898, 234; Lorine Swainston Goodwin, *The Pure Food, Drink, and Drug Crusaders,
1879–1914* (Jefferson, N.C.: McFarland, 1999); "Where Does the Hotel Employee
Stand?" *The Caterer* 28, no. 8 (1917): 17. Other journals, of course, also took strong
stances against extravagant eating, but they either did not have the circulation
and longevity of *What to Eat* (as in the case of *The Table*) or did not have an urban
middle-class audience with extensive opportunities to shape dining culture
(as in the case of *Cooking Club*). For examples, see "Refinements of the Table,"
The Table 1, no. 2 (1873): 31; and "Dinner Custom Changes," *Cooking Club* 9, no. 1
(1903): 15.

51 For more on Chatfield-Taylor, see "Arbiter of the Elegancies," *Newark Daily Advocate*, July 1, 1893, 2.

52 H. C. Chatfield-Taylor, "The Philosophy of Gastronomy," *What to Eat*, August 1896, 3.

53 Ibid., 4.

54 Ibid., 3.

55 On Roosevelt, see "Simpler and Cheaper Meals," *What to Eat*, August 1904, 93–94.

56 Ibid.

57 "The Art of Eating Enough and Eating Right," *What to Eat*, March 1904, 106.

58 "Simpler and Cheaper Meals," 93–94.

59 Marila Pemberton and Paul Pierce, "New York Adopts Simple Life," *What to Eat*, October 1905, 146.

60 Frank Luther Mott, *A History of American Magazines*, vol. 3, 1865–1885 (Cambridge: Harvard University Press, 1930); Frank Luther Mott, *A History of American Magazines*, vol. 4, 1885–1905 (Cambridge: Harvard University Press, 1930), 42, 745, 766, 690. In 1903, the *Ladies' Home Journal* had a circulation of nearly a million and the *Saturday Evening Post* had about 500,000 subscribers. In 1898, the *Atlantic Monthly* (admittedly in a slump) had only 7,000 readers. *Survey*, at the height of its influence in 1910, had about 20,000 subscribers. Highbrow middle-class journals such as *Outlook* and *Century* had circulations of 100,000 and 150,000 respectively.

61 *N. W. Ayer and Son's American Newspaper Annual and Directory* (1893; 1897). In 1897, Ayer and Son listed *What to Eat*, but circulation numbers were not available. By 1911, however, *What to Eat* (retitled *National Food Magazine*) had a circulation of 45,000, *Cooking Club* 38,000, *The Boston Cooking School Magazine* 25,850, and *Vegetarian Magazine* 15,333. *Table Talk* had declined to 10,500 and would soon merge with *What to Eat (National Food Magazine)*.

62 "Good Food Makes a Bow," *Good Food* 1, no. 1 (1906): 5; "Rudimentary Principles of Food Cooking Need to Be Emphasized," *Good Food* 2, no. 2 (1907): 5; "The Sated Millionaire," *Good Food* 2, no. 7 (1907): 22.

63 "Value of Good Food," *Cooking Club* 8, no. 3 (1902): 3.

64 "Simplicity," *Cooking Club* 8, no. 7 (1902): 3.

65 "Dinner Custom Changes," 15.

66 Maria Parloa, *Home Economics: A Guide to Household Management* (New York: Century Co., 1898), 258. See also Corson, *Every-Day Cookery and Hints for the Laundry*, 79; Juliet Corson, *Miss Corson's Practical American Cookery and Household Management* (New York: Dodd, Mead & Co., 1885), 128; M. L. Holbrook, *Eating for Strength; or, Food and Diet in Relation to Health and Work* (New York: M. L. Holbrook, 1888), 94.

67 Daniel Horowitz, *The Morality of Spending: Attitudes toward the Consumer Society in America, 1875–1940* (Baltimore: Johns Hopkins University Press, 1985), 90–108. See also Levenstein, *Revolution at the Table*, 86–172.

68 "Does the Human Family Eat Too Much?" *What to Eat*, October 1904, 149.

69 For a general discussion of the New York press, see M. H. Dunlop, *Gilded City:*

Scandal and Sensation in Turn-of-the-Century New York (New York: W. Morrow, 2000), xix. Not all of the publicity was unwanted. As the numbers of wealthy in New York swelled during the Gilded Age, parvenus sought press coverage of their homes, parties, and charitable events to bolster their claims to society membership. Many elite women hired personal secretaries who acted as press agents. For a contemporary (fictional) account, see Edgar Fawcett, *New York: A Novel* (New York: F. Tennyson Neely, 1898), 155–56.

70 Lloyd R. Morris, *Incredible New York* (New York: Arno Press, 1975), 241; Frederick Townsend Martin, *Things I Remember* (New York: John Lane, 1913), 238–43. The Bradley-Martins were relatively new to society. Both were from upstate New York; she was the daughter of a railroad magnate and he was a banker.

71 Lately Thomas, *Delmonico's: A Century of Splendor* (Boston: Houghton Mifflin, 1967), 320; Kate Simon, *Fifth Avenue: A Very Social History* (New York: Harcourt Brace Jovanovich, 1978), 117; Edward Tarrisse, "Some Freak Dinners," *Table Talk*, January 1913, 50. Thomas misstates the date of the event as 1900.

72 Dixon Wecter, *The Saga of American Society: A Record of Social Aspiration, 1607–1937* (New York: Scribner, 1970), 371; Simon, *Fifth Avenue*, 118. "A Notable Society Function Given at Sherry's in New York," *The Chef* 11, no. 4 (1901): 958.

73 "The Café Madrid may still be called a lively spot in the early morning hours. . . . You may see there people who are in Lobster Palace Society but not in the Four Hundred and–hist!—you may also see some people who are in both. It is extraordinary how the two sets overlap each other at the edges—people from Fifth Avenue are such climbers, anyway." Julian Street, "Lobster Palace Society," *Everybody's Magazine* 1910, 654.

74 Nancy Groce, *New York: Songs of the City* (New York: Watson-Guptill Publications, 1999), 39.

75 Respectable restaurants, at least in fiction, were not immune from criticism. In David Graham Phillips's *Susan Lenox: Her Rise and Fall*, Susan's fall from respectability includes meals bought for her at expensive restaurants. In Edgar Fawcett's 1898 *New York*, George Oliver's fall from social grace (and his efforts to restore his name) begins when he is tempted by a woman and plied with drink at the Hoffman House. David Graham Phillips, *Susan Lenox: Her Fall and Rise*, 2 vols. (New York: D. Appleton, 1917); Fawcett, *New York*, 9–11.

76 W. R. Stewart, "Banquet in Modern American Life," *Cosmopolitan*, March 1904, 618.

77 Tarrisse, "Some Freak Dinners," 50. For a further critique, see "A Society Dog Lunch," *The Caterer* 23, no. 12 (1912): 28. The middle class did not restrict its criticism of dietary excess to elites, but often middle-class critiques of the poor were tempered by compassion. "The reason of the monotonous one course which characterizes the dinner of these classes is, undoubtedly, due to the necessity which exists in such cases for the saving of time and trouble, otherwise it is difficult to account for the austere and conservative nature of their culinary economy." A. C., "Unsatisfactory Dinners," *The Table* 1, no. 8 (1873): 172.

78 Stearns, *Fat History*, 8–9; Editors, *The Caterer* 3, no. 8 (1885): 323.

79 Robert Tomes, *The Bazar Book of Decorum* (New York: Harper and Brothers, 1870), 184–85. Even some of the more sober guides, while recommending moderation, felt it was rude to refuse a course when offered. See, for example, a guide first published in 1857, Samuel R. Wells, *How to Behave: A Pocket Manual of Republican Etiquette, and Guide to Correct Personal Habits* (New York: Fowler and Wells, 1887), 75.

80 "Quacks," *The Chef* 8, no. 8 (1898): 352.

81 "What the New York Diner out Orders for His Dinner," *New York Times*, December 28, 1913, sec. Sunday Magazine, 7. World War I helped to change wealthy dining habits. F. Reichenbach, a butler working in New York, claimed in 1918 that "the rich folk are helping in many ways. In the saving of food and the foregoing of their favorite dinners and dishes they are doing wonders." "Society's Changed Diet in War Times," *The Caterer* 30, no. 3 (1918): 32.

82 "True Art in Simplicity," *The Cook*, March 30, 1885, 8.

83 Thomas J. Murray, "Less Variety and Better Quality," *The Cook*, August 17, 1885, 4. "The best hotels, it gives me pleasure to state, are fast moving in the direction of simplicity of bill of fare. In New York the leading house of the American plan does not provide its table with much more than one-half the variety of dishes one may have offered at second rate pretentious concerns through the country." "Americans Rounding Out," *The Cook*, August 3, 1885, 5. See also *Hotel Mail*, "Short Bills of Fare," *The Caterer* 3, no. 3 (1884): 122.

84 "Woman Can Order Dinners," *New York Times*, August 7, 1898, 14.

85 William Griffith, "The New Yorker and His Dinner," *New York Times*, March 26, 1905, sec. 3, 1.

86 *New York World*, "Too Much on Menu," *Washington Post*, December 2, 1906, sec. E, 4.

87 Menu, "Carte Du Jour," Brevoort House, New York, N.Y., November 10, 1886, Box 4 (1886-76a [a-b]), Buttolph Menu; Menu, "Dinner: Café and Restaurant," Waldorf-Astoria, New York, N.Y., November 17, 1905, Box 128 (1905-875), Buttolph Menu. A November 18, 1905, menu for dinner in the Garden restaurant is similar enough to suggest that this was the standard size of the Waldorf-Astoria's menus. Menu, "Dinner: Garden," Waldorf-Astoria, New York, N.Y., November 18, 1905, Box 128 (1905-867), Buttolph Menu.

88 John A. Ewins, "How Are We Going to Satisfy Our Guests at the Present Cost of Food Supplies?" *The Steward* 7, no. 9 (1912): 17 (emphasis added).

89 "Simpler and Cheaper Meals," *What to Eat*, August 1904, 93-4. Women were often credited for restaurants' willingness to adopt lighter fare. Marila Pemberton told readers of *What to Eat* in 1906 that "many of New York's business men have adopted the custom [of doing without luncheon] from women, who seem to thrive on it, and have abandoned the midday restaurant lunch." Marila Pemberton, "Fads and Fancies of Gotham: The 'Doing without Luncheon' Fad," *What to Eat*, April 1906, 130. But it is important to note that while the movement to reduce the

bill of fare took root in the early twentieth century and received a boost during the voluntary rationing of World War I, restaurants evolved slowly and the battle for simpler meals was waged in industry journals well into the 1930s. For later examples, see "Hotel Men Cut Bill-of-Fare," *The Caterer* 28, no. 4 (1916): 48; "Cliff Lewis Advocates Small Menu, Americanized," *The Caterer* 28, no. 6 (1917): 45; and "War Time Menus in New York Hotels," *The Caterer* 28, no. 10 (1917): 18–20.

90 "Is This a 'Perfect Dinner'?" *The Caterer* 24, no. 12 (1913): 59. Likewise, *Good Food* favorably contrasted a massive 1857 menu to the modern menus of hotels and restaurants. "A Square Meal," *Good Food* 2, no. 8 (1907): 7.

91 "In 'Lobster Palaces.' Scenes in Broadway Restaurants after the Theatre," *New York Daily Tribune*, May 3, 1903, sec. Illustrated Supplement, 6.

92 Jessup Whitehead, *The Steward's Handbook and Guide to Party Catering* (Chicago: J. Anderson, 1889), 58.

93 "A Day's Experience of Hotel High Life," *Cooking Club* 9, no. 3 (1903): 220–22.

94 "In 'Lobster Palaces,'" 6.

95 The high prices were not solely the result of à la carte dining. Food prices rose significantly in the early twentieth century.

96 Menu, "Menu," Planter's Hotel, St. Louis, Mo., 1905, Box 128 (1905-848), Buttolph Menu.

97 August Stender, "Reform Menus," *The Caterer* 28, no. 3 (1916): 45; "The Long Bill of Fare Drives Customers from Hotel Restaurants," *The Caterer* 20, no. 5 (1908): 22; "The 'after-Theater' Business," *The Caterer* 15, no. 10 (1904): 28.

98 Charles Fellows, *The Menu Maker: Suggestions for Selecting and Arranging Menus for Hotels and Restaurants* (Chicago: Hotel Monthly Press, 1910), 57.

99 "Getting Served in New York," *New York Times*, May 2, 1909, sec. 5, 3. Similar stories abound. See *Chicago Evening Post*, "Bluffed It Out," *The Southern Hotel Journal* 1, no. 9 (1911): 63.

100 "A head waiter has to know all the tricks of the trade, and they are many. You have to watch them closely, for if you don't they will make more money than the proprietor. To keep their checks straight is a task in itself. Every system of checks has been outdone by the waiter. Some of them won't stay in places where they cannot make a fair salary by scheming." James Joseph Flanagan, *The Waiter* (Providence: Star Printing, 1903), 42.

101 The "Liberty Lunch" was a fixed price meal that might or might not have been served on a single plate but encouraged dinners to think of the meal as a single entity. (A similar menu titled "Eat and Grow Thin" was offered at the Hotel Pantlind in Grand Rapids, Michigan, before the war.) "High-Class and Cheaper Diet," *The Caterer* 29, no. 1 (1917): 6; "Cliff Lewis Advocates Small Menu, Americanized," 48–49. Meanwhile, the U.S. Food Administration recommended single-plate dining in 1917 and issued an order that made it "taboo" to serve more than one meat at a single meal in 1918. U.S. Food Administration, "Time to Try out the Club Plan," *The Caterer* 29, no. 4 (1917): 70; "Food Administration Decrees a One-Meat Meal," *The Caterer* 30, no. 4 (1918): 31. For more on World War I rationing,

see Helen Zoe Veit, "'We Were a Soft People': Asceticism, Self-Discipline and American Food Conservation in the First World War," *Food, Culture and Society* 10, no. 2 (2007): 167–90.

102 "Plate Dinners Are Popular," *The Steward* 13, no. 8 (1918): 27.

103 Precursors to the plate dinner were common in Great Britain and were occasionally served in American hotels and boarding houses in the nineteenth century. Railroads adopted individual portions before World War I, and these meals may have been the inspiration for restaurant plate dinners. However, the practice was criticized "as a prodigious test of the powers of digestion" in some etiquette guides. Tomes, *Bazar Book of Decorum*, 186–87; "Railroad Individual Dishes," *The Caterer* 27, no. 1 (1915): 45; Charles Peters, ed., *The Girl's Own Indoor Book* (Philadelphia: J. B. Lippincott, 1888), 400.

104 "Bans on Foreign Names on Our Menus Urged as First Culinary Congress Is Organized," *New York Times*, November 7, 1939, 25. During the war years, the plate dinner was not the only effort at simplifying dining. A variable-price table d'hôte menu where the patron would check off selections was also applauded by culinary writers. In 1918, editors at *Table Talk* declared the "coupon" meal a "revolution in public dining" that might serve as an alternative to the "old time extravagant, ill balanced meal served by small town hotels." The editors extolled the new model as "a nicely arranged dinner, served with due regard to proteins and carbohydrates and calories and digestive systems." However, restaurateurs continued to struggle with balancing the expectations of elite customers with practical reforms, even as World War I forced compromises. The issue would not be complete resolved for over twenty years. Editors, "A Revolution in Public Dining," *Table Talk, the National Food Magazine*, December 1918; Stender, "Reform Menus," 44; "High-Class and Cheaper Diet," 36; "Whitman and Cuisine," *The Caterer* 29, no. 6 (1918): 17.

105 Charles Ranhofer, *The Epicurean: A Complete Treatise of Analytical and Practical Studies on the Culinary Art* (New York: C. Ranhofer, 1894).

106 "Dancing at the hotels and restaurants in New York seems fair to be fully as popular this season as it was last, for it is noticed that more and more of the institutions that held aloof from the popular craze in the past have yielded to the demands of their patrons, while those places that introduced dancing in the earlier days, are certain to continue. Among the very latest of the ultra conservative places that have at last given way is Delmonico's, where dancing will be held every afternoon during the week in what is known as the roof garden." "Notes and Notions," *The Steward* 9, no. 8 (1914): 25. Nonetheless, the introduction of orchestras and later dance floors in restaurants was the source of much lamentation by the stewards of the aristocratic restaurants. Jacques Kraemer, manager of the celebrated Hotel Carlton, London, declared in 1914: "We would not have tea dancing at the Carlton; nor would we have supper dancing. I think these do a lot of harm to a restaurant. They rather spoil its 'cachet.'" "Praises and Criticizes American Hotels and Food," *The Steward* 9, no. 3 (1914): 29. Many shared

the sentiment. See the comments of George Newton, proprietor of the Hotel St. George, in 1914: "Notes and Notions," 18. See also Lewis A. Erenberg, *Steppin' Out: New York Nightlife and the Transformation of American Culture, 1890–1930* (Westport, Conn.: Greenwood Press, 1981); "Where Music Soothes While Lobsters Broil," *New York Times*, April 24, 1910, sec. Sunday Magazine, 7.

107 "Great Relief to Him," *The Steward* 14, no. 8 (1919): 17.

108 Emily Post, *Etiquette: The Blue Book of Social Usage* (New York: Funk and Wagnalls, 1937), 187–88. Similar changes in the menu were taking place in Europe at roughly the same time. As in this study, those changes have been attributed, at least in part, to changes in restaurant patronage. See, for example, Hans-Jürgen Teuteberg, "The Rising Popularity of Dining Out in Germany in the Aftermath of Modern Urbanization," in *Eating Out in Europe: Picnics, Gourmet Dining, and Snacks since the Late Eighteenth Century*, ed. Marc Jacobs and Peter Scholliers (Oxford: Berg, 2003), esp. 286–88; and Peter Scholliers, *Food Culture in Belgium* (Westport, Conn.: Greenwood Press, 2009), 24–25.

109 On the political dimensions of the search for greater access to consumer goods, especially in the post–World War II era, see Lizabeth Cohen, *A Consumer's Republic: The Politics of Mass Consumption in Postwar America* (New York: Vintage Books, 2003).

110 "A Restaurant Revolt," *Washington Post*, April 10, 1910, 4. The *Washington Post* suggested vaguely that these patrons were wealthy and fashionable; however, many if not most of the patrons of Broadway restaurants were, by this time, middle-class urbanites and tourists. See Erenberg, *Steppin' Out*; Richard Barry, "Transient Society for the Transients Made to Order at the Cabarets," *New York Times*, November 24, 1912, sec. 10, 1.

CHAPTER 6

1 "Mrs. Blatch to Sue the Hoffman House," *New York Times*, August 6, 1907, 1.

2 Harriot Stanton Blatch was a political activist and sought-after lecturer. Five years earlier, she had returned from England tutored in the British suffrage movement and influenced by Fabian socialism. More radical than her mother, Blatch broke new ground by encouraging New York suffragists to engage in activist politics, to participate in mass demonstrations (in particular, parades), and to reach out to working-class women both socially and politically. Ellen Carol DuBois, *Harriot Stanton Blatch and the Winning of Woman Suffrage* (New Haven: Yale University Press, 1997), 60–87, 97.

3 "Mrs. Blatch to Sue the Hoffman House," 1.

4 Mrs. John T. Trow, chairman of the New York Equal Suffrage League legislative committee, told the *New York Times* on the eve of the Blatch trial that she was unaware of any case that had previously challenged the right of public accommodations—including hotels, restaurants, and railroads—to exclude women. She was incorrect. In 1897, Clara Foltz, the first woman lawyer in California and an advocate of Progressive legal reforms and women's rights, sued a New York hotel

and restaurant after the proprietor forced her and her daughter to leave because the restaurant would not admit unescorted women after 9 P.M. They filed for $5,000 damages. In 1903, a similar case was brought before the New York State Supreme Court. Rebecca Israel's suit against the Café Boulevard, an upscale French restaurant, was made under provisions of the state's racial civil rights laws passed in 1895. Justice Greenbaum ruled that since the escort policy had been applied uniformly, no discrimination had taken place. I have not located any similar court challenges prior to 1897, although the local character of these cases makes any comprehensive claim impossible. "Suffragists Aid Mrs. Blatch's Suit," *New York Times*, October 5, 1907, 11; "Clara Foltz Is Mad," *Los Angeles Times*, February 28, 1897, 3; "Restaurant Keepers' Rights: Court Upholds Defendant Who Refused to Serve a Woman Because She Had No Male Escort," *New York Times*, May 17, 1903, 3.

5 "Mrs. Blatch to Sue the Hoffman House," 1 (emphasis added).

6 "Hotels May Bar Lone Women Diners," *New York Times*, February 6, 1908, 14.

7 Ibid.

8 Members of the Consumer League, the City Federation of Women's Clubs, and the New York Equal Suffrage League accompanied Blatch to the trial. Before the trial, there had been talk of civil disobedience if the court ruled against Blatch. Emma Hunt told members of the Equal Suffrage League that she "would be very glad to go and make a test case myself" if Blatch's suit was "not sufficient to make the desired point." "Suffragists Aid Mrs. Blatch's Suit," 11. But no further action was taken, and the suit is not mentioned in Blatch's autobiography or a subsequent biography. See Harriot Stanton Blatch and Alma Lutz, *Challenging Years: The Memoirs of Harriot Stanton Blatch* (New York: G. P. Putnam's Sons, 1940).

9 "The Active Woman," *New York Times*, October 6, 1907, 10.

10 Noah Brooks, "Restaurant Life of San Francisco," *Overland Monthly*, November 1868, 466–67.

11 Edith Harman Brown, "Where Old New Yorkers Ate," *What to Eat*, July 1904, 4–5.

12 Brooks, "Restaurant Life of San Francisco," 467. The strong association between sexual license and public eating in the mid-nineteenth century drew on two images: the concert saloon waitress and the "hot corn" girl. The concert saloon was a bar, a primitive restaurant, and a dance hall. The more risqué concert halls employed waitresses, dressed in wench costumes—high-cut skirts and low-cut blouses—to serve drinks to rowdy male crowds. Some of the waitresses were prostitutes. "Hot corn" girls were street vendors who were widely suspected of selling sex. The "hot corn" girls became a notorious symbol of urban vice after the agricultural editor of the *New York Tribune*, Solon Robinson, published a series of temperance tales titled "Hot Corn" in 1854. Although Robinson did not claim that the women, some as young as thirteen or fourteen, were prostitutes, other reformers sexualized the image of the "hot corn" girl in order to draw the

social boundaries of respectability. On concert saloons, see Michael Batterberry and Ariane Ruskin Batterberry, *On the Town in New York: The Landmark History of Eating, Drinking, and Entertainments from the American Revolution to the Food Revolution* (New York: Routledge, 1999), 102; Luc Sante, *Low Life: Lures and Snares of Old New York* (New York: Vintage Books, 1992), 109–11; and Matthew Hale Smith, *Sunshine and Shadow in New York* (Hartford: J. B. Burr and Company, 1869), 424. On "hot corn" girls, see Solon Robinson, *Hot Corn: Life Scenes in New York Illustrated* (New York: De Witt and Davenport, 1854), 18.

13 Lately Thomas related the exception that proves the rule. Victoria and Tennessee Woodhull

> were . . . sensational "lady stock brokers" who played the market on tips from Commodore Vanderbilt, and who advocated spiritualism, free love, and votes for women. . . . Seating themselves boldly in Delmonico's restaurant, without escort, the sisters . . . ordered, "Tomato soup for two." The waiter regretted that he could not take their order. They called for Charles Delmonico, who appeared all smiles. He liked the pair, and good-naturedly he offered to cover their retreat by strolling to the door with them, engaging them in conversation, so diners might assume they had merely dropped in to speak to him. By no means, they responded; they had come to dine, and if the presence of a man was indispensable, they would provide that accessory.

The driver of a horse cab was summoned and seated at their table and Victoria ordered "Tomato soup for three." Lately Thomas, *Delmonico's: A Century of Splendor* (Boston: Houghton Mifflin, 1967), 200–201.

14 Emmeline Stuart Wortley, *Travels in the United States, Etc.: During 1849 and 1850* (New York: Harper and Brothers, 1855), 38.

15 Isabella Lucy Bird, *The Englishwoman in America* (Madison: University of Wisconsin Press, 1966), 100. See also *Where and How to Dine in New York: The Principal Hotels, Restaurants and Cafes of Various Kinds and Nationalities Which Have Added to the Gastronomic Fame of New York and Its Suburbs* (New York: Lewis, Scribner, 1903), 19.

16 Brooks, "Restaurant Life of San Francisco," 467.

17 Tunis G. Campbell, *Hotel Keepers, Head Waiters, and Housekeepers' Guide* (Boston: Coolidge and Wiley, 1848), 41–42.

18 Editors, *Hotel World*, November 2, 1876, 6.

19 Bird, *Englishwoman in America*, 149–50.

20 "Mallard's Moves," *New York Times*, October 15, 1908, 5. For various exceptions, see "Varieties," *Appleton's Journal*, July 29, 1871, 139; "Mistaken for a Handsome Man," *New York Times*, July 4, 1884.

21 Batterberry and Batterberry, *On the Town in New York*, 92; "Women Lunch at Cafes," *Chicago Daily Tribune*, June 19, 1896, 12.

22 Batterberry and Batterberry, *On the Town in New York*, 92.

23 Restaurateurs were slow to identify women as a potential market. Early accounts suggest that women ordered too little, lingered too long, and complained too much to be profitable. See "The Woman in the Restaurant," *New York Times*, July 18, 1876, 3; and "Nice but Unprofitable," *New York Times*, May 30, 1886, 6.

24 "'Home' Coffee and Lunch Rooms," *Overland Monthly*, December 1888, n.p.

25 Cindy R. Lobel, "Consuming Classes: Changing Food Consumption Patterns in New York City, 1790–1860" (PhD diss., City University of New York, 2003), 105.

26 Thomas, *Delmonico's*, 199.

27 Mary P. Ryan, *Women in Public: Between Banners and Ballots, 1825–1880* (Baltimore: Johns Hopkins University Press, 1990), 73.

28 "Lady," in *The Century Dictionary: An Encyclopedia Lexicon of the English Language*, ed. William Dwight Whitney (New York: Century Company, 1911), 3328. Other terms (regularly employed by restaurateurs) such as "respectable" had more complex meanings but were also closely linked to wealth. "Respectable," in *The Century Dictionary*, 5109.

29 "Any Woman's a Lady Who Behaves That Way," *New York Times*, January 12, 1907, 8. Lately Thomas tells a similar story without naming Vanderbilt. According to Thomas, Charles Delmonico recognized a grande dame but asked her to leave because she did not have a male escort. The rebuffed lady took the incident as a "compliment to Mr. Delmonico and his excellently moral establishment." Thomas, *Delmonico's*, 200.

30 Marila Pemberton, "Fads and Fancies of Gotham: Short Skirts for Dining Room Costumes," *What to Eat*, January 1906, 31; Marila Pemberton, "Mrs. Belmont's Restaurant Dress," *What to Eat*, January 1906, 32; "Restaurant Gowns and Wraps," *New York Times*, April 16, 1911, sec. Sunday Magazine, n.p.; Mary Eleanor O'Donnell, "Smart Costumes for Restaurant and Theater Wear," *Chicago Daily Tribune*, January 2, 1910, sec. F, 1. Restaurant dresses remained popular, although not short, through the beginning of the second decade of the twentieth century.

31 Cited in Thomas, *Delmonico's*, 199–200, 239–40.

32 Samuel Paynter Wilson, *Chicago by Gaslight* (Chicago: n.d., c. 1910), 146.

33 Gertrude Atherton, "The New Aristocracy," *Cosmopolitan*, April 1906, 624.

34 Jan Whitaker, *Tea at the Blue Lantern Inn: A Social History of the Tea Room Craze in America* (New York: St. Martin's Press, 2002), 19.

35 Richard Barry, "The Tea Rooms, Where Society and Business Meet," *New York Times*, December 1, 1912, sec. 10, 1.

36 Cassandra Tate, *Cigarette Wars: The Triumph of "The Little White Slaver"* (New York: Oxford University Press, 1999).

37 George G. Foster and Stuart M. Blumin, *New York by Gas-Light and Other Urban Sketches* (Berkeley: University of California Press, 1990), 135.

38 Genie H. Rosenfeld, "Notes Dramatic," *What to Eat*, November 1903, 157.

39 "Women Who Smoke Rare," *New York Times*, December 9, 1894, 18.

40 Anhelm, "What Women Do: Separate Lunch for Women and Men at Delmo-

nico's," *Los Angeles Times*, June 10, 1894, 18. See also the various descriptions of dining in Edith Wharton, *The Age of Innocence* (New York: Modern Library, 1948). See also the recollections of *Vanity Fair* editor Frank Crowninshield. Frank Crowninshield, "Personal Glimpses: How New York Society Got That Way," *Literary Digest*, January 20, 1923, 44.

41 For a thorough discussion of the role of publicity and privacy in upper-class New York, see Maureen E. Montgomery, *Displaying Women: Spectacles of Leisure in Edith Wharton's New York* (New York: Routledge, 1998), esp. 9, 32–38, 150–57.

42 Elaine S. Abelson, *When Ladies Go a-Thieving: Middle-Class Shoplifters in the Victorian Department Store* (New York: Oxford University Press, 1989).

43 For some of the voices of concern, see Katherine Barber, "The College Girl as a Cook," *What to Eat*, September 1899, 93; "The Kitchen: 'The Heart of the Home,'" *What to Eat*, January 1904, 31; "Women and Waiters," *What to Eat*, July 1899, 30; "The Woman Wage-Earner's Luncheon," *What to Eat*, November 1902, 194; Rosenfeld, "Notes Dramatic," 157; Mary Margaret McBride, "I Come to New York," *Scribner's Magazine*, March 1931, 316; "Woman Can Order Dinners," *New York Times*, August 7, 1898, 14; and "The Maid and the Menu: Can a Woman Order a Dinner?" *New York Times*, October 30, 1904, sec. 2, 6. For an alternative view, see "Women in Restaurants: Where They Usually Show Their Superiority over Men," *New York Times*, July 10, 1892, 15.

44 For negative accounts of women's skill at ordering dinner, see "Men and Women Cooks Compared," *Hotel World*, November 2, 1876, 7; E. J., "The 'Original' Walker," *The Table* 1, no. 7 (1873): 142; *The Spectator*, "How Women Give an Order," *Washington Post*, January 29, 1888, 9; and "Ladies Fare at Lunch: Capricious Taste Shown in Her Orders at the Restaurants," *Washington Post*, December 13, 1896, 13. For a later, more positive account, see "Sexes in Restaurants," *Chicago Daily Tribune*, May 29, 1904, 23.

45 Amelia Gere Mason, "Decadence of Manners," *Century*, August 1900, 536.

46 Thomas Beer, "Menu: Conversation on Food and Restaurants, European and American," *Scribner's Magazine*, December 1932, 347.

47 Harry E. Lewis quoted in "Blames Lights for Immorality: Justice Lewis Wants More Illumination in Cafes as a Check for Lawlessness," *New York Times*, April 18, 1926, 12.

48 In 1882, the Hotel Brunswick sullied its reputation when Billy McGlory, the proprietor of a notorious "concert saloon," tricked the hotel into hosting a party composed of gamblers and prostitutes. In 1907, the popularity of the Paul Potter play *The Girl from Rector's* (and later, the Ziegfeld Follies song "If a Table at Rector's Could Talk") seemed to foreshadow the decline of Rector's restaurant. Both restaurants failed years after they were implicated in scandal, but the idea that scandal could ruin a restaurant persisted. On the Hotel Brunswick, see Batterberry and Batterberry, *On the Town in New York*, 156–58. On Rector's, see Albin Pasteur Dearing, *The Elegant Inn: The Waldorf-Astoria Hotel, 1893–1929* (Secaucus, N.J.: L. Stuart, 1986), 153; and John F. Mariani, *America Eats Out: An Illustrated His-*

tory of Restaurants, Taverns, Coffee Shops, Speakeasies, and Other Establishments That Have Fed Us for 350 Years (New York: Morrow, 1991), 59.

49 It became more common for women to travel with their husbands and dine in restaurants in the last quarter of the nineteenth century. See *New York Tribune*, "Arrivals at the Hotels," *Hotel World*, September 14, 1876, 8.

50 "In the Realm of Women," *New York Times*, August 28, 1898, 14.

51 "Fair Women at Lunch," *New York Times*, December 20, 1885, 4; "Unlucky Man in a Woman's Restaurant," *New York Times* May 17, 1903, sec. Sunday Magazine, 15.

52 "Women Lunch at Cafes," 12.

53 Mariani, *America Eats Out*, 113–17.

54 G. Sudley, "Luncheon for a Million," *Munsey's Magazine*, March 1901, 845.

55 *Philadelphia Times*, "Restaurants for Women," *Los Angeles Times*, September 1, 1893, 4.

56 "The Tea Room Habit Has Come to Stay," *New York Times*, April 3, 1904, sec. Sunday Magazine, 7. The *New York Times* dates the tearoom craze to about 1895. For an excellent discussion of the social history of tearooms, see Whitaker, *Tea at the Blue Lantern Inn*.

57 M. M. Maxwell, "Hotels for Women," *New York Times*, October 21, 1910, 6. Escort policies were still common enough in 1899 for Dorothy Stanhope to find it remarkable that Cuban women lunched together without male escorts and to predict that "the force of American example will cause the Cubans to break through their old customs." Dorothy Stanhope, "Food in Havana Is Poor," *New York Times*, April 16, 1899, 25.

58 Class distinctions are difficult to categorize in the United States. In the examples given, the class of the female transgressors is rarely clear. A few of these women may have been elite society women; however, I argue that changes in restaurant culture were possible because of larger shifts in the class of the consuming public, which destabilized traditional social categories.

59 Barry, "Tea Rooms," 1.

60 "Women's Equality Union," *New York Times*, February 10, 1898, 7.

61 "Any Woman's a Lady Who Behaves That Way," 8.

62 The article was reprinted in newspapers across the country, and Waldorf-Astoria historian Albin Dearing contends that the policy was widely imitated. *New York Times*, "Who's a Lady?" *Washington Post*, January 13, 1907, sec. E, 4; "Definition of 'Lady' Wanted," *Los Angeles Times*, January 24, 1907, sec. 2, 3; Dearing, *Elegant Inn*, 196, 197, 211.

63 "Any Woman's a Lady Who Behaves That Way," 8.

64 Ibid.

65 Ibid.

66 Ibid.

67 Ibid.

68 Whitaker, *Tea at the Blue Lantern Inn*, 25. The event took place in 1913.

69 Richard M. Ohmann, *Selling Culture: Magazines, Markets, and Class at the Turn of the Century* (London: Verso, 1996), 67–68.

70 Janet Thurston, "Women Often Pay the Check, Man Helps to Eat the Meal," *Chicago Daily Tribune*, August 23, 1908, sec. D, 8. See also *New York Sun*, "Women Who Pay," *Los Angeles Times*, March 1, 1908, sec. 7, 2; and "Women in Business Life: Feminine Wage-Earners Need a Code of Etiquette," *Chicago Daily Tribune*, October 17, 1897, 46.

71 "Epicurean Miscellany," *The Caterer* 19, no. 1 (1907): 49.

72 There were a few exceptions. For example, there was some controversy about women frequenting bars in New York, and city elders in Boston made concrete efforts to prevent single women from patronizing any establishment that served alcohol. See "The First Ladies' Bar," *The Caterer* 24, no. 10 (1913): 30; and "Curbing Bohemianism in Boston," *The Southern Hotel Journal* 1, no. 10 (1912): 43.

73 In 1883 (or 1889; accounts vary), Café Martin was the first restaurant to allow male patrons to smoke in the public dining rooms. Before the new policy, men retired to the restaurant's male saloon for a postprandial cigar or cigarette. "Not All May Smoke: Gotham Restaurants Puzzled Over Woman's Rights," *Washington Post*, January 5, 1908, 10; "Ladies May Smoke: On New Year's Eve, and Perhaps Afterward, in at Least One Restaurant," *New York Times*, December 30, 1907, 2.

74 Cecil B. Hartley, *The Gentlemen's Book of Etiquette, and Manual of Politeness: Being a Complete Guide for a Gentleman's Conduct in All His Relations Towards Society* (Boston: DeWolfe Fiske, 1873), 203. See also S. Annie Frost, *Frost's Laws and By-Laws of American Society: A Condensed but Thorough Treatise on Etiquette and Its Usages in America* (New York: Dick and Fitzgerald, 1869), 102.

75 Henry Collins Brown, *In the Golden Nineties* (Hastings-on-Hudson, N.Y.: Valentine's Manual, 1928), 128. Lobster Palaces attracted some middle-class men (especially young men) and, toward the end of the phenomenon, tourists. But it was wealthy elites who set the tone. "From 12 until 3 or 4 o'clock in the morning the huge supper restaurants are wide open. . . . Here, again, the man who has not a plethoric purse and the woman who is not fashionably gowned is out of place." On both the diversity of Lobster Palace guests and the primacy of the rich, see "New York That Never Sleeps," *New York Times*, January 8, 1905, sec. Sunday Magazine, 2. On Chicago's less licentious "millionaire's bohemia," see "Saturday Night in Chicago. How Millionaires Amuse Themselves in the 'Lobster Palaces' after the Theater," *Chicago Daily Tribune*, January 12, 1908, sec. D, 8.

76 As early as the 1890s, American women, especially middle-class women, seized upon cigarettes as a symbol of the "new woman." U.S. Department of Health and Human Services, *Reducing Tobacco Use: A Report of the Surgeon General* (Washington, D.C.: Department of Health and Human Services, U.S. Public Health Service, 2000), 36–37. For a comparable treatment of smoking in Canada that associates the trend with the middle class, see Jarrett Rudy, *The Freedom to Smoke: Tobacco Consumption and Identity* (Montreal: McGill–Queen's University Press,

2005). For a contrasting view, see Tate, *Cigarette Wars*, esp. 97. Tate suggests that upper-class women were more accepting of cigarettes than middle-class women but admits that due to the stigma often associated with women smoking, turn-of-the-century behavior is "difficult to document." Ultimately, the sources do not provide direct clues as to the class of the women who publicly smoked in the second decade of the twentieth century, and it is reasonable to suggest that some of the women were members of the upper class. However, the close association between suffragists, the "new woman," and smoking as well as the specific location of the first major incident—a New Year's party at Martin's—suggests that middle-class women were involved.

77 Reports prior to 1908 suggest that public smoking by women had been quietly on the rise for much of the decade. An article in the *Washington Post* in 1905 recounted the story of two women who were asked to stop smoking at a restaurant and complied. "Inquiry afterward revealed the fact that such a scene is a not uncommon occurrence at restaurants nowadays, but so far public sentiment favors the management." "Had to Give up Her Cigarette," *Washington Post*, November 26, 1905, sec. A, 6.

78 "Two Restaurants Let Women Smoke; but the Fifth Avenue Places Will Stick to the Old Rule at Present," *New York Times*, January 2, 1908, 3. James Martin had been considering the "experiment" for some time and had recently built a smoking parlor on the second floor for women. It may not be a coincidence that a month before Martin's new policy, the *New York Times* ran an editorial criticizing women who smoked in public. "Ladies May Smoke," 2; "The Women Who Smoke," *New York Times*, December 3, 1907, 8.

79 "Not Many Women Smoked," *New York Times*, January 1, 1908, 2.

80 "Two Restaurants Let Women Smoke," 3. See also "Ladies May Smoke," 2.

81 "Not All May Smoke," 10.

82 "Two Restaurants Let Women Smoke," 3. See also "Ladies May Smoke," 2.

83 "Two Restaurants Let Women Smoke," 3; "Smoking by Women Popular," *Washington Post*, January 3, 1908, 2.

84 "Femininity and Cigarettes," *Washington Post*, January 14, 1908, 6.

85 "Found No Women Smoking in Chicago," *New York Times*, January 2, 1908, 3.

86 "Femininity and Cigarettes," 6.

87 "No Public Smoking by Women Now," *New York Times*, January 21, 1908, 1. The politics of the smoking ban speaks volumes about the class interests at stake. Rumor held that the legislation was revenge by a "well-known politician," probably "Little Tim" Sullivan, who had been denied a reservation at a prominent city restaurant. True or not, Sullivan must have viewed a bill that would bar the "smart set" from smoking in the city's elite restaurants as a populist cause. "Women Mustn't Smoke," *New York Times*, January 22, 1908, 4. Sullivan had previously earned a reputation as "the Bowery moralist" when he forced theater managers to "cover the billboards [showing] the undraped limbs of well-favored women." "Bars Woman Smokers," *Washington Post*, January 7, 1908, 3. Although

"none of the Aldermen nor any one else about the City Hall regards [the smoking ordinance] very seriously," the measure, with Tammany Hall support, passed unanimously in both the Committee on Laws and Legislation and the Board of Aldermen (despite the widespread belief that the ordinance was illegal). "Sullivan Controls Board," *New York Times*, January 7, 1908, 4; "Forbids Women to Smoke," *Washington Post*, January 22, 1908, 3; "Women Mustn't Smoke," 4; "No Public Smoking by Women Now," 1. "Little Tim" acknowledged that the law might not hold up in the court of appeals if challenged but expected that "he 'can get away with his ordinance,' even if it does infringe slightly upon woman's inherent and constitutional rights." "Bars Woman Smokers," 3. Curiously, a bill to ban the sale of cigarettes to minors introduced a week later was allowed to languish in the Committee on Laws and Legislation. "New War on Cigarettes," *New York Times*, January 29, 1908, 1.

Katie Mulcahey (age twenty-nine) was the only woman arrested under the Sullivan Ordinance. She was picked up for smoking outside a Bowery Street home and fined five dollars but imprisoned when she refused on principle to pay. Curiously, the ordinance did not prohibit smoking outside, nor did it call for individual smokers to be fined. "Arrested for Smoking," *New York Times*, January 23, 1908, 1. The *Times* did not note the misapplication of the law.

88 "Women Mustn't Smoke," 4.

89 "Sullivan the Lesser's Motion," *New York Times*, January 8, 1908, 8.

90 "Mayor Lets Women Smoke: Vetoes 'Little Tim' Sullivan Ordinance Restricting Them," *New York Times*, February 4, 1908, 1. McClellan's publicly stated reasons for vetoing the ordinance should be taken with a grain of salt. McClellan, although anti-Prohibition, was a champion of the city's Sunday blue laws and employed similar regulations to keep nickelodeons closed on Sunday. Not coincidentally, the Sullivan family was invested in nickelodeons. Roberta E. Pearson and William Uricchio, "Corruption, Criminality and the Nickelodeon," in *Hop on Pop: The Politics and Pleasures of Popular Culture*, ed. Henry Jenkins, Tara MacPherson, and Jane Shattuck (Durham, N.C.: Duke University Press, 2002).

91 "No Public Smoking by Women Now," 1.

92 "Ban on Woman Smokers," *New York Times*, January 12, 1908, sec. 2, 1.

93 "Smoking by Women Called Deplorable," *New York Times*, January 24, 1908, 4.

94 "Not All May Smoke," 10. Boston was particularly intolerant of women smoking and especially quick to see the habit as foreign. "It's quite the custom in the South Sea islands to go nude in the best society, but it wouldn't do in America. And so on as to any other revolting habit of any other land." "Stopped the Lady's Smoke," *The Caterer* 24, no. 6 (1913): 42.

95 "Smoking Women under Ban in Washington Restaurants," *Washington Post*, November 13, 1911, 2.

96 "Women Smoke? Babies Weak," *Chicago Daily Tribune*, January 13, 1908, 3.

97 "Woman Smoked in the Ritz-Carlton: Puffed Away Undisturbed at Her Cigarette, Not a Soul Interfered," *New York Times*, December 18, 1910, 14.

98 By 1908, both the Waldorf and the Savoy in London allowed women to smoke. "Women Smoke Less," *New York Times*, November 28, 1908, 12.

99 "Woman Smoked in the Ritz-Carlton," 14.

100 Since the mid-1800s, middle-class reform movements had opposed smoking in public for both sexes. The Women's Christian Temperance Union (WCTU) launched the largest anti-smoking campaign in the United States, and by 1901 eleven states had some form of anti-smoking law. These laws, passed at a time when few women smoked, were aimed primarily at male smokers and minors. While the WCTU continued to argue against tobacco use, it formally abandoned its legislative efforts in 1919 at a time when women's smoking was on the rise. In New York, where "new women" heralded the cigarette as a sign of liberation, most middle-class anti-smoking campaigns did not specifically target women. Dr. Charles G. Pease formed the Non-Smoking Protective League in 1910 to promote legislation against smoking in "public and semi-public places" by both men and women, and in 1909 he successfully encouraged the city to pass a ban on smoking in the subway. "Form Non-Smoker's League," *New York Times*, May 10, 1910, 18. Similarly, in 1912 the *New York Times*, once cynical about Sullivan's proposal, endorsed a broad effort to prevent both men and women from smoking in restaurants. "The Criminality of Ill-Bred Smoking," *New York Times*, July 27, 1912, 6. As a letter writer from Utica, New York, told readers of the *Times* during the 1911 debate over a citywide ordinance banning women from smoking: "There is infinitely more that is offensive to the sight done by [man] than by woman, and it would surely be lamentable if the City Fathers should strain at a gnat and swallow a camel." "Aldermen and Smoking Women," *New York Times*, October 14, 1911, 12. See also U.S. Department of Health and Human Services, *Reducing Tobacco Use*, 29–37.

101 "Stopped Women Smokers," *New York Times*, January 9, 1911, 1.

102 *New York Press*, "Smoking among Women," *Washington Post*, July 30, 1911, sec. E, 4.

103 "'Tobacco-Smoking Females': Aldermen Moved to Invoke the Corporate Counsel against Them," *New York Times*, October 11, 1911, 1.

104 There were holdouts. James B. Reagan of the Knickerbocker Hotel "said that women were never permitted to smoke" in his hotel, and Oscar Tschirky of the Waldorf-Astoria promised a private room for women who wanted to smoke. However, these were short-lived exceptions. P. C. Jennings, "New York Letter," *The Southern Hotel Journal* 1, no. 11 (1912): 57.

105 Ibid.

106 "Women Smokers Objected to by Some Managers," *New York Times*, March 16, 1919, sec. 7, 2. A few of the more conservative family hotels discovered a niche market by banning women smokers, but even they acknowledged that women had a legitimate right to make their own choices about behavior. The manager of the Woodstock Hotel told the *New York Times*: "I don't care whether a woman smokes or not. Far be it from me to lay down the law controlling the personal

habits of others. But I find that, from a business standpoint, it pays to enforce a rule of that kind" (2).

107 Ibid.

108 The Santerer (pseud.), "Notes and Notions," *The Steward* 5, no. 11 (1911): 32.

109 Claudia Roth Pierpont, "The Silver Spire: How Two Men's Dreams Changed the Skyline of New York," *New Yorker*, November 18, 2002, 74–75.

110 Richard Duffy, "New York at Table," *Putnam's and the Reader*, February 1909, 569; Sudley, "Luncheon for a Million," 845.

111 "Women Who Smoke," 8. Similarly, see "Smoking Women under Ban in Washington Restaurants," 2.

112 "Hotels to Let Men Dine Coatless; Spread of Custom Is up to Women," *Washington Post*, August 13, 1916, sec. ES, 2.

113 "Women Smokers Objected to by Some Managers," 2.

114 A. Steele Penn (pseud.), "Smoke and Dust: Second Puff," *The Table* 1, no. 7 (1873): 159–60.

115 Historians generally date the emergence of companionate marriage to the first three decades of the twentieth century. With companionate marriage came a new form of sociability that advocates of cosmopolitanism celebrated. In contrast to upper-class society, which continued to seek out venues that segregated men and women at the turn of the century, middle-class Americans gathered as couples. On the history of companionate marriage, see Steven Mintz and Susan Kellogg, *Domestic Revolutions: A Social History of American Family Life* (New York: Free Press, 1988), 107–19; and Elaine Tyler May, *Great Expectations: Marriage and Divorce in Post-Victorian America* (Chicago: University of Chicago Press, 1980), 75–91.

116 Clarence E. Edwords, *Bohemian San Francisco: Its Restaurants and Their Most Famous Recipes* (San Francisco: P. Elder, 1914), 6.

117 Nan Enstad, *Ladies of Labor, Girls of Adventure: Working Women, Popular Culture, and Labor Politics at the Turn of the Twentieth Century* (New York: Columbia University Press, 1999), 48–51.

118 In 1914, a restaurant manager objected, despite the hot weather, to a woman who removed her hat in his restaurant. Miss Florence De Witt and her escort, Mr. William B. Wette, offended, tried to leave. The restaurant owner, William Weimann, asked that the couple pay for their meal and when they refused, had them arrested. The police quickly released the couple, and they promptly sued Weimann for $5,000 in damages. "Suit over Woman's Hat," *New York Times*, September 4, 1914, 16. Similar lawsuits were brought in 1917 against hotels that tried to police morality. In one case, hotel security detained Sadie Disbrow Hurd, the wife of a real estate broker, for kissing her husband outside the door to his room. She sued the Hotel Astor and was awarded damages. In the second case, Mrs. Mary Boyce, the wife of a marine engine manufacturer, received $8,000 in damages from the McAlpin after her husband was detained for visiting her room at night. "Hotel Astor Loses: Mrs. Hurd, Questioned for Kissing Husband,

Gets $2,500 Damages," *New York Times*, June 15, 1917, 9; "Woman Wins Hotel Suit: $8,000 Verdict against Mcalpin for Alleged Insult," *New York Times*, May 16, 1917, 8.

119 "Include Women in Dry Law," *New York Times*, March 8, 1918, 9 (emphasis added).

CHAPTER 7

1 August J. Bock, *Knight of the Napkin: Memoirs of Fifty Years' Experiences in Many Lands* (New York: Exposition Press, 1951), 31, 28–27.

2 "Piker" is American slang for someone who is both petty and stingy. It is roughly synonymous with "penny-pincher" or "cheapskate."

3 Bock, *Knight of the Napkin*, 28–27, 37.

4 Ibid., 28.

5 Kerry Segrave, *Tipping: An American Social History of Gratuities* (Jefferson, N.C.: McFarland, 1998), 5–6; Ofer H. Azar, "The History of Tipping from Sixteenth-Century England to United States in the 1910s," Department of Economics, Northwestern University, http://econwpa.wustl.edu/wpawelcome.html (accessed December 2, 2004). Although tipping was rare prior to the Civil War, it was not unheard of. Tunis Campbell, a headwaiter with experience in Boston and New York, warned proprietors to pay their waiters well to eliminate their need for tips in his 1848 waiter's manual. Tunis G. Campbell, *Hotel Keepers, Head Waiters, and Housekeepers' Guide* (Boston: Coolidge and Wiley, 1848), 8–9.

6 Eustace Williams, "Growth of Tipping Habit: Fifty Years Ago American Servants Rejected Gratuities," *Washington Post*, September 11, 1905, 9. Waiters may have also played a role in promoting tipping, especially in the 1870s and 1880s as more and more hotels hired European immigrant waiters accustomed to receiving tips. While tipping was generally viewed as a European vice, African Americans were blamed for transforming a reward into an obligation. The *Steward's Handbook* of 1889 reported that "in regard to the headwaiter's 'tips' the subject is much mixed, because it depends upon the kind of man he is whether he receives much or anything in that way, but it is a fact that very few *white* headwaiters ever receive 'tips,' unless, perhaps in a general way, the guests make up a purse at the end of a season or at Christmas." Jessup Whitehead, *The Steward's Handbook and Guide to Party Catering* (Chicago: J. Anderson, 1889), 185. (Europeans, ironically, were aghast at the influence that American travelers had on tipping in Europe. Europeans regarded American visitors as spendthrift tippers who continually drove up the cost of good service. Some European restaurants, it was reported, eliminated wages altogether and charged the waiters a portion of their tips for the privilege of waiting tables.)

7 Nineteenth-century hotels and restaurants were far less distinguished by food—they all served similar, French-inspired menus—than by clientele. Anglophobes might favor a particular restaurant, Wall Street men another, Republicans another, society matrons another; as a result, those who dined out established rou-

tine habits and often dined out regularly at the same restaurant. They might even request the same waiter time after time and continue to guarantee good service with regular large tips. In contrast, tipping in the twentieth century is largely an act of social control. Most people today tip to reward good service or punish bad service not because they ever expect to see the same waiter or waitress again but because they hope that their tip will have an overall positive effect on the level of service when dining out.

8 Winfield Forrest Cozart, *A Technical Treatise on Dining-Room Service: The Waiters' Manual* (Chicago: H. J. Bohn and Brother, 1898), 13.

9 "Feeing Waiters," *The Cook*, July 13, 1885, 10.

10 James Joseph Flanagan, *The Waiter* (Providence: Star Printing, 1903), 36.

11 Cozart, *Technical Treatise*, 104. See also Campbell, *Hotel Keepers, Head Waiters, and Housekeepers' Guide*, 54–55.

12 Flanagan, *The Waiter*, 30.

13 Charles Beadle, *A Trip to the United States in 1887* (London: J. S. Virtue, 1887), 69–70.

14 Flanagan, *The Waiter*, 26–27.

15 Edwin L. Sabin, "The Waiter," *What to Eat*, October 1907, 138 (abridged).

16 Thorstein Veblen, *The Theory of the Leisure Class: An Economic Study of Institutions* (New York: Modern Library, 1934), 63.

17 "Society," *Washington Post*, October 6, 1907, 7.

18 Alvin Harlow, "Our Daily Bribe," *Forum & Century* 99 (April 1938): 231, as quoted in Segrave, *Tipping*, 5–6. On tipping as a pernicious foreign influence, see also Frank Crane, "A Big Store and the Tipping Nuisance," *Syracuse (N.Y.) Herald*, May 9, 1916, 8; and Mary Marshall Duffee, "The Right Thing at the Right Time: How Much to Tip," *Indianapolis Star*, November 1, 1917, 7.

19 "The Tipping Evil," *Lincoln (Ill.) Daily News*, April 7, 1915, 6.

20 "Tips and Wages," *Newark Daily Advocate*, April 13, 1915, 4.

21 Azar, "History of Tipping."

22 "Tip or Do Without: Practice Has Reached Haughty Zenith in New York," *Washington Post*, March 19, 1905, 3. See also Crane, "A Big Store and the Tipping Nuisance," 8.

23 "The Custom of Tipping," *What to Eat*, January 1901, 31.

24 "A Terrible Revelation," *What to Eat*, October 1897, 89. Accusations about disgruntled waiters contaminating food were so common that it is perhaps best to view most of these events as urban legends and evidence of middle-class insecurity more than as actual occurrences. However, Joseph Ettor may have advised members of the International Hotel Workers' Union to poison the food of restaurant guests in 1913. "Food and Criminal Speech," *The Caterer* 24, no. 7 (1913): 17.

25 Segrave, *Tipping*, 14.

26 H. C. Bierwirth, "The Ethics of 'Tips,' Fees, and Gratuities," *Andover Review*, August 1886, 169.

27 "On the Custom of Tipping," *The Southern Hotel Journal* 1, no. 10 (1912): 9.

28 "Tyranny of Tipping," *Living Age*, May 23, 1908, 509, reprinted from the British journal *Spectator*.

29 Flanagan, *The Waiter*, 9.

30 Williams, "Growth of Tipping Habit," 9.

31 Joseph Hatton, "The Idler's Club," *Idler* 3 (July 1893): 681, as quoted in Segrave, *Tipping*, 13. Of course, advocates of tipping argued that middle-class patrons should not go to restaurants where they could not afford to tip. See Experienced, "The Tipping Question Again," *The Caterer* 23, no. 1 (1911): 28.

32 William Dean Howells, "Editor's Easy Chair: Tipping," *Harper's Monthly Magazine*, July 1913, 312.

33 First prize went to Clarence Loeb of Brooklyn for "I am not rich enough to be eccentric." "The Contest to Find the Missing Answer," *New York Times*, January 19, 1908, sec. 5, 11.

34 Ibid., 11. Waiters themselves were generally reluctant to admit that they pressured dinner guests into giving higher tips although they did admit that tips purchased better service. As the unusually candid James Flanagan argued, "Surely if the people who patronize these first-class houses and restaurants expect extraordinary attention, I think the service should be paid for in tips." Flanagan, *The Waiter*, 44. See also "Waiters," *The Cook*, July 27, 1885, 10.

35 Howells, "Editor's Easy Chair," 312.

36 Bierwirth, "Ethics of 'Tips,' Fees, and Gratuities," 167.

37 Richard Barry, "Tips," *Everybody's Magazine*, January 1913, 65.

38 "Why Not Get Rid of It?" *Syracuse Herald*, September 5, 1920, 3.

39 "Tip for Restaurateurs," *Outlook*, February 4, 1920, 187. Middle-class concern about tipping had its altruistic aspect. Not only did tipping distort the democracy of consumption, it also perverted the political independence of waiters. "Let us not congratulate the servants on their gain," one writer penned, "for no servant takes a tip without losing something of manhood or womanhood." Likewise, Frank Crane, a syndicated columnist, contended that the tip put waiters "into a class with the beggar, or the receiver of a bribe," and "break[s] down the self-respect of a worker who is engaged in a perfectly honorable calling." Granted, the altruistic argument against tipping was put forth more fiercely when the middle class itself was threatened. In 1905, the mayor of Portland, Maine, drew national attention when he criticized college students who degraded themselves by accepting jobs as waiters and accepted tips at summertime resorts. Barry, "Tips," 68; Crane, "A Big Store and the Tipping Nuisance," 8; "Komura's 'Tips' at the Waldorf," *New York Times*, August 9, 1905, 6. See also "Tyranny of Tipping," 508.

40 "War on Tips Spreads," *Washington Post*, December 24, 1911, 5; "The Anti-Tipping Crusade Is Dead: Waiters Read Papers and Got Cold Feet," *Syracuse Herald*, October 31, 1913.

41 N. Q. R. in *Town and Country*, "One Man Who Praises the Tipping Custom," *Washington Post*, June 24, 1905, 3 (punctuation changed). On etiquette, see Duffee, "Right Thing at the Right Time," 7; and Mrs. Chester Adams, "Advice on Social

Customs: The Tipping Problem," *Indianapolis Star*, March 19, 1911. The percent-age system seems to have originated in France.

42 Hollis W. Fields, "The Ten Per Cent. Tip Idea," *Washington Post*, June 17, 1905, 8. See also *New York Sun*, "The Waiter Needs His Tips," *Washington Post*, April 12, 1903, sec. E, 10.

43 Adams, "Advice on Social Customs." See also Frederic J. Haskins, "The Ten Per-cent Tip," *Fitchburg (Mass.) Daily Sentinel*, August 20, 1919, 4.

44 Segrave, *Tipping*, 36. On tipping in the Senate restaurant, see "Antitipping Rule Broken: Senate Lunchroom Falls Back into Former Practices," *Washington Post*, April 18, 1910, 14; "Editorial," *New York Times*, April 4, 1910, 8.

45 Segrave, *Tipping*, 37. Kentucky considered, and may also have passed, an anti-tipping law in 1912. For the text of an anti-tipping law, see "Iowa's Anti-Tipping Law," *The Caterer* 27, no. 2 (1915): 34.

46 Roy K. Moulton, "On the Spur of the Moment," *Elyria (Ohio) Chronicle-Telegram*, November 26, 1920.

47 Segrave, *Tipping*, 38. A legal fight in Iowa that resulted in the state supreme court ruling the Iowa anti-tipping law unconstitutional may have had a chilling effect on other states.

48 "Tipping and Its Remedy," *New York Times*, January 23, 1911, 6, as quoted in Segrave, *Tipping*, 38. Even many critics of tipping opposed boycotts and other forms of collective action. The *New York Times* labeled tipping "the vilest of our imported habits" but generally dismissed both legislation and boycotts against tipping as unrealistic. In a 1911 editorial response to the National League of Com-mercial Travelers' threatened boycott of hotels, the *Times* warned that a "con-spiracy in restraint of trade" might warrant legal action under the Sherman Anti-Trust Act. "An Appeal Likely to Be Heard," *New York Times*, November 4, 1911, 12. Three months earlier, a letter writer had offered a more genteel solution to readers of the *Times*. In an August 5, 1911, letter, J. K. M. suggested that those who disliked tipping might seek refuge in private clubs where tipping was prohibited. "Certainly any business man can find among his acquaintances some one who belongs to one of these clubs, and who would vouch for him." "No 'Tips' at Clubs: More General Patronage of Clubs Would Diminish the Evil," *New York Times*, August 5, 1911, 6.

49 George Brunswick, "Chance to Abolish Tips," *New York Times*, June 14, 1903, 6.

50 Middle-class reforms such as the plate dinner had the unintended effect of rein-forcing the tipping system. By simplifying service, the plate dinner eliminated the one incentive restaurants had to combat tipping, the cost incurred by restau-rants when waiters pandered for tips by providing patrons with extra food. Once a curse for restaurateurs, tipping now worked to their advantage; it produced the illusion of lower prices by shifting the burden of paying the wait staff directly to the customer.

51 "Another Poor Defense of Tipping," *New York Times*, June 2, 1905, 8. See also "Topics of the Times," *New York Times*, November 21, 1899, 6; and "Chicago

Waiter Lives in Luxury on Money He Gets as Tips," *Chicago Daily Tribune*, January 13, 1907, sec. F, 2.

52 Don R. Egbert, "Mr. Man! Do You Know You Are Spending a Fortune Every Year in Tips in Indianapolis So You Won't Be Called a Piker?" *Indianapolis Sunday Star*, March 31, 1912, sec. magazine, 1.

53 Howells, "Editor's Easy Chair," 313.

54 George R. Chester, "The Millennium in Dining," *What to Eat*, May 1900, 133.

55 Warren Belasco, "Future Notes: The Meal-in-a-Pill," in *Food in the USA: A Reader*, ed. Carole Counihan (New York: Routledge, 2002), 62–63; David W. Miller, "Technology and the Ideal: Production, Quality and Kitchen Reform in Nineteenth-Century America," in *Dining in America, 1850–1900*, ed. Kathryn Grover (Amherst and Rochester: University of Massachusetts Press and the Margaret Woodbury Strong Museum, 1987), 50–51. See illustrations in Carlotta Cherryholmes Greer, *A Text-Book of Cooking* (Boston: Allyn and Bacon, 1915). One published report claimed there was a restaurant in Brooklyn in 1902 that served "compressed" food, including, the article implied, some foods in pill form. This report could not be confirmed. "Tabloid Food," *Cooking Club* 8, no. 4 (1902): 38.

56 Harvey A. Levenstein, *Revolution at the Table: The Transformation of the American Diet* (New York: Oxford University Press, 1988), 19; M. Alden, "Automatic Dinner," *Delineator*, October 1912, 252. On manufacturing, see Levenstein, *Revolution at the Table*, 37. On goods, see Ruth Schwartz Cowan, *More Work for Mother: The Ironies of Household Technology from the Open Hearth to the Microwave* (New York: Basic Books, 1983), 72–73. See also Susan Strasser, *Satisfaction Guaranteed: The Making of the American Mass Market* (New York: Pantheon Books, 1989), 6; A Housewife, "Labor-Saving Devices for the Home," *Table Talk*, January 1913, 7–10; Roger Horowitz, *Putting Meat on the American Table: Taste, Technology, Transformation* (Baltimore: Johns Hopkins University Press, 2006).

57 Cowan, *More Work for Mother*, 122. Dudden, like Cowan, argues that at first the new technology raised standards for homemakers and domestics alike without decreasing the total amount of household labor; however, by the early twentieth century, the growing difficulties of acquiring domestic help as well as the increasing efficiency of household technologies made it possible to eliminate live-in servants from the middle-class home. Faye E. Dudden, *Serving Women: Household Service in Nineteenth-Century America* (Middletown, Conn.: Wesleyan University Press, 1983), 127, 240. When Sarah Rorer updated her 1886 cookbook in 1902, she acknowledged the servantless household by including a new section titled "Serving Dinner without a Maid." Rorer warned that serving a dinner without domestic help was "a difficult task," and she provided a minute-by-minute choreography of how the hostess could accomplish the feat, from when to remove her apron and sleevelets to when to pop into the kitchen to make the coffee. Hostesses were told that no apologies were necessary: "[T]ake your seat, and resume conversation as if you had not left the table." Sarah Tyson Heston Rorer,

Mrs. Rorer's New Cook Book: A Manual of Housekeeping (Philadelphia: Arnold, 1902), 653, 667–68.

58 John F. Kasson, *Civilizing the Machine: Technology and Republican Values in America, 1776–1900* (New York: Grossman Publishers, 1976), 183.

59 In 1888, vending machines offered subways riders in New York City a mechanical way to buy gum. By 1920, vending machines could pour you a cup of soda. In 1900, Charles Seeberger transformed a Coney Island novelty ride, the escalator, into an alternative to the attended elevator. In the following decade, the New York subway adopted coin-operated turnstiles to eliminate cheating by subway employees. In 1917, William Ghiglieri of San Francisco patented an automatic traffic light, eliminating the need for traffic cops.

60 Carroll W. Pursell, *The Machine in America: A Social History of Technology* (Baltimore: Johns Hopkins University Press, 1995), 204.

61 Technology played a critical role in the expansion of the modern restaurant industry at the turn of the century. See Adel P. den Hartog, "Technological Innovations and Eating Out as a Mass Phenomenon in Europe," in *Eating Out in Europe: Picnics, Gourmet Dining, and Snacks since the Late Eighteenth Century*, ed. Marc Jacobs and Peter Scholliers (Oxford: Berg, 2003), 263–80.

62 Only a few of the patents were specifically labeled as "waiterless" restaurants. Under classification number 186, however, are collected patents for mechanical devices that deliver service in an eating establishment. Limiting the count to patents that were issued between 1880 and 1925 and devices that might be used to deliver food in a moderately upscale restaurant, there were twenty patents. See, for example, U.S. Patent and Trademark Office numbers 659057, 746615, 1147831, 1215536, 1222943, and 1487179.

63 U.S. Patent and Trademark Office 358149 (February 22, 1887), 649520 (May 15, 1900), 1,389,690 (September 6, 1921) (available online at http://www.uspto.gov/).

64 For a fuller discussion of the utopian technological ideal as applied to dining, see Belasco, "Future Notes," 59–72. Belasco ascribes four motives to the development of the meal-in-a-pill idea: a desire for mobility, a rejection of European decadence, a faith in engineering, and an acknowledgment of scientific eating. The waiterless restaurant embodied these ideals but involved not only a rejection of European decadence but also a re-envisioning of the public sphere.

65 John F. Mariani, *America Eats Out: An Illustrated History of Restaurants, Taverns, Coffee Shops, Speakeasies, and Other Establishments That Have Fed Us for 350 Years* (New York: Morrow, 1991), 116–18. See also Alec Tristin Shuldiner, "Trapped behind the Automat: Technological Systems and the American Restaurant, 1902–1991" (PhD diss., Cornell University, 2001), 46; "New-York's Restaurants," *New York Daily Tribune*, October 14, 1888, 15.

66 Mariani, *America Eats Out*, 116–18; Shuldiner, "Trapped behind the Automat", 78–85.

67 On Quisiana, see "Automatic Lunch Counter," *Scientific American*, December 5,

1896, 408. See also *Scientific American*, "Cafe without Waiters," *Los Angeles Times*, March 29, 1897, 5.

68 "Editorial," *What to Eat*, July 1897, 22.

69 "Automat Lunch Room," *Philadelphia Evening Bulletin*, June 7, 1902, 2, as quoted in Shuldiner, "Trapped behind the Automat," 26. See also Shuldiner, "Trapped behind the Automat," 23; Mariani, *America Eats Out*, 116–18; "Push and Pull Restaurants," *The Caterer* 28, no. 8 (1917): 50.

70 Horn and Hardart promoted the fact that there was no tipping. Shuldiner, "Trapped behind the Automat," 19.

71 "A Nickel-in-the-Slot Lunch," *What to Eat*, May 1897, 239.

72 "Automat Lunch Room" quoted in Shuldiner, "Trapped behind the Automat," 15.

73 Accounts of the 1902 Automat suggest that some customers were not impressed with the no-service restaurant from the start. "[Theater-goers] unaccustomed to the idea, insisted in [*sic*] personal service by rapping on the panes of the small enclosures containing the food they sought. Employees found it necessary to go among the customers, explaining how the nickel-in-the-slot apparatus worked." Quoted in Shuldiner, "Trapped behind the Automat," 50.

74 The Automat continued to evolve, and Horn and Hardart made efforts to appeal to the middle-class white tablecloth dinner crowd by broadened the menu and reintroducing full dinners after 1916. In the 1930s, Horn and Hardart even hired a Cordon Bleu–trained executive chef. Shuldiner, "Trapped behind the Automat," 19, 65 n. 109, 70, 77.

75 "Automatic Restaurant," *Scientific American*, July 18, 1903, 49–50; Genie H. Rosenfeld, "Meals Served by Electricity," *What to Eat*, April 1903; "A Waiterless Restaurant," *National Food Magazine*, October 1908, 155.

76 "Slot-Machine Restaurant," *Lima (Ohio) Times-Democrat*, January 18, 1901, 7.

77 "An Eat-as-You-Go Lunch Room," *Literary Digest*, December 24, 1921, 21–22.

78 Typical was a 1903 article in *What to Eat* on a tube system that promised to deliver meals from a central commissary to individual homes. The article ended with the statement that "the tube plan is being tried in Katonah, New York." To date, however, I have found no evidence that this scheme was ever implemented. Rosenfeld, "Meals Served by Electricity," 120–21. Some restaurants installed more modest technologies, including elevators for waiters and toy train tracks. See "Facilitating Dining Room and Cafe Service," *The Caterer* 23, no. 12 (1912): 31; "The 'Dragon Room' at Murray's," *The Caterer* 20, no. 4 (1908): 31.

79 An equally ambitious restaurant was also planned for Paris by George Knap, whose electric house had received attention in the press. However, as in the case of the American restaurants, there is little evidence that the restaurant was ever opened. Describing the possibilities, *The Southern Hotel Journal* wrote that at the Electra Feria, "you sit down, press the button at your elbow, and the lamp on your table asks for your order." "Hurrah! It's Coming: The 'Tipless' Hotel," *The Southern Hotel Journal* 2, no. 8 (1912): 73; "Electra Feria—Marvel of Science," *Popular Electricity and the World's Advance*, June 1914, 193.

80 Christopher Gray, "Streetscapes," *New York Times* (1996), http://query.nytimes
    .com/search/article-page.html?res=9C06E6DE1439F935A25755C0A960958260
    (accessed May 1, 2003).

81 "Restaurant De Luxe to Seat 5,000 Diners," *New York Times*, August 14, 1908, 7.

82 Ibid.

83 "Waiterless Restaurant," 155.

84 "Restaurant De Luxe to Seat 5,000 Diners," 7. Erkins envisioned an elegant res-
    taurant with "prices as high as in any restaurant," and the failure of the venture
    may have reflected the problem of attracting enough wealthy patrons to fill a
    restaurant that served thousands. As "one of the sagest of Broadway observers"
    told the *New York Times* in 1908, "New Yorkers only want to go to places where
    they can't get a seat." Erkins may have been more successful had he targeted the
    burgeoning middle class.

85 John F. Daschner, "The New Service—The Waiterless Dining Room," *The Stew-
    ard* 8, no. 6 (1913): 53. Daschner's plan did not entirely eliminate waiters. How-
    ever, waiters would work underground, and only about half the usual number of
    waiters would be needed. To compensate for the loss of tips, Daschner suggested
    that male waiters, usually paid ten dollars a week, could be paid twenty-five dol-
    lars, or alternatively women might be hired at ten dollars a week.

86 "Every Table Has Its Own Dumbwaiter," *The Caterer* 28, no. 4 (1916): 51.

87 Daschner, "The New Service—The Waiterless Dining Room," 52–53.

88 "Every Table Has Its Own Dumbwaiter," 51. See also "Putting Daschner Right,"
    The Caterer 28, no. 5 (1917): 76.

89 A search of the United States Trademark and Patent Office database indicates
    that John Daschner received a patent in 1917, four years after he announced his
    plans (USTPO 1,223,943, www.patft.ustpo.gov, October 2003). A second patent
    was awarded a few years later.

90 "Enlarging the Unique Restaurant," *The Caterer* 28, no. 5 (1916): 76. Details re-
    garding Daschner's failed restaurant are not available, but four months after
    announcing his planned expansion, Daschner was living in Palm Beach, Flor-
    ida, and four months later he took a job in Palisades, New York. In the 1930s
    and 1940s, Daschner's waiterless tables were installed as novelties in a few res-
    taurants. Ultimately, Daschner's obituary attributed the overall failure of the
    idea to the high cost of the needed equipment. "Daschner at Palm Beach,"
    The Caterer 28, no. 8 (1917): 65; "Daschner Returns to New York," *The Caterer*
    28, no. 12 (1917): 29; "Dining Room Auto Service," *The Caterer* 29, no. 6 (1918):
    46–48.

91 Robert Tomes, *The Bazar Book of Decorum* (New York: Harper and Brothers,
    1870), 188.

92 Ibid., 13–14.

93 Abby Buchanan Longstreet, *Social Etiquette of New York* (New York: D. Appleton,
    1883), 106; Harriet Prescott Spofford, *The Servant Girl Question* (Boston: Hough-
    ton, Mifflin, 1881), 12.

94 The aristocratic rules that governed dining were so complex that many middle-class publications conceded that newcomers were unlikely to master table etiquette. *The Caterer* conceded that "the truth is, luxury and invention push table appliances so far that few can be expected to know the particular convention that may be considered good form in any diversified society." "Napkin Etiquette," *The Caterer* 3, no. 7 (1885): 280.

95 This middle-class critique of the aristocratic table has an explicit parallel in recent scholarly debates over Jürgen Habermas's description of a vigorous and influential public sphere in eighteenth-century European coffeehouses and salons. Jürgen Habermas, *The Structural Transformation of the Public Sphere: An Inquiry into a Category of Bourgeois Society* (Cambridge: MIT Press, 1989), 36; Nancy Fraser, "Rethinking the Public Sphere: A Contribution to the Critique of Actually Existing Democracy," in *Habermas and the Public Sphere*, ed. Craig Calhoun (Cambridge: MIT Press, 1996), 109–42.

96 See Lizabeth Cohen, *A Consumer's Republic: The Politics of Mass Consumption in Postwar America* (New York: Vintage Books, 2003), 21. Cohen argues that the "consumer's republic" was a post–World War II envisioning of abundance and maintains that it was different than its antecedents. Yet while she focuses more on Progressive campaigns rather than technological utopias, Cohen might have included the idealization of the waiterless restaurant in what she considers the "first-wave consumer movement."

97 Daschner, "The New Service—The Waiterless Dining Room," 53.

98 The democracy of consumer isolation that the waiterless restaurant symbolized is not unlike the democratic isolation created by many of the twentieth century's most cherished inventions—the television and the Internet, to name but two. Historically, it echoed Thorstein Veblen's evolutionary theory of technology. Veblen argued that "the machine technology takes no cognizance of conventionally established rules of precedence; it knows neither manners nor breeding and can make no use of any of the attributes of worth." In time, Veblen argued that industrial man could be disciplined by the machine and would come to abandon such traditional rights as property. Industrial man would then find himself in opposition to the pecuniary man (the capitalist) and his profits. Thorstein Veblen, *The Theory of Business Enterprise* (New York: C. Scribner's Sons, 1904), 311.

99 Belasco, "Future Notes," 61.

100 For a discussion of social engineering in turn-of-the-century utopian novels, see Howard P. Segal, "The Technological Utopians," in *Imagining Tomorrow: History, Technology, and the American Future*, ed. Joseph J. Corn (Cambridge: MIT Press, 1986), 119–36.

CHAPTER 8

1 The Ohio Society of New York was established in 1886 and claimed to be the first state association to be formed in the city. In the first year, 300 members joined, including 113 merchants, 9 physicians, 24 attorneys, 9 railway men, 7 insurance

executives, 29 bankers, 3 real estate agents, 6 hotel proprietors, 26 journalists, 2 clergymen, 11 artists, and over 30 others, notably "the Vice-President of the United States, the Chief-Justice of the United States Supreme Court, the Governor of Ohio and two ex-Governors, the Secretary of State and one ex-Secretary, several United States Senators and Members of Congress from Ohio and other States with which they have since become identified." Henry Howe, *Historical Collections of Ohio*, vol. 1 (Columbus: C. J. Krehbiel, 1888), 180–81.

2 Catherine Mackenzie, "From Kitchen to Banquet Tables," *New York Times*, February 16, 1936, sec. Sunday Magazine, 16.

3 Alice Foote MacDougall, *The Secret of Successful Restaurants* (New York: Harper and Brothers, 1929), 127. It is reasonable to assume that MacDougall was not intending to slight ethnic food. She built her restaurant empire on a waffle shop, but by the mid-1920s at least one of her restaurants was Italian-themed.

4 *Washington Star*, "What They Go By," *Iowa City Daily Press*, January 12, 1912, 2.

5 Constance Cary Harrison, "French in the Restaurant," *The Southern Hotel Journal* 2, no. 2 (1912): 46. Reprinted from the *California Tourist and Hotel Reporter*.

6 "Why French Names?" *Washington Post*, July 8, 1917, sec. fashion, 5 (punctuation changed).

7 Gail Hamilton, "Hotel of the Future," *Scribner's Monthly*, November 1875, 111.

8 "Concerning Words," *The Cook*, May 11, 1885, 4.

9 Thomas J. Murray, "Less Variety and Better Quality," *The Cook*, August 17, 1885, 4.

10 Ibid. Radicalized, *The Cook* also poked fun at an American summer hotel that "set down grandiloquently in the bill of fare" *gateaux de gingembre* for the "simple ginger-snap." "Kitchen English in France," *The Cook*, August 24, 1885, 9.

11 "Opposed to the Spread of Knowledge," *The Cook*, May 18, 1885, 10. *The Cook* claimed that professional chefs used "cook's French" to prevent recipes from being widely disseminated so that only those who could afford to hire a chef, or for that matter eat in a restaurant, could enjoy French cooking.

12 *Philadelphia Call*, "Innocent Children," *The Cook*, April 13, 1885, 12. On linguistic disguises, see also "French Bills of Fare," *Washington Post*, October 9, 1923, 6.

13 Many of the early complaints were good-natured, or in the case of *The Caterer*, tentative. In a lead editorial in 1885, *The Caterer* initially claimed that the use of French in English-speaking countries was "ridiculous" and had little justification other than to "follow what the fashionable diner affects." However, midway through the editorial the journal shifted position and called merely for an "improvement in the quality of the French used." "The Modern Bill of Fare and the French and English of It," *The Caterer* 3, no. 5 (1885): 165–66.

14 Donald G. Ross, "Food Luxuries of America," *What to Eat*, December 1897, 169.

15 August E. Gans, "Ze Million Peegs in Our Ma-Niews," *Kitchen Craft and Cuisine*, May 1907, 256.

16 *Keeler's Hotel Weekly*, "That Menu in English," *The Steward*, December 1920, 26.

17 Max Bloch, "Menus in French," *New York Times*, April 19, 1909, 8.

18 A. H. La Mont, "Wants to Eat in English," *New York Times*, April 21, 1909, 6.

19 *New York Globe*, "A Good System," *The Southern Hotel Journal* 2, no. 9 (1912): 57.

20 "Reform the Menu!" *Washington Post*, September 28, 1910, 6. The article "Reform the Menu!" appeared in the *Washington Post* with the tag "From the *Louisville Courier-Journal*" and the subtitle "Col. Watterson Wants French Terms Eliminated in All Cafes." Netter is only briefly quoted, so the ideas in the article may be those of the reporter and not Netter. Netter, within a year, became the international buyer for Louis Martin, the New York restaurateur, and is sometimes mentioned as the acting manager of Martin's restaurant. The Geneva White Cross Society was founded in 1907 as an international pure food organization modeled after the Red Cross Society. In 1908, its chief spokesperson, Swiss senator Auguste Calvet, visited the United States to drum up support for the organization and apparently spoke with both President Theodore Roosevelt and Dr. Harvey Wiley of the Bureau of Agriculture. In general, the Swiss senator refused to comment on food adulteration in the United States until further research had been conducted, but he did express concern about the contamination of French cooking in the United States: "There have been, of course, in this country, many adulterated imitations of French food and wines." "A White Cross Society Needed: Senator Auguste Calvet Tells of Geneva's Fight against Poisoned Food," *New York Times*, June 21, 1908, sec. Sunday Magazine, 5.

21 Unkel David, "Unkel David's Letter," *Field and Stream*, December 1912, 900.

22 "The Humor of the Menu," *The Caterer* 30, no. 1 (1918): 24.

23 "Cook French Has Its Advantages," *New York Times*, April 22, 1909, 8.

24 Laura A. Smith, "Why the French Menu Has Become So Universally Popular," *New York Times*, May 16, 1909, sec. Sunday Magazine, 11.

25 Frank Tryon Charles, "French Menus," *What to Eat*, December 1899, 182–83; Frank Tryon Charles, "French Menus," *What to Eat*, December 1900, 29. Cos lettuce is commonly called romaine in the United States.

26 See for example, "Some English Definitions of Culinary Terms," *Restaurant Bulletin* 2, no. 15 (1905): 15; "Cheap and Dainty Feast," *New York Times*, October 17, 1897, sec. 10, 6; and "'Covers for Two': A Gastronomic Study," *New York Times*, September 2, 1906, sec. Sunday Magazine, 2.

27 Charles, "French Menus," 183.

28 "Humor of the Menu," 24.

29 "Cook French Has Its Advantages," 8.

30 Jessup Whitehead, *The Steward's Handbook and Guide to Party Catering* (Chicago: J. Anderson, 1889), 50, 48.

31 "High Living in New-York," *New York Daily Tribune*, February 16, 1890, 15.

32 George H. Ellwanger, *The Pleasures of the Table: An Account of Gastronomy from Ancient Days to Present Times* (New York: Doubleday Page, 1902), ix–x. Spelling in original. Similar lists of literal translations of French dishes were quite common. For an early example, see "Gastronomic Pickings," *The Caterer* 2, no. 10 (1884): 389.

33 "Mr. Regan on Current Topics," *The Steward* 5, no. 11 (1911): 19.

34 "A Hint to Some Proprietors," *The Caterer* 11, no. 2 (1900): 26.

35 Menu, "Dinner/Diner," Waldorf-Astoria, New York, N.Y., November 11, 1895, Box 22 (1895-28 or 1895-179), Buttolph Menu. Menus are used throughout this chapter. Menus are fantastic sources that have not been used for a major historical work on restaurants in the past. However, working with menus poses some challenges. No collection of menus (including the Buttolph Menu Collection, the archive used most often in this work) is complete. Most collections from the late nineteenth and early twentieth centuries include more banquet and special event menus than everyday menus. None of the collections are extensive enough to offer more than a snapshot of the dining community at any given time, and when trying to demonstrate change over time, the limits of these collections— marvelous as they are—become even more apparent. In this chapter, menus are used cautiously to illustrate concepts only when other sources suggest that the examples are representative of historically significant trends.

36 "Too Well Advertised, St. Regis Man Laments," *New York Times*, November 6, 1904, 12; Menu, "Breakfast," Hotel St. Regis, New York, N.Y., June 10, 1905, Box 124 (1905-446), Buttolph Menu; Menu, "Dinner," Hotel St. Regis, New York, N.Y., June 25, 1905, Box 125 (1905-512), Buttolph Menu; Menu, "Supper," Hotel St. Regis, New York, N.Y., June 10, 1905, Box 124 (1905-447), Buttolph Menu.

37 Menu, "Dinner," Waldorf-Astoria, New York, N.Y., September 10, 1914, Box 281 (1914-0909C), Buttolph Menu; Menu, "Dinner," Waldorf-Astoria, New York, N.Y., September 5, 1914, Box 281 (1914-0903D), Buttolph Menu. Menu research is difficult since the menus are rarely preserved with any notation. A Waldorf-Astoria menu for September 16, 1914 (days after the previously cited menus), was folded at the center and included an English menu on the left and a French menu on the right. Like the other cited menus from this time period, it was an à la carte menu, apparently a dinner menu. It featured a similar selection of dishes and essentially the same prices. The Waldorf-Astoria had numerous dining rooms, and it is possible that the difference reflects the more formal service in one of the restaurants (although one might expect to see a greater difference in the food offered and the prices charged if this was the case). Equally plausible, the second menu might have been prepared in small quantities for international guests.

38 Menu, "Fifteenth Annual Meeting of the Colorado Bar Association," The Antlers Hotel, Colorado Springs, Colo., July 12, 1912, Box 242 (1912-0514), Buttolph Menu.

39 Menu, "Supper," Hotel Cadillac, Detroit, Mich., hand-dated September 29, 1911, Box 231 (1911-0670), Buttolph Menu.

40 Menu, "Mid-Day Meal," Thayer's Hotel, Littleton, N.H., August 18, 1915, Box 291 (no item number), Buttolph Menu.

41 Menu, "Petit Salon," Schrafft's, New York, N.Y., hand-dated September 26, 1911, Box 231 (1911-0667), Buttolph Menu.

42 Menu, "Macy's Restaurant," Macy's Restaurant, New York, N.Y., n.d. (c. 1905), Box 129 (1905-0955), Buttolph Menu.

43 "Eating in American," *Literary Digest*, October 10, 1914, 702. See also "Menus Are Now Neutral in Chicago Restaurants," *Washington Post*, September 25, 1914, 5.

The Caterer, in contrast, condemned the new menus as "foolish" given the lack of "war heat" in the United States. "How Unmasked Menus Look," *The Caterer* 27, no. 1 (1915): 75.

44 "Foreign Menus Not Favored," *The Steward* 12 (1917): 41; "Manhattan Waiters' Association," *The Caterer* 28, no. 10 (1917): 65.

45 "'Oeufs' on Leviathan's Menu Rouse Britten; Wants Eggs," *Washington Post*, October 8, 1923, 4. Britten's protest garnered national attention. See, for example, "French Menus under Fire," *Los Angeles Times*, October 8, 1923, sec. 1, 1. He also was the victim of a smear campaign in the society and gossip columns. See "Post-Scripts," *Washington Post*, October 12, 1923, 1; and "By-Products," *New York Times*, October 14, 1923, sec. E, 6.

46 Laszlo Tehel, "American Cookery," *Washington Post*, July 7, 1925, 6.

47 Menu, "The Bar Association of the City of Boston Seventeenth Triennial Dinner," Copley-Plaza, Boston, Mass., December 28, 1914, Box 284 (1914-1057), Buttolph Menu.

48 Menu, "Banquet tendered the American Seed Trade Association by the Chicago Seedmen on the Occasion of the 30th Annual Convention," Hotel Sherman, Chicago, Ill., June 26, 1912, Box 242 (1912-0487), Buttolph Menu.

49 Mayonnaise, although a French preparation, was in common use in America and was not capitalized on the menu, so it was not counted as one of the five French items. Menu, "Carte du Jour," St. Denis Hotel, New York, N.Y., December 15, 1912, Box 248 (1912-0879), Buttolph Menu.

50 Jeanette Young, "Cafe des Beaux-Arts, Where Fame and Fashion Meet and Dine," *Table Talk* 26, no. 4 (1911): 223.

51 Menu, "Table d'Hôte," Café des Beaux-Arts, New York, N.Y., July 11, 1912, Box 242 (1912-0513), Buttolph Menu.

52 Criticism of French cooking both in the United States and France became increasingly common in the twentieth century. See, for example, Dora M. Morrell, "French Cookery," *What to Eat*, March 1902, 139.

53 The *Century Dictionary*, a comprehensive dictionary from the turn of the century, defined a cuisine as "the manner or style of cooking," but the term is possibly best understood as encompassing both manner (techniques) *and* style (agreed-upon ingredients). "Cuisine," in *The Century Dictionary: An Encyclopedia Lexicon of the English Language*, ed. William Dwight Whitney (New York: Century Company, 1911), 1390. The line between what is and what is not a cuisine is necessarily somewhat arbitrary, and each of the characteristics that kept American cuisine from appearing cohesive at the turn of the century became, in turn, a keystone of America's later culinary revolutions. James Beard, for example, created a nationally recognized cuisine by drawing on America's regional dishes, Alice Waters turned the abundance of America's larder into a culinary movement, and William and Samuel Childs, Fred Harvey, and, most important, Ray Kroc, created a model of kitchen organization and efficiency that became influential worldwide.

54 Fannie C. W. Barber, "American Cooking," *What to Eat*, July 1897, 8. First published in the *Chautauquan*.

55 Ellwanger, *Pleasures of the Table*, 248–49. If Ellwanger was dismissive about American cooking, his contemporaries in Rochester, New York, were puzzled by this native son's fascination with European cooking. "His epicurean tastes were a constant source of bewilderment and even revulsion to many of his acquaintances, but were a delight shared by a few." Natalie F. Hawley, "Literature in Rochester, 1865–1905," *Rochester History* 10, no. 1 (1948): 18.

56 *Chicago Daily Tribune*, "The High Cost of Living," *The Steward* 5, no. 10 (1910): 56.

57 "Discovered, American Restaurant; Chances Are It's the Only One Alive," *Chicago Daily Tribune*, October 9, 1910, sec. I, 4.

58 Although now recognized as the first "American" cookbook, Amelia Simmons's 1798 cookbook was not widely known at the turn of the century. An *Atlantic Monthly* article in 1909 discussed the work, but the author did not know the date it was published and did not suggest that it was uniquely American. In the next decade or so, its fame increased significantly. Amelia Simmons, *American Cookery, or the Art of Dressing Viands, Fish, Poultry, and Vegetables, and the Best Modes of Making Pastes, Puffs, Pies, Tarts, Puddings, Custards, and Preserves, and All Kinds of Cakes, from the Imperial Plum to Plain Cake* (Hartford: Printed for Simeon Butler, Northhampton, 1798); Theodora Taylor, "Amelia Simmons: An American Orphan," *Atlantic Monthly*, September 1909.

59 Ellwanger, *Pleasures of the Table*, 251–52.

60 Ross Hasbrouck, "American Cooks," *New York Times*, May 2, 1909, 10; Jean-Robert Pitte, *French Gastronomy: The History and Geography of a Passion*, trans. Jody Gladding (New York: Columbia University Press, 2002), 82–84. See also Edwin Tarrisse, "French Food Dainties," *Table Talk*, June 1914, 339.

61 Mary E. Parmelee, "Practical Housekeeping: February," *Table Talk*, February 1905, 64. American cooking was easier to recognize when abroad. See Harvey A. Levenstein, *Seductive Journey: American Tourists in France from Jefferson to the Jazz Age* (Chicago: University of Chicago Press, 1998), 91–92.

62 H. C. Chatfield-Taylor, "The Philosophy of Gastronomy," *What to Eat*, August 1896, 3.

63 "High Cost of Living," 56.

64 Aubrey Fullerton, "Queer Eating Places," *Table Talk*, February 1905, 68. See also Auguste Escoffier, "Secret of Good Cooking," *Harper's Bazaar*, October 1908, 1008–11.

65 The late-nineteenth-century culinary journal *The Table* used a discussion of the British raconteur of dining, Thomas Walker, to make the case that as long as the French controlled the language of dining, French cuisine would stifle the development of a national cuisine. E. J., "The 'Original' Walker," *The Table* 1, no. 7 (1873): 143.

66 John Ferguson, "Why Are Americans Not Cooks?" *The Steward* 4, no. 4 (1909): 25.

See also Christine Terhune Herrick, "The Times' Answers by Experts: Women of One Dish," *Los Angeles Times*, December 22, 1902, 13.

67 "Our Cooks Will Be the Best: American Dinners Will One Day Be the Best on Earth," *New York Times*, January 5, 1896, 29.

68 Juliet Corson, *Miss Corson's Practical American Cookery and Household Management* (New York: Dodd, Mead & Co., 1885).

69 On regional recipes, see, for example, Parmelee, "Practical Housekeeping," 64; and Constance Fuller McIntyre, "The Old Time Colored Cook," *Table Talk*, February 1906, 52. On the Boston School of Cooking, see Laura Shapiro, *Perfection Salad: Women and Cooking at the Turn of the Century* (New York: Farrar Straus and Giroux, 1986), 63.

70 "Delicacies in France," *The Steward*, May 1909, 46; Charles J. Rosebault, "A Word for Our Native Cookery," *New York Times*, March 27, 1921, sec. Book Review, 5. Eventually the federal government conducted a survey of American dining as part of the Federal Writers' Project. The initiative was started in 1935 and was intended to culminate in 1945 with a book-length manuscript called "America Eats" to be edited by Lyle Saxon. The work acknowledged and celebrated local and regional differences in cooking and eating, but it was hoped that it would help develop a greater sense of national unity, as the Federal Writer's Project travel guides had done. The project failed, although Nelson Algren's account of midwestern foodways and a few other partial accounts were eventually published. The Library of Congress now houses the "America Eats" collection. Nelson Algren and David E. Schoonover, *America Eats* (Iowa City: University of Iowa Press, 1992). See also Christine Bold, *The WPA Guides: Mapping America* (Jackson: University Press of Mississippi, 1999).

71 Menu, "Dinner, Cosmopolitan . . . Hotel," Cosmopolitan Hotel, New York, N.Y., January 15, 1905, Box 119 (1905-028), Buttolph Menu.

72 Menu, "Carte du Jour," New Grand Hotel, New York, N.Y., June 14, 1905, Box 125 (1905-460), Buttolph Menu.

73 "[American Food]," *The Steward* 8, no. 3 (1913): 15.

74 "All-American Menu Contest," *New York Times*, November 14, 1923, 17. Formally, the Société did not endorse English-only menus until the 1930s when it allied itself with the Chefs de Cuisine Association of America and the Vatel Club. In 1939, the Société participated in a "culinary congress" held at the Waldorf-Astoria where the first industry-wide resolution to adopt an "American bill of fare" was proposed. "Bans on Foreign Names on Our Menus Urged as First Culinary Congress Is Organized," *New York Times*, November 7, 1939, 25. The 1923 contest was prompted in part by the protest of the *Leviathan*'s menu launched by Congressman Britten. For an overview of the Société, see "The Societe Culinaire Philanthropique," *The Chef* 8, no. 1 (1898): 5–8.

75 Menu, "Regular Dinner," The Arlington, Washington, D.C., May 10, 1871, Box 2 (1871-73-30248), Buttolph Menu. See also E. M. Collingham, *Curry: A Tale of Cooks and Conquerors* (Oxford: Oxford University Press, 2006), 161–62.

76 H. T. Finck, "Mulitiplying the Pleasures of the Table," *Century*, December 1911, 220–28.

77 Menu, "Carte du Jour: Luncheon," Hotel Astor, New York, N.Y., April 15, 1927, Box 311 (not numbered), Buttolph Menu. See, in contrast, Menu, "Menu," Hotel Astor, New York, N.Y., January 21, 1905, Box 119 (1905-045), Buttolph Menu.

78 Menu, "Menu," Fifth Avenue Restaurant, New York, N.Y., December 14, 1912, Box 248 (1912-0875), Buttolph Menu.

79 Menu, "Luncheon," Fifth Avenue Restaurant, New York, N.Y., n.d. (c. 1910), Box 218 (1910-5415), Buttolph Menu. Both the sausage and the beef dish are ambiguous. Depending on the preparation, these may have been French provincial dishes, but at the very least they would have appealed to diners interested in German and English cuisines.

80 For *Macaroni à l'Italienne*, see Menu, "Dinner," The Waldorf, New York, N.Y., November 11, 1895, Box 22 (1895-28 or 1895-179), Buttolph Menu; Menu, "Carte du Jour," Fred Harvey Union Station Restaurant, Chicago, Ill., November 15, 1905, Box 128 (1905-859), Buttolph Menu. Harvey's restaurant included both *Macaroni au Gratin* and *Spaghetti, Italian* on its vegetable menu. For a definition of *l'Italienne* as "brown or white sauce with wine, shallots, mushrooms, etc.," see Whitehead, *Steward's Handbook*, 350.

81 Menu, "Garret Restaurant," Garret Restaurant, New York, N.Y., n.d. (c. 1914), Box 281 (1914-0887), Buttolph Menu; Menu, "Bill of Fare," Jeo's Restaurant, Brooklyn, N.Y., September 1, 1914, Box 281 (1914-0878), Buttolph Menu. For the reference to "real native Italian style," see Menu, "The Place to Dine," Hotel Princesa Café and Restaurant, New York, N.Y., n.d. (c. 1914), Box 281 (1914-0892), Buttolph Menu.

82 Rodenbaugh and Morris, "Midwestern Hotel Items," *The Steward*, April 1912, 20. Other restaurants experimented with Italian dinners. See "A Novel Italian Dinner," *The Caterer* 28, no. 4 (1916): 71.

83 Menu, "Our German Specialties," New Grand Hotel, New York, N.Y., June 15, 1905, Box 125 (1905-469 Item A), Buttolph Menu; "In and About New York," *The Caterer* 20, no. 4 (1908): 46.

84 Menu, "Specialties for Dinner," New Washington Hotel, Seattle, Wash., April 13, 1913, M35–2.jpg, Historical Menu Collection, University of Washington Libraries, Seattle, http://content.lib.washington.edu/u?/menus,123 (accessed August 10, 2009).

85 *Where and How to Dine in New York: The Principal Hotels, Restaurants and Cafes of Various Kinds and Nationalities Which Have Added to the Gastronomic Fame of New York and Its Suburbs* (New York: Lewis, Scribner, 1903), 201. Later restaurant guides featured ethnic fare as well. See Rupert Hughes, *The Real New York* (New York: Smart Set, 1904); and George S. Chappell, *The Restaurants of New York* (New York: Greenberg, 1925). A fuller discussion of these guides appears in the conclusion.

86 Menu, "Bill of Fare," Levy's, Los Angeles, Calif., n.d. (c. 1900–1910), Regional

History Menu Collection, Los Angeles Public Library, Los Angeles, California, http://www.lapl.org/resources/en/menu_collection.html (accessed May 1999). Levy's, in addition to its tamales, offered customers *Wiener Schnitzel with Paprica [sic] or Garni Sauce, Imported Frankfurters and Sauerkraut*, or *Finnan Haddie*, a Scottish cured white fish, boiled, broiled, or in a chafing dish—all with the option of Spanish sauce on the side.

87 "News from San Antone," *The Southern Hotel Journal* 2, no. 4 (1912): 32–33.

88 Menu, "A Merry Christmas," The Windsor, New York, N.Y., December 25, 1895, Box 22 (1895-184 or 1895-2246), Buttolph Menu; "Detroit's Mexican Restaurant," *The Caterer* 28, no. 3 (1916): 26–27.

89 "Chinese Dinner in Atlanta," *The Caterer* 27, no. 3 (1915): 40–43; "An Oriental Evening," *The Caterer* 27, no. 8 (1916): 59.

90 "Thirteen Club Dines in Pekin," *The Caterer* 27, no. 5 (1915): 57; "Chinese Dishes Served Daily at a Big New York Hotel," *The Steward*, March 1919, 16–17.

91 "Chicago Letter," *The Southern Hotel Journal* 2, no. 12 (1913): 32. As the cosmopolitan ideal took hold, expensive fine dining establishments that specialized in more obscure cuisines opened in the heart of major American cities. See, for example, an article on the opening of an upscale Middle Eastern restaurant, "'Kalil's' Is Opened," *Restaurant Bulletin* 2, no. 19 (1905): 29.

92 Xenophon Kuzmier, "Cooks and Cookery," *The Caterer* 29, no. 2 (1917): 59.

93 "Bills of Fare in Fashionable Restaurants," *Washington Post*, May 21, 1898, 7.

94 "Dinner under Ground at New Astor Hotel," *New York Times*, August 29, 1904, 7.

95 "Catering to Culinary Sentiment," *The Caterer* 30, no. 12 (1919): 29.

96 "In and About New York," 46.

97 Menu, "Diet Menu/Dinner," The Homestead, Hot Springs, Va., November 22, 1915, Box 292 (no number), Buttolph Menu.

98 Menu, "Refreshments," St. Charles Hotel, New Orleans, La., February 1, 1913, Box 251 (1913-0144), Buttolph Menu; "The Hotel St. Charles' Famous Italian Garden," *The Caterer* 23, no. 10 (1912): 40–41.

99 Hughes, *Real New York*, 100.

100 "Where Music Soothes While Lobsters Broil," *New York Times*, April 24, 1910, sec. Sunday Magazine, 7.

101 Menu, "Carte du Jour," Hotel Brunswick, New York, N.Y., 1879, Box 2 (1878-1879 19a [a-b]), Buttolph Menu; Menu, "Welcome Home Dinner to Lieut. James W. Carlin, U.S.N.," Bohemian Club, San Francisco, Calif., 1889, San Francisco Public Library, San Francisco, California, http://dbase1.1spl.org/scripts/dbtcgi.ex . . . SSword=&sDISPLAY_FORM=MENUS&sNODISPLAY=0 (accessed July 11, 2005). See also "A Supper at Rector's Restaurant," *The Caterer* 19, no. 4 (1907): 39; "Decorated Menu Folders," *The Caterer* 19, no. 10 (1908): 66.

102 Kristin L. Hoganson, *Consumers' Imperium: The Global Production of American Domesticity, 1865–1920* (Chapel Hill: University of North Carolina Press, 2007), 14, 49. Hoganson provides a thorough overview of the growing importance of foreign goods to American identity, but her focus is on gender and domesticity, and

she tends to conflate middle-class and upper-class consumers while understating the evolution of their experiences over time. For the definitive discussion of orientalism, see Edward W. Said, *Orientalism* (New York: Pantheon Books, 1978). On American orientalism, see Holly Edwards, ed., *Noble Dreams, Wicked Pleasures: Orientalism in America, 1870–1930* (Princeton: Princeton University Press, 2000).

103 Hoganson, *Consumers' Imperium*, 11.

104 William Leach, *Land of Desire: Merchants, Power, and the Rise of a New American Culture* (New York: Pantheon Books, 1993), 105–11.

105 Holly Edwards, "A Million and One Nights: Orientalism in America, 1870–1930," in *Noble Dreams, Wicked Pleasures: Orientalism in America, 1870–1930*, ed. Holly Edwards (Princeton: Princeton University Press, 2000), 45.

106 For a discussion of oriental images in American mass marketed products, see ibid., 42–45.

107 For an example of the middle-class commitment to "authentic" experiences, see S. Bosse, "Giving a Chinese Luncheon Party," *Harper's Bazaar* 1913, 135. Sara Bosse suggested that before making a Chinese dish at home, middle-class housewives should try the dish in a Chinatown restaurant. For a contemporary treatment of the meaning of eating foreign cuisine and the search for authenticity, see Lisa M. Heldke, *Exotic Appetites: Ruminations of a Food Adventurer* (New York: Routledge, 2003).

108 Hoganson, *Consumers' Imperium*, 124, 151.

109 "New York's Restaurant Trade: Value of Distinct Features," *The Steward*, June 1911, 24–25.

110 "Adrian Tenu Heat Victim," *New York Times*, July 3, 1901, 1; "Waldorf-Astoria's Chef Dies," *New York Daily Tribune*, July 3, 1901, 3.

111 "Foreign News: Art, Sauces, Honor," *Time*, July 5, 1926, 13 (emphasis added).

112 Ibid., 13. The name of the court is as it appeared in the original. The reference is to the Cour d'assises.

113 The story was not covered in other English-language sources, including the *New York Times* and the London *Times*, and it does not appear in French papers either. In addition, none of the major sources on French cuisine list Berthelin as one of the great chefs of France.

114 "Haute Cuisine," in *Oxford English Dictionary* (Oxford: Oxford University Press, 1989).

115 Bertram Gordon examined the role of French culture in America by studying the number of entries for France (and all things French) in the *Readers' Guide to Periodical Literature*. The first entries for "Cookery, French" do not appear until 1915, and the listings (as a percentage of total entries) declined until the 1960s when Julia Child sparked interest in French cooking. As Gordon explains:

> Despite the increases in the twentieth century, the gastronomy series shows a long-term pattern of decline for France when measured by the American series projected back to England in the eighteenth century.

If one takes the proportion of French entries in only the totals of the international cookery listings . . . the figures for French cookery in the eighteenth century, as measured in England's *Gentlemen's Magazine*, are 52 percent. The corresponding figures for the nineteenth-century *Poole's* are 40 percent. French cookery as a proportion of the international listings held at an average 29.1 percent for the five-year periods from the appearance in the *Readers' Guide* of the French subcategory in 1915–19 through 1934–39, but then declined to an average 15 percent for the years from 1940 through 1994, as the American culinary world expanded into Chinese, Italian, and Mexican, to name just a few.

Gordon's analysis suggests that interest in French food declined only after 1939. But Gordon overestimates the influence of French cooking from 1915 through 1939, because he mistakenly assumes that the lack of an entry for French cooking means there was no interest in French food prior to 1915. The opposite is true. The *Readers' Guide* created a category for French cookery only when it lost its hegemonic status; before 1915, French cookery was so prevalent that it was essentially synonymous with the more general heading "cookery." The *Readers' Guide*'s decision to give French cooking its own entry in 1915 should be interpreted as evidence that it was coming to be viewed as just one among a number of competing ethnic cuisines. Once this error is corrected, Gordon's analysis offers compelling support for the contention that interest in French cuisine began to decline in the early twentieth century. Bertram M. Gordon, "The Decline of a Cultural Icon: France in American Perspective," *French Historical Studies* 22, no. 4 (1999): 644–45.

116 The war years, although often blamed for Delmonico's demise, were generally good years for restaurants. Ralph C. Epstein of Harvard University used data collected by the federal government during the war to calculate the relative profitability of certain wartime industries. In Epstein's analysis, restaurants fared well. Restaurants experienced a 27.96 percent rate of return on their investments, which placed them in the top 50 percent of the businesses that he examined. Ralph C. Epstein, "Industrial Profits in 1917," *Quarterly Journal of Economics* 39, no. 2 (1925): 241–66.

117 Lately Thomas, *Delmonico's: A Century of Splendor* (Boston: Houghton Mifflin, 1967), 333–34.

118 Clarence E. Edwords, *Bohemian San Francisco: Its Restaurants and Their Most Famous Recipes* (San Francisco: P. Elder, 1914), 6–7.

119 E. P. Thompson, *The Making of the English Working Class* (New York: Pantheon Books, 1964), 9–10.

120 Adolphe Meyer, "As to Food Conservation," *Table Talk, the National Food Magazine*, February 1918, 64. See also Adolphe Meyer, "Concerning Menus and Culinary Fantasy," *International Culinary Magazine* 1 (1914): 149. Although opposed to eliminating luxury, Meyer was an early advocate of English-language menus.

121 Menu, "A Happy New Year: Menu," The Plaza, New York, N.Y., December 31, 1912, Box 248 (1912-091), Buttolph Menu; Menu, "New Year's Eve: Menu," St. Charles, New York, N.Y., December 31, 1913, Box 284 (1914-1069), Buttolph Menu.

122 In 1911, New York's Lafayette Restaurant introduced an eight-course table d'hôte, including *cassoulet of lobster* and *pâté de la maison en gelée* at the very middle-class price of two dollars. French cuisine no longer demanded high prices. When French cuisine enjoyed a revival in fine-dining establishments in the late 1920s, it was the small, intimate, and casual bistro, not the grand hotels, that attracted middle-class patrons. James Trager, *The Food Chronology: A Food Lover's Compendium of Events and Anecdotes from Prehistory to the Present* (New York: Henry Holt, 1995), 405. Michael Batterberry and Ariane Ruskin Batterberry, *On the Town in New York: The Landmark History of Eating, Drinking, and Entertainments from the American Revolution to the Food Revolution* (New York: Routledge, 1999), 227.

123 "A La Carte Menus Found Outmoded: President of Waldorf Advises Nation's Chefs That Selective Meals Will Win Favor," *New York Times*, November 8, 1939. See also "Bans on Foreign Names on Our Menus Urged as First Culinary Congress Is Organized," 25.

124 "Bans on Foreign Names on Our Menus Urged as First Culinary Congress Is Organized," 25. Sprinzing was opposed by Camille Den Dooven of Boston, who argued for the "showmanship" of French.

125 H. I. Phillips, "The Once Over: The Dining Out Problem," *Washington Post*, November 18, 1939, 9.

126 "How New York Eats," *The Steward*, November 1920, 22.

CONCLUSION

1 Charles J. Rosebault, "Lost Tribe of New York," *New York Times*, February 13, 1921, sec. Book Review, 5.

2 Harvey A. Levenstein, *Paradox of Plenty: A Social History of Eating in Modern America* (New York: Oxford University Press, 1993), 46.

3 Belief in the individuality of taste not only was consistent with the middle-class celebration of diversity but also was sanctioned by science. "Different persons are differently constituted with respect to the chemical changes which their food undergoes and the effect produced, so that it may be literally true that 'one man's meat is another man's poison,'" reported the culinary journal *Good Food*. "Agreement of Food with Individuals," *Good Food* 2, no. 9 (1907): 7.

4 George S. Chappell, *The Restaurants of New York* (New York: Greenberg, 1925), 1.

5 Josée Johnston and Shyon Baumann, "Democracy versus Distinction: A Study of Omnivorousness in Gourmet Food Writing," *American Journal of Sociology* 113, no. 1 (2007): 169.

6 Richard A. Peterson, "Problems in Comparative Research: The Example of Omnivorousness," *Poetics* 33, no. 5–6 (2005): 264.

7 Priscilla Parkhurst Ferguson, *Accounting for Taste: The Triumph of French Cuisine* (Chicago: University of Chicago Press, 2004), 17.

8 *Appleton's Hand-book of American Travel: Northern and Eastern Tour* (New York: D. Appleton, 1876), 10 (abridged).

9 *Lippincott's General Guide to the United States and Canada* (Philadelphia: J. B. Lippincott, 1876), 14–15. While the following travel guides may mention restaurants in passing, all provide only limited treatments of restaurant cuisine: *Morrison's Strangers' Guide to the City of Washington, and Its Vicinity* (Washington: W. M. Morrison, 1844); Edward Alfred Pollard, *The Virginia Tourist: Sketches of the Springs and Mountains of Virginia : Containing an Exposition of Fields for the Tourist in Virginia* (Philadelphia: J. B. Lippincott, 1870); *Illustrated New York* (New York: International Publishing, 1888); Edwin M. Bacon, *Boston: A Guide Book* (Boston: Ginn and Company, 1918); Frederick Wilkinson Kilbourne, *Chronicles of the White Mountains* (Boston: Houghton Mifflin Company, 1916). A few guides were a little more descriptive. Appleton's "Southern Tour" provided more information than most (including the Appleton's "Northern and Eastern Tour"). For example, the guide reported that "the Restaurants of New Orleans have long been famous for the excellence of their cuisine. *Victor's*, 185 Canal Street; the *Maison Dorée*, 144 Canal; and the *Restaurant Moreau*, have no superiors in the South. *Galpin's*, 32 Royal Street (steaks and chops); *Pino's*, 23 St. Charles; and *Rivas* (oysters), 156 Dryades Street, are among the best of their class in the city." (Italics in original.) Edward Hepple Hall, *Appleton's Hand-book of American Travel: The Southern Tour; Being a Guide through Maryland, District of Columbia, Virginia, North Carolina, Georgia and Kentucky* (New York: D. Appleton, 1866), 108. See also *Visitor's Guide to New Orleans* (New Orleans: J. C. Waldo, 1875), 172. This guide to New Orleans contained an advertising section that noted restaurants and hours. Typical is the advertisement for McCloskey's: "The best the market affords at prices to suit the times."

10 Karl Baedeker (firm) and James F. Muirhead, *The United States, with an Excursion into Mexico, Cuba, Porto Rico, and Alaska* (New York: Charles Scribner's Sons, 1909), xxiv–xxv. Earlier editions did not significantly differ. See Karl Baedeker (firm) and James F. Muirhead, *The United States, with an Excursion into Mexico; Handbook for Travellers* (New York: C. Scribner's Sons, 1904); and Karl Baedeker and M. J. Muirhead, *The United States with an Excursion into Mexico* (Leipsig: Karl Baedeker Publisher, 1893).

11 While the author is unknown, the title suggests familiarity with two European works printed by the publishing house of G. Richards and Pall Mall Publications: Nathaniel Newnham-Davis, *Dinners and Diners: Where and How to Dine in London* (London: G. Richards, Pall Mall Publications, 1899); and Roland Strong, *Where and How to Dine in Paris, with Notes on Paris Hotels, Waiters and Their Tips* (London: G. Richards, 1900). Notably, Roland Strong was the Paris correspondent for a number of papers including the *New York Times*, and his work would have been familiar to the author of *Where and How to Dine in New York*. The British books, however, substantially differ from the American in that they included information on cuisine.

12 *Where and How to Dine in New York: The Principal Hotels, Restaurants and Cafes of Various Kinds and Nationalities Which Have Added to the Gastronomic Fame of New York and Its Suburbs* (New York: Lewis, Scribner, 1903), 2–3.

13 Ibid., 29.

14 Ibid., preface.

15 "Kinds of Restaurants: How They Vary According to Place and Purpose," *New York Daily Tribune*, November 1, 1896, sec. 3, 6.

16 The rare article anticipated restaurant reviewing. In what was perhaps one of the first published restaurant reviews in the United States, *The Caterer* wrote about the opening of the Moulin Rouge on Broadway in 1917. "We also offer the suggestion that either more waiters must be obtained, or that those on hand must be better trained, or held in better control than were those the night it was our pleasure to be in the place." "Moulin Rouge," *The Caterer* 28, no. 9 (1917): 60.

17 Chappell, *The Restaurants of New York*, 4.

18 Ibid., 8, 7.

19 Ibid., 40.

20 Ibid., 122, 148, 133.

21 Clarence E. Edwords, *Bohemian San Francisco: Its Restaurants and Their Most Famous Recipes* (San Francisco: P. Elder, 1914); Jack L. Dodd and Hazel Blair Dodd, *Bohemian Eats of San Francisco* (San Francisco: n.p., 1925).

22 Dodd and Dodd, *Bohemian Eats of San Francisco*, n.p. Many early guides to restaurants were paid advertisements. *Bohemian Eats of San Francisco* had a sponsor, the Hupp Motor Company, but it is unclear whether restaurants paid promotional fees for appearing in the booklet. Regardless, the restaurant descriptions go well beyond the usual descriptions found in contemporary guides.

23 "A History of the Michelin Guides: Press Release," Michelin, http://www.michelinman.com/difference/releases/pressrelease02232005b.html (accessed April 2005).

24 Levenstein, *Paradox of Plenty*, 46–47; Duncan Hines, *Adventures in Good Eating* (Bowling Green, Ky.: Adventures in Good Eating, 1946); Louis Hatchett, *Duncan Hines: The Man Behind the Cake Mix* (Macon, Ga.: Mercer University Press, 2001); David Schwartz, "Duncan Hines: He Made Gastronomes out of Motorists," *Smithsonian*, November 1984, 86–97. Hines's fame and credibility sold goods. In 1957, Proctor & Gamble acquired the use of his name and reputation as well as a cake mix formula that they marketed nationally.

25 Bryan Miller, "Craig Claiborne, 79, *Times* Food Editor and Critic, Is Dead," *New York Times*, January 24, 2000, sec. A, 1.

26 Lawrence Van Gelder, "New Yorkers, Etc.," *New York Times*, April 25, 1979, sec. C, 14. See also Chris Chase, *The Great American Waistline: Putting It on and Taking It Off* (New York: Penguin Books, 1982), 53.

27 Reviewers offered advice, but they could not dictate the individual diner's response to the food he or she consumed. Historically, taste has been recognized as something both personal and shared. These tensions constrained the influence of the reviewer. As Stephen Mennell observed, "Taste and opinion always

have been, and always will be, produced in *imperfect markets.*" Stephen Mennell, "Eating in the Public Sphere in the Nineteenth and Twentieth Centuries," in *Eating Out in Europe: Picnics, Gourmet Dining, and Snacks since the Late Eighteenth Century,* ed. Marc Jacobs and Peter Scholliers (Oxford: Berg, 2003), 257. For a fuller discussion of these ideas, see Michael Shaffer, "Taste, Gastronomic Expertise, and Objectivity," in *Food and Philosophy: Eat, Think and Be Merry,* ed. Fritz Allhoff and Dave Monroe (Oxford: Blackwell Publishing, 2007), esp. 85; and Carolyn Korsmeyer, *Making Sense of Taste: Food and Philosophy* (Ithaca: Cornell University Press, 1999), esp. 38–67.

28 On middle-class efforts to remake the nation in its own image, see Michael E. McGerr, *A Fierce Discontent: The Rise and Fall of the Progressive Movement in America, 1870–1920* (New York: Free Press, 2003). See also Suellen M. Hoy, *Chasing Dirt: The American Pursuit of Cleanliness* (New York: Oxford University Press, 1995); and Robert H. Wiebe, *The Search for Order, 1877–1920* (New York: Hill and Wang, 1967).

29 C. Wright Mills, *White Collar: The American Middle Classes* (London: Oxford University Press, 1951; reprint, 1981), ix.

30 "Both in New York and Philadelphia, first-class restaurants at first refused to serve men [attired in shirt waists]—those in charge taking their stand on the ground that it was against the rules of the establishment to serve men in their shirt sleeves, not realizing that society had laid down the decision that a fancy shirt that is called a shirt waist is not a shirt, and that shirt waist sleeves are not (despite their appearances) shirt sleeves." "The Man in the Shirt Waist," *The Caterer* 11, no. 1 (1900): 27. In this case, shirt waist refers to a manufactured men's shirt with attached collar and cuffs.

31 "Manager Hilliard Cauterizes a London Hotel Statement," *The Caterer* 24, no. 4 (1912): 57.

32 The literature on how shared preferences and shared oppositions create collective identities is extensive. For a discussion, with particular relevance to food studies, see Peter Scholliers, "Meals, Food Narratives, and Sentiments of Belonging in Past and Present," in *Food, Drink and Identity: Cooking, Eating and Drinking in Europe since the Middle Ages,* ed. Peter Scholliers (Oxford: Berg, 2001), esp. 6–7, 9, 14.

33 James Surowiecki, *The Wisdom of Crowds: Why the Many Are Smarter Than the Few and How Collective Wisdom Shapes Business, Economies, Societies, and Nations* (New York: Doubleday, 2004). See also Korsmeyer's discussion of David Hume. Korsmeyer, *Making Sense of Taste,* 51–53.

34 Strictly speaking, the middling folks did not have to see themselves as a class to exercise power in the marketplace. The more they identified with the cosmopolitan ideal, however, the more they constituted a class with shared interests. The more they thought of themselves as a class, the more others did too, and their power in the marketplace increased.

35 E. P. Thompson, "The Moral Economy of the English Crowd in the Eighteenth Century," *Past and Present*, no. 50 (1971): 76–136. Thompson believed that moral economies existed only in societies that were transitioning from traditional to market economies. Other scholars have argued that Thompson's theory can be used to explain modern, market capital societies as well. See for example, Thomas Clay Arnold, "Rethinking Moral Economy," *American Political Science Review* 95, no. 1 (2001): 85–95.

36 "Where the elite meet to eat" was the catch phrase of *Duffy's Tavern*, a radio program set in an Irish bar that featured Hollywood stars like Bing Crosby, not New York City's fashionable Four Hundred.

37 Scudder Middleton, *Dining, Wining and Dancing in New York* (New York: Dodge Publishing, 1938), 112 13.

In the late 1930s, French food and high prices could be found at many of the fashionable nightclubs and a number of the most important restaurants in New York (culminating in 1939 with the popularity of Henri Soulé's restaurant at the World's Fair and the opening of Le Pavillion in New York). In 1961, the publication of Julia Child, Simone Beck, and Louisette Bertholle's *Mastering the Art of French Cooking* (as well as Child's subsequent PBS television show) sparked a widespread revival of French cuisine. But French cooking remained but one cuisine among many. Le Pavillion soon faced competition from self-consciously American restaurants such as the Four Seasons, and Child's success spurred the emergence of popular chefs who promoted both international cuisines and American classics. On various efforts to revive French cuisine, see Krishnendu Ray, "Ethnic Succession and the New American Restaurant Cuisine," in *The Restaurants Book: Ethnographies of Where to Eat*, ed. David Beriss and David Sutton (New York: Berg, 2007), 97–114; Patric Kuh, *The Last Days of Haute Cuisine* (New York: Viking, 2001); and Laura Shapiro, *Julia Child* (New York: Lipper/Penguin, 2007).

38 "Fifty Kinds of Public Eating Places," *The Caterer* 30, no. 2 (1918): 67.

39 An industry term for vacuum sealing in plastic.

40 David Leite, "Perfection? Hint: It's Warm and Has a Secret," *New York Times* (2008), http://www.nytimes.com/2008/07/09/dining/09chip.html?_r=1&ref=dining &oref=slogin (accessed July 9, 2008).

41 This work is about the lives of consumers, but it is worth noting that unrestrained consumption has consequences for producers and the environment. In the nineteenth century, for all the luxurious wastefulness of the aristocratic restaurant, the damage was limited to the horrible abuses at Chicago meatpacking plants chronicled in *The Jungle*, the overfishing of oysters, terrapin, and canvasback ducks, and the rising cost of lobster. Mass consumption has multiplied those effects, threatening the destruction of rain forests and fishing beds and widening the global gap between those who eat steak and those who struggle to acquire enough rice to survive.

BIBLIOGRAPHY

ARCHIVAL COLLECTIONS

Buttolph Menu Collection, New York Public Library, New York, New York

Centennial Exhibition Digital Collection, Free Library of Philadelphia, Philadelphia,
Pennsylvania, http://libwww.library.phila.gov/CenCol/

R. G. Dun & Company Collection, Baker Library, Harvard Business School,
Cambridge, Massachusetts

Senator John Heinz History Center, Library and Archives, Pittsburgh, Pennsylvania

Historical Menu Collection, University of Washington Libraries, Seattle,
Washington, http://content.lib.washington.edu/menusweb/index.html

National Restaurant Association, Library and Archives, Washington, D.C.

Patent Full-Text and Image Database, United States Patent and Trademark Office,
Washington, D.C., http://www.uspto.gov/patft/index.html

Regional History Menu Collection, Los Angeles Public Library, Los Angeles,
California, http://www.lapl.org/resources/en/menu_collection.html

NEWSPAPERS AND PERIODICALS

American City	*The Chef*
American Cookery	*Chef, Steward and Housekeeper*
American Magazine	*Chicago Daily Tribune*
American Mercury	*Collier's*
American Restaurant	*Commonweal*
Andover Review	*Contemporary Review*
Appleton's Journal	*The Cook*
Arena	*Cooking Club*
Atlantic Monthly	*Cooking Club Magazine*
Bookman	*Cornhill Magazine*
Boston Cooking-School Magazine	*Cosmopolitan*
Boston Daily Globe	*Country Life*
The Caterer	*Critic*
Catholic World	*Current Literature*
Century	*Current Opinion*
Charleston Daily Mail	*Delineator*
Chautauquan	*Denton (Md.) Journal*

Dial

The Dining Room Magazine

Education

Elyria (Ohio) Chronicle-Telegram

Everybody's Magazine

Field and Stream

Fitchburg (Mass.) Daily Sentinel

Fortune

Forum

Frank Leslie's Popular Monthly

Good Food

Good Housekeeping

Harper's Bazar

Harper's Monthly Magazine

Harper's New Monthly Magazine

Harper's Weekly

Hotel World

Independent

Indianapolis Star

International Culinary Magazine

Iowa City Daily Press

Journal of American Folk-Lore

Journal of Home Economics

Kitchen Craft and Cuisine

Ladies' Home Journal

Lima (Ohio) Times-Democrat

Lincoln (Ill.) Daily News

Lippincott's Monthly Magazine

Literary Digest

Living Age

Los Angeles Times

McClure's Magazine

Municipal Affairs

Munsey's Magazine

Nation

National Food Magazine

Newark Daily Advocate

New England Magazine

New Republic

New York Daily Tribune

New York Times

Nineteenth Century

Outlook

Overland Monthly

Pacific Coast Gazette

Public

Putman's Magazine

Restaurant Bulletin

Restaurant Man

Saturday Evening Post

Scientific American

Scribner's Magazine

Scribner's Monthly

The Southern Hotel Journal

The Steward

Survey

Syracuse (N.Y.) Herald

System

The Table

Table Talk

Travel

Trenton Evening Times

Washington Post

What to Eat

Woman's Home Companion

World's Work

World To-Day

SELECT WORKS CONSULTED

Abelson, Elaine S. *When Ladies Go a-Thieving: Middle-Class Shoplifters in the Victorian Department Store.* New York: Oxford University Press, 1989.

Algren, Nelson, and David E. Schoonover. *America Eats.* Iowa City: University of Iowa Press, 1992.

Anderson, E. N. *The Food of China.* New Haven: Yale University Press, 1988.

Appiah, Kwame Anthony. *Cosmopolitanism: Ethics in a World of Strangers.* New York: W. W. Norton, 2006.

———. "Cosmopolitan Patriots." In *For Love of Country: Debating the Limits of Patriotism*, edited by Martha Craven Nussbaum and Joshua Cohen, 21–29. Boston: Beacon Press, 1996.

Appleton's Hand-book of American Travel: Northern and Eastern Tour. New York: D. Appleton, 1876.

Archer, Melanie, and Judith R. Blau. "Class Formation in Nineteenth-Century America: The Case of the Middle Class." *Annual Review of Sociology* 19 (1993): 17–41.

Arnold, Matthew. *Civilization in the United States: First and Last Impressions of America*. Boston: Cupples and Hurd, 1888.

Arnold, Thomas Clay. "Rethinking Moral Economy." *American Political Science Review* 95, no. 1 (2001): 85 95.

Aron, Cindy Sondik. *Ladies and Gentlemen of the Civil Service: Middle-Class Workers in Victorian America*. New York: Oxford University Press, 1987.

———. *Working at Play: A History of Vacations in the United States*. New York: Oxford University Press, 1999.

Aron, Jean Paul. *The Art of Eating in France: Manners and Menus in the Nineteenth Century*. New York: Harper and Row, 1975.

Avakian, Arlene Voski, and Barbara Haber, eds. *From Betty Crocker to Feminist Food Studies: Critical Perspectives on Women and Food*. Amherst: University of Massachusetts Press, 2005.

Azar, Ofer H. "The History of Tipping from Sixteenth-Century England to United States in the 1910s." Department of Economics, Northwestern University, http://econwpa.wustl.edu/wpawelcome.html (accessed December 2, 2004).

Bacon, Edwin M. *Boston: A Guide Book*. Boston: Ginn and Company, 1918.

Baedeker, Karl, and James F. Muirhead. *The United States with an Excursion into Mexico*. Leipsig: Karl Baedeker Publisher, 1893.

———. *The United States, with an Excursion into Mexico; Handbook for Travellers*. New York: C. Scribner's Sons, 1904.

———. *The United States, with an Excursion into Mexico, Cuba, Porto Rico, and Alaska*. New York: Charles Scribner's Sons, 1909.

Baker, Houston A. "Critical Memory and the Black Public Sphere." In *The Black Public Sphere: A Public Culture Book*, edited by Black Public Sphere Collective, 7–37. Chicago: University of Chicago Press, 1995.

Banks, William P. *Two Great Foundations*. Philadelphia: n.p., 1878.

Bannister, Robert C. *Social Darwinism: Science and Myth in Anglo-American Social Thought*. Philadelphia: Temple University Press, 1979.

Barbas, Samantha. "'I'll Take Chop Suey': Restaurants as Agents of Culinary and Cultural Change." *Journal of Popular Culture* 36, no. 4 (2003): 669–84.

Barr, Andrew. *Drink: A Social History of America*. New York: Carroll and Graf, 1999.

Bates, Edwin, and the U.S. Bureau of Foreign and Domestic Commerce. *The San Francisco Restaurant Industry*. Washington, D.C.: Government Printing Office, 1930.

Batterberry, Michael, and Ariane Ruskin Batterberry. *On the Town in New York: The Landmark History of Eating, Drinking, and Entertainments from the American Revolution to the Food Revolution*. New York: Routledge, 1999.

Beadle, Charles. *A Trip to the United States in 1887*. London: J. S. Virtue, 1887.

Beck, Louis J., ed. *New York's Chinatown: An Historical Presentation of Its People and Places*. New York: Bohemia Publishing, 1898.

Beckert, Sven. *The Monied Metropolis: New York City and the Consolidation of the American Bourgeoisie, 1850–1896*. Cambridge: Cambridge University Press, 2001.

Bederman, Gail. *Manliness and Civilization: A Cultural History of Gender and Race in the United States, 1880–1917*. Chicago: University of Chicago Press, 1995.

Beecher, Catharine Esther, and Harriet Beecher Stowe. *The American Woman's Home; or, Principles of Domestic Science*. New York: J. B. Ford, 1869.

Belasco, Warren. "Future Notes: The Meal-in-a-Pill." In *Food in the USA: A Reader*, edited by Carole Counihan, 59–72. New York: Routledge, 2002.

———. *Meals to Come: A History of the Future of Food*. Berkeley: University of California Press, 2006.

Belasco, Warren James, and Philip Scranton, eds. *Food Nations: Selling Taste in Consumer Societies*. New York: Routledge, 2002.

Bellows, Albert J. *Philosophy of Eating*. Boston: Houghton Mifflin, 1870.

Benson, Susan Porter. *Counter Cultures: Saleswomen, Managers, and Customers in American Department Stores, 1890–1940*. Urbana: University of Illinois Press, 1986.

Bercovici, Konrad. *Around the World in New York*. New York: Century Co., 1924.

Berger, Frances de Talavera, and John Parke Custis. *Sumptuous Dining in Gaslight San Francisco*. Garden City, N.Y.: Doubleday, 1985.

Berger, Molly W. "A House Divided: The Culture of the American Luxury Hotel, 1825–1860." In *His and Hers: Gender, Consumption, and Technology*, edited by Roger Horowitz and Arwen Mohun, 39–66. Charlottesville: University Press of Virginia, 1998.

Bethea, D. A. *Colored People's Blue-Book and Business Directory of Chicago, Ill., 1905*. Chicago: Celerity Print, 1905.

Bird, Isabella Lucy. *The Englishwoman in America*. Madison: University of Wisconsin Press, 1966.

Bishop, E. C. *Twenty-First Biennial Report of the State Superintendent of Public Instruction to the Governor of the State of Nebraska*. Lincoln, Nebraska: Department of Public Instruction, 1911.

Bjelopera, Jerome P. *City of Clerks: Office and Sales Workers in Philadelphia, 1870–1920*. Urbana: University of Illinois Press, 2005.

Blackford, Mansel G. *A History of Small Business in America*. Chapel Hill: University of North Carolina Press, 2003.

Blatch, Harriot Stanton, and Alma Lutz. *Challenging Years: The Memoirs of Harriot Stanton Blatch*. New York: G. P. Putnam's Sons, 1940.

Bledstein, Burton J. *The Culture of Professionalism: The Middle Class and the Development of Higher Education in America*. New York: Norton, 1976.

Bledstein, Burton J., and Robert D. Johnston, eds. *The Middling Sorts: Explorations in the History of the American Middle Class*. New York: Routledge, 2001.

Blumin, Stuart M. *The Emergence of the Middle Class: Social Experience in the American City, 1760–1900*. Cambridge: Cambridge University Press, 1989.

Bock, August J. *Knight of the Napkin: Memoirs of Fifty Years' Experiences in Many Lands*. New York: Exposition Press, 1951.

Bold, Christine. *The WPA Guides: Mapping America*. Jackson: University Press of Mississippi, 1999.

Bonner, Arthur. *Alas! What Brought Thee Hither? The Chinese in New York, 1800–1950*. Madison, N.J.: Fairleigh Dickinson University Press, 1997.

Bourdieu, Pierre. *Distinction: A Social Critique of the Judgment of Taste*. Cambridge: Harvard University Press, 1984.

Bourg, Gene. "New Orleans Foodways." In *New Encyclopedia of Southern Culture*, edited by John T. Edge, 85. Chapel Hill: University of North Carolina Press, 2007.

Bourget, Paul. *Outre-Mer: Impressions of America*. New York: C. Scribner's Sons, 1895.

Bowles, Samuel. *Across the Continent: A Summer's Journey to the Rocky Mountains, the Mormons, and the Pacific States, with Speaker Colfax*. New York: Samuel Bowles and Company, 1865.

Braynard, Frank O. "Leviathan." In *Ships of the World: An Historical Encyclopedia*, edited by Lincoln P. Paine, 299–300. Boston: Houghton Mifflin, 1997.

Brooks, Joanna. "The Early American Public Sphere and the Emergence of a Black Print Counterpublic." *William and Mary Quarterly* 62, no. 1 (2005): 67–92.

Brown, Henry Collins. *Brownstone Fronts and Saratoga Trunks*. New York: E. P. Dutton, 1935.

———. *Delmonico's: A Story of Old New York*. New York: Valentine's Manual, 1928.

———. *In the Golden Nineties*. Hastings-on-Hudson, New York: Valentine's Manual, 1928.

Browne, Junius Henri. *The Great Metropolis: A Mirror of New York*. Hartford: American Publishing, 1869.

Brumberg, Joan Jacobs. *Fasting Girls: The History of Anorexia Nervosa*. New York: Vintage Books, 2000.

Burnham, John C. *Bad Habits: Drinking, Smoking, Taking Drugs, Gambling, Sexual Misbehavior, and Swearing in American History*. New York: New York University Press, 1993.

Burris, Val. "The Discovery of the New Middle Class." *Theory and Society* 15, no. 3 (1986): 317–49.

Bushman, Richard L. *The Refinement of America: Persons, Houses, Cities*. New York: Vintage Books, 1992.

Butsch, Richard. *For Fun and Profit: The Transformation of Leisure into Consumption*. Philadelphia: Temple University Press, 1990.

Campbell, Tunis G. *Hotel Keepers, Head Waiters, and Housekeepers' Guide*. Boston: Coolidge and Wiley, 1848.

Carter, Dale. "A Bridge Too Far? Cosmopolitanism and the Anglo-American Folk Music Revival." *European Journal of American Culture* 29, no. 1 (2010): 35–52.

Chandler, Alfred Dupont. *The Visible Hand: The Managerial Revolution in American Business*. Cambridge, Mass.: Belknap Press, 1977.

Chaney, David. "Cosmopolitan Art and Cultural Citizenship." *Theory, Culture and Society* 19, no. 1–2 (2002): 157–74.

Chang, Iris. *The Chinese in America: A Narrative History*. New York: Viking, 2003.

Chappell, George S. *The Restaurants of New York*. New York: Greenberg, 1925.

Chase, Chris. *The Great American Waistline: Putting It On and Taking It Off*. New York: Penguin Books, 1982.

Chen, Jack. *The Chinese of America*. San Francisco: Harper and Row, 1980.

Chen, Yong. *Chinese San Francisco, 1850–1943*. Stanford: Stanford University Press, 2000.

Child, Lydia Maria Francis. *The Frugal Housewife*. London: T. T. and J. Tegg, 1832.

Christ, J. X. "A Short Guide to the Art of Dining, Slumming, Touring, Wildlife, and Women for Hire in New York's Chinatown and Chinese Restaurants." *Oxford Art Journal* 26, no. 2 (2003): 71–92.

Chu, Louis H. "The Chinese Restaurants in New York City." Master's thesis, New York University, 1939.

Chudacoff, Howard P. *The Age of the Bachelor: Creating an American Subculture*. Princeton: Princeton University Press, 1999.

Chudacoff, Howard P., and Judith E. Smith. *The Evolution of American Urban Society*. Upper Saddle River, N.J.: Pearson/Prentice Hall, 2005.

Clark, Priscilla P. "Thoughts for Food I: French Cuisine and French Culture." *French Review* 49, no. 1 (1975): 32–39.

———. "Thoughts for Food II: Culinary Culture in Contemporary France." *French Review* 49, no. 2 (1975): 198–205.

"Clementine Paddleford Is Dead; Food Editor of Herald Tribune." *New York Times*, November 14, 1967, 47.

Cmiel, Kenneth. *Democratic Eloquence: The Fight over Popular Speech in Nineteenth-Century America*. New York: W. Morrow, 1990.

Cobble, Dorothy Sue. *Dishing It Out: Waitresses and Their Unions in the Twentieth Century*. Urbana: University of Illinois Press, 1991.

Cocks, Catherine Campbell. "'A City Excellent to Behold': Urban Tourism and the Commodification of Public Life in the United States 1850–1915." PhD diss., University of California, Davis, 1997.

———. *Doing the Town: The Rise of Urban Tourism in the United States, 1850–1915*. Berkeley: University of California Press, 2001.

Coe, Andrew. *Chop Suey: A Cultural History of Chinese Food in the United States*. New York: Oxford University Press, 2009.

Cohen, Lizabeth. *A Consumer's Republic: The Politics of Mass Consumption in Postwar America*. New York: Vintage Books, 2003.

Collingham, E. M. *Curry: A Tale of Cooks and Conquerors*. Oxford: Oxford University Press, 2006.

Conwell, Russell Herman. *Why and How? Why the Chinese Emigrate*. Boston: Lee and Shepard, 1871.

Corson, Juliet. *Every-Day Cookery and Hints for the Laundry*. Chicago: Adams and Westlake Manufacturing, 1884.

———. *Miss Corson's Practical American Cookery and Household Management*. New York: Dodd, Mead & Co., 1885.

Cousine, Clara L. *The Columbia Ideal Account Book*. Chicago: Columbia Publisher, 1894.

Cowan, Ruth Schwartz. *More Work for Mother: The Ironies of Household Technology from the Open Hearth to the Microwave*. New York: Basic Books, 1983.

Cozart, Winfield Forrest. *A Technical Treatise on Dining-Room Service: The Waiters' Manual*. Chicago: H. J. Bohn and Brother, 1898.

Crook, J. Mordaunt. *The Rise of the Nouveaux Riches: Style and Status in Victorian and Edwardian Architecture*. London: John Murray, 1999.

Cummings, Richard Osborn. *The American and His Food: A History of Food Habits in the United States*. Chicago: University of Chicago Press, 1941.

Curtis, Waldo J. *Visitor's Guide to New Orleans*. New Orleans: J. C. Waldo, 1875.

Dale, Elizabeth. "'Social Equality Does Not Exist among Themselves, nor among Us': Baylies vs. Curry and Civil Rights in Chicago, 1888." *American Historical Review* 102, no. 2 (1997): 311–39.

Davidson, Alan. *Oxford Companion to Food*. Oxford: Oxford University Press, 1999.

Dearing, Albin Pasteur. *The Elegant Inn: The Waldorf-Astoria Hotel, 1893–1929*. Secaucus, N.J.: L. Stuart, 1986.

Dedmon, Emmett. *Fabulous Chicago*. New York: Random House, 1953.

Degler, Carl N. *At Odds: Women and the Family in America from the Revolution to the Present*. New York: Oxford University Press, 1980.

De Gouy, Louis Pullig. *Chef's Cook Book of Profitable Recipes*. Stamford, Conn.: The Dahls, 1939.

Denker, Joel. *The World on a Plate: A Tour through the History of America's Ethnic Cuisines*. Boulder: Westview Press, 2003.

Derks, Scott. *The Value of a Dollar: Prices and Incomes in the United States, 1860–1999*. Lakeville, Conn.: Grey House, 1999.

DeWitt, Frederic M. *An Illustrated and Descriptive Souvenir and Guide to San Francisco: A New Handbook for Strangers and Tourists*. San Francisco: Frederick M. DeWitt, 1897.

Dickens, Charles. *American Notes for General Circulation and Pictures from Italy*. London: Chapman & Hall, 1914.

Diner, Hasia R. *Hungering for America: Italian, Irish, and Jewish Foodways in the Age of Migration*. Cambridge: Harvard University Press, 2001.

Dodd, Jack L., and Hazel Blair Dodd. *Bohemian Eats of San Francisco*. San Francisco: n.p., 1925.

Domosh, Mona. "Those 'Gorgeous Incongruities': Polite Politics and Public Space on the Streets of Nineteenth-Century New York City." *Annals of the Association of American Geographers* 88, no. 2 (1998): 209–26.

Douglas, Mary, ed. *Food in the Social Order: Studies of Food and Festivities in Three American Communities*. New York: Russell Sage, 1984.

Dreiser, Theodore. *American Diaries, 1902–1926*. Philadelphia: University of Pennsylvania Press, 1982.

DuBois, Ellen Carol. *Harriot Stanton Blatch and the Winning of Woman Suffrage*. New Haven: Yale University Press, 1997.

Dudden, Faye E. *Serving Women: Household Service in Nineteenth-Century America*. Middletown, Conn.: Wesleyan University Press, 1983.

Duis, Perry. *Challenging Chicago: Coping with Everyday Life, 1837–1920*. Urbana: University of Illinois Press, 1998.

———. *The Saloon: Public Drinking in Chicago and Boston, 1880–1920*. Urbana: University of Illinois Press, 1983.

Dumenil, Lynn. *Freemasonry and American Culture, 1880–1930*. Princeton: Princeton University Press, 1984.

Dunlop, M. H. *Gilded City: Scandal and Sensation in Turn-of-the-Century New York*. New York: W. Morrow, 2000.

Edwards, Holly, ed. *Noble Dreams, Wicked Pleasures: Orientalism in America, 1870–1930*. Princeton: Princeton University Press, 2000.

Edwords, Clarence E. *Bohemian San Francisco: Its Restaurants and Their Most Famous Recipes*. San Francisco: P. Elder, 1914.

Ehrenreich, Barbara. *Fear of Falling: The Inner Life of the Middle Class*. New York: Pantheon Books, 1989.

Elias, Norbert. *The Civilizing Process*. Oxford: B. Blackwell, 1982.

Ellet, Elizabeth Fries Lummis. *The Practical Housekeeper: A Cyclopaedia of Domestic Economy*. New York: Stringer and Townsend, 1857.

Elliott, R. N. *Tea Room and Cafeteria Management*. Boston: Little, Brown, 1926.

Ellwanger, George H. *The Pleasures of the Table: An Account of Gastronomy from Ancient Days to Present Times*. New York: Doubleday Page, 1902.

Enstad, Nan. *Ladies of Labor, Girls of Adventure: Working Women, Popular Culture, and Labor Politics at the Turn of the Twentieth Century*. New York: Columbia University Press, 1999.

Epstein, Ralph C. "Industrial Profits in 1917." *Quarterly Journal of Economics* 39, no. 2 (1925): 241–66.

Erenberg, Lewis A. *Steppin' Out: New York Nightlife and the Transformation of American Culture, 1890–1930*. Westport, Conn.: Greenwood Press, 1981.

Escoffier, A. *Le Guide Culinaire: The First Complete Translation into English*. New York: Mayflower Books, 1979.

Ewen, Stuart. *All Consuming Images: The Politics of Style in Contemporary Culture*. New York: Basic Books, 1988.

Farmer, Fannie Merritt. *The 1896 Boston Cooking-School Cook Book*. New York: Gramercy Books, 1997.

Fawcett, Edgar. *New York: A Novel*. New York: F. Tennyson Neely, 1898.

Featherstone, Mike. "Cosmopolis: An Introduction." *Theory, Culture and Society* 19, no. 1–2 (2002): 1–16.

Fellows, Charles. *The Menu Maker: Suggestions for Selecting and Arranging Menus for Hotels and Restaurants*. Chicago: Hotel Monthly Press, 1910.

Fenster, J. M. "The Taste of Time: All across America There Are Restaurants That Serve Up the Spirit and Conviviality." *American Heritage*, April 1997, 38–48.

Ferguson, Priscilla Parkhurst. *Accounting for Taste: The Triumph of French Cuisine*. Chicago: University of Chicago Press, 2004.

Filippini, Alexander. *The Table: How to Buy Food, How to Cook It, and How to Serve It*. New York: Baker & Taylor, 1895.

Finck, Henry Theophilus. *The Pacific Coast Scenic Tour, from Southern California to Alaska, the Canadian Pacific Railway, Yellowstone Park and the Grand Cañon*. New York: C. Scribner's Sons, 1890.

Fine, Gary Alan. *Kitchens: The Culture of Restaurant Work*. Berkeley: University of California Press, 1996.

———. "Wittgenstein's Kitchen: Sharing Meaning in Restaurant Work." *Theory and Society* 24, no. 2 (1995): 245–69.

Finkelstein, Joanne. *Dining Out: A Sociology of Modern Manners*. New York: New York University Press, 1989.

Flanagan, James Joseph. *The Waiter*. Providence: Star Printing, 1903.

Foster, George G., and Stuart M. Blumin. *New York by Gas-Light and Other Urban Sketches*. Berkeley: University of California Press, 1990.

Francatelli, Charles. *Francatelli's New Cook Book Francatelli's Modern Cook: A Practical Guide to the Culinary Art in All Its Branches*. Philadelphia: D. McKay, 1895.

Frank, Dana. *Purchasing Power: Consumer Organizing, Gender, and the Seattle Labor Movement, 1919–1929*. Cambridge: Cambridge University Press, 1994.

Fraser, Nancy. "Rethinking the Public Sphere: A Contribution to the Critique of Actually Existing Democracy." In *Habermas and the Public Sphere*, edited by Craig Calhoun, 109–42. Cambridge: MIT Press, 1996.

Fraser, Steve, and Gary Gerstle. *Ruling America: A History of Wealth and Power in a Democracy*. Cambridge: Harvard University Press, 2005.

Frost, S. Annie. *Frost's Laws and By-Laws of American Society: A Condensed but Thorough Treatise on Etiquette and Its Usages in America*. New York: Dick and Fitzgerald, 1869.

Furet, François. "Democracy and Utopia." *Journal of Democracy* 9, no. 1 (1998): 65–79.

Gabaccia, Donna. *We Are What We Eat: Ethnic Food and the Making of Americans*. Cambridge: Harvard University Press, 2000.

Garvey, Ellen Gruber. *The Adman in the Parlor: Magazines and the Gendering of Consumer Culture*. New York: Oxford University Press, 1996.

Gault, Henri, and Christian Millau. *A Parisian's Guide to Paris*. New York: Random House, 1969.

Gilfoyle, Timothy J. *City of Eros: New York City, Prostitution, and the Commercialization of Sex, 1790–1920*. New York: W. W. Norton, 1992.

Gilkeson, John S. *Middle-Class Providence, 1820–1940*. Princeton: Princeton University Press, 1986.

Gilmore, Glenda Elizabeth. *Gender and Jim Crow: Women and the Politics of White Supremacy in North Carolina, 1896–1920*. Chapel Hill: University of North Carolina Press, 1996.

Glenn, Norval D., and Jon P. Alston. "Cultural Distances among Occupational Categories." *American Sociological Review* 33, no. 3 (1968): 365–82.

Goodrich, Samuel G. *Peter Parley's Geography for Beginners*. New York: Huntington and Savage, 1845.

Goodwin, Lorine Swainston. *The Pure Food, Drink, and Drug Crusaders, 1879–1914*. Jefferson, N.C.: McFarland, 1999.

Gordon, Bertram M. "The Decline of a Cultural Icon: France in American Perspective." *French Historical Studies* 22, no. 4 (1999): 625–52.

———. "Going Abroad to Taste: North Americans, France, and the Continental Tour, the Late Nineteenth Century to the Present." Paper presented at the Twenty-fifth Annual Meeting of the Western Society for French History, Greeley, Colorado, 1999.

Gottdiener, Mark. *The Theming of America: Dreams, Media Fantasies, and Themed Environments*. Boulder: Westview Press, 2001.

Gould, Stephen Jay. *The Mismeasure of Man*. New York: Norton, 1981.

Greer, Carlotta Cherryholmes. *A Text-Book of Cooking*. Boston: Allyn and Bacon, 1915.

Grier, Katherine C. *Culture and Comfort: Parlor Making and Middle-Class Identity, 1850–1930*. Washington: Smithsonian Institution Press, 1997.

Griffiths, Sian, and Jennifer Wallace, eds. *Consuming Passions: Food in the Age of Anxiety*. Manchester: Manchester University Press, 1998.

Groce, Nancy. *New York: Songs of the City*. New York: Watson-Guptill Publications, 1999.

Groth, Paul Erling. *Living Downtown: The History of Residential Hotels in the United States*. Berkeley: University of California Press, 1994.

Grover, Kathryn, ed. *Dining in America, 1850–1900*. Amherst and Rochester: University of Massachusetts Press and the Margaret Woodbury Strong Museum, 1987.

Grund, Francis J. *Aristocracy in America*. London: R. Bentley, 1839.

Guidry, John A., and Mark Q. Sawyer. "Contentious Pluralism: The Public Sphere and Democracy." *Perspectives on Politics* 1, no. 2 (2003): 273–89.

Gvion-Rosenberg, Liora. "Why Do Vegetarian Restaurants Serve Hamburger? Toward an Understanding of a Cuisine." *Semiotica* 80, no. 1–2 (1990): 61–79.

Gyory, Andrew. *Closing the Gate: Race, Politics, and the Chinese Exclusion Act*. Chapel Hill: University of North Carolina Press, 1998.

Habermas, Jürgen. *The Structural Transformation of the Public Sphere: An Inquiry into a Category of Bourgeois Society.* Cambridge: MIT Press, 1989.

Hall, Edward Hepple. *Appletons' Hand-book of American Travel: The Southern Tour; Being a Guide through Maryland, District of Columbia, Virginia, North Carolina, Georgia and Kentucky.* New York: D. Appleton, 1866.

Halle, David. "The Audience for Abstract Art: Class, Culture, and Power." In *Cultivating Differences: Symbolic Boundaries and the Making of Inequality,* edited by Michèle Lamont and Marcel Fournier, 131–51. Chicago: University of Chicago Press, 1992.

Halttunen, Karen. *Confidence Men and Painted Women: A Study of Middle-Class Culture in America, 1830–1870.* New Haven: Yale University Press, 1982.

Hamilton, Richard F. "The Marginal Middle Class: A Reconsideration." *American Sociological Review* 31, no. 2 (1966): 192–99.

Hamlin, Ina Marie, and Arthur Harry Winakor. *Department Store Food Service.* Urbana: University of Illinois, 1933.

Harcourt, Mrs. Charles. *Good Form for Women: A Guide to Conduct and Dress on All Occasions.* Philadelphia: John C. Winston, Co., 1907.

Hardman, Jacob Benjamin Salutsky. *American Labor Dynamics in the Light of Post-War Developments.* New York: Harcourt, 1928.

Harris, Neil. "The Gilded Age Reconsidered Once Again." *Archives of American Art Journal* 23, no. 4 (1983): 8–18.

Hartley, Cecil B. *The Gentlemen's Book of Etiquette, and Manual of Politeness: Being a Complete Guide for a Gentleman's Conduct in All His Relations Towards Society.* Boston: DeWolfe Fiske, 1873.

Hatchett, Louis. *Duncan Hines: The Man behind the Cake Mix.* Macon, Ga.: Mercer University Press, 2001.

Hawkins, Mike. *Social Darwinism in European and American Thought, 1860–1945.* Cambridge: Cambridge University Press, 1997.

Hays, Samuel P. *The Response to Industrialism, 1885–1914.* Chicago: University of Chicago Press, 1995.

Hechter, Michael, and Christine Horne. *Theories of Social Order: A Reader.* Stanford: Stanford Social Sciences, 2003.

Heldke, Lisa M. *Exotic Appetites: Ruminations of a Food Adventurer.* New York: Routledge, 2003.

Henderson, Helen Weston. *A Loiterer in New York.* New York: George H. Doran, 1917.

Hess, John L., and Karen Hess. *The Taste of America.* New York: Penguin Books, 1977.

Hines, Duncan. *Adventures in Good Eating.* Bowling Green, Ky.: Adventures in Good Eating, 1946.

Hofstadter, Richard. *The Age of Reform from Bryan to F.D.R.* New York: Knopf, 1955.
———. *Social Darwinism in American Thought.* Boston: Beacon Press, 1992.

Hoganson, Kristin L. *Consumers' Imperium: The Global Production of American Domesticity, 1865–1920.* Chapel Hill: University of North Carolina Press, 2007.

Holbrook, M. L. *Eating for Strength; or, Food and Diet in Relation to Health and Work*. New York: M. L. Holbrook, 1888.

Holman, Andrew Carl. *A Sense of Their Duty: Middle-Class Formation in Victorian Ontario Towns*. Montreal: McGill–Queen's University Press, 2000.

Homberger, Eric. *Mrs. Astor's New York: Money and Social Power in a Gilded Age*. New Haven: Yale University Press, 2002.

Horowitz, Daniel. "Frugality or Comfort: Middle-Class Styles of Life in the Early Twentieth Century." *American Quarterly* 37, no. 2 (1985): 239–59.

———. *The Morality of Spending: Attitudes toward the Consumer Society in America, 1875–1940*. Baltimore: Johns Hopkins University Press, 1985.

Horowitz, Roger. *Putting Meat on the American Table: Taste, Technology, Transformation*. Baltimore: Johns Hopkins University Press, 2006.

Houghton, Walter R. *Rules of Etiquette and Home Culture; or, What to Do and How to Do It*. Chicago: Rand, McNally, 1893.

Hoy, Suellen M. *Chasing Dirt: The American Pursuit of Cleanliness*. New York: Oxford University Press, 1995.

Hughes, Rupert. *The Real New York*. New York: Smart Set, 1904.

Humble, Nicola. *Culinary Pleasures: Cookbooks and the Transformation of British Food*. London: Faber, 2005.

Huneker, James. *New Cosmopolis: A Book of Images*. New York: Scribner, 1915.

Huston, James L. *Securing the Fruits of Labor: The American Concept of Wealth Distribution, 1765–1900*. Baton Rouge: Louisiana State University Press, 1998.

Iacobbo, Karen, and Michael Iacobbo. *Vegetarian America: A History*. Westport, Conn.: Praeger, 2004.

Illustrated New York. New York: International Publishing, 1888.

Inness, Sherrie A. *Dinner Roles: American Women and Culinary Culture*. Iowa City: University of Iowa Press, 2001.

———, ed. *Kitchen Culture in America: Popular Representations of Food, Gender, and Race*. Philadelphia: University of Pennsylvania Press, 2001.

Jackson, Helen Hunt. *Bits of Talk about Home Matters*. Boston: Roberts Brothers, 1873.

Jackson, Kenneth T. *Crabgrass Frontier: The Suburbanization of the United States*. New York: Oxford University Press, 1985.

Jacobs, Marc, and Peter Scholliers, eds. *Eating Out in Europe: Picnics, Gourmet Dining, and Snacks since the Late Eighteenth Century*. Oxford: Berg, 2003.

Jakle, John A., and Keith A. Sculle. *Fast Food: Roadside Restaurants in the Automobile Age*. Baltimore: Johns Hopkins University Press, 1999.

Jochnowitz, Eve. "Dining Out and Spectacle in Russian Jewish New York." In *The Restaurants Book: Ethnographies of Where to Eat*, edited by David Beriss and David E. Sutton, 115–32. New York: Berg, 2007.

Johnston, Josée, and Shyon Baumann. "Democracy versus Distinction: A Study of Omnivorousness in Gourmet Food Writing." *American Journal of Sociology* 113, no. 1 (2007): 165–204.

Johnston, Robert D. "Re-democratizing the Progressive Era: The Politics of

Progressive Era Political Historiography." *Journal of the Gilded Age and Progressive Era* 1, no. 1 (2002): 68–92.

Jones, Colin. "The Great Chain of Buying: Medical Advertisements, the Bourgeois Public Sphere, and the Origins of the French Revolution." *American Historical Review* 101, no. 1 (1996): 13–40.

Jones, Howard Mumford. *America and French Culture, 1750–1848.* Chapel Hill: University of North Carolina Press, 1927.

Kammen, Michael G. *American Culture, American Tastes: Social Change and the 20th Century.* New York: Alfred A. Knopf, 1999.

Kasson, John F. *Civilizing the Machine: Technology and Republican Values in America, 1776–1900.* New York: Grossman Publishers, 1976.

———. *Rudeness and Civility: Manners in Nineteenth-Century Urban America.* New York: Hill and Wang, 1990.

Keeler, Charles. *San Francisco and Thereabout.* San Francisco: California Promotion Committee, 1903.

Kellogg, E. E. *Science in the Kitchen: A Scientific Treatise on Food Substances and Their Dietetic Properties.* Battle Creek, Mich.: Health Publishing, 1892.

Kellogg, John Harvey. *Plain Facts for Old and Young; Embracing the Natural History and Hygiene of Organic Life.* Burlington, Iowa: I. F. Segner, 1890.

Kelly, Ian. *Cooking for Kings: The Life of Antonin Carême, the First Celebrity Chef.* New York: Walker and Co., 2003.

Kiefer, Nicholas M. "Economics and the Origins of the Restaurant." *Cornell Hotel and Restaurant Administration Quarterly* 43, no. 4 (2002): 58–65.

Kilbourne, Frederick Wilkinson. *Chronicles of the White Mountains.* Boston: Houghton Mifflin, 1916.

Kipling, Rudyard. *American Notes.* New York: Arcadia House, 1950.

Klein, Maury. *The Flowering of the Third America: The Making of an Organizational Society, 1850–1920.* Chicago: Ivan R. Dee, 1993.

Kliebard, Herbert M. *Forging the American Curriculum: Essays in Curriculum History and Theory.* New York: Routledge, 1992.

Koczanowicz, Leszek. "Cosmopolitanism and Its Predicaments." *Studies in Philosophy and Education* 29, no. 2 (2010): 141–49.

Korsmeyer, Carolyn. *Making Sense of Taste: Food and Philosophy.* Ithaca: Cornell University Press, 1999.

Kraditor, Aileen S. *Up from the Pedestal: Selected Writings in the History of American Feminism.* Chicago: Quadrangle Books, 1968.

Kuh, Patric. *The Last Days of Haute Cuisine.* New York: Viking, 2001.

Labaree, David F. "Curriculum, Credentials, and the Middle Class: A Case Study of a Nineteenth Century High School." *Sociology of Education* 29, no. 1 (1986): 56.

Lacour-Gayet, Robert. *Everyday Life in the United States before the Civil War, 1830–1860.* New York: F. Ungar, 1969.

Lamont, Michèle. *Money, Morals, and Manners: The Culture of the French and American Upper-Middle Class.* Chicago: University of Chicago Press, 1992.

Lamster, Mark. *Spalding's World Tour: The Epic Adventure That Took Baseball around the Globe—and Made It America's Game*. New York: Public Affairs, 2006.

Landau, Loren B., and Iriann Freemantle. "Tactical Cosmopolitanism and Idioms of Belonging: Insertion and Self-Exclusion in Johannesburg." *Journal of Ethnic and Migration Studies* 36, no. 3 (2010): 375–90.

Lathrop, Elise. *Early American Inns and Taverns*. New York: Arno Press, 1977.

Latimer, John Francis. *What's Happened to Our High Schools?* Washington: Public Affairs Press, 1958.

Leach, William. *Land of Desire: Merchants, Power, and the Rise of a New American Culture*. New York: Pantheon Books, 1993.

Lears, T. J. Jackson. "The Concept of Cultural Hegemony: Problems and Possibilities." *American Historical Review* 90, no. 3 (1985): 567–93.

———. *No Place of Grace: Antimodernism and the Transformation of American Culture, 1880–1920*. Chicago: University of Chicago Press, 1994.

Leavitt, Sarah Abigail. *From Catharine Beecher to Martha Stewart: A Cultural History of Domestic Advice*. Chapel Hill: University of North Carolina Press, 2002.

Lee, Anthony W. *Picturing Chinatown: Art and Orientalism in San Francisco*. Berkeley: University of California Press, 2001.

Leslie, Miriam. *California: A Pleasure Trip from Gotham to the Golden Gate*. New York: G. W. Carleton, 1877.

Levenstein, Harvey A. "Immigration, Travel, and the Internationalization of the American Diet." In *Food Selection: From Genes to Culture*, edited by Harvey Anderson, John Blundell, and Matty Chiva, 153–73. Levallois-Perret, France: Danone Institute, 2002.

———. *Paradox of Plenty: A Social History of Eating in Modern America*. New York: Oxford University Press, 1993.

———. *Revolution at the Table: The Transformation of the American Diet*. New York: Oxford University Press, 1988.

———. *Seductive Journey: American Tourists in France from Jefferson to the Jazz Age*. Chicago: University of Chicago Press, 1998.

Levine, Lawrence W. *Highbrow/Lowbrow: The Emergence of Cultural Hierarchy in America*. Cambridge: Harvard University Press, 1988.

Levine, Susan. "The Culture of Consumption Reconsidered." *Journal of Women's History* 19, no. 1 (2007): 10–16.

Lewis, Dio. *Talks about People's Stomachs*. Boston: Fields, Osgood and Company, 1870.

Liechty, Mark. *Suitably Modern: Making Middle-Class Culture in a New Consumer Society*. Princeton: Princeton University Press, 2003.

Lifshey, Earl. *The Housewares Story: A History of the American Housewares Industry*. Chicago: National Housewares Manufacturers Association, 1973.

Lincoln, Mary J. *Mrs. Lincoln's Boston Cook Book: What to Do and What Not to Do in Cooking*. Boston: Roberts Brothers, 1884.

Lippincott's General Guide to the United States and Canada. Philadelphia: J. B. Lippincott, 1876.

Liu, Haiming. "Chop Suey as Imagined Authentic Chinese Food: The Culinary Identity of Chinese Restaurants in the United States." *Journal of Transnational American Studies*, 1, no. 1 (2009), http://escholarship.org/uc/item/2bc4k55r (accessed May 10, 2010).

Lloyd, B. E. *Lights and Shades in San Francisco*. San Francisco: A. L. Bancroft and Company, 1876.

Lobel, Cindy R. "Consuming Classes: Changing Food Consumption Patterns in New York City, 1790–1860." PhD diss., City University of New York, 2003.

Long, Clarence Dickinson, and the National Bureau of Economic Research. *Wages and Earnings in the United States, 1860–1890*. Princeton: Princeton University Press, 1960.

Longone, Jan. "Professor Blot and the First French Cooking School in New York, Part 1." *Gastronomica* 1, no. 2 (2001): 65–71.

———. "Professor Blot and the First French Cooking School in New York, Part 2." *Gastronomica* 1, no. 3 (2001): 53–59.

Longstreet, Abby Buchanan. *Social Etiquette of New York*. New York: D. Appleton, 1883.

Lutz, Catherine, and Jane Lou Collins. *Reading National Geographic*. Chicago: University of Chicago Press, 1993.

Maccannon, E. A. *Commanders of the Dining Room: Biographic Sketches and Portraits of Successful Head Waiters*. New York: Gwendolyn, 1904.

MacDougall, Alice Foote. *The Secret of Successful Restaurants*. New York: Harper and Brothers, 1929.

Malatesta, Maria. "The Landed Aristocracy during the Nineteenth and Early Twentieth Centuries." In *The European Way: European Societies during the Nineteenth and Twentieth Centuries*, edited by Hartmut Kaelble, 44–67. New York: Berghahn Books, 2004.

Mann, Patricia S. *Micro-Politics: Agency in a Postfeminist Era*. Minneapolis: University of Minnesota Press, 1994.

Mariani, John F. *America Eats Out: An Illustrated History of Restaurants, Taverns, Coffee Shops, Speakeasies, and Other Establishments That Have Fed Us for 350 Years*. New York: Morrow, 1991.

Martin, Frederick Townsend. *Things I Remember*. New York: John Lane, 1913.

Matthews, Glenna. *The Rise of Public Woman: Woman's Power and Woman's Place in the United States, 1630–1970*. New York: Oxford University Press, 1992.

May, Elaine Tyler. *Great Expectations: Marriage and Divorce in Post-Victorian America*. Chicago: University of Chicago Press, 1980.

McAllister, Ward. *Society as I Have Found It*. New York: Cassell, 1890.

McCarthy, James Remington, and John Rutherford. *Peacock Alley: The Romance of the Waldorf-Astoria*. New York: Harper and Brothers, 1931.

McFeely, Mary Drake. *Can She Bake a Cherry Pie? American Women and the Kitchen in the Twentieth Century*. Amherst: University of Massachusetts Press, 2000.

McGerr, Michael E. *A Fierce Discontent: The Rise and Fall of the Progressive Movement in America, 1870–1920*. New York: Free Press, 2003.

McLeod, Alexander. *Pigtails and Gold Dust: A Panorama of Chinese Life in Early California*. Caldwell, Idaho: Caxton Printers, 1947.

Mennell, Stephen. *All Manners of Food: Eating and Taste in England and France from the Middle Ages to the Present*. Oxford: B. Blackwell, 1985.

———. "Eating in the Public Sphere in the Nineteenth and Twentieth Centuries." In *Eating out in Europe: Picnics, Gourmet Dining, and Snacks since the Late Eighteenth Century*, edited by Marc Jacobs and Peter Scholliers, 245–60. Oxford: Berg, 2003.

Middleton, Scudder. *Dining, Wining and Dancing in New York*. New York: Dodge Publishing, 1938.

Miller, David W. "Technology and the Ideal: Production, Quality and Kitchen Reform in Nineteenth-Century America." In *Dining in America, 1850–1900*, edited by Kathryn Grover, 47–84. Amherst and Rochester: University of Massachusetts Press and the Margaret Woodbury Strong Museum, 1987.

Miller, Michael Barry. *The Bon Marché: Bourgeois Culture and the Department Store, 1869–1920*. Princeton: Princeton University Press, 1981.

Miller, Stuart Creighton. *The Unwelcome Immigrant: The American Image of the Chinese, 1785–1882*. Berkeley: University of California Press, 1969.

Mills, C. Wright. *The Power Elite*. New York: Oxford University Press, 1956.

———. *White Collar: The American Middle Classes*. London: Oxford University Press, 1951. Reprint, 1981.

Milne-Smith, Amy. "Clubland: Masculinity, Status, and Community in the Gentlemen's Clubs of London, c. 1880–1914." PhD diss., University of Toronto, 2006.

Mintz, Sidney Wilfred. *Sweetness and Power: The Place of Sugar in Modern History*. New York: Penguin Books, 1986.

———. *Tasting Food, Tasting Freedom: Excursions into Eating, Culture, and the Past*. Boston: Beacon Press, 1996.

Mintz, Steven, and Susan Kellogg. *Domestic Revolutions: A Social History of American Family Life*. New York: Free Press, 1988.

Miriam Leslie. *California: A Pleasure Trip from Gotham to the Golden Gate*. New York: G. W. Carleton, 1877.

Model, John. "Patterns of Consumption, Acculturation, and Family Income Strategies in Late Nineteenth-Century America." In *Family and Population in Nineteenth-Century America*, edited by Tamara K. Hareven and Maris Vinovskis, 206–40. Princeton: Princeton University Press, 1978.

Montgomery, David. *The Fall of the House of Labor: The Workplace, the State, and American Labor Activism, 1865–1925*. Cambridge: Cambridge University Press, 1987.

Montgomery, Maureen E. *Displaying Women: Spectacles of Leisure in Edith Wharton's New York*. New York: Routledge, 1998.

Morris, Lloyd R. *Incredible New York*. New York: Arno Press, 1975.

Morrison's Strangers' Guide to the City of Washington, and Its Vicinity. Washington: W. M. Morrison, 1844.

Moskowitz, Marina. *Standard of Living: The Measure of the Middle Class in Modern America*. Baltimore: Johns Hopkins University Press, 2004.

Moss, Frank. *The American Metropolis: From Knickerbocker Days to the Present Time*. New York: P. F. Collier, 1897.

Moss, Sidney Phil. *Charles Dickens' Quarrel with America*. Troy, N.Y.: Whitston, 1984.

Mott, Frank Luther. *A History of American Magazines*. Vol. 3, 1865–1885. Cambridge: Harvard University Press, 1930.

———. *A History of American Magazines*. Vol. 4, 1885–1905. Cambridge: Harvard University Press, 1930.

Narayan, Uma. *Dislocating Cultures: Identities, Traditions, and Third-World Feminism*. New York: Routledge, 1997.

Nasaw, David. "Gilded Age Gospels." In *Ruling America: A History of Wealth and Power in a Democracy*, edited by Steve Fraser and Gary Gerstle, 123–48. Cambridge: Harvard University Press, 2005.

———. *Going Out: The Rise and Fall of Public Amusements*. New York: Basic Books, 1993.

Nascher, I. L. *The Wretches of Povertyville: A Sociological Study of the Bowery*. Chicago: J. J. Lanzit, 1909.

Nava, Mica. *Visceral Cosmopolitanism: Gender, Culture and the Normalisation of Difference*. New York: Berg, 2007.

Neill, Deborah. "Finding the 'Ideal Diet': Nutrition, Culture, and Dietary Practices in France and French Equatorial Africa, c. 1890s to 1920s." *Food and Foodways* 17, no. 1 (2009): 1–28.

Nelson, Elizabeth White. *Market Sentiments: Middle-Class Market Culture in Nineteenth-Century America*. Washington, D.C.: Smithsonian Books, 2004.

Neuhaus, Jessamyn. *Manly Meals and Mom's Home Cooking: Cookbooks and Gender in Modern America*. Baltimore: Johns Hopkins University Press, 2003.

Newman, Louise Michele. *Men's Ideas/Women's Realities: Popular Science, 1870–1915*. New York: Pergamon Press, 1985.

Newnham-Davis, Nathaniel. *Dinners and Diners: Where and How to Dine in London*. London: G. Richards, Pall Mall Publications, 1899.

Norris, Frank. *McTeague: A Story of San Francisco*. Mineola, N.Y.: Dover Publications, 2004.

Nugent, Walter. "Tocqueville, Marx and American Class Structure." *Social Science History* 12, no. 4 (1988): 327–47.

N. W. Ayer and Son's American Newspaper Annual and Directory. Philadelphia: N. W. Ayer and Son, 1893, 1897, 1911.

O'Connell, Daniel. *The Inner Man: Good Things to Eat and Drink and Where to Get Them*. San Francisco: Bancroft Company, 1891.

Ohmann, Richard M. *Selling Culture: Magazines, Markets, and Class at the Turn of the Century*. London: Verso, 1996.

Orvell, Miles. *The Real Thing: Imitation and Authenticity in American Culture, 1880–1940*. Chapel Hill: University of North Carolina Press, 1989.

Ovington, Mary White. *Half a Man: The Status of the Negro in New York*. New York: Longmans, Green, 1911.

Parkin, Katherine J. *Food Is Love: Food Advertising and Gender Roles in Modern America*. Philadelphia: University of Pennsylvania Press, 2006.

Parloa, Maria. *Home Economics: A Guide to Household Management*. New York: Century Co., 1898.

Patterson, Jerry E. *The First Four Hundred: Mrs. Astor's New York in the Gilded Age*. New York: Rizzoli, 2000.

Pearson, Roberta E., and William Uricchio. "Corruption, Criminality and the Nickelodeon." In *Hop on Pop: The Politics and Pleasures of Popular Culture*, edited by Henry Jenkins, Tara MacPherson, and Jane Shattuck, 376–88. Durham, N.C.: Duke University Press, 2002.

Peiss, Kathy Lee. *Cheap Amusements: Working Women and Leisure in Turn-of-the-Century New York*. Philadelphia: Temple University Press, 1986.

Peterson, Richard A. "Problems in Comparative Research: The Example of Omnivorousness." *Poetics* 33, no. 5–6 (2005): 257–82.

Peterson, Richard A., and Roger M. Kern. "Changing Highbrow Taste: From Snob to Omnivore." *American Sociological Review* 61, no. 5 (1996): 900–907.

Peterson, Richard A., and Albert Simkus. "How Musical Tastes Mark Occupational Status Groups." In *Cultivating Differences: Symbolic Boundaries and the Making of Inequality*, edited by Michèle Lamont and Marcel Fournier, 152–86. Chicago: University of Chicago Press, 1992.

Peterson, T. Sarah. *Acquired Taste: The French Origins of Modern Cooking*. Ithaca: Cornell University Press, 1994.

Pierpont, Claudia Roth. "The Silver Spire: How Two Men's Dreams Changed the Skyline of New York." *New Yorker*, November 18, 2002, 74–75.

Pieterse, Jan Nederveen. *White on Black: Images of Africa and Blacks in Western Popular Culture*. New Haven: Yale University Press, 1992.

Pillsbury, Richard. *From Boarding House to Bistro: The American Restaurant Then and Now*. Boston: Unwin Hyman, 1990.

———. *No Foreign Food: The American Diet in Time and Place*. Boulder, Colo.: Westview Press, 1998.

Pinkard, Susan. *A Revolution in Taste: The Rise of French Cuisine, 1650–1800*. Cambridge: Cambridge University Press, 2009.

Pitte, Jean-Robert. *French Gastronomy: The History and Geography of a Passion*. Translated by Jody Gladding. New York: Columbia University Press, 2002.

Plante, Ellen M. *The American Kitchen, 1700 to the Present: From Hearth to Highrise*. New York: Facts on File, 1995.

Poling-Kempes, Lesley. *The Harvey Girls: Women Who Opened the West*. New York: Paragon House, 1989.

Polk's Pittsburgh City Directory. Pittsburgh: R. L. Polk, 1869–70, 1874–75, 1879–80, 1885, 1890, 1895, 1900, 1905, 1910, 1915, 1920, 1925, 1930.

Pollard, Edward Alfred. *The Virginia Tourist: Sketches of the Springs and Mountains of Virginia*. Philadelphia: J. B. Lippincott, 1870.

Porterfield, James D. *Dining by Rail: The History and the Recipes of America's Golden Age of Railroad Cuisine*. New York: St. Martin's Press, 1993.

Post, Emily. *Etiquette: The Blue Book of Social Usage*. New York: Funk and Wagnalls, 1937.

Pursell, Carroll W. *The Machine in America: A Social History of Technology*. Baltimore: Johns Hopkins University Press, 1995.

Ranhofer, Charles. *The Epicurean: A Complete Treatise of Analytical and Practical Studies on the Culinary Art*. New York: C. Ranhofer, 1894.

Rauch, Jonathan. "Seeing around Corners." *Atlantic Monthly*, April 2002, 35.

Ray, Krishnendu. "Ethnic Succession and the New American Restaurant Cuisine." In *The Restaurants Book: Ethnographies of Where to Eat*, edited by David Beriss and David Sutton, 97–114. New York: Berg, 2007.

Read, Jason. *The Micro-Politics of Capital: Marx and the Prehistory of the Present*. Albany: State University of New York Press, 2003.

Rees, Albert. *Real Wages in Manufacturing, 1890–1914*. Princeton: Princeton University Press, 1961.

Research Department of the American Restaurant Magazine. *A Market Analysis of the Restaurant Industry*. Chicago: Patterson Publishing, 1930.

Richards, David. *Poland Spring: A Tale of the Gilded Age, 1860–1900*. Hanover, N.H.: University Press of New England, 2005.

Robbins, Derek. *Bourdieu and Culture*. London: SAGE, 2000.

Roberts, J. A. G. *China to Chinatown: Chinese Food in the West*. London: Reaktion Books, 2002.

Robinson, Solon. *Hot Corn: Life Scenes in New York Illustrated*. New York: De Witt and Davenport, 1854.

Rodgers, Daniel T. *Atlantic Crossings: Social Politics in a Progressive Age*. Cambridge, Mass.: Belknap Press of Harvard University Press, 1998.

Rogan, Michael P., and John L. Shrover, eds. *Political Change in California: Critical Elections and Social Movements, 1890–1966*. Westport, Conn.: Greenwood, 1970.

Root, Waverley. *Food: An Authoritative and Visual History*. New York: Simon and Schuster, 1980.

Rorer, Sarah Tyson Heston. *Mrs. Rorer's New Cook Book: A Manual of Housekeeping*. Philadelphia: Arnold, 1902.

Rosenzweig, Linda W. *The Anchor of My Life: Middle-Class American Mothers and Daughters, 1880–1920*. New York: New York University Press, 1993.

Rosenzweig, Roy. *Eight Hours for What We Will: Workers and Leisure in an Industrial City, 1870–1920*. Cambridge: Cambridge University Press, 1983.

Rubin, Joan Shelley. *The Making of Middle/Brow Culture*. Chapel Hill: University of North Carolina Press, 1992.

Rudy, Jarrett. *The Freedom to Smoke: Tobacco Consumption and Identity*. Montreal: McGill–Queen's University Press, 2005.

Ryan, Mary P. *Cradle of the Middle Class: The Family in Oneida County, New York, 1790–1865*. Cambridge: Cambridge University Press, 1981.

———. *Women in Public: Between Banners and Ballots, 1825–1880*. Baltimore: Johns Hopkins University Press, 1990.

Rydell, Robert W., and Rob Kroes. *Buffalo Bill in Bologna: The Americanization of the World, 1869–1922*. Chicago: University of Chicago Press, 2005.

Said, Edward W. *Orientalism*. New York: Pantheon Books, 1978.

Sandage, Scott A. *Born Losers: A History of Failure in America*. Cambridge: Harvard University Press, 2005.

Sante, Luc. *Low Life: Lures and Snares of Old New York*. New York: Vintage Books, 1992.

Sarasúa, Carmen. "Upholding Status: The Diet of a Noble Family in Early Nineteenth-Century La Mancha." In *Food, Drink and Identity: Cooking, Eating and Drinking in Europe since the Middle Ages*, edited by Peter Scholliers, 37–61. Oxford: Berg, 2001.

Scapp, Ron, and Brian Seitz, eds. *Eating Culture*. Albany: State University of New York Press, 1998.

Schehr, Lawrence R., and Allen S. Weiss, eds. *French Food: On the Table, on the Page, and in French Culture*. New York: Routledge, 2001.

Schelling, Thomas C. *Micromotives and Macrobehavior*. New York: Norton, 1978.

———. "Models of Segregation." *American Economic Review* 59, no. 2 (1969): 488–93.

Schlereth, Thomas J. *Victorian America: Transformations in Everyday Life, 1876–1915*. New York: HarperPerennial, 1992.

Schmidt, Leigh Eric. *Consumer Rites: The Buying and Selling of American Holidays*. Princeton: Princeton University Press, 1995.

Schneirov, Matthew. *The Dream of a New Social Order: Popular Magazines in America, 1893–1914*. New York: Columbia University Press, 1994.

Schnetzer, Amanda Watson. "The Golden Age of Cooking." *Policy Review* 97 (October/November 1999): 53–66.

Schofield, Mary Anne. *Cooking by the Book: Food in Literature and Culture*. Bowling Green, Ohio: Bowling Green State University Popular Press, 1989.

Scholliers, Peter. *Food Culture in Belgium*. Westport, Conn.: Greenwood Press, 2009.

———, ed. *Food, Drink and Identity: Cooking, Eating and Drinking in Europe since the Middle Ages*. Oxford: Berg, 2001.

Schorman, Rob. *Selling Style: Clothing and Social Change at the Turn of the Century*. Philadelphia: University of Pennsylvania Press, 2003.

Schwartz, David. "Duncan Hines: He Made Gastronomes out of Motorists." *Smithsonian*, November 1984, 86–97.

Schwartz, Hillel. *Never Satisfied: A Cultural History of Diets, Fantasies, and Fat*. New York: Free Press, 1986.

Scobey, David. "Anatomy of the Promenade: The Politics of Bourgeois Sociability in Nineteenth-Century New York." *Social History* 17, no. 2 (1992): 203–27.

Segal, Howard P. "The Technological Utopians." In *Imagining Tomorrow: History, Technology, and the American Future*, edited by Joseph J. Corn, 119–36. Cambridge: MIT Press, 1986.

Segrave, Kerry. *Tipping: An American Social History of Gratuities*. Jefferson, N.C.: McFarland, 1998.

Shaffer, Michael. "Taste, Gastronomic Expertise, and Objectivity." In *Food and Philosophy: Eat, Think and Be Merry*, edited by Fritz Allhoff and Dave Monroe, 73–87. Oxford: Blackwell Publishing, 2007.

Shammas, Carole. "A New Look at Long-Term Trends in Wealth Inequality in the United States." *American Historical Review* 98, no. 2 (1993): 412–31.

Shapiro, Laura. *Julia Child*. New York: Lipper/Penguin, 2007.

————. *Perfection Salad: Women and Cooking at the Turn of the Century*. New York: Farrar Straus and Giroux, 1986.

————. *Something from the Oven: Reinventing Dinner in 1950's America*. New York: Viking, 2004.

Sherwood, Mary Elizabeth Wilson. *Manners and Social Usages*. New York: Harper and Brothers, 1887.

Shortridge, Barbara Gimla, and James R. Shortridge, eds. *The Taste of American Place: A Reader on Regional and Ethnic Foods*. Lanham, Md.: Rowman and Littlefield, 1998.

Shuldiner, Alec Tristin. "Trapped behind the Automat: Technological Systems and the American Restaurant, 1902–1991." PhD diss., Cornell University, 2001.

Simmons, Amelia. *American Cookery*. Hartford: Printed for Simeon Butler, Northampton, 1798.

Simon, Kate. *Fifth Avenue: A Very Social History*. New York: Harcourt Brace Jovanovich, 1978.

Smith, Andrew F. *Eating History: 30 Turning Points in the Making of American Cuisine*. New York: Columbia University Press, 2009.

Smith, Matthew Hale. *Sunshine and Shadow in New York*. Hartford: J. B. Burr, 1869.

Smith-Rosenberg, Carroll. "The Female World of Love and Ritual: Relations between Women in Nineteenth-Century America." *Signs* 1, no. 1 (1975): 1–29.

Spang, Rebecca L. *The Invention of the Restaurant: Paris and Modern Gastronomic Culture*. Cambridge: Harvard University Press, 2000.

Spann, Edward K. *The New Metropolis: New York City, 1840–1857*. New York: Columbia University Press, 1981.

Spencer, Ethel, Charles Hart Spencer, Michael P. Weber, and Peter N. Stearns. *The Spencers of Amberson Avenue: A Turn-of-the Century Memoir*. Pittsburgh: University of Pittsburgh Press, 1983.

Spencer, Herbert. *The Principles of Sociology*. Westport, Conn.: Greenwood Press, 1975.

Spofford, Harriet Prescott. *The Servant Girl Question*. Boston: Houghton, Mifflin, 1881.

Springsteed, Anne Frances. *The Expert Waitress*. New York: Harper and Brothers, 1912.

Stansell, Christine. *City of Women: Sex and Class in New York, 1789–1860*. Urbana: University of Illinois Press, 1987.

Stearns, Peter N. *Fat History: Bodies and Beauty in the Modern West*. New York: New York University Press, 1997.

———. "The Middle Class: Toward a Precise Definition." *Comparative Studies in Society and History* 21, no. 3 (1979): 377–96.

Steckel, Richard H., and Carolyn M. Moehling. "Rising Inequality: Trends in the Distribution of Wealth in Industrializing New England." *Journal of Economic History* 61, no. 1 (2001): 160–83.

Steevens, G. W. *The Land of the Dollar*. New York: Dodd, Mead, 1897.

Sterngass, Jon. *First Resorts: Pursuing Pleasure at Saratoga Springs, Newport, and Coney Island*. Baltimore: Johns Hopkins University Press, 2001.

Stevenson, Louise L. *The Victorian Homefront: American Thought and Culture, 1860–1880*. New York: Twayne Publishers, 1991.

Strand, Torill. "Introduction: Cosmopolitanism in the Making." *Studies in Philosophy and Education* 29, no. 2 (2010): 103–9.

Strasser, Susan. *Never Done a History of American Housework*. New York: Pantheon Books, 1982.

———. *Satisfaction Guaranteed: The Making of the American Mass Market*. New York: Pantheon Books, 1989.

Street, Julian. *Abroad at Home: American Ramblings, Observations and Adventures of Julian Street*. New York: Century, 1915.

Strong, Roland. *Where and How to Dine in Paris, with Notes on Paris Hotels, Waiters and Their Tips*. London: G. Richards, 1900.

Stuart, Emmeline Wortley. *Travels in the United States, Etc.: During 1849 and 1850*. New York: Harper and Brothers, 1855.

Surowiecki, James. *The Wisdom of Crowds: Why the Many Are Smarter Than the Few and How Collective Wisdom Shapes Business, Economies, Societies, and Nations*. New York: Doubleday, 2004.

Susman, Warren. *Culture as History: The Transformation of American Society in the Twentieth Century*. New York: Pantheon Books, 1984.

Takaki, Ronald T. *Strangers from a Different Shore: A History of Asian Americans*. Boston: Back Bay Books, 1998.

Tannahill, Reay. *Food in History*. New York: Stein and Day, 1973.

Tate, Cassandra. *Cigarette Wars: The Triumph of "The Little White Slaver."* New York: Oxford University Press, 1999.

Taylor, Bayard. *Eldorado, or, Adventures in the Path of Empire: Comprising a Voyage to California Via Panama, Life in San Francisco and Monterey*. 2 vols. New York: George P. Putnam, 1850.

Taylor, Benjamin F. *Between the Gates*. Chicago: S. C. Griggs, 1878.

Taylor, William Robert. *In Pursuit of Gotham: Culture and Commerce in New York*. New York: Oxford University Press, 1992.

———. *Inventing Times Square: Commerce and Culture at the Crossroads of the World*. New York: Russell Sage Foundation, 1991.

Tchen, John Kuo Wei. *New York before Chinatown: Orientalism and the Shaping of American Culture, 1776–1882*. Baltimore: Johns Hopkins University Press, 1999.

Teuteberg, Hans-Jürgen. "The Rising Popularity of Dining Out in Germany in the Aftermath of Modern Urbanization." In *Eating Out in Europe: Picnics, Gourmet Dining, and Snacks since the Late Eighteenth Century*, edited by Marc Jacobs and Peter Scholliers, 281–99. Oxford: Berg, 2003.

Theophano, Janet. *Eat My Words: Reading Women's Lives through the Cookbooks They Wrote*. New York: Palgrave, 2002.

Thomas, Lately. *Delmonico's: A Century of Splendor*. Boston: Houghton Mifflin, 1967.

Thompson, E. P. *The Making of the English Working Class*. New York: Pantheon Books, 1964.

———. "The Moral Economy of the English Crowd in the Eighteenth Century." *Past and Present* 50, no. 1 (1971): 76–136.

Thompson, John R. *Where We Foregather*. Chicago, n.d., c. 1922.

Thorne, Robert. "Places of Refreshment in the Nineteenth-Century City." In *Buildings and Society: Essays on the Social Development of the Built Environment*, edited by Anthony D. King, 228–54. London: Routledge and Kegan Paul, 1980.

Thudichum, John Louis William. *Cookery: Its Art and Practice*. London: Frederick Warne, 1895.

Tomes, Robert. *The Bazar Book of Decorum*. New York: Harper and Brothers, 1870.

Trager, James. *The Food Chronology: A Food Lover's Compendium of Events and Anecdotes from Prehistory to the Present*. New York: Henry Holt, 1995.

Trollope, Frances Milton. *Domestic Manners of the Americans*. Edited by Donald Arthur Smalley. New York: Vintage Books, 1949.

Trubek, Amy B. *Haute Cuisine: How the French Invented the Culinary Profession*. Philadelphia: University of Pennsylvania Press, 2000.

Trumbull, Matthew M. "Aristocracy in America." *The Nineteenth Century* 18, no. 102 (1888): 209–17.

Tsai, Shih-Shan Henry. *The Chinese Experience in America*. Bloomington: Indiana University Press, 1986.

Twain, Mark. "Essays on Paul Bourget." Salt Lake City: Project Gutenberg, 2004, http://www.gutenberg.org/etext/3173 (accessed March 7, 2005). Originally published in 1895.

Twitchell, James B. *Living It Up: Our Love Affair with Luxury*. New York: Columbia University Press, 2002.

Urry, John. *The Tourist Gaze: Leisure and Travel in Contemporary Societies*. London: Sage Publications, 1990.

U.S. Bureau of the Census. *Fifteenth Census of the United States, 1930, Population.* Washington, D.C.: Government Printing Office, 1933.

U.S. Bureau of the Census. *Special Reports. Occupations at the Twelfth Census.* Washington, D.C.: Government Printing Office, 1904.

U.S. Department of Health and Human Services. *Reducing Tobacco Use: A Report of the Surgeon General.* Washington, D.C.: Department of Health and Human Services, U.S. Public Health Service, 2000.

U.S. Food Administration and U.S. Bureau of Education. *Food Saving and Sharing: Telling How the Older Children of America May Help Save from Famine Their Comrades in Allied Lands across the Sea.* Garden City: Doubleday, Page, 1918.

Veblen, Thorstein. *The Theory of Business Enterprise.* New York: C. Scribner's Sons, 1904.

———. *The Theory of the Leisure Class: An Economic Study of Institutions.* New York: Modern Library, 1934.

Veenstra, Gerry. "Can Taste Illumine Class? Cultural Knowledge and Forms of Inequality." *Canadian Journal of Sociology/Cahiers canadiens de sociologie* 30, no. 3 (2005): 247–79.

Veit, Helen Zoe. "'We Were a Soft People': Asceticism, Self-Discipline and American Food Conservation in the First World War." *Food, Culture and Society* 10, no. 2 (2007): 167–90.

Vertovec, Steven, and Robin Cohen. *Conceiving Cosmopolitanism: Theory, Context and Practice.* New York: Oxford University Press, 2002.

Visitor's Guide to New Orleans. New Orleans: J. C. Waldo, 1875.

Wall, Diana diZerega. *The Archaeology of Gender: Separating the Spheres in Urban America.* New York: Plenum Press, 1994.

Wang, Xinyang. *Surviving the City: The Chinese Immigrant Experience in New York City, 1890–1970.* Lanham, Md.: Rowman and Littlefield, 2001.

Warde, Alan, and Linda Martens. "The Prawn Cocktail Ritual." In *Consuming Passions: Food in the Age of Anxiety,* edited by Sian Griffiths and Jennifer Wallace, 118–22. Manchester: Manchester University Press, 1998.

Wason, Elizabeth. *Cooks, Gluttons and Gourmets: A History of Cookery.* Garden City, N.Y.: Doubleday, 1962.

Wecter, Dixon. *The Saga of American Society: A Record of Social Aspiration, 1607–1937.* New York: Scribner, 1970.

Weems, Robert E. *Desegregating the Dollar: African American Consumerism in the Twentieth Century.* New York: New York University Press, 1998.

Weigley, Emma Seifrit. *Sarah Tyson Rorer: The Nation's Instructress in Dietetics and Cookery.* Philadelphia: American Philosophical Society, 1977.

Wells, Jonathan Daniel. *The Origins of the Southern Middle Class, 1800–1861.* Chapel Hill: University of North Carolina Press, 2004.

Wells, Samuel R. *How to Behave: A Pocket Manual of Republican Etiquette, and Guide to Correct Personal Habits.* New York: Fowler and Wells, 1887.

Welter, Barbara. "The Cult of True Womanhood: 1820–1860." *American Quarterly* 18 (1966): 151–74.

Wheaton, Barbara Ketcham. *Savoring the Past: The French Kitchen and Table from 1300 to 1789*. Philadelphia: University of Pennsylvania Press, 1983.

Whelpton, P. K. "Occupational Groups in the United States, 1820–1920." *Journal of the American Statistical Association* 21, no. 155 (1926): 335–43.

Where and How to Dine in New York: The Principal Hotels, Restaurants and Cafes of Various Kinds and Nationalities Which Have Added to the Gastronomic Fame of New York and Its Suburbs. New York: Lewis, Scribner, 1903.

Whitaker, Jan. *Service and Style: How the American Department Store Fashioned the Middle Class*. New York: St. Martin's Press, 2006.

———. *Tea at the Blue Lantern Inn: A Social History of the Tea Room Craze in America*. New York: St. Martin's Press, 2002.

Whitehead, Jessup. *The Steward's Handbook and Guide to Party Catering*. Chicago: J. Anderson, 1889.

Whyte, William Foote. *Human Relations in the Restaurant Industry*. New York: McGraw-Hill, 1948.

Wiebe, Robert H. *The Search for Order, 1877–1920*. New York: Hill and Wang, 1967.

Wiese, Andrew. "The House I Live In: Race, Class, and African American Suburban Dreams in the Postwar United States." In *The New Suburban History*, edited by Kevin Michael Kruse and Thomas J. Sugrue, 99–119. Chicago: University of Chicago Press, 2006.

Williams, Susan. *Savory Suppers and Fashionable Feasts: Dining in Victorian America*. New York: Pantheon Books, 1985.

Williamson, Jeffrey G., and Peter H. Lindert. *American Inequality: A Macroeconomic History*. New York: Academic Press, 1980.

Wilson, Lucy Langdon. *Handbook of Domestic Science and Household Arts for Use in Elementary Schools: A Manual for Teachers*. New York: Macmillan, 1900.

Wilson, Samuel Paynter. *Chicago by Gaslight*. Chicago, n.d., c. 1910.

Woloson, Wendy A. *Refined Tastes: Sugar, Confectionery, and Consumers in Nineteenth-Century America*. Baltimore: Johns Hopkins University Press, 2002.

Wyllie, Irvin G. "Social Darwinism and the Businessman." *Proceedings of the American Philosophical Society* 103, no. 5 (1959): 629–35.

Wyman, Roger E. "Middle-Class Voters and Progressive Reform: The Conflict of Class and Culture." *American Political Science Review* 68, no. 2 (1974): 488–504.

Zavisca, Jane. "The Status of Cultural Omnivorism: A Case Study of Reading in Russia." *Social Forces* 84, no. 2 (2005): 1233–55.

Zeckhauser, Richard. "Distinguished Fellow: Reflections on Thomas Schelling." *Journal of Economic Perspectives* 3, no. 2 (1989): 153–64.

Zhang, Jie. "Transplanting Identity: A Study of Chinese Immigrants and the Chinese Restaurant Business." PhD diss., Southern Illinois University at Carbondale, 1998.

Zunz, Olivier. *Making America Corporate, 1870–1920*. Chicago: University of Chicago Press, 1990.

INDEX

Académie Culinaire de France, 30–31

Académie de Cuisine. *See* Académie Culinaire de France

Adventures in Good Eating (Duncan Hines), 229

Alice Adams (Booth Tarkington), 46, 60

All-American Restaurant Competition, 209

American Cookery (Amelia Simmons), 315 (n. 58)

American Tragedy (Theodore Dreiser), 60

Aristocracy: defined, 2, 237 (n. 6); size of, 21, 56, 246 (nn. 10, 14); and conspicuous consumption, 22–23; imitation of, 49–56, 61–63; excesses of, 135–36, 152–54, 232; contact with middle class, 264 (n. 3)

Aristocratic restaurants: origins of, 24, 28–29, 250 (nn. 57, 58), 251 (n. 60); and French cuisine, 27–29, 325 (n. 37); and French chefs, 29–32, 250 (n. 52); and French-language menus, 32–33, 193–95; waiters at, 33–37; patronage of, 37–38, 302 (n. 7); as arbiters of culture, 193; decline of, 219–20, 222

Astor, Ava Lowle Willing (Mrs. John Jacob Astor IV), 119

Atwater, Wilbur O., 129, 284 (n. 83)

Battle Creek Sanitarium, 127

Beecher, Catharine Esther, 127

Belmont, August, 23

Berthelin, Chef, 217

Billings, C. K. G., 135

Bird, Isabella Lucy, 149

Blatch, Harriot Stanton, 145–48, 161, 291 (n. 2)

Blot, Pierre, 24

Bock, August J., 171–72

Bohemian, 279 (n. 82), 282 (n. 7)

Bohemian Eats of San Francisco (Jack L. Dodd and Hazel Blair Dodd), 228–29, 323 (n. 22)

Bohemian San Francisco (Clarence Edwords), 228

Boomer, Lucius, 220–21

Boston Cooking School, 129, 208

Bourdieu, Pierre, 39, 90–91

Bradley-Martin Ball, 135, 254 (n. 100)

Britten, Fred A., 204–5

Brooks, Noah, 148

Browne, Junius Henri, 68

Burt, Stephen Smith, 41–42

Campbell, Tunis G., 149–50

Carême, Marie-Antoine, 30, 31

Centennial Exhibition (Philadelphia), 92–95, 226, 273 (n. 3); ethnic food at, 93–94

Chatfield-Taylor, H. C., 130–32

Chefs: French, 29–32; American, 208

Child, Julia, 325 (n. 37)

Civil and Political Equality League (New York), 158

Claiborne, Craig, 230

Consumerism, 223, 232–34, 310 (n. 96)

Cooking Club, 134

Cooking schools: Boston, 128; New York, 128; Philadelphia, 128

Cook's French, xiii, 32–33, 198, 311 (nn. 10–11)

Corson, Juliet, 128, 208

Cosmopolitanism: influence of, 9, 223–24, 232; as nationalism, 110; defined, 110–11, 116–17, 121, 169; New York, 111–12; San Francisco, 112–14; Los Angeles, 114; Washington, D.C., 114; Boston, 114–15; contrast with orientalism, 215; internal contradiction in, 223–24, 239 (n. 21); and restaurant reviews, 230; compared with omnivorism, 240 (n. 23), 280 (n. 97)

Cuisine: New England, 81; southern, 81; ethnic, 95–98, 104–5, 210–13; American, 206–10, 316 (nn. 70, 74); defined, 314 (n. 53)

Culinary congress (1939), 220–21

Cultural capital, 39; examples of, 218–19; as class consciousness, 219; limits of, 219

Daschner, John F., 186–89, 309 (nn. 85, 89–90)

Delmonico's, 3, 20, 24–25, 38, 53, 59, 123, 137, 151, 152, 159–60, 192, 218, 254 (n. 100); influence of, 25; menu, 54 (ill.)

Dickens, Charles, 19–21, 245 (nn. 5, 7); *Martin Chuzzlewit*, 19

Edgerly, Webster, 127

Erkins, Henry, 185–86, 309 (n. 84)

Escoffier, Auguste, 30, 252 (n. 80)

Ethnic restaurants, 98, 276 (n. 48); Chinese, 2, 103–4, 107, 213, 278 (nn. 62, 64); German, 98–99, 104, 212, 226, 273 (n. 14); French, 100, 325 (n. 37); Italian, 100–101, 211–12, 274 (n. 27); in San Francisco, 101; in Los Angeles, 101–2; in Washington, D.C., 102; gentrification of, 106–9, 277 (n. 55), 278 (n. 62); Mexican, 212

Etiquette, 51–53, 60, 152, 259 (nn. 37, 41); and middle class, 105–9; and Emily Post, 143–44

Farmer, Fanny, 130; influence of, 284 (n. 35)

Foster, George G., 24, 70

French-language menu: and accessibility, 32–33; campaign against, 194–96; use of as conspiracy, 195; rationale for use of, 198. *See also* Cook's French

Geneva White Cross Society. *See* Netter, Gaston G.

Girl from Rector's, The (Paul Potter), 295 (n. 48)

Good Food, 134

Gould, Jay, 119

Graham, Hettie Wright, 145–48

Graham, Sylvester, 126

Guide Michelin, Le, 229

Haan, R. M., 124–26, 167

Harrison, Constance Cary, 193–94

Haute cuisine: defined, 217–18; popularity of, 319 (n. 115)

Hoffman House, 44, 145–47

Hotels: growth of, 122; plans of service, 122–23, 283 (n. 12)

House of Mirth (Edith Wharton), 60

Jackson, Helen Hunt, 127

Kellogg, Ella, 127

Kellogg, John Harvey, 127

Ladies' ordinary, 149

Leviathan, 204

Lewis, Dio, 64–65

Lincoln, Mary, 129

Martin, J. B., 138

Martin Chuzzlewit (Charles Dickens), 19

Martin's Café, 162–64

McAllister, Ward, 24, 28, 31, 37, 41, 50, 56, 260 (n. 54)

McAlpin, Hotel, 1, 3, 172, 213

McGlory, Billy, 253 (n. 84), 295 (n. 48)

McTeague (Frank Norris), 47

Menus: as sources, 313 (n. 35)

Micromotives: defined, 85, 270 (n. 69); and restaurants, 85–87, 263 (n. 86); influence of, 224, 233

Middle class: in early nineteenth century, 45; defined, 46–48, 120, 257 (nn. 18, 19), 282 (n. 6); size of, 47, 120, 258 (n. 25); salaries of, 57; culinary adventurism of, 103–5, 275 (n. 36), 276 (n. 48); middle-class vanguard, 120–21; formation of, 233; and working class, 240 (n. 24), concerns about health, 275 (n. 37); African American, 282 (n. 6)

Modern Instance, A (William Dean Howells), 76

Murray's Roman Gardens, 185

N. W. Ayer and Son, 130

National Restaurant Association, 13

Netter, Gaston G., 193, 196–97, 312 (n. 20)

New Year's Day, 43–44, 220

New York School of Cooking, 128

Ohio Society (New York), 192, 310 (n. 1)

Omnivorism. *See* Cosmopolitanism

Orientalism, 214–16, 318 (n. 102)

"Our Artist's Dream of the Centennial Restaurants" (Walter Brown), 92–93, 93 (ill.)

Paddleford, Clementine, 229–30

Pemberton, Marila, 133

Philadelphia School of Cooking, 128

Pierce, Paul, 130–33, 285 (n. 50)

Plate dinner. *See* Simple eating

Plaza Hotel, 160, 167

Progressive movement, 8

Public sphere, 263 (n. 86), 310 (n. 95)

Pure food movement, 285 (n. 50)

R. G. Dunn Company, 12

Ralston Health Club, 127

Ranhofer, Charles, 24, 142, 248 (n. 31)

Republican table, 189, 310 (n. 95)

Restaurant dresses, 294 (n. 30)

Restaurant reviews, 223–30

Restaurants: economics of, 12, 216; growth of restaurant industry, 12–13, 72–73, 265 (nn. 16–18); and advertising, 13, 267 (n. 24); influence of, 15; cost of, 57–58, 261 (n. 56); for businessmen, 70–71; demand for, 71, 74–75, 83–85, 86, 89; lunchrooms, 76–78; table d'hôte, 78–79; beefsteak, 79–80; American, 80–81, 268 (n. 43); at department stores, 81; buffets, 81, 183; Automats, 81, 184–85, 308 (nn. 73–74); coffee and cake saloons, 81–82, 268 (n. 53); rate of failure of, 82–83, 269 (n. 55); restaurant critics, 87; music and dancing at, 87–88, 214, 222, 271 (n. 80), 290 (n. 106); lobster palaces, 135–36, 162, 297 (n. 75); types of service at, 139–40; ice cream parlors, 150; women's, 150, 151, 154–57; cafeterias, 157, 183–84; tearooms, 157; waiterless, 185–89, 307 (n. 62), 308 (nn. 78–79), 309 (nn. 84–90); exotic atmosphere at, 213–14

Restaurants of New York, The (George S. Chappell), 227–28

Richards, Ellen, 130, 284 (n. 83)

Rise of Silas Latham, The (William Dean Howells), 60

Ritz-Carlton Hotel, 166–67

Rorer, Sarah, 128–29, 284 (n. 37)

Sacralization of culture, 7

St. Regis Hotel, 124–26, 200

Sala, George Augustus Henry, 24

Salisbury, James, 127

Servant problem, 71–72

Simple eating: aristocratic attitudes toward, 118–19, 133, 136; and domestic science, 127–30; Sarah Rorer and, 128–29; and restaurants, 138; plate dinner as, 141–42, 289 (n. 101), 290 (nn. 103–4), 305 (n. 50)

Smoking, 161–68, 297 (nn. 73, 76), 298 (n. 77); and Martin's Café, 162–64; campaigns against, 165, 167, 300 (n. 100)

Social Darwinism, 39–41, 255 (n. 109)

Société Culinaire Philanthropique, 209

Société des Cuisiniers Français, 31

Spaghetti, 211–12, 274 (n. 27)

Street, Julian, 118

Sullivan, Timothy (Little Tim), 163–64, 298 (n. 87)

Sullivan Ordinance, 164, 298 (n. 87), 299 (n. 90)

Susan Lennox: Her Fall and Rise (David Graham Phillips), 60

Technology, 182–83; for household, 182, 306 (n. 57); for restaurants, 183–89, 190; utopian, 191, 307 (n. 62); democratic, 307 (n. 59)

Tenu, Adrein, 217

Tipping, 58; origin of, 172, 302 (nn. 6–7); advantage of for elites, 173–74; as undemocratic, 175, 178–79; psychological effect of, 175–76; cost of, 176–77; and ten-percent rule, 179; legislation on, 180; as harmful to waiters, 304 (n. 39); boycotts on, 305 (n. 48)

Tocqueville, Alexis de, 4

Travel guides, 225–26, 322 (nn. 9–10)

Tschirky, Oscar, 138

Upper class. See Aristocracy

Veblen, Thorstein, 38

Waiters: appearance of, 34; race of, 34–35, 253 (nn. 88, 89), 254 (n. 90); deference of, 35–37; responsibilities of, 35–37, 173–74; unscrupulousness of, 141, 176, 289 (n. 100), 303 (n. 24); discretion of, 174; middle-class concern for, 304 (n. 39)

Waldorf Astoria, 44, 53, 135, 158–59, 200

What to Eat, 130–32; and simple eating, 132–33; circulation of, 133

Where and How to Dine in New York, 226–27, 322 (n. 11)

Women: in public, 151; as ladies, 151–52, 157–61, 294 (nn. 28–29); excesses of, 152–54; and simple eating, 288 (n. 89); legal challenges to discrimination, 291 (n. 4), 292 (n. 8), 301 (n. 118); concert saloon waitresses, 292 (n. 12); "hot corn" girls, 292 (n. 12)

Woodhall, Tennessee, 293 (n. 13)

Woodhall, Victoria, 293 (n. 13)

World War I, 141–42, 170, 204, 288 (n. 81)

Wortley, Emmeline Stuart, 149